DATA BASE MANAGEMENT

WILLIAM C. HOUSE, EDITOR
PROFESSOR OF MANAGEMENT
UNIVERSITY OF ARKANSAS

FIRST EDITION

petrocelli books. New York 1974

Library of Congress Cataloging in Publication Data

House, William C   comp.
    Data base management.

    Includes bibliographies.
    1. Electronic data processing. 2. Information
storage and retrieval systems. I. Title.
QA76.H69   001.6'4   73-18383
ISBN 0-88405-051-3

CONTENTS

PART V. METHODS OF PROCESSING DATA: BATCH VERSUS CONTINUOUS PROCESSING 323

PART VI. INFORMATION RETRIEVAL AND DISPLAY CONCEPTS, ALTERNATIVES, AND DEVICES 399

PREFACE

This collection of readings reflects current developments in hardware, software, and data base technology as they affect the characteristics and capabilities of data base systems. The reader is encouraged to consult the index for a listing of key topic areas and page numbers where discussion of each topic may be found. Further study of each key topic area is possible through study of selected references in the bibliography at the end of each part. The study of selected references may also be useful in providing insights into the full implications of the discussion questions included at the end of each part.

The development, updating, and editing of this reading collection has been a long, painful process covering a period of approximately eight years. I am extremely grateful to Jane Rogers Tonero, managing editor, and Richard Nolan, consulting editor, for their patience, assistance, and advice during the preparation of this manuscript. I am also very grateful to my wife Adrian, my daughter Melinda Ann, and my wife's parents, Sam and Maude Musselwhite, who were kind enough to assist me during the developmental stage of manuscript. I sincerely hope the results of these endeavors will convey to the reader some indication of the vast scope and intense depth of the emerging field of data base systems.

INTRODUCTION TO DATA BASE MANAGEMENT

The functions commonly performed by data base systems include data collection, data communication, data organization and storage, data processing, and information retrieval and display. In addition, there has been the emergence of the function of data base management, which combines such processes as data organization, storage, processing, and retrieval under the guidance of a single systems manager. It may also be helpful to observe that very sophisticated subsystems can be developed to perform the functions of data collection, data transmission, data storage, data processing, and information display. The operations of the various subsystems must then be coordinated to ensure effective, efficient, and economical operation of the total data base system. The coordination and control of the various subsystems is largely the responsibility of the data base management system.

The system designed must select the composite aggregation of methods, media, and devices (or alternately, subsystems) that will permit systems functions to be performed rapidly, accurately, and completely enough to meet the user's information requirements at a reasonable cost in terms of resources used (for example, money, manpower, materials, and machine time). Since it is rarely possible to achieve fully information system goals such as fast response times, economical and reliable system operation, convenience and flexibility of access to stored data, and so on, in one system, the systems developer should carefully evaluate tradeoffs between desirable objectives in terms of resources required and relative importance of each objective. The articles in this collection have been selected to familiarize the reader with the nature of each function, to emphasize factors that are important in deciding how each function should be performed, and to illustrate problems that typically arise in the performance of the various functions.

The articles in Part I discuss instances when source data-capturing devices should be used instead of keypunching data and also the various possibilities that now exist for narrowing the gap between input-output speeds and internal computer processing speeds. The factors that should be considered in deciding whether source data automation is to be used instead of other methods of data collection and the most suitable types of applications for SDA are also discussed. Particular attention is paid to the prospects and problems of utilizing optical scanners, key-to-tape, and key-to-disk devices as keypunch replacements.

The types of data transmission terminals, channels, and services available for transmitting collected data from remote collection stations to central processing points are presented in Part II along with key factors to be considered in designing data collection and transmission systems. In addition, the importance and functions of "smart" and "dumb" terminals are discussed in articles contained in this section.

Part III deals with the function of data organization and storage. The articles selected discuss the characteristics, benefits, limitations, and most promising applications for physical sequential, indexed sequential, and random methods of file organization used in conjunction with serial access and direct-access storage devices. The characteristics and applications of magnetic cores and other storage devices to main memories and mass memories in computer systems are also discussed, as well as key factors that should be considered in designing files to be stored on direct-access systems. Special attention is also paid to the important concept of virtual storage.

Part IV is devoted to considerations of the benefits, limitations, and implications of integrated data bases as opposed to conventional file structures. The factors that should be considered in designing the data base are presented in the light of their relative importance and the tradeoffs that must be made in determining an acceptable design. Finally, the characteristics of data management systems and the importance of such systems in making the process of organizing, processing, retrieving, and displaying data/information simpler, more flexible, and more automatic from the standpoint of the information user are discussed fully.

Part V focuses on the problems of determining the best possible mix of batch and continuous processing methods for a given set of applications as well as the most effective manner of using remote batch processing and dedicated computers. The articles selected for inclusion in this section indicate how such considerations as response-time requirements, human effectiveness, machine efficiency, systems development and operating costs, accuracy and reliability require-ments, and the application itself must be weighed to reach the best possible decision on the method of processing to be employed. Methods used to collect, organize, and store data must also be considered in deciding how data will be processed. Key factors to be considered when using time-sharing systems or services are presented in considerable detail.

The articles in Part VI emphasize the problems encountered in the process of retrieving and displaying information. The characteristics of various types of printers are discussed and some attention is paid to ways in which the effectiveness of such devices can be measured. The types of digital data display systems currently available and factors that should be considered when selecting a data display system are also treated in some detail. The benefits and implications of computer output to microfilm systems for information storage and display are carefully considered. The benefits, limitations, and implica-tions of computer graphics and interactive visual display for man-agerial decision making are presented in a very straightforward manner. Finally, the types of problem-solving tasks best suited for men and for machines are explored in considerable detail.

PART I

DATA COLLECTION: MINIMIZING TIME, COST, AND ERROR BOTTLENECKS

One of the most widely discussed approaches to reducing the input bottleneck is the introduction of source data automation to the data collection process. Source data automation is the process of capturing business data in a machine-readable form as the by-product of the typing or punching of a source document (that is, using typewriters, cash registers, and adding machines with special attachments). Once data is captured in machine-usable form, it is relatively easy to convert such data to other machine-readable forms (for example, from punched cards to magnetic tape). In essence, source data automation reduces the time required to collect and prepare data for further processing, reduces the opportunities for errors, lowers clerical costs, and permits a wider range of data to be processed than comparable data collection systems.

Source data automation is most applicable to data collection activities with large input volumes, high error rates, some data repetition, sizable clerical personnel requirements, extensive computer processing, and fast response-time requirements for processed data. A careful systems analysis of present workloads, personnel, documents, and other requirements in relation to available equipment characteristics and costs is essential before a logical decision about source data automation can be made. Careful consideration should be given to input, processing, and output needs in such a way that the data collection process complements rather than impedes the processing and output operations. Ideally, the source data automation evaluation study should be comparable in intensity and scope to the feasibility study conducted prior to the selection of an electronic computer.

Man-machine interface with the computer is the real data processing bottleneck, according to Schwab and Sitter. Keypunching of cards or paper tape is relatively slow compared with the internal processing speeds of electronic computers. Buffered units and overlapped input-output have narrowed but not closed the input-output gap. Turnaround documents can reduce keypunch costs for applications best suited to the use of punched cards. Unbalanced data-handling speeds and unoperational formats are the major remaining data collection problems.

Key-to-tape units, mark sensing, magnetic ink character recognition equipment, and optical character recognition (OCR) units are feasible keypunch alternatives. Key-to-tape and OCR systems are more economical than the keypunch as volumes increase. In making the choice of data collection methods, the user must consider data volumes, processing times, data sources, reliability and accuracy, the form of data input, and information output requirements. Input-output equipment represents a significant portion of total system costs as well as the greatest data processing bottleneck.

Key-to-tape units cut data processing time, reduce errors, and speed up verify/search operations. Key-to-cassette units eliminate the need for separate verifiers, work at electronic speeds, and capture data in directly machine-readable form. Optical character readers with handprint reading, multiformat, and multifont characteristics are economical for large data volumes and can be connected directly to a central processing unit. Shared processors (for example, key-to-disk) can handle multiple keystations, unlimited record lengths and formats, and large data volumes. Combined OCR–Shared-Processor units offer real promise of finally breaking the input bottleneck.

As Ferrara and Nolan point out, two approaches to improving computer data entry have emerged in recent years: keypunch replacements (buffered keypunch, keytape, key-disk) and source data entry (direct entry of handwritten, typed, or printed information). Thus, the major data entry alternatives include keypunch and keypunch replacements, OCR (for example, bar-code, mark-sense, and optical character readers), and terminal systems.

Keytape and keydisk systems offer faster, more accurate, and more flexible data entry than keypunch systems. The significant features of OCR equipment that affect its use include cost, reject handling, and operating flexibility. Fast response time, on-line updating of data bases, and error checking are three advantages frequently claimed for terminal systems. Cathode-ray tube and typewriter terminals are the most common keyboard terminals. In evaluating data entry alternatives, consideration should be given to potential productivity increases through decreased personnel and machine requirements as well as intangible factors such as training and data integrity improvements.

Data preparation and entry costs have risen faster than other data processing costs, according to studies conducted by Lybrand, the

Ross brothers, and Montgomery as reported in *Administrative Management* and the *Lybrand Ross Newsletter*. Improving productivity and machine utilization can lower input costs by 20 percent to 30 percent. In some cases, shifting from standard keypunches to buffered keypunches, keytape units, or shared-processor systems can lower data collection costs, reduce errors, and result in faster, more automatic operation. Standard operating data developed for various types of data collection equipment permits accurate assessment of savings in time and costs before equipment changes are actually made.

Within the span of five years, keyboard to magnetic tape data entry has become one of the most popular methods of data collection. The major types of key-to-tape equipment include stand-alone data tape recorders, a data inscriber (which uses either a tape cartridge or a tape cassette), and a key-processing system that controls a number of keystations and uses key-to-disk units. Key-to-tape operations are generally more efficient, more economical, and more accurate (as well as being quieter) than card keypunching. Many companies have found that key-to-tape entry of data requires fewer machines, fewer operators, and less time to read data into a computer than punched card operations.

Stand-alone data tape recorders using tape reels were the first type of key-to-tape data entry unit introduced and are still popular for many applications. Cartridge- or cassette-loaded data inscribers are somewhat more expensive but do avoid the problems associated with loading and unloading tape reels. The key-to-disk system receives data from a number of keystations, edits and formats the data under the guidance of a control program, stores data on the disk, and periodically dumps data in computer-ready form onto magnetic tape. Key-processing systems in some cases replace not only keypunches and verifiers but certain tabulating machines as well. In choosing a particular type of key-to-tape unit, the user should carefully consider the volumes of data to be handled, equipment capabilities, reliability, and the availability of service.

Although computer systems have become cheaper per unit of throughput, the data preparation cost per unit has increased for keypunching operations. Key-to-tape operations are decidedly faster and more accurate than keypunching. Although typical key-to-tape units cost about three times as much as a keypunch, one organization has found that total data preparation costs have been reduced through increased efficiency in keying and verifying data, in operations between data capture and computer input, and in backup equipment required. Key-to-tape operations are considerably faster than keypunching when the input involves considerable duplication, skipping, and zero fills. (The number of backup machines required in case primary equipment is down varies with data volume and severity of response-time requirements.) Both keypunch operators and typists learn to operate the recorders after several weeks of training and many operators consider them to be more glamorous than the more conventional keypunch. User installations have found not only that keypunches and verifiers can be reduced in number but that in some cases even sorters, collators, and other EAM equipment can be eliminated. Although off-line operation is the most common mode of operation now, on-line entry of data directly from the key-to-tape unit into the computer system is also possible if desired.[1]

Stanley Greenblatt has pointed out that key-to-storage systems promise reduced costs, faster processing speeds, and lower card and storage requirements. Key-to-tape machines can be used for both entry and verification, and tape keying is easier than keypunching.[2] Buffered keypunches are more competitive than regular keypunches with keytape units but still rent for twice as much as conventional keypunches.

Key-cassette/cartridge units are desirable if data is to be collected directly at several outlying points. Shared-processor systems have greater data entry/editing, and error-correcting capabilities, and more automatic operation than stand-alone units. Such systems require high data volumes to be economical and carry a risk of complete system shutdown if one machine malfunctions.

Key-to-storage devices bypass card punching, require buffer memories for temporary data and program storage, and provide error-correcting capabilities. Errors undetected at the entry stage are difficult and costly to correct once data is stored, so source data are frequently displayed and keyed twice before actual entry. Key-to-storage units may be placed in remote locations and connected to a computer via communications channels.

Bieser points out that keytape data entry and typewriter/optical scanning data entry increase operator efficiency about 20 percent and reduce input costs about 20 percent. Input systems that detect and correct errors at the point of entry permit significant savings in time and cost. Shared-processor systems allow faster, easier, more flexible,

[1] For a more complete discussion of the experiences of an organization with key-to-tape equipment, see Dennis G. Price, "Whither Keypunch?" *Datamation,* June 1967, pp. 32–34.
[2] See S. Greenblatt, "Delete Delays and Dollars with Direct Data Entry," *Infosystems,* September 1972, pp. 20–25, for amplification of these points.

and more efficient keying operations. The key/disk shared-processor system eliminates the need for pooling and adds improved editing capabilities. Such systems with data communications links added have become extremely popular in industry.

Murphy discusses keytape stations, shared processor keytape systems, and keydisk systems. Keytape stations generally have keyboards and display consoles and produce outputs of computer-compatible tape, cassette tape, or cartridge tape. Shared-processor keytape systems can handle large data volumes, permit expanded record lengths and formats, and entail lower hardware requirements and costs. Shared-processor keydisk systems eliminate the need for multiple tape transports, provide greater data-handling capabilities, permit increased processing power, and allow greater flexibility than keytape systems.

Feidelman indicates that optical readers are the ultimate example of source data automation and can be divided into three classes: barcode readers, mark-sense readers, and optical character readers. Bar-code readers are low in cost but limited in operational flexibility. Mark-sense readers are moderate in cost, very reliable, and limited format devices. Optical character readers can be either single font or multifont, are high-cost units, and in some cases can read "handwritten" numerics. Remote scanners utilizing data transmission facilities are now being used more widely than ever before. When comparing optical readers to keyboard-to-tape units, the user should give consideration to such factors as data volumes to be handled, training and ease of use, on-line capability, verification, and cost.

Eisdorfer points out that there are two major types of optical readers: document readers and page readers. Optical character readers can also be characterized by reading speeds, by single font versus multifont capabilities, and by whether or not they can read numeric handprinting. OCR can be used in lieu of a keying operation (such as keypunching) or as a means of capturing data at the source. Type scanning is just as accurate, just as fast, and is less costly than keypunching when sufficient volumes of data are involved. The real payoff is in source data collection where OCR use can reduce personnel numbers and costs and also improve accuracy.

For large data volumes, according to Philipson,[3] optical character recognition is often more economical than keypunching. If reentry costs are significant, an OCR system may prove to be uneconomical,

---

[3] H. L. Philipson, "Optical Character Recognition: The Input Answer," *Data Processing Annual*, Vol. X (1966), pp. 119–130.

so reliability of OCR units is a vital factor in the selection process. OCR systems perform the functions of reading, recognition (vocabulary control), paper handling, format definition, and on-line processing. Problems that occur at any of these stages can seriously impair the efficiency and effectiveness of the OCR operation.

Limitations as to format flexibility, type fonts read, form size, and document shapes handled are often crucial elements in successful OCR applications. On-line processing (editing, accuracy checking, and so on) can increase the economic benefits of optical character recognition equipment. Promising OCR applications include document processing in printing and publishing, education, government activities, airline ticket handling, and banking.

Data can be communicated from man to the computer using voice recognition, signals generated by direct keyboard entry, punched cards or paper tape, or documents containing either magnetic or optical characters. Optical scanners, which read typewritten, printed, or handwritten characters, provide a rapid and efficient method for feeding human-generated data to computers. However, there are some serious problems with optical scanning. Scanners that can read multifonts at very high speeds are very expensive while lower-priced machines can be used only for limited, highly standardized applications. Paper-handling problems on most machines are as important as difficulties in recognizing characters. No machines currently available can read general-purpose script. Despite these drawbacks, continued expansion of OCR applications in future years seems probable.[4]

Paper-handling, printing, and scanning problems associated with optical scanners and higher throughput rates achieved with key-to-tape devices have inhibited the growth of optical scanning. However, declining research costs and font standardization have produced lower-cost optical scanners that can read a variety of sizes and shapes of documents. Document readers, journal tape readers, and reader punches have tended to be cheaper than page readers because of simpler movement problems and smaller scanning areas. Multifont readers that will handle a variety of type fonts and sizes are becoming more readily available but are still quite expensive.[5]

The use of OCR equipment can be expected to increase as demand for EDP equipment increases, as unit costs decrease, and as

[4] See Jacob C. Rabinow, "Whither OCR?," *Datamation*, July 1969, pp. 38–42, for a fuller discussion of OCR problems and prospects.
[5] See Elinor Gebremedhin, "Optical Character Recognition Performance up, Prices down," *Data Processing*, June 1970, pp. 42–51, for a more complete discussion of OCR benefits, drawbacks, and implications.

more EDP users gain experience with OCR systems. Control of print quality is the essential requirement for efficient and effective use of OCR systems. Page readers, which use typed documents that can be produced faster, more accurately, and more economically than punched cards, are the most flexible and widely used type of OCR equipment. Document readers, which read turnaround source documents (for example, in utility and insurance applications) require a high degree of document control and are less flexible than page readers, but they are more economical to use and operate. Optical reader card punches are widely used to process large volumes of sales invoices (such as oil company credit card tickets) but do encounter considerable problems in print quality. Journal tape readers are used to read printed cash register, adding machine, or accounting machine tapes at high speeds. The various types of OCR machines now available can be either leased or purchased and their use has been proved in practice.

Optical character recognition has been widely heralded as a promising approach to overcome the gap between computer input and processing speeds, to reduce data collection costs, and to alleviate a possible shortage of keypunch operators. Despite this, the adoption rate has been relatively slow, largely because of the high price of scanners and rigid specifications for input documents. If data volumes are large, OCR units can perform data collection functions faster and more cheaply than any other method of data entry. Companies that do not have sufficient volume to justify exclusive use of an OCR reader can utilize the facilities of a data processing service center. Two new OCR services are now available using either remote terminals via telephone lines or data conversion to microfilm prior to scanning.

Self-punch, journal tape, document, and page readers are being used for such applications as mail-order handling, bank customer accounting, insurance policy updating, and computerized typesetting. The greatest advantage of optical scanning is the elimination of costly, error-producing, and time-consuming data transcription, provided that data can be generated initially in OCR acceptable form. Problems arising from the use of OCR equipment include rigid paper-handling requirements, rigid type-font requirements, and lack of flexibility in handling different applications. Standardization of type fonts and paper documents to make OCR less expensive is one approach to overcoming present OCR problems. The development of economical OCR equipment that will read conventional type fonts rapidly and accurately is an equally promising alternative.

1.

ECONOMIC ASPECTS OF COMPUTER INPUT-OUTPUT EQUIPMENT

By Bernhard Schwab
and Robert Sitter

Editor's Note: From FINANCIAL EXECUTIVE, September 1969, pp. 75–87. Reprinted by permission of the publisher, Financial Executives Institute, and authors.

By now almost everybody has heard of the rapid development of computer technology during the last two decades. Many people may even be aware that the pace of development has not slowed down yet, even if the computer industry may not have made major headlines since the introduction of third generation computer systems three or four years ago. However, is modern business sufficiently informed and sufficiently adaptable to make full use of the latest technological achievements?

We believe the answer to this question is no—at least in part. Discrepancies do exist between the current state of the art of computer technology and the mode of operation of many data processing facilities in business. This is particularly true for computer peripherals, which have recently gone through a phase of exceptionally dynamic development. A variety of new equipment and techniques has been introduced on the market to alleviate the often critical bottleneck of data input/output in computer operations; some of these newer approaches have proved to be highly successful in a number of applications.

Nevertheless, many data processing facilities still operate around the standard keypunch-printer approach. It is the purpose of this article to review some of the newer techniques for computer input/ output, and to explore the economic implications of various alternatives. If cost-performance relationships are essential to the business manager, he will have to reappraise his data processing operations periodically in the light of a rapidly advancing technology. It is hoped that this article will aid him in such reappraisal for the important area of computer input/output peripherals.

MAN-MACHINE INTERFACE

In order to solve problems on computers, man has to communicate with the machine. First, he has to prepare the program which tells the machine what to do; secondly, he has to prepare the data in machine-readable form. Upon completion of the solution process by the computer, output information has to be prepared in a form that can be readily interpreted by the user.

Man-machine interface has become the real bottleneck in computing. Since the advent of computers, significant break-throughs have occurred in the design of central processing units (CPU); we have seen vacuum tubes replaced by transistors, transistors by integrated circuits. Each stage of development resulted in startling improvements of cost/performance ratios.

But advances in the area of man-machine interface, though important, have not been able to match development in other areas. Input/output (I/O) has often become the bottleneck in computing, and it is safe to predict that for some time to come research and development in computer systems will concentrate in the field of computer peripherals.[1]

In our discussion of input/ouput problems, we shall not be concerned with computer programming; programming is an area of enough importance to merit separate study in detail. Rather, our emphasis will be on analyzing data preparation, both by man for the machine and by the computer for the user. To illustrate its importance, we may note that costs associated with the interchange of information between man and machine may well constitute the largest expense of operating a computer. For example, the federal government in the U.S. was spending $550 million yearly to convert data into machine readable form in the mid-1960s.[2] A single large insurance firm in

---

[1] Berul, L. H., "Survey of IS & R Equipment," *Datamation*, March, 1968, pp. 27–32.
[2] *Clearinghouse*, U.S. Department of Commerce, Springfield, Va., PB 176 911, January, 1967, p. 259.

1966 was spending $4,800,000 yearly on conversion of data to machine usable form.[3] For industrial uses of computers, keypunching alone can run as high as 50 per cent of total equipment costs.[4]

Needless to say, computer manufacturers and systems analysts show continuing concern for reducing the costs of data preparation and interpretation. Recent rapid developments in this area become understandable. And certainly, there are no grounds for considering the state of the art fixed at this time; further improvements can be expected.

CONVENTIONAL KEYPUNCH

To some degree, I/O equipment preceded modern computers. Punched cards and paper tapes have been used for 50 years or more. In the late 1800s, Hollerith used punched cards to aid compilation of the U.S. census. To facilitate data summation, a mechanical card sorter was developed. Similarly, paper tapes have been used in business for a variety of applications.

With the advent of high-speed computers, adaptations of previously used techniques have become increasingly inadequate. Central processing units of modern computers are able to operate many times faster than data can be fed in or out by conventional electro-mechanical equipment. Necessary input volume often has increased enormously, and volume of output by standard printers can become such that interpretation and comprehension by management is made nearly impossible. This dilemma has led to the I/O "bottleneck." [5, 6]

Before discussing some of the alternatives which may alleviate this bottleneck, let us briefly review the operation of conventional punched card machines and line impact printers, which are still the standard I/O equipment in most data processing installations in industry.

There are four steps typically involved in preparing input data with the standard manual keypunch. The first step is, of course, the

[3] Philipson, H. L., "Optical Character Recognition: The Input Answer," *Data Processing*, Vol. X, June, 1966, pp. 119–130.
[4] Lee, M. K., "The Demise of the Keypunch," *Datamation*, March, 1968, pp. 51–55.
[5] Spiro, B. E., "Man-Machine Interface in System's Design," *Data Processing*, Vol. XI, Oct., 1966, pp. 118–138.
[6] Nievergelt, J., "Computing—past, present, and future," *I.E.E.E.*, Spectrum, 5, 1, January, 1968, pp. 57–61.

keypunching itself. Since we may expect the frequency of errors in keypunching to be 2 to 4 per cent, error verification is normally required as a second step, adding to the cost of the keypunching operation. Following preparation of punched cards, a card reader translates the coded information into binary format to be stored on magnetic tapes, from which the computer can request it automatically as the actual processing is initiated. Auxiliary equipment may be required to facilitate interpreting, verifying, sorting, and collating the punched cards.

To illustrate some of the basic unbalances of such a system, a keypunch operator can punch and verify roughly two to four cards per minute, an electro-mechanical card reader can read about 1000 cards per minute, and a modern central processor of average size may process the information contained on about 100,000 cards per minute.

Punched paper tape systems are similar to the punched card system except that paper tape on reels replaces punched cards, and paper tape equipment replaces punched card equipment. Performance characteristics vary to some extent, but the basic problem of unbalance remains.

On the output side, the basic problem is often not the mismatching of various data handling and processing speeds, even if mismatching exists. If cards or tape have to be punched to record the output of the computer, speed—or lack of it—may remain the main factor of consideration. However, with printing speeds of 10,000 characters or more per second, the primary concern on the output side is often with the problem of interpretation of stacks of printer output by the user rather than with increasing printer speeds. The basic problem becomes one of selection and format of presentation rather than one of lack of quantity.

INITIAL IMPROVEMENTS

Given the obvious discrepancies in processing speeds between the fully electronic central processing unit of a computer and its mostly electromechanical peripheral attachments, it became obvious fairly early in the development of computers that solutions to the ensuing problems had to be found if economical operation of the total system was to be achieved. Clearly, it would violate any notion of efficient use of resources if the expensive central processing unit were to sit idle for over 80 per cent of its time waiting for peripheral units to accomplish input and output operations. Early efforts were aimed mainly at allowing the central processing unit to pursue other computational tasks while waiting for input and output operations to take place, thus avoiding wasteful idle times. Buffers, "off-line" input-output, and "overlapped" input and output were highly successful results of these endeavors. High-speed electronic storage devices of limited capacity are used temporarily to "buffer" all communications between the CPU and peripheral devices. For example, a buffer may receive character by character the information recorded on a punched card as it is read by a card reader, at a rate of roughly 700 characters per second. Once all the information on this card is stored in the buffer, this information can be transferred to the central processing unit at a rate of 50,000 characters per second upon the appropriate instruction from the CPU. The CPU is free to work on other problems while the buffer gradually receives information from the next card; processing of problems by the CPU and performance of input/output operations can "overlap."

Carrying the same concept further, a small independent computer may be responsible for coordinating all input/output operations under control of the system's main processor. Or data may be transferred from, for example, punched cards to magnetic tape "off-line" by a card reader and a tape handler as an operation which is completely separated from the main computer. The magnetic tapes are then transferred to the tape drives of the main computer and, again, can be processed from there at speeds of 50,000 characters per second or more. Similarly, CPU output can be written on magnetic tape, and printing can be performed off-line. With magnetic tape encoding speeds as high as 300,000 characters per second and impact printing speeds of 10,000 characters per second or less, the opportunity for increased efficiency in regard to CPU is obvious. (It should be noted that a reel of magnetic tape costing $50 can hold more than 10 million characters and is reusable.)

To reduce keypunching costs, turnaround documents have been used successfully in some systems. To illustrate, a computer produces a punched card which is sent to a customer as an invoice. When the customer returns the card with payment, the document can be fed directly into the reader, thus avoiding repunching information. Also, in some systems, cards or paper tape are punched as a by-product of the original preparation of source documents. The punched cards or paper tape are accumulated and processed in a conventional manner when required. Invoicing, inventory control, ordering, payroll, and bookkeeping tasks are often streamlined by use of such techniques, but the handling of cards or paper tape still persists.

In order to alleviate the bottleneck resulting from relatively slow printer speeds, electro-static printers have been designed. Utilizing electrical and chemical processes, printing speeds up to 5000 lines per minute are possible, whereas the conventional impact printer, subject to electro-mechanical limitations, is capable of only 1200 lines per minute. However, we have seen that at such speeds the problem of information selection and comprehension by the user can become a new bottleneck, thus stressing the need for experimenting with radically new formats of output.

Even after the significant improvements in standard keypunch and printer operations by the techniques described were made, the basic issues of unbalanced speeds and unoperational formats remained. It became clear that in order to ameliorate the basic problems of input and output, concepts fundamentally different from the conventional would have to be used in developing alternatives to the standard keypunch-printer approach. A number of such new concepts has already led to highly successful alternatives, and further developments suggesting even more radical improvements are well under way. Following are some of the alternatives which are currently available and which have proven themselves in an operational environment.

• Key-to-tape systems involve methods and equipment which enable the elimination of paper by keying information from source documents directly onto magnetic tape. A keying machine is used to encode source data onto magnetic tape in a format which is directly suitable for computer processing. Keying is done off-line, and data can then be used by the CPU as required at speeds vastly superior to punched card readers. In advanced systems of this type, the keying and verification is done under the control of a small, peripheral computer. That is, a special CPU is employed to assist simultaneously up to 32 key operators in data entry and verification. Storage and output to magnetic tape is accomplished under full control of the special CPU. In comparison to standard punched card operations, it is estimated the input error rates can be reduced by roughly 30 per cent, and keying costs are reduced by approximately 20 per cent.

• Mark-sensing is a technique in which paper documents (mostly cards) are marked in appropriate places with a special conductive-lead pencil (or with a normal pencil if more advanced optical recognition equipment is used). They can then be automatically punched or scanned. This method has proven useful where information of a standard, repetitive format has to be recorded in the field away from places where a keypunch would be readily accessible.

It eliminates manual keypunching of such information upon receipt of the source documents at the computing center. Successful applications include use by public utility companies, forest inventory compilers, and college registrars.

• With magnetic ink character recognition (MICR), information is printed on documents in the form of standardized characters with magnetic ink. These magnetic ink characters can be read automatically by machines, the speed being limited only by the rate at which documents can be moved physically through the reading machine. Following encoding in magnetic ink, an MICR reader transfers data directly to magnetic tape from which it can be processed by the CPU. Magnetic ink coding, which preceded general optical character recognition, has been found particularly useful where users need to be able to reread periodically the coded information, the most familiar application example being the use of magnetic-ink encoded checks.

• Devices for general optical character recognition (OCR) have been developed which are capable of reading automatically standardized type fonts, such as the U.S.A. Standard Character Set for Optical Character Recognition, directly from the source document. More advanced equipment, such as the "Electronic Retina Computing Reader" (ERCR) is able to read practically any type font that is machine printed and is equal to or better in quality than normal typewritten copy. The task of preparing data in machine-readable form is reduced to normal typing, which is considerably less expensive than keypunching. Processing time varies with document size and the number of lines to be read, but speeds of several hundred documents per minute are often attainable. In some European countries, banks have bypassed the MICR stage, having gone directly to optical character recognition in their check handling operation. Other examples include Philco's 6200 Optical Address Reader, which automatically reads and sorts mail addressed in standard machine written fonts. Farrington's Series III Model 2030 reads full pages of typewritten information or scans an entire page in search of particular information. Presently, more than 10 different manufacturers offer over 25 models of optical scanning equipment on the market.

In recent years, the reliability of OCR has attained the necessary level to make these systems fully operational in industrial applications; in fact, the error rate of a good OCR system is likely to be considerably below error rates in standard keypunching operations. It should be pointed out, however, that automatic reading of characters does not imply automatic understanding of any meaning which may be conveyed by a text in ordinary language. Significant problems will have to be overcome before we can look for an automatic reading and understanding of general text.

• In some data processing systems, at least a partial elimination of source documents is feasible. Details of a transaction are captured at the time of occurrence and fed directly into the computer for processing. Input may be accomplished by remote terminals of various types which are located at the point of transaction occurrence, and paper documents become unnecessary. This concept, which is widely used in the area of computerized process control, is becoming increasingly popular in business; e.g. in processing production information, orders, sales, etc. For example, NCR's 420-2 can read journal tapes from sales registers, accounting machines, or adding machines (at a rate of over a thousand characters per second) directly into the computer for automatic processing.

• On the output side, automatic plotting—which again has been used for some time in engineering applications—is becoming a more widely used tool in the business environment. The common wisdom that "one picture may be worth a thousand words" may be rephrased as "one graph may be worth a thousand numbers." The human mind is notoriously poor at absorbing and remembering large quantities of numerical information. However, it can often be conveyed successfully in the form of graphs. Time series of sales or profits, probability distributions of future returns, or business forecasts are but a few common examples. A variety of digital or digital-to-analog plotters with varying performance and cost characteristics to suit a wide spectrum of application needs are readily available on the market to produce hard-copy graphs, either on-line or off-line. Even time-sharing terminals can now be augmented by attaching a plotter (e.g. the Calcomp plotter) and, as the official of a time-sharing service firm recently pointed out, it is a wonder more people do not have them.

• Cathode Ray Tubes (CRT) are the basis of some of the newest input/output equipment to become widely operational. In essence, visual information is displayed by the computer on TV screens at electronic speeds. In some of the more advance installations, the screen can also be used for data input, as a kind of scratchpad, by means of a light-pen which is activated by the user. Such CRT's, while still somewhat expensive, are highly versatile and may well become increasingly popular in the industrial environment. Hard copies can be produced by attaching microfilming equipment to the CRT.

   An example of equipment utilizing a processor, CRT's, and microfilming auxiliaries is the SC-4060, which translates data coded on punched cards or magnetic tape into alpha-numeric or graphic form on the CRT. A recent article in the *Harvard Business Review* discusses in some detail the benefits which may be gained from a CRT system.[7] Again, a variety of models have appeared on the market in a relatively short time-span from over 20 different manufacturers with purchase prices ranging anywhere from $1,500 to $150,000, depending on performance characteristics, to suit a variety of different needs and budgets.

AN APPLICATION

To illustrate the potential of some of the alternatives discussed, consider the following example of a large-scale input operation. A firm has to prepare input data amounting to 40 million characters each month. Assume the task at hand is to uncode these data from paper source documents onto magnetic tape. With a conventional keypunch operation, approximately 1.6 million cards would have to be prepared (assuming an average of 25 characters per card). A keypunch operator may punch 8000 strokes per hour, for 157.5 hours a month. The cost of one keypunch operator and keypunch machine may be roughly as follows: [8]

Salary	$400 per month
Overhead	77 "
Equipment rental	65 "
Card stock (44,000 cards)	38 "
Total	$580 per month

The cost of keypunching would come out to 46 cents per 1000 strokes. Thirty-two keypunch machines and operators are required, plus the additional hardware and operators required for verification. Verification would vary somewhat with the specific application; in one particular case it was found to be 31 cents per 1000 strokes, which would result in total data preparation costs of 77 cents per 1000 keypunched characters, or a total of $31,500 per month for our application (this includes the cost of a card reader).

Let us consider as a first alternative to conventional keypunching a direct key-to-magnetic-tape system, such as "Key-Processing" manu-

[7] M. S. Morton and A. M. McCosh, "Terminal Costing for Better Decisions," *Harvard Business Review*, May-June, 1968, pp. 147–156.
[8] Philipson, H. L., *op. cit.*, pp. 119–130.

factured by Computer Machinery Corporation, in which keying is done under the control of a special CPU. Due to faster keying and easier verification and correction, operator keying rates of 8000 strokes per hour should be achievable, including verification. The cost breakdown per operator:

Salary	$400 per month	
Overhead	70	"
Equipment rental	82	"
Total	$552 per month	

This would result in costs of 44 cents per 1000 strokes, and 32 keying stations would be required. Considering monthly costs of a processor, disk-storage and auxiliaries at $4000, total costs for the operation would be roughly $22,000 per month.

A further alternative which ought to be analyzed is the operation of a system in which source documents are typed in some standard format acceptable to OCR equipment. The cost per typist may be as follows:

Salary	$400 per month	
Overhead	65	"
Equipment rental, paper and ribbons	27	"
Total	$492 per month	

With ordinary typing, it is generally safe to assume an effective typing rate of 12,000 strokes per hour or better, thus yielding costs of 26 cents per 1000 strokes. The problem of verification is considerably eased when typing is compared to keypunching, since typewritten copy can be partially verified by sight. In one study, the error rates for typing and for keypunching were found to be 0.79 per cent and 2.9 per cent respectively. Furthermore, verification costs for typed material are considered to be only 40 per cent of keypunch verification costs, or approximately 13 cents per 1000 strokes. Total cost of typing may be assumed approximately at 39 cents per 1000 strokes, or $15,600 per month for the case under consideration. (Twenty-one typists plus verifiers would be required.) If, for example, a Scan-Data 300 System OCR Page Reader were employed to read the output of the typists, the monthly cost, including a full-time operator, would be $9,500, thus yielding total operation costs of $25,100, as compared to the $31,500 to do the same task with a conventional keypunch operation.

Figure 1.1 shows costs as a function of data input volume for each

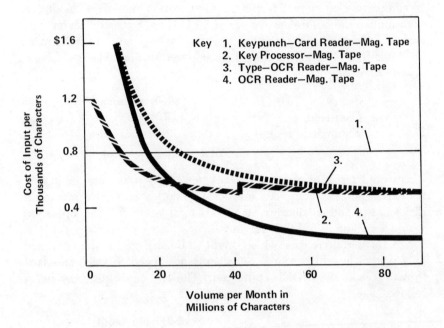

1.1   METHOD OF CONVERTING SOURCE DOCUMENT TO MAGNETIC TAPE

of the three alternatives. While conventional keypunching may be economically optimal at very low volumes, a key-to-tape system provides significant advantages beyond a volume of roughly 10 million characters per month. The OCR oriented system continues to decrease in unit cost per character at volumes even beyond 40 million characters per month, hence being particularly suited for large volumes of data. Obviously, the costs of an OCR system are effectively reduced by a significant amount if the typed source documents are themselves required within the organization, so that only a small fraction of the costs of preparing these documents may need to be allocated to data input preparation for the computer. A cost-curve like (4) in Figure 1.1 could easily result, placing the OCR system in a very favorable position, even for relatively low data volumes.

It should be noted that Figure 1.1 has been presented to facilitate illustration of a concept. In practice, a decision would be based on the specific costs involved in each alternative available to the firm. For example, a firm faced with the task of processing large volumes of cards will likely require a considerable amount of unit record equipment for sorting, merging, and so on. If this were the case, the cost curve (1) in Figure 1.1 would be shifted upwards, thus reducing the breakeven point between keypunching and other methods. Another factor which could have considerable effect on card oriented systems is storage cost. Card storage costs for a firm handling 1.6 million cards per month could be substantial.

A number of companies have been able to attain significant savings by following through with a systematic analysis of alternatives as illustrated above. Following are some examples of systems departing from the conventional keypunch approach which have proven themselves in a business operating environment.

• Using Data-Recorders manufactured by Mohawk Data Sciences, savings of up to 30 per cent were experienced in file conversions, file updating, program entry, and program editing. Savings were attributed primarily to faster keying, easier verification and correction, fewer steps between data capture and computer input, elimination of cards and use of reusable magnetic tapes, and cheaper requirements for backup equipment.[9]

• Optical font sales registers and adding machines which make their entries on printed tapes in a series of stylized numbers and operating codes are used in the retailing industry. Tapes are read directly into the data processing system through optical tape reader peripherals. This procedure is used for accounts receivable updating and for control of inventory.[10]

• In Florida, a group of 20 newspapers are using an Electronic Retina Computing Reader (ERCR), manufactured by Recognition Equipment, to read 10 to 20 pages of newscopy per minute. The ERCR transfers the characters to magnetic tape, which is then used to drive type-setting equipment automatically.[11]

• The Chicago Board of Education, the U.S. Army, United Air Lines, and Swedish banking firms are among the other users of ERCR. In the case of United Air Lines, the ERCR reads ticket numbers, route, fare, and tax information from 87,000 tickets each day. The savings to United are reported to be $10,000 to $15,000 per month. The U.S. Army's ERCR recognizes 360 upper and lower case letters in several different type fonts.

• *TV Guide* magazine reports installation of OCR equipment manufactured by Farrington which resulted in increased speed, accuracy, and cost savings over a conventional keypunch operation which simply

[9] Price, D. G., "Whither Keypunch?" *Datamation*, June, 1967, pp. 32–34.
[10] Lee, M. K., *op. cit.*, pp. 51–55.
[11] Philipson, H. L., *op. cit.*, pp. 119–130.

was not able to handle seasonal peaks of over 500,000 renewal subscriptions in a six-week period before Christmas. Quoting from a recent report by the company's EDP-manager: "At the conclusion of our 1966 Christmas season, we compared our results with the same three months of 1965. We had employed 55 operators in our card processing department versus 75. In 1966, we worked 2,488 overtime hours versus 4,108 in 1965. Meanwhile, our order volume had increased to 1,531,000 versus 1,284,000 in 1965, and our costs had decreased. The most gratifying factor was that all orders delivered into our cashiering department by our cutoff date were processed into the Christmas issue, a far cry from 1965 when 200,000 remained behind." [12]

CHOOSE YOUR SYSTEM

It seems obvious that the first step in choosing any data processing equipment must be a clear specification of the tasks to be accomplished. Regarding data input/output, questions such as the following will have to be answered:

1. What is the volume of data to be processed? What are average volumes and what peak demands can be expected, both today and in the future?

2. How often will each type of information processing be required?

3. What are the requirements regarding processing times?

4. What degrees of reliability and accuracy are required? Consequently, what verification and error detection procedures are necessary?

5. What types and quality of output documents are required? Are hard copies required; are turnaround documents desirable?

6. Where and how is the original source information generated?

Only after these questions have been answered can one reasonably proceed with an evaluation of specific techniques and equipment: equipment selection has to be preceded by systems design, not vice versa. In proceeding with the equipment selection phase, good comparative listings of electronic data processing equipment and their characteristics are often useful, at least for an initial assessment

[12] Rizzo, A. J., "OCR for Handling Publication Subscriptions," *Datamation*, December, 1968, pp. 67–71.

of alternatives. Such listings are available from the following sources, among others:

Auerbach Standard EDP—Reports, published by the Auerbach Corporation, Philadelphia, Pa.
1968 Guide to Data Processing Equipment, Woods Gordon and Company, Toronto, Ontario.
June issue of each year of *Computers and Automation.*
September issue of each year of *Business Automation.*

It should be pointed out that much of the specialized, modern input/output equipment is not produced by the major computer manufacturers but rather by smaller firms which specialize in the area of computer peripherals. Hence, systems proposals from major manufacturers are not necessarily based on a complete analysis of input/output alternatives as proposed above. In fact, this may be one of the reasons for some of the existing gaps between current technical know-how and actual operations. Once a number of alternatives has been identified as viable in the light of the initial system's specifications, a comparative cost and performance analysis as outlined above will indicate the course of action to be pursued.

CONCLUSIONS

We have seen that the process of transposing data from common man-usable formats into computer code and vice versa has become a major bottleneck in many data processing systems. Most conventional input/output equipment is based on electro-mechanical processes which restrict data handling speeds significantly. Considerable human effort is required for manual data preparation and for interpretation of unwieldy computer outputs. Thus, input/output functions entail a major portion of total costs in many EDP installations in business. New processes and equipment have been developed in recent years to ameliorate the input/output bottleneck, yet business is generally not making sufficient use of tools presently available. Certainly, additional significant improvements can be expected in the future, as testified by current research in areas such as automatic reading of handwritten documents, graphic input devices, and voice response systems. However, present achievements in areas such as optical character recognition, graphic output, and the others discussed often warrant a critical reappraisal of current conventional modes of operation without waiting for the ultimate solution of the future. Important savings may be achieved by analyzing systematically the economic aspects of available computer input/output alternatives, and by integrating system design and equipment selection so as to obtain the optimum in regard to cost and performance.

2.

NEW LOOK AT COMPUTER DATA ENTRY

By Raymond Ferrara
and Richard L. Nolan

Editor's Note: From the JOURNAL OF SYSTEMS MANAGEMENT, February 1973, pp. 24–33. Reprinted by permission of the publisher, the Association for Systems Management, and authors.

The research for this article was supported by the Associates of the Harvard Business School, working drafts were reviewed as CBIS (Computer-Based Information Systems) Working Paper #3.

The technology of most aspects of computing has changed so rapidly as to be barely recognizable from the technology of a mere seven years ago. We have seen several hundredfold improvements in internal processing speeds and on-line mass storage. Software operating systems have allowed a more efficient utilization of increasingly more powerful computers. Communications capability has added an entirely new dimension to the scope of computer applications. Most companies have quickly assimilated computing advancements and have benefited from the performance improvements. Business, especially big business, would find it difficult to operate if it weren't for these advancements. The volume of work would simply be too great to handle manually or with first or even second-generation computers.

However, there is one notable exception to business' rapid assimilation of new computer technology: data entry. Broadly defined, data entry is the process by which information is generated in a form suitable to be read by the computer. Here, we will be concerned primarily with volume data entry—how an organization's standardized, repetitive information can be captured as opposed to, say, textual data entry (word-processing) or program data entry.

Until the mid-60's, volume data entry was nearly synonymous with keypunching. Although a much wider range of alternative methods now is available, keypunching still accounts for the large majority of computer data requirements. Considering the performance progress in other areas of the technology, it is rather surprising to note that this vast bulk of data is being prepared on equipment initially designed for the 1890 U. S. Census. The keypunch's standard medium, the 80-column, 12-row punch card, was developed more recently, in 1924, but its origins extend even further back to the card-controlled weaving machines of the 1850's.

Are the keypunch and the punched card, like the wheel, designs that cannot be fundamentally improved? The punch card does have some obvious advantages: it can be read by both man and machine; it is largely resistant to environmental conditions, and, like the keypunch, it is relatively inexpensive. But the disadvantages are just as apparent. The information able to be contained on any one card is limited, leading to troublesome multiple-card records. The speed at which cards can be input to the computer is 10 to 100 times slower than with other recording media such as magnetic tape; and, most important, card preparation is time-consuming and highly labor-intensive.

The design of better data entry systems has been approached from two basic directions. *Keypunch replacement* focuses on improving or replacing the keypunch, yet still retaining an operator dedicated to keying data from source documents to a computer-readable medium. Data entry systems utilizing the buffered keypunch, key-tape units, or key-disk systems fall into this category. *Source data entry,* on the other hand, implies eliminating the intermediate operators necessary in a keypunch or keypunch replacement system. Optical character recognition equipment, for example, translates handwritten, typed, or printed information directly from a source document.

Most terminal systems, even keyboard terminal systems, are used as source data entry systems. An airline reservation agent, although he may often key from a prepared document just like a keypunch operator, isn't employed solely to type into a terminal. He would be there, terminal or not; the terminal is simply a device allowing him to obtain rapid confirmation of passenger requests. A byproduct of this activity is that the information he keys is obtained in computer readable form.

BASIS FOR REVIEWING ALTERNATIVES

Data entry typically accounts for 20-40 percent of EDP expenditures. Consequently, the decisions concerning the types of data entry to be used in an organization are likely to have major cost ramifications. Equally important, these decisions can affect the timeliness and accuracy of the organization's information flow. But keypunch replacement and especially source data entry may never be investigated without some co-operation and prodding by top management.

Even if there is an awareness of the potential savings to be gained in data entry, there is little incentive for change. Performance is not always measured in financial terms. The premium can be on maximizing the quality and reliability of service rather than minimizing cost. Source data entry methods are also especially hard to implement, since these require commitment and cooperation across departmental boundaries.

But, with computer manufacturers leading the way, managers at all levels are becoming aware of the benefits of on-line keyboard terminals. On-line keyboard terminals probably will be the general purpose data entry devices of the future, but it is also clear that we are in a transition stage, with most companies possessing neither the resources nor the need to convert all their data entry workloads to on-line systems. Moreover, it would be misleading to associate the benefits of on-line keyboard terminals *only* with on-line keyboard terminals. Rapid communication with a central computer can be achieved through remote batch terminals or even an off-line network (e.g., key-tape unit to off-line tape station). Response capability is also possible through a batch or off-line network provided immediate response is not required. Finally, cost-effective source data entry can be achieved through a wide variety of devices, from flexowriters to industrial data collection systems, without the heavy central computer utilization and communications line charges which continuously on-line terminals incur.

MAJOR DATA ENTRY ALTERNATIVES

The major data entry alternatives can be grouped into (1) keypunch and keypunch replacement, (2) optical character recognition and related equipment, and (3) terminal systems. Figure 2.1 shows the projected trends in installed units for the keypunch and the three

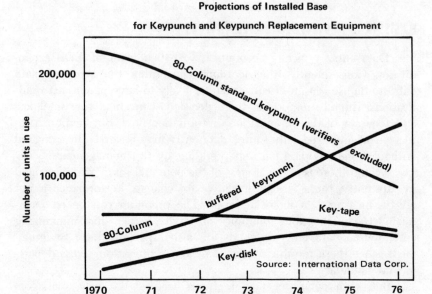

2.1 PROJECTIONS OF INSTALLED BASE FOR KEYPUNCH AND KEYPUNCH REPLACEMENT EQUIPMENT

major types of keypunch replacement equipment: buffered keypunch, key-tape, and key-disk.

All three types of replacement equipment share some fundamental advantages over the standard keypunch. Each unit can function in both data entry and verify [1] modes, eliminating the necessity for separate verification equipment. Another common feature is the electronically buffered keyboard. Because characters are imprinted *after* a record is complete, the operator does not have to "wait" on formerly mechanically-constrained actions like card registration, skipping, and duplicating. Nor does the operator have to rekey the whole record upon detecting an error. The operator simply backspaces and rekeys the correction. Though individual operators may have trouble becoming accustomed to a buffered keyboard, most users have experienced productivity increases from 10–25 percent over standard keypunchers and verifiers.[2]

[1] Verification is a step employed in most keypunch installations to reduce errors. Basically, each card is re-keyed by another operator on another machine. If there are any discrepancies, the card is returned for correction.
[2] The June 1970 *Datamation* includes seven articles on the keypunch replacement.

Aside from the keyboard, the buffered keypunch is basically equivalent to standard models. Univac, the originators, had the market entirely to themselves from 1968 to 1971, until IBM announced a buffered keypunch for standard 80-column cards and another for the newer System/3 96-column cards.[3] IBM's entrance is expected to give a tremendous boost to buffered keypunch sales; chances are the buffered models will outnumber standard models by late 1974.

With key-tape, the operator keys directly onto magnetic tape, bypassing the card entirely. With tape, records lengths can be variable, thus avoiding multiple card records. Tape is also a faster, more accurate medium than cards for computer input. In practice, however, tape has proved cumbersome for the installation that is characterized by a large variety of data entry jobs. The operator must mount new tapes frequently or key different batches on the same tape. The latter method requires pooling,[4] or separating appropriate records onto appropriate tapes. Pooling has proved a time-consuming and expensive process in installations with a large job mix.

Key-tape manufacturers, the pioneers of keypunch replacement, are facing a semi-saturated market. Some of the more recent models offer communications options for users desiring an off-line data entry network, but with many former key-tape installations converting to key-disk or on-line terminal entry, retirements are expected to exceed sales, leading to the projected decline in the installed base.

Key-disk systems avoid the pooling problem and offer other positive advantages. The basic concept of a key-disk system is to link several buffered keystations to a small controller or minicomputer. Data records can be keyed, extensively checked and validated using the minicomputer, and stored on its disk. When complete batches are accumulated, the data can be automatically re-recorded on magnetic tape for input to a central computer.

The first key-disk system was introduced in 1969, followed by at least 10 other introductions within a year. Many of these "early" systems were large 16 to 64 keystation systems. But several companies

---

A descriptive article on key-tape can be seen in September-October 1968 *Data Processing Magazine*. Three user experiences with key-disk are reported in August-September 1971, *Data Dynamics*.

[3] 96-column buffered keypunches are not included in Figure 1.1. Except for installations with System/3 computers, 96-column keypunches will rarely be used as standard keypunch replacements.

[4] If the key-tape unit records on computer-compatible tape, then pooling may be performed on a host computer or on a specialized off-line device called a pooler. If the unit records are on noncompatible tape (e.g., cassette or cartridge), then pooling must be performed on an off-line device which also produces computer-compatible tapes.

are now providing smaller-scale, reasonably priced key-disk systems.[5] Over 80 percent of the present keypunch population is located at sites with less than 16 machines,[6] so key-disk should penetrate quite deeply.

In the past year, there have been several announcements of small computer systems which are functionally very similar to key-disk. Each can support a number of keystations, and also peripherals such as line printers, card reader/punches, and communications interfaces allowing disk-accumulated data to be transmitted directly to a host computer. These systems, although they may be more expensive on a per-keystation basis, combine the advantages of key-disk and remote batch processing.

OPTICAL CHARACTER RECOGNITION

Optical Character Recognition (OCR), heralded during the 60's as the coming solution for data entry problems, has yet to fulfill its promise. All but a few of the OCR systems produced to date have been sophisticated and expensive. They have been attractive primarily in high-volume, specialized applications but of little use to smaller installations.

Besides the cost of the equipment, a difficulty with OCR lies in the resystematization that is necessary to accommodate its use. Forms have to be redesigned, using special OCR papers and ink. Ribbons and printing elements are readily available, both for computer printers and Selectric typewriters, but the forms redesign may be rather expensive, since printing an OCR form is a complex process. Besides the special paper requirements, the form may have portions pre-printed in OCR-readable inks (e.g., standard information, field separation) and in nonreadable inks (e.g., instructions). With minimum setup charges above $500 and minimum running charges above $5 per 1,000, an OCR form cannot be printed economically for low-volume applications. General-purpose forms can be used, but this puts the burden on the OCR typist. For example, she would be required to locate information such as field and record separation. Efficient OCR typing requires training equivalent to that of a keypunch operator.

The principal features of OCR equipment which affect potential users are reject handling and operating flexibility. Some scanning units

[5] See Figure 7.7 for representative price ranges for keypunch and keypunch replacement equipment.
[6] *Data Entry Equipment*, International Data Corporation, 1972.

can read only selected portions of an input document (e.g., one or two lines) and thus restrict potential applications.[7] The ease with which new forms can be accommodated is also important. Machine specific higher-level languages exist, but their complexity and flexibility vary. Usually the manufacturer will provide support in this area, helping the user design and accommodate new forms.

OCR readers differ in how they handle rejects or unreadable data. Some have a rescan feature which may help to cut down the incidence of rejects. An increasing number of readers are being equipped with one or more graphic displays and keyboards. Unreadable characters are projected on the display; the operator keys in his interpretation.

	Typed input	Handprinted input	Computer-printed input
Supervised preparation	Less than 1%	1–3%	negligible
Unsupervised but familiar with OCR rules	Less than 5%	Less and 10%	negligible

2.2 TYPICAL OCR REJECT RATES

This technique can reduce the reject rate enormously, but may result in significant lower OCR throughput speeds because the reader must pause until the reject is processed. Whatever the methods for handling rejects, the critical features are that clear, convenient techniques exist for (1) identifying the rejected data, (2) correcting it, and (3) maintaining batch integrity while avoiding data duplication.

Some manufacturers also emphasize reading speed and multifont capability as important features. Neither of these is likely to warrant a price premium for most potential users. Reading speeds should be checked to ensure that the projected workload can be handled in a reasonable time, but most users will find there is time to spare. Multi-

---

[7] Within the OCR industry, there has been a distinction between page and document readers. Page readers typically handle larger forms (e.g., 8½" by 11" or more), and operate faster than document readers. The price differential between the two types of readers exists mainly within the vendors' product lines, not so much across the industry. Several manufacturers produce combined document/ page readers.

font capability (e.g., reading more than one type of OCR font) is becoming less important with OCR "A" emerging as American industry's standard font.

The ability to read handprinted numeric characters is available. Provided some fairly basic rules are followed, character-substitution error rates of less than one-tenth of one percent are achievable.[8] Except on two lower-priced OCR terminals, however, the handprint feature can be found only on equipment costing over $100,000. There are also at least two machines with alphanumeric handprint options.

As a source data entry system, OCR has been most successful where much of the information to be captured can be pre-printed (e.g., the return stub on a computer printed utility bill), or where some degree of control can be exercised in preparing the form. A high reject rate will offset the advantages of OCR, since rejected documents will have to be retyped or even cycled back to the source for correction. Providing that reasonable care is exercised to separate out folded or mutilated documents beforehand, the following reject rates are typical of users' experiences.[9]

As a keypunch replacement, OCR is feasible where the cost of OCR equipment can be offset by a reduction in keypunch and EAM equipment rentals and by the increased productivity of typists. Wages for typists are generally lower than for keypunch operators, but productivity will be much higher when sight-verification can be substituted for key-verification.[10]

Figure 2.3 shows the projected trends for OCR equipment. The steadily upward trend is expected to accelerate with the introduction of lower cost, minicomputer based OCR units. Four systems now on the market sell for less than $50,000. Given a limited number of source data entry jobs, this lower cost OCR equipment could be a cost effective replacement for as few as five or six keypunches. Several OCR manufacturers have announced combined OCR disk systems. Data read through the OCR unit is stored on disk; corrections to this data as well as entirely new batches of data may be entered through the keyboards.

As a data entry method, OMR has limited applicability. It can

[8] A character-substitution error occurs when the machine processes a character but reads it incorrectly. Rejects, on the other hand, occur when the machine will not process the character(s) at all. Many manufacturers will quote character-substitution error rates for their machines, but very few will quote on the reject rate since this depends heavily on the particular application.

[9] *AUERBACH On Optical Character Recognition* (Philadelphia: AUERBACH Publishers, Inc., 1971).

[10] "Improvements in Data Entry," *EDP Analyzer* (September-October 1971).

Projections of Installed Base for Optical Character and Optical Mark Readers

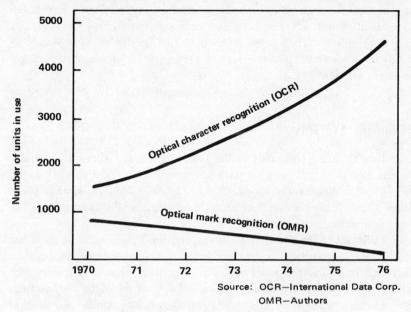

Source: OCR—International Data Corp.
OMR—Authors

Optical mark readers (OMR) cannot "read" characters
as true OCR units do; they can only detect the presence
or absence of marks on a paper form. Because of OMR's
inherently simpler recognition logic, the price of these
units is substantially lower than OCR. Some sell for as
low as $2,000 but the average is closer to $25,000.

2.3 PROJECTIONS OF INSTALLED BASE FOR OPTICAL CHARACTER AND OPTI-
CAL MARK READERS

be useful on documents where responses are limited to "yes-no" or
multiple choice answers, but it is an inaccurate, clumsy way of handling alphanumeric data. OMR's present installed base is less than
half of the OCR's on a per-unit basis. Many OMR installations are
now switching to OCR with numeric handprint capability, so OMR's
installed base is probably on a permanent decline, despite several new
product announcements.

Bar code and Magnetic Ink Character Recognition (MICR) are
even less common data entry methods. Except for its entrenched position in the banking industry, MICR is unsuited for volume data
entry. Document control is at least as difficult as with conventional
OCR, the machines are just as expensive, and most MICR readers can
translate only the numeric font used by the banking industry.

Bar code readers have alphanumeric capability,[11] but require mechanical devices (e.g., embossers, modified typewriters) for source document generation. Bar code has not been extensively promoted as a general purpose data entry method. A further decline is probable as OCR becomes less expensive, since bar code offers no other advantages over conventional OCR.

TERMINAL SYSTEMS

In comparing terminals to the other data entry alternatives, more is involved than just data preparation; transmission and reception can be equally important considerations. Figure 2.4 helps clarify these lines of comparison as well as provide a basic classification scheme for terminal data entry systems.

In an integrated terminal system, terminal equipment is used for both data preparation and transmission. In a composite system, the terminal equipment is used only for data transmission; virtually any stand-alone data entry equipment can be used for data preparation. In practice, paper tape and cards are the most popular preparation media, since reliable inexpensive transmission terminals for these are readily available.

All the terminal systems in Figure 2.4 can transmit information to a central site more rapidly than we would expect with a non-terminal system. However, transmission will be a major expense with any remote terminal system.[12] If terminal lines extend more than, say, 2000 feet from the host computer or cross a public right-of-way, then communications must be by way of telephone or slower speed telegraph lines. Large-scale alternative communications methods (i.e. via independent companies with microwave or satellite relays) will appear 3–5 years from now, at best.

Some costs for transmission via telephone lines are: (1) line charges. Leased line: $5 mile/month plus conditioning charges. Dial-up line: same rates as normal business telephone. One line can support several terminal units. Transmission speeds may vary from 300 to 1600 characters per second. Higher-capacity lines are available. (2) modems ($75/mo. up) or acoustic couplers ($10/mo. up). These must be connected at both ends of the communications line. Prices vary

---

[11] Bar code readers read characters encoded as vertical lines. Some devices print normal typed characters above or below the bar code.

[12] For a further discussion, see *The Future of Telecommunications*, by James Martin (Prentice-Hall, 1971).

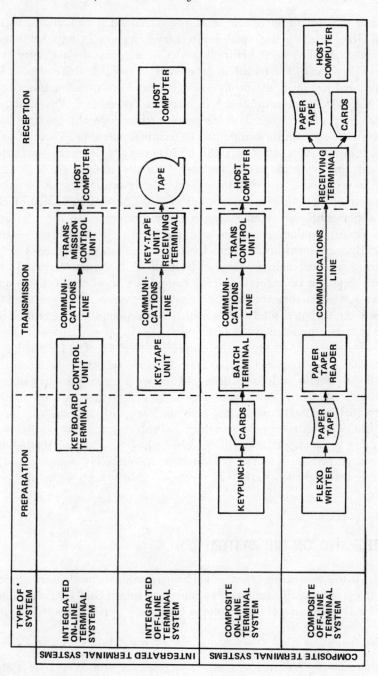

2.4   TYPE OF TERMINAL SYSTEMS

widely depending on transmission speed and error correction ability.

Other things being equal, rapid entry to a central computer should be an established need before considering a terminal data entry system. Then even if a terminal data entry is needed, there should be additional justifications for an on-line entry. For an installation to go on-line, several prerequisites will have to be satisfied. Physically, it needs a relatively large, fast computer with an operating system and teleprocessing monitor compatible to terminal operation. Then a front-end transmission control unit will be necessary to interface communications lines with the main computer.[13] Finally, the process of designing, programming, and maintaining on-line applications is considerably more complex than with batch applications. Consequently skilled technical personnel will assume a much greater importance.

On-line updating of data bases and error checking are two frequently mentioned justifications for on-line operation. Neither of these is usually a sufficient justification in itself. With off-line terminal systems, data can be entered quickly enough for most applications, and there are alternative methods for controlling errors (e.g., verification, check digits, batch totals, etc.) which can be employed regardless of the type of equipment used.

Response capability is the only characteristic of a terminal system that really requires on-line operation. By response, we mean the ability to obtain additional data and return it for display or printing within a relatively short time. This is in contrast to "echoes" of the data just entered. Several key-tape and key-disk systems are quite sophisticated in their echo capability—displaying the full record, performing error checks and minor calculations, or allowing limited retrieval of previously keyed information. Nevertheless, echoing is still a long way from the variety of response capable with an on-line system.

INTEGRATED ON-LINE SYSTEMS

Of the two major types of keyboard terminals used in integrated on-line systems, alphanumeric cathode ray tube (CRT) terminals are by far the more popular for volume data entry applications.[14, 15] Type-

[13] See the August, 1972 *Datamation* or the February, 1972 *Computer Decision* for an explanation and market survey for this type of equipment.
[14] Alphanumeric CRT terminals possess a keyboard and cathode ray tube capable of producing only character images. Graphic CRT terminals, on the other hand, can produce and manipulate curves and lines as well as characters, but because

writer terminals (e.g. Teletypes) are used by those desiring hard copy with data entry, but the projected growth for this type of terminal will come largely through time-sharing and remote job entry applications rather than data entry.

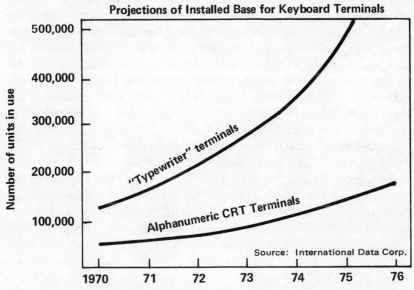

Projections of Installed Base for Keyboard Terminals

(y-axis: Number of units in use; values 100,000 – 500,000; x-axis: 1970, 71, 72, 73, 74, 75, 76)

"Typewriter" terminals

Alphanumeric CRT Terminals

Source: International Data Corp.

2.5   PROJECTIONS OF INSTALLED BASE FOR KEYBOARD TERMINALS

Alphanumeric CRT terminals are included in the product lines of all the major computer manufacturers. In addition, there are over 30 independent manufacturers of CRT terminals. Prices range from below $2,000 to over $10,000 per unit.[16] Price, however, is not usually a major selection criterion, since the terminal by itself usually represents a relatively minor cost in an on-line system. Terminal design considerations such as screen size and clarity, editing capability, and especially transmission methods are likely to assume important roles.

There is a definite trend towards increasing the terminal's local editing and processing power, thereby cutting down the load on the host computer and reducing communications line charges. Some ter-

of the expense and CPU overhead required for graphic CRT's, they are not normally considered appropriate for volume data entry.

[15] Several companies have developed inexpensive line printers or photographic display reproduction techniques for use with alphanumeric CRT terminals.

[16] For price/performance information on all types of terminal equipment see *AUERBACH Terminal Equipment Digest* (Philadelphia, AUERBACH Publishers, 1971).

minals include this power in the terminal itself, while others depend on local minicomputer control units. The latter may be able to support peripherals (e.g. line printers), provide intermediate storage, and even operate off-line, although transmission is performed on-line.

Key-tape or key-disk equipment can form the basis for an integrated off-line terminal system. The only other terminal equipment which generally fit into this category are industrial data collection systems and point-of-sale systems. Both of these terminal systems are designed for specific applications: industrial data collection for the factory floor and point-of-sale for the retail store. In their own applications, they deserve close consideration, since their specialized design—resulting in source data entry—may prove more economical than any generalized form of data entry.

After some initial set-backs, the point-of-sale concept seems set for rapid growth. Singer, the principal vendor, already claims over a $100 million order backlog, and at least four other major companies are now involved in producing modified cash registers for data entry. Industrial data collection represents a more mature but still underdeveloped market. These systems generally incorporate badge or card readers, time clocks, and simple keyboards for gathering data from the production floor. There are now six vendors sharing an installed base close to $150 million.

FRAMEWORK FOR EVALUATING ALTERNATIVES

With the large array of data entry equipment and methods, selecting the reasonable, cost-effective system can be a complex process. Here we will focus mainly on the economics of equipment selection —the operating and conversion costs for each alternative. Of course, non-economic factors should enter into any selection process. Reliability, operator convenience, and ease of conversion may not find their way into the numbers, but are very real considerations nonetheless. What a cost comparison of alternatives can do is provide the background against which these non-economic factors can be assessed.

Examining the keypunch replacement decision first provides a sense for the basic economics of data entry. Then we will develop a more general framework, a "top-down" approach suitable for evaluating a wider variety of data entry alternatives.

Figure 2.6 summarizes the cost characteristics of a typical keypunch operation. Only those costs which are likely to vary with the

Cost Category	% of Direct Cost	Potential Source of Cost Savings	Assumptions
Operator wages	74	Productivity increases	$500/mo., 22 days/ mo., 8,000 keystrokes/ hr., 7 productive hrs./day.
Keypunch and verifier rental	17	–	keypunch–$125/mo. verifier–$100/mo.
CPU charges	7	Reduced CPU charges	200 cards/minute processing speed, $40/CPU hour
Card costs	2	No cards With tape input	$1 per 1000 cards

Direct Cost/Character=$.0012
Direct Cost/Card   =4.8¢ (40 columns keyed and verified)

2.6   COST CHARACTERISTICS OF TYPICAL KEYPUNCH OPERATION

keypunch replacement decision are included. Occupancy, supervisory expenses, etc. are excluded for this reason.

Card costs are a real though minor savings with key-tape and key-disk, but reduced CPU utilization may not be. Unless the installation can get rid of the computer's card reader or rents computer time on the outside, CPU savings are more apparent than real. The exception is the conversion of former unit record machine applications (e.g., sorting) to the main computer. Although computer utilization might actually increase, the reduction in unit record equipment rental could more than balance this, and be included as a cost savings in this category.

Productivity increases are potentially the most important source of savings. Does keypunch replacement result in productivity increases? Yes, almost invariably. Productivity increases can result from four separate factors, three of which are susceptible to some degree of measurement and prediction.

The first measurable factor is the reduction in operator "idle" time. The standard keypunch duplicates at 18 card columns per second, skips up to 80 columns/second, and takes approximately a quarter of a second for card registration. For an operator keying, say, 1400 cards per day with an average of 20 columns skipped and 20 columns duplicated per card, this means 12% of the time (50 minutes) is spent waiting on the machine. With a buffered keyboard, the operator can spend virtually all this time actively keying.

Improved accuracy and verification procedures also affect productivity, albeit indirectly. A typical keypunch installation might spend 5% of its time on error correction. All of the sources we have referenced indicate 10% to 90% first-pass error reduction with keypunch replacement.[17] Usually this reduction is not significant enough to bypass the need for verification, but it does make for easier verification. And the verification step itself is simplified, since the verifier operator can make corrections on the spot without recycling the record back to be re-keyed.

The third "measurable" factor, applicable to most key-tape and key-disk systems, results from reformatting card records for tape input. Extraneous columns with blank fill or, in multiple card records, card identifiers and repetitive information can all be eliminated. Essentially, operators can prepare the same information with less keystrokes.

The unpredictable factor is operator acceptance. In general, most trained operators seem to react favorably to keypunch replacement equipment,[18] particularly if the keyboard arrangement and audible keystroke "click" remain much the same as on the standard keypunch. Due to the intangible "operator image enhancement" features of keypunch replacement, it is not at all unusual to see productivity increase more than one would expect from a consideration of the three measurable factors. However, any intangible factors leading to abnormally high productivity may not be persistent, as many early key-tape users have noted.

Any savings from productivity increases must be realized indirectly through decreased personnel and machine requirements. This is common sense. If the same number of operators are kept working on the same number of machines as before, the net result will be a jump in direct costs—keypunch replacement equipment

[17] The degree of error reduction will depend upon the error prevention checks built into the equipment (e.g. field-length checks, numeric only checks, etc.) and the operator incentive system.
[18] See "The Human Side of Data Input," April 1971, *Data Dynamics;* "Improvements to Data Entry," Sept.-Oct., *EDP Analyzer,* and footnote 2.

Standard Equipment	Buffered Keypunch	Key-Tape	Key-Disk
Keypunch: $44-110	Units: $69-150	Units: $120-240	Units:
Verifier: $80-85		PLUS	$50-125
		Pooler(s) and	Controller:
		Pooler Operating	$560 up
		Personnel	

2.7 MONTHLY RENTALS FOR KEYPUNCH AND KEYPUNCH REPLACEMENT EQUIPMENT (OPTIONS EXCLUDED)

is always more expensive on an equivalent unit basis than standard keypunches and verifiers.

Determining whether keypunch replacement equipment will pay off overall is relatively straightforward *if* productivity increases are predicted with a reasonable degree of accuracy. In an installation with cost characteristics similar to those in Figure 2.6, one can expect a 10 percent productivity increase with buffered keyboards, and another 10 percent from reformatting some multiple card records to tape. Before conversion costs and rental charges for replacement equipment are taken into account, monthly savings as a percentage of direct costs can be calculated as shown in Figure 2.8.

Suppose the sample installation is presently employing 15 operators on 15 keypunch/verifier machines and incurring $10,000 per month in direct costs. The bottom line of Figure 2.8 tells us that the installation could spend up to $2,440 for monthly rental of buffered keypunches or up to $3,380 for key-disk or key-tape and still realize a net savings. How much the savings would be depends on the rental for the equipment actually selected. If we chose, say, 14 buffered keypunches with an aggregate monthly rental of $1,750 (Avg. unit rental = $125) (see Figure 2.7), net direct cost savings would be on the order of $700 per month. If we choose a 12-station key-disk system renting for $1,800, savings should approximate $3,380 minus $1,800, or $1,580 per month.

Factors other than rental cost may be taken into consideration at this point. With the buffered keypunch, there are no conversion problems other than some minimal operator training. With key-type and key-disk, operator training may be slightly more complicated, but still not a major problem. Any manufacturer will provide help in this re-

Cost Category	Cost Category Percent of Direct Cost	Buffered Keypunch		Key-Tape		Key-Disk	
	A	Source of Savings	Savings as Percent of Direct Cost	Source of Savings	Savings as Percent of Direct Cost	Source of Savings	Savings as Percent of Direct Cost
	A	B	$A \times B$	C	$A \times C$	D	$A \times D$
Operator Wages	74	10% from buffered keyboard	7.4	10% from buffered keyboard and 10% from formatting	14.8	10% from buffered keyboard and 10% from reformatting	14.8
Keypunch and Verifier Rental	17	100%, new equipments costs will be taken into account later	17	100%, new equipments costs will be taken into account later	17	100%, new equipment costs will be taken into account later	17
CPU Charges	7	None	0	None	0	None	0
Punch Cards	2	None	0	approximately 100% no cards, tapes are reusable	2	approximately 100% no cards, tapes are reusable	2
Totals	100		24.4		33.8		33.8

2.8 SAMPLE CALCULATION OF MONTHLY SAVINGS BEFORE EQUIPMENT RENTAL

spect with short on-site training sessions. Because operator productivity should be the critical factor in determining whether keypunch replacement is economical, a trial period of several weeks' duration is usually justified. But even if this cannot be arranged, potential customers will benefit by taking a close look at the projected workload. If most jobs cannot take advantage of reformatting or the increased skipping and duplicating speeds, then there may be no justification for keypunch replacement.

Converting computer programs to accept tape input can be a difficulty, though certainly not an insurmountable one. Another tape-oriented consideration is how errors detected during the computer validation run will be corrected. If the device does not have a full-record display (only a few key-disk systems do) and search capability, post-validation correction can be a recurring headache. In general, tape loses its attractiveness as an input medium if the installation processes many small jobs.

Finally, help in judging factors like system reliability, vendor maintenance policies, and vendor stability should be sought wherever possible. Comments from other users usually prove invaluable.

GENERALIZING THE FRAMEWORK

A large organization's data entry workload usually consists of different input streams which run the gamut for volume, accuracy requirements, and timeliness of entry and response. By tracing through each of the major input streams, we are likely to find most of it is not time-critical. As a general rule, it will not be worthwhile to enter this data through an integrated on-line system. This is not so much because of the cost of terminal equipment—most keyboard terminals are less expensive than keypunches—but because of the conversion and operating expense for an on-line system.

However, if on-line applications are already up and running, the point at which it is desirable to cross over to on-line entry may not be so clear-cut, especially if true source data entry can be achieved. Most of the costs for hardware/software conversion, and the technical expertise necessary to accommodate on-line operation will have been incurred. Intermediate operator wages account for up to 75 percent of the direct cost of keypunching. The elimination of these costs can go a long way toward financing communications charges and modern terminal equipment rental. There may be other desirable alternatives to process some or all of this workload. In a large organization, OCR might be feasible, or perhaps some data entry might remain key-punch-oriented but decentralized to branch office locations with existing batch terminals.

Figure 2.9 shows a worksheet method for analyzing the economic implications of this and similar decisions. Three types of costs are considered: one-time conversion costs, monthly variable costs, and monthly fixed costs. Meaningful comparisons *between* alternatives can be made by defining these as follows:

1. *Monthly Fixed Costs.* Those costs which will be continuously incurred if the data entry alternative is used regardless of the number and type of jobs processed using that alternative (e.g. OCR equipment rental).
2. *Monthly Variable Costs.* Those costs which will be continuously incurred, over and above any fixed costs, if a particular alternative is used on a particular type of job.
3. *Conversion Costs.* A. Fixed: One-time costs which will be incurred if an alternative is used, regardless of the number and type of jobs processed. B. Variable: One-time costs which will be incurred, over and above any fixed conversion costs, if a particular alternative is used on a particular type of job.

Some of the major items which would be included in each cost category are identified in Figure 2.9. In this case we assume comparisons are being made relative to a central-site keypunch operation.

Four major alternatives are listed in this example. In practice, we would list only the particular alternatives being considered and eventually include specific manufacturers' data entry equipment. Since monthly and conversion variable costs are dependent on the type of job for which the alternative is used, these would have to be listed separately for each type of job included in the evaluation.

Some care must be taken in determining the relevant job classification for that portion of data entry workload being analyzed. If job classifications are defined too broadly, or include separate rate input streams, one may not be able to obtain meaningful cost estimates on, say, reject rates for OCR forms or productivity increases. Jobs should be classified so that one can estimate costs by alternative and by job.

Getting reasonable cost estimates should be the most difficult part of all, especially for large on-line networks. As with any cost analysis some common sense rules must be observed. Any cost items which vary across the set of alternatives and jobs being considered should be included. Those which do not vary should not be included and may bias the results if they are. For example, in a department with exist-

ALTERNATIVE	TYPE OF COST	MONTHLY FIXED COST	CONVERSION FIXED COST	JOB TYPE "A" MONTHLY VARIABLE COST	JOB TYPE "A" CONVERSION VARIABLE COST	JOB TYPE "B" MONTHLY VARIABLE COST	JOB TYPE "B" CONVERSION VARIABLE COST
PRESENT KEYPUNCHING	OPERATORS	0		ACTUAL DIRECT EXP.	0		
	EQUIPMENT	0	0	ACTUAL DIRECT EXP.	0		
	CPU CHARGES	0	0	ACTUAL DIRECT EXP.	0		
	SUPPLIES		0	ACTUAL DIRECT EXP.			
	OTHER	SUPERVISORY AND OCCUPANCY EXPENSE	0	INDIRECT EXP. PREPARATION AND MAILING TO CENTRAL SITE	0		
OCR	OPERATORS	OCR OPERATORS	TRAINING	OCR TYPISTS*	TRAINING 0		
	EQUIPMENT	OCR EQUIPMENT	0	TYPEWRITERS*	TESTING 0		
	CPU CHARGES	0	0	CPU OVERHEAD	FORMS DESIGN		
	SUPPLIES	0		FORMS			
	OTHER	0	ADD. CORE?	INDIRECT EXP. AND REJECT HANDLING*	REPROGRAMMING FOR OCR DIRECT OR TAPE INPUT		
INTEGRATED ON-LINE SYSTEM	OPERATORS	0	0	TERMINAL OPERATORS	TRAINING 0		
	EQUIPMENT	TRANSMISSION CONTROL EQUIPMENT	0	KEYBOARD TERMINALS, CONTROL UNITS, MODEMS*	TESTING 0		
	CPU CHARGES	0	0	CPU OVERHEAD			
	SUPPLIES	0	0	0			
	OTHER	OS CONVERSION TP MONITOR	EDUCATION FOR PROGRAMMING STAFF	COMMUNICATIONS CHARGES	REPROGRAMMING		
COMPOSITE ON-LINE SYSTEM (REMOTE BATCH TERMINALS WITH KEYPUNCH)	OPERATORS	BATCH TERMINAL OPERATORS	0	OPERATOR WAGES AND KEYPUNCHES AT REMOTE LOCATION	0		
	EQUIPMENT	TRANSMISSION CONTROL EQUIPMENT BATCH TERMINALS	0	0	0		
	CPU CHARGES	0	0	CPU OVERHEAD			
	SUPPLIES	0	0	CARDS	TESTING 0		
	OTHER	OS CONVERSION TP MONITOR LEASED LINES	EDUCATION FOR PROGRAMMING STAFF	0	REPROGRAMMING		

*MOST OF THE COST ASSOCIATED WITH THIS ITEM WOULD NOT APPLY IF THE JOB IS SUSCEPTIBLE TO SOURCE DATA ENTRY.

2.9   EVALUATING DATA ENTRY ALTERNATIVES

ing batch terminal expenses for transmission, equipment and software teleprocessing monitors should be included in evaluating new applications only to the extent additional charges for these items would be incurred.

Setting cost estimates in this framework may not make economic implications immediately obvious. But once the framework is established, the mechanics of estimating total costs are straightforward. The way in which the cost structure has been defined permits the evaluation and comparison of total costs for any single alternative or mix of alternatives over any given time span.

SUMMARY

An organization's data entry system is an area for potential cost savings, and provides an opportunity to improve the performance of the overall computer activity. For a variety of industry and organizational reasons, the data entry system of the organization may not have been reassessed recently. Nevertheless, within the past few years data entry technology has undergone considerable improvement.

Evaluating both the tangible and intangible factors of data entry system alternatives within the context of an organization can get quite complex. An approach is to start with a consideration of the tangible economic factors benchmarked on the existing data entry system. Within the background of the economic factors, the less tangible factors such as training and data integrity improvements can be successively considered. The worksheet approach is a useful technique for getting into the analysis.

3.

SIGNIFICANT COST SAVINGS POSSIBLE IN DATA PREPARATION

Editor's Note: From LYBRAND NEWSLETTER, March 1971. Reprinted by permission of the publisher, Coopers and Lybrand. See also "Workable Ways to Cut Input Costs," *Administrative Management*, August 1971, pp. 66–67 for another version of the same article.

Computer users of all sizes may save 20 percent to 30 percent or more of their current keypunching costs by increasing operator productivity, reducing verification, improving scheduling, or acquiring new equipment. Computers, systems, and programming have been constantly refined to their current level of sophistication, but data preparation has largely been neglected, with many companies still preparing and entering input as they did in the early days.

While each succeeding computer generation has decreased cost per computation about tenfold, data preparation costs have actually risen because of the extra personnel expense incurred to process the burgeoning input that today's faster and more productive computers can handle. Management is often unaware of the opportunity for cost reduction and control in data entry. Take, for example, the following broad observations made during recent Lybrand engagements:

- Data entry costs (keypunch and closely related activities) can represent 20 percent to 50 percent of total recurring EDP expenses, and these tend to rise faster than processing costs.
- The critical factors are operator productivity and machine utilization, which affect the quantity per dollar of the EDP "product"; and error control and scheduling, which affect the

accuracy and timeliness of the information (the quality of the "product").

- Equipment alone will not solve data entry problems. Potential "trade-offs," with preceding source data preparation and following computer processing, must be investigated. Formats, procedures, and managerial controls must also be scrutinized. In fact, careful analysis of the critical factors affecting data entry may help achieve significant economies without any equipment changes.
- Actions taken in this area must be consistent will overall EDP and corporate objectives.

The same studies uncovered several typical inefficient practices, including:

- Keypunch operators leaving their machines to get small, unscheduled batches of work.
- Supervisors unaware of (1) individual performance (since it had never been measured) or (2) "normal" production (since there were no established standards).
- Formats forcing operators to search for out-of-sequence data.
- A policy of 100% verification despite the noncritical nature of most information.

DATA ENTRY EQUIPMENT—MAJOR CHARACTERISTICS

	Standard Keypunch	"Buffered" Keypunch	Key-tape	Shared Processor Key-Disc-Tape
Operator productivity				
Is operator limited by machine speeds of duplicating, skipping, and card positioning?	Yes	No	No	No
Is job setup easy and fast?	No	Yes	Yes [1]	Yes
Are more than two formats readily available to an operator?	No	In most cases	No	Yes
Is it easy and fast to correct detected errors?	No	Yes	Yes	Yes
Can on-line editing reduce the need for verification?	No	No	No	Yes

Error control

Is batch balancing an available option?	No	Yes	Yes	Yes
Are edit checks possible (beyond the usual field definition controls)?	No	No	No	Yes

Machine utilization

Can one machine both enter and verify data?	No	In most cases	Yes	Yes

Management control

Are operator productivity and error statistics easy to obtain?	No	No [2]	No [2]	Yes
Does the equipment facilitate good, close supervisory control?	No	No	No	Yes

Operating costs

What is the relative unit cost of equipment?	Low	Medium	Medium	From medium to high, depending on the number of operator stations
What is the cost of supplies?	High	High	Low	Very low
Can subsequent computer processing costs be reduced?	No	No	Somewhat	Yes
Is a special physical environment required?	No	No	In some cases	In some cases
What are the operating conditions?	Poor	Poor	Good	Good
Is the system vulnerable to equipment failure?	No	No	Somewhat	Yes

[1] With automatic program load option; otherwise, job setup requires keying in a new program.
[2] Most key entry devices can be equipped with registers to record production and error statistics, but these must be accumulated and analyzed by hand.

It has been found that much operator verification time can be eliminated by computer editing *, and more realistic scheduling may level out workloads and raise productivity. In addition, simply measuring operator performance may increase productivity and decrease errors. New equipment may also offer some further savings and better control. Many manufacturers of keypunch replacements ("buffered" keypunch, keyboard-to-tape, and keyboard-to-disc-to-tape) are actively

* Having the computer verify the accuracy of the data by a variety of logic checks.

promoting their equipment as a way to save from 10 percent to 50 percent of data entry costs.

The accompanying chart of major data entry equipment characteristics illustrates the general advantages and disadvantages of each category. It does not, however, tell the whole story. In all instances, an individual appraisal of a company's requirements, correlated with a detailed analysis of the critical factors, is needed before a clear picture of the actual gains emerges.

Operator productivity is most important, and hard to assess. Experience with data input/output automation has led to the development of a technique for establishing data preparation times (without physical observation of a job) before actual installation. The technique is reasonably accurate, permitting a quick and easy judgment of the effect on operator productivity of various equipment, formats, or methods. Preparation times are based on predetermined standards for each individual machine and human element required in a data entry job. For example, consider a data entry job of 30-character records in an 80-column card "image" (20 key-entered, 10 duplicated, 50 skipped). Assuming an even mixture of alphanumeric data, an ideal source document, and an operator-detected and corrected-error rate of 7 per 1,000 keystrokes, our studies showed a productivity factor of .76 for key-tape.

In other words, this job can be prepared on key-tape in 76 percent of the time it would take on standard keypunch equipment. Even greater operator productivity could be realized on this job during verification because of the ease with which detected errors can be corrected. Evaluation of major jobs, using this approach, will establish the productivity gains and economic benefits that could be achieved by changing equipment.

One company, which had to replace its current equipment for compatibility with a new computer system, expects to save four out of 14 operators by data entry measurement and control, and another two because of improved equipment. Before beginning any active operations, a large government group set up an entirely new medical claims program for which it selected equipment, designed forms and formats, and staffed (200 operators) a system for typing and then optically reading information. Another company, by applying basic production and schedule controls, and revising formats, reduced errors to one-fifth of the previous level, increased operator productivity by 25 percent, brought back in-house work (which had been done by a service bureau), and decreased its workforce *without* changing its key-tape equipment.

4.

KEY-TO-TAPE AND KEY-TO-DISK SYSTEMS

By Albert H. Bieser

Editor's Note: From MODERN DATA, December 1971, pp. 32–36. Reprinted by permission of the publisher, Modern Data Services, Inc., and author.

A little over two years ago a new sub-industry was born as a direct result of market needs. Unlike many other computer-related innovations, it was not heralded as a revolutionary engineering or technological marvel, and simply involved configuring some existing equipment and techniques together into an economical and practical input system to prepare and enter data for computers.

This sub-industry is known as the keyboard-to-disk-to-magnetic tape or shared processor data entry system industry. In such systems a number of keyboard terminals share a minicomputer that collects, controls, edits, and organizes input data into tape files that are ready for mainframe computer processing. The keyboard data entry terminals have display capabilities (display tube, CRT, hard-copy), and input data on tape via minicomputer-disk memory control. Other peripherals, such as teleprinters or line printers, can also be included in key-disk systems as supervisory console options.

The two primary ancestors of key-disk systems were key-tape data entry, and typing for optical scanning, both being employed as a means of replacing keypunches. Both systems allowed the keyboard operator to enter new data without having to wait for the card punch to mechanically duplicate information previously entered or to skip through areas where no information was to be entered.

The end result of these keypunch replacement methods was an

approximate 20 percent increase in operator efficiency and a 20 percent reduction in input cost. However, both methods had a drawback that was common to punched cards. The cards, tapes, or typed pages had to be entered into a satellite computing system that would convert these batch entry items to magnetic tape.

KEY-DISK ADVANTAGES

By considering the various elements of a data entry system and relating them to key-disk systems, the advantages and characteristics of key-disk data entry can be illustrated.

Data Entry Operations & Errors

The first step in the data entry process is one that 95% of all the information destined for computers must undergo—operator keying of data from source documents.

The next step is verification, where the original input is checked for accuracy. This generally takes the form of a second operator re-keying the data that has already been entered. The key verification machine notifies the second operator whenever the keystroking varies from the original. The operator then has the option of deciding that: (1) the original entry was incorrect and must be changed; (2) the verification was incorrect and the original should remain; or (3) a new record should be entered. Rejected items must be sent back to the entry station, entered and reverified, and the resulting data integrated with the original data so that batch integrity is maintained.

Additional error detection usually occurs in the satellite computer which converts the punched cards to magnetic tape and frequently performs minor data checks. If an error is found at this stage, it must be set aside and then processed through the clerical function, which may involve manual retrieval of the source document and then recycling through the entire entry verification—reentry—reverification process. The high-density magnetic tape is then sent to the mainframe computer, which usually performs additional checks. The additional errors it catches go once again through the entire chain. As these steps become increasingly longer, the cost of handling errors rises.

The most expensive error corrections occur when the person who ultimately receives the data is involved. For example, when a customer receives an incorrect invoice, he notifies the invoicing company who then must reprocess it through the entire system.

In some instances the cost of an error at this stage can be even more extreme. It is an unfortunate fact that a person who is billed more than he owes will complain loudly, but someone who is billed less will often pay only the lower amount. Similarly, if checks are written for too-large an amount, there is a good possibility they will be cashed.

Figure 4.1 and the associated table show the operation and cost of a typical input system with a volume of 500,000 documents a month. The table shows the labor costs of input operation and error handling. The cash figures do not show the hardware costs or the cost that is hardest to put a dollar value on—the cost of an unhappy customer.

A perusal of these figures shows that an input system that detects and corrects errors at the entry level, rather than down-line, provides significant savings for data entry operations.

Operator Factors

Other often overlooked elements of any data entry system are factors involving the operator who enters the data. Any input system should have keyboard stations that are comfortable and as easy as possible for the operator to use. Keyboards should be designed for easy operator transition from typing, keypunch, or tenkey adding machines. The keyboard must permit operators to key data at top speeds making "n-key rollover" essential. This feature prevents character loss if the keys are depressed rapidly, and gives the operator a self-assurance that normally results in speed increases of up to 20 percent. N-key rollover assures that if the keys are struck in the proper sequence, the keyboard output will be correct.

Shared processor systems allow for an overall reduction in personnel because of the much faster keying rates and operator efficiency. Because the keyboard arrangements are more flexible, the need for highly-trained operators is eliminated; this saves the user time and money in the hiring and training of operator personnel.

Other cost reductions occur in the error correction area. Because errors are found and corrected at the entry level while the source document is in front of the operator, the high cost of correcting an error that reaches the mainframe computer is eliminated. These errors can run as high as $10 apiece.

One user who installed a key-disk system reduced the number of keyboard operators from 88 to 55, and eliminated a satellite model 360/30 computer and four down-line 360/65 programs because of the input system sophistication and editing capabilities. This user estimates savings at more than $250,000 a year.

Other Advantages

Key-disk systems allow longer and more flexible record lengths

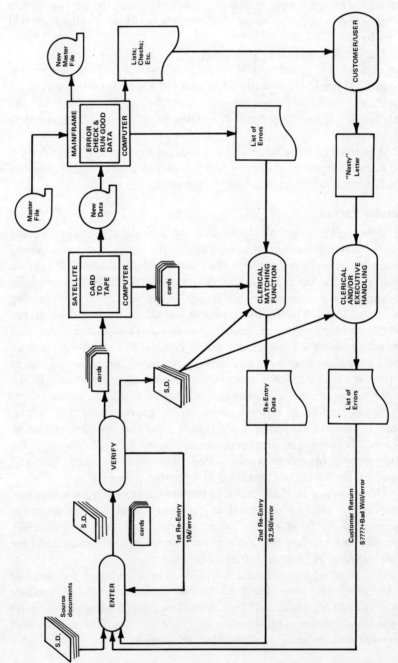

4.1 DATA INPUT FLOW FOR KEYPUNCH OPERATION (500,000 DOCUMENTS PER MONTH)

TABLE 4.1 DATA INPUT COSTS FOR KEYPUNCH OPERATION
(500,000 Documents Per Month)

OPERATION	INITIAL ENTRY (500,000 documents)	FIRST RE-ENTRY (3.6% = 18,000 documents)	SECOND RE-ENTRY (0.4% = 2,000 documents)	CUSTOMER RETURN (unknown)
KEYPUNCH	$12,000/mo.	$900/mo.	$100/mo.	$???/mo.
KEY VERIFY	$8,000/mo.	$900/mo.	$100/mo.	$???/mo.
SATELLITE PROCESSOR	$1,000/mo.	————	————	————
CLERICAL RESEARCH	————	————	$3,400/mo.	$????/mo.
LOSS DUE TO DELAY & RECYCLE	————	————	$1,400/mo.	$????/mo.
CUSTOMER LOSS (cancels, underpay, etc.)	————	————	————	$????/mo. + Bad Will
	$21,000/mo.	$1,800/mo.	$5,000/mo.	$????/mo. + Bad Will

and formats than card equipment, higher electronic operation speeds than the mechanical rates of punches, and more advanced error detection and correction. Key-disk systems offer users a large number and variety of program formats, editing and validation routines, simultaneous data entry and verification, complete record display, and peripheral and communications system options. A direct cost advantage in the key-disk systems are the savings realized from eliminating cards. The approximate cost of $1 per 1000 cards can be doubled or tripled when storage, handling, record keeping, and other functions associated with cards are added.

With many key-disk systems the displayed data is an acknowledgement of the system rather than an independent keyboard response. The data displayed is the same data that is received and processed by the data controller. By performing extensive edits during the first pass entry, second pass verification is reduced to a minimum. Every keyboard in a shared processor system can be used for entry, update, or verification for any of the jobs processed. There are no idle keyboards.

Contrasted to keypunch equipment, the key-disk stations are noticeably more quiet and attractive, making the data entry room a more efficient place to work.

KEY-DISK VS. KEY-TAPE

The two direct advantages of key-disk systems over key-tape devices are the elimination of the pooling process necessary in stand-alone key-tape operations, and the editing capability of the shared processor system. Key-disk input is accomplished directly through the system processor. The result is a single edited tape. Because of these two advantages, a user can generally increase his throughput from 15 to 20 percent over key-tape units by using key-disk systems.

Advantages accrue to the key entry supervisor of the key-disk system as well. Statistics are available on the performance of every operator and keyboard. The supervisor can assemble batches in any order without the hazard of spilling boxes of cards. Job batches can be printed for spot checks; new programs can be entered and verified simultaneously during data entry without interrupting regular work flow; batch to tape can be written concurrently with data entry. The supervisor can also schedule work as the daily requirements dictate —temporarily terminating one batch of data part way through entry, and re-opening it when priority jobs have been finished.

Key-disk systems provide clean tapes for the user's mainframe; rejects have already been resolved and corrected in the data entry area. There are no costly and time-consuming delays incurred by waiting for up-dates. This complete and sophisticated front-end editing provides for much more effective and economical use of mainframe power.

Since shared processor systems do not use a preprocessing computer, it is essential that system software be complete, available, flexible, and proven in user environments. Some manufacturers have placed great emphasis on this area of development, making the installation and implementation of a key-disk system a quick and easy task. Other related benefits of hardware and software flexibility allow the tailoring of a key-disk system to the unique needs of the user.

COMMUNICATIONS ASPECTS

The use of shared processor key-disk systems for remote site data entry is one of the fastest growing areas in the industry. In such applications, keyboard terminals are located at remote data entry sites, and are connected to the central shared processor via communications links. The flexible system software and hardware of key-disk allow for a gradual expansion to remote site operation without major changes and a disruption of regular on-site data entry.

Burlington Northern employs one of its five key-disk systems in a communications mode data entry operation. This 29-terminal system is used in a payroll accounting application with the data controller and five keyboard terminals located at St. Paul, and other terminals at Portland, Oregon; Whitefish, Montana; Willmar, Minnesota; Omaha; and Chicago. Payroll information is entered at these various locations and transmitted over communications lines to the railroad's St. Paul headquarters for processing.

Neiman-Marcus, the famed Dallas-based specialty store, installed a key-disk system with 11 keyboard stations at its central data processing facility in January, 1971. The system is used to enter data for a variety of store applications, including daily sales information, sales audit, accounts payable for both store merchandise and normal business expenses, sales commissions, and gift bond debits and credits. About two months after the system was installed, Neiman-Marcus had reduced its keying staff from 15 to 11, or almost 30 percent, through attrition, in addition to adding applications for a new store in Florida. The data processing facility serves five stores.

According to Gene Campbell, the store's EDP manager, many edits were put into the key-disk system that were on the main computer system. Although the mainframe still runs through them, the data is clean, so there are no rejects. He adds that when new programs are written for the central processing system, they will not have to include the edit routines that are performed by the key-disk system. He also explains that special edits and software programs were supplied with the system, such as validity tables, that were required for their applications.

Mr. Campbell feels they could have installed a simpler shared processor system that would have been sufficient for the short term, but they were looking ahead to the company's growth and expansion. Neiman-Marcus has announced plans to expand throughout the United States; as a result he feels they will expand the key-disk system to solve the firm's total data capture problems and will use its communications capabilities.

THE MARKET

Key-disk systems made their debut on the EDP scene early in 1970. During that year, a large number of manufacturers appeared —and disappeared—1970 being a year of severe depression in the computer industry. The total number of systems delivered during the year was considerably less than projections. This business environment made it difficult for the prospective user to determine what was failing—the system, due to technological problems; or the manufacturer, due to the economy. 1971 has pretty well proved it to be the latter case, as sales volume has grown impressively. There are now about 11 surviving manufacturers in the key-disk field and approximately 1000 installations of such systems worldwide, with about 25 percent outside the United States.

Most industry research experts concur that sales of non-punched card data entry equipment will reach $250 million annually by 1975, with key-disk systems accounting for $135 million and key-tape for $115 million. Although key-tape systems have out-sold key-disk systems in the past, predictions are that key-disk will experience the stronger growth of the two methods during the next years. In fact, the General Services Administration, the U.S. Government purchasing arm, estimates that the federal government will order some 2400 shared processor systems within the next two years.

Most everyone, manufacturers and users alike, agrees that the key-disk market will grow, both domestically and internationally, and that most of the growth will be associated with solving larger, more complex input problems.

5.

KEY-TO-TAPE DATA ENTRY

By John A. Murphy

Editor's Note: From MODERN DATA, December 1971, pp. 37–38. Reprinted by permission of the publisher, Modern Data Services, Inc., and author.

Key-to-magnetic tape data entry has come a long way since Mohawk first introduced a buffered key-tape keypunch replacement station back in the mid 1960's. The single stand-alone station key-to-tape concept has evolved into multi-station shared processor systems used in medium to high volume data entry operations. Key-to-tape data entry has also attracted the attention of the interactive terminal manufacturers—the CRT display and keyboard printer makers—who now offer magnetic tape cassette or cartridge options with their terminals.

The hierarchy of keyed data entry goes from the keypunch to the shared processor key-to-disk-to-tape system, with intermediate ranks occupied by the buffered keypunch, the stand-alone key-tape station, and the shared processor key-tape system. The equipments described in this Profile are primarily used for key-to-tape data entry; buffered keypunches will be covered next month, and the interactive cousins to key-to-tape equipments—the CRT display and teleprinting terminals—were described in the May and July, 1971 issues of MODERN DATA.

KEY TAPE STATIONS

The basic components of a stand-alone key-to-tape station or terminal are: the operator keyboard and display console; the tape transport; and the internal buffer and logic circuitry that controls the data entry and formating operations.

Keyboards are laid out in keypunch style, or in arrangements similar to those used on a standard typewriter. Special format and function keys and switches used to control key station operation are also included. Adding machine or numeric-only key-pads are also available as options or additions to the above.

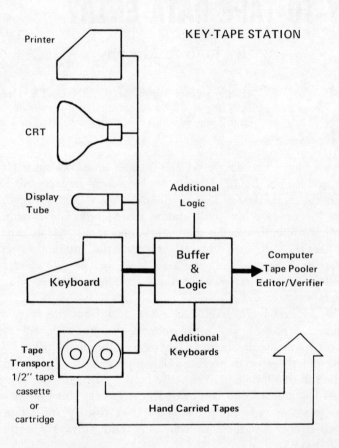

5.1 KEY-TAPE STATION

Display consoles consist of control and function panel lights, and some form of alphanumeric display—display tube, CRT screen, and/or hard copy printer. Stations equipped with display tube consoles display the last or last few characters keyed and the column designations. The more costly CRT and hard copy terminals display or print complete record or document formats.

Tape output of key-tape stations can be mainframe computer-compatible ½-inch tape, cassette tape, or cartridge tape. Cassette or cartridge tape is pooled onto ½-inch computer compatible tape either by hand carrying the tape containers to the pooling station or by on-line connection to the pooler via a direct or telephone line link. Some ½-inch key-tape stations may also employ pooling to merge many tapes and decrease tape handling.

Buffer and logic circuitry control the data entry, formatting and display operations of the key station. Such circuitry may range from hardware to control 80-column, 2 format, display tube stations, to more complex (and costly) logic used to operate long record length, multi-format, CRT or hard-copy display terminals.

Some key-tape stations have the ability to expand, adding more buffer and logic to increase operational capabilities. Others can serve as master terminals for several slave keyboards, having the ability to expand into shared processor key-tape systems.

SHARED PROCESSOR KEY-TAPE SYSTEMS

Evolving to meet the needs of higher volume key data entry operations, shared processor key-to-tape systems are configured around a central processor with one or more ½-inch mainframe compatible tape transports. A number of operator keyboard stations share the processing and tape capabilities of this central facility, reducing the buffer and logic needed at each station and the total number of tape transports required by the overall key-tape operation, and lowering the per station costs for multi-station operations. This sharing also provides expanded record length and format capabilities, each station having access to—and being serviced by—the more powerful shared processor.

The individual keyboard stations can be located at the central shared processor site or can operate at remote sites, communicating over telephone lines. Some stations may be equipped with tape transports (usually cassette or cartridge) for off-line data entry, on-line pooling with the shared processor and central tape units; others share the central tape facilities directly and have no tape capabilities at the station site.

Optional features of shared processor key-tape systems allow for supervisory input/output via teleprinter or line printer peripherals, providing program format loading, data printout and data entry

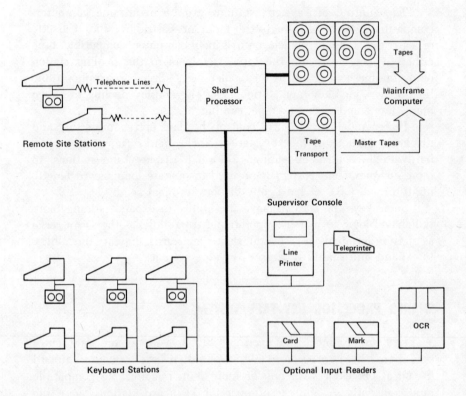

5.2   SHARED PROCESSOR KEY-TAPE SYSTEM

capabilities. Other options include input by card, mark or OCR readers, and direct on-line data entry to the mainframe computer.

KEY-DISK SYSTEMS

The most powerful of key data entry systems, key-to-disk-to-tape systems expand upon the shared processor concept by the addition of disk or disk-drum memory units. The disk memory contains the format program library and the operating system routines, and serves as a mass storage area for key station input. A number of keyboard stations share the processing, disk memory, and tape storage capabilities of the central key-disk facility much in the way as in key-tape systems.

The difference between shared processor key-disk and key-tape systems is the increased processing power and flexibility of the central facility. Shared processor key-disk systems provide greater data

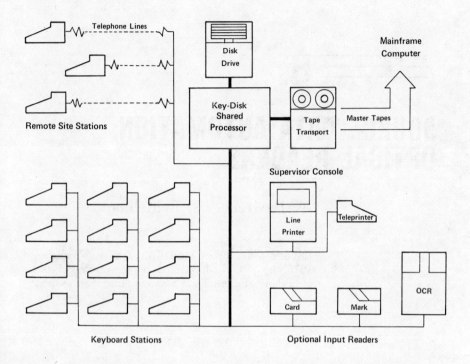

Telephone Lines

Remote Site Stations

Disk Drive

Key-Disk Shared Processor

Tape Transport

Master Tapes

Mainframe Computer

Supervisor Console

Line Printer

Teleprinter

Keyboard Stations

Card

Mark

OCR

Optional Input Readers

5.3 KEY-DISK SYSTEM

handling capabilities such as expanded record lengths, format program libraries, edit checks, etc. Key-disk also allows for a higher degree of operator and supervisor interaction with the system.

Key-disk eliminates the need for multiple tape transports at the central facility—a requirement of some shared processor key-tape systems. Data is entered via the shared processor and disk memory onto a single master tape; a redundant tape transport is used only as a backup or for entering data onto different track/density tape.

Other features of shared processor key-disk systems allow for the generation of status, keyboard utilization, and operator efficiency reports. Options include card, mark and OCR readers, display consoles (CRT, printer), and remote site communications.

6.

SOURCE DATA AUTOMATION: OPTICAL READERS

By Lawrence A. Feidelman

Editor's Note: From MODERN DATA, November 1970, pp. 56–57. Reprinted by permission of the publisher, Modern Data Services, Inc., and author.

The optical reader represents the prime example of Source Data Automation equipment. Unlike keyboard data entry devices, optical readers are designed to eliminate any manual retranscription of data. Rather than data being entered manually at a keyboard, data enters the system automatically by optically scanning printed or coded material. The ultimate goal of optical reading is to "read" any type of handwritten data. This goal is still far in the future, but the technology has presently progressed to reliable reading of typed characters and numeric hand-printed characters under strictly controlled conditions.

Optical readers fall into three distinct classes: bar code readers, mark-sense readers, and character readers.

BAR CODE READERS

Bar code readers "read" a character indirectly by recognizing an associated bar code. The bar codes are usually placed on the paper by either an embossed card or keyboard imprinter. The easily machine-readable font shown in Fig. 6.1 results in a highly reliable

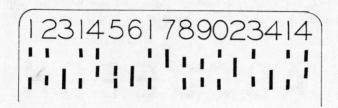

6.1 BAR CODE OPTICAL FONT

low-cost ($10,000 to $20,000 range) optical reader. The basic disadvantages are the requirement for a specialized preparation device and a limited numeric character set.

MARK-SENSE READERS

Mark-sense readers "read" characters indirectly by detecting marks recorded by hand in specific locations on the paper. The mark-sense reader is moderate in cost (from $20,000 to $40,000) and highly reliable. The disadvantages relate to a fixed preprinted format and difficulty in human readability.

OPTICAL CHARACTER READERS

The optical character reader (OCR) recognizes the character directly by its shape. Optical character readers are usually classified by their ability to read different types of characters. Most single font readers (selling at $30,000 to $100,000) are designed to read the standard character font developed by the United States of America Standards Institute (USASI), shown in Fig. 6.2. Arguments on its

ABCDEFGH
IJKLMNOP

6.2 USASI OCR-A FONT

aesthetics, however, have led certain manufacturers to implement the International Standards Organization (ISO) font B as shown in Fig. 6.3.

ABCDEFGH
IJKLMNOP

6.3   ISO OCR-B FONT

Most multi-font readers can only recognize a limited number of specified fonts, of which one is the U.S. standard. These readers sell in the range of $150,000 to $400,000. Multi-font readers which can recognize a large variety of character fonts (mainly from type-writers) sell in the one to three million dollar range. Multi-font OCR readers are used by banks, publications, the U.S. Post Office, and others. At present, all fonts must be defined to the reader. However, experimental OCR readers exist which read new fonts by a learning process.

Although handprinting readers may technically be classified under multi-font readers, their present development demands particular emphasis. Most commercially-available handprinting readers only read numerics. At present, handprinted character readers must be employed with caution in a highly controlled environment. The costs of handprinting readers vary from $100,000 to $300,000.

REMOTE SCANNERS

A newer concept connected with optical readers has been the remote scanner terminal used to transmit optically read data over communication lines (usually telephone lines). The scanner terminal may contain only the scanning optics and transmit analog data to a central computer for recognition, or it may contain the complete scanner and recognition unit and transmit digitally coded data. Prices range from $2,000 for a numeric-only terminal, to $35,000 for an alphanumeric OCR reader terminal. Of course, completely self-contained terminals may also be used off-line as low-cost OCR readers.

OPTICAL READERS VS. KBT

Since an optical reader is basically an alternative to a keyboard-to-tape (KBT) system, there are common features of each type of equipment category that can be compared:

FACTOR	OPTICAL READER	KEYBOARD-TO-TAPE
Volume	Primarily for large volumes of document data	For smaller volumes (e.g., less than can be handled by 8 keypunch operators) and/or where data is not in document form
Training	Typist level	Keypunch level
Ease of Use	Special care required for initial data preparation	As easy or easier to use than standard keypunch equipment
On-line Capability	Remote scanner terminals	Remote KBT or pooler terminals
Verification	Proofreading	Visual verification or manual re-entry
Cost	High initial equipment and system costs; can provide lowest cost/document	Lower initial cost; cost/record largely dependent on number of keystrokes

SUMMARY

The optical reader is an advanced SDA equipment permitting direct data reading and, thereby, elimination of keypunching. Due to its relatively high cost, a large volume of data is required to justify its utilization. Different types of optical readers exist to meet different reading applications, depending upon preparation controls, character set, volume, and on-line, real-time requirements.

7.

A STUDY OF OPTICAL CHARACTER RECOGNITION

By Alfred Eisdorfer

Editor's Note: From the JOURNAL OF SYSTEMS MANAGEMENT, November 1970, pp. 19–22. Reprinted by permission of the publisher, the Association for Systems Management, and author.

Data collection through Optical Character Recognition is an extensive area of study. Here we will be concerned only with an overview of several of the major factors involved in a scanning system. These are: 1. Optical Scanning Equipment; 2. Software; 3. Fonts (Character sets); 4. Single Font versus Multi-Font; 5. Handprinting; 6. Applications.

Optical Character Recognition or scanning, as it is better known, is just another means of capturing data so that it can be manipulated by computers. Optical readers work on a simple principle; they recognize the difference or contrast between printed, typed or hand-printed characters and marks, and the background on which they are printed. This is done by using a principle of light reflectance and non-reflectance and optics. An intense light is beamed onto the document so that the optics can sense those areas which do not reflect light. These are the areas where data are present. This information is then picked up, a character at a time, and compared with patterns stored in the machine's memory. After the correct comparison is made the character is converted to its Binary Form and is ready for use in an EDP mode.

The two main types of Optical Readers are the document reader and the page reader. The document reader is normally a device which will read computer turn-around documents, that is computer output, such as subscription billings, can be re-entered into the computer system automatically when it is returned by subscribers with their payments. Another major use for document readers is to capture data from credit card forms and airline tickets. Document readers normally scan 1, 2 or 3 lines on a document of tab card size or slightly larger. The through-put speed is up to and in excess of 1,000 documents per minute depending on the number of lines scanned and the speed of the particular reader.

PAGE READER

The page reader can use the same optical character recognition concepts as a document reader but it is engineered to read more information on a single page and consequently the through-put per page is much less. Character through-put however, may be more since an 8½" x 11" page or larger can hold much more data than a smaller document. A page reader will normally read either consecutive lines, single or double spaced, or can be programmed to read only selected information.

Until recently, all the emphasis on fast paper handling was put on the document reader rather than on the page reader, since the document reader was geared to read a large volume of documents. Now page readers can read reliably at increased speeds. Speed is very difficult to calculate for a page reader application since much depends on how much information is being scanned on each document, the effective reading speed of the particular scanner being used and the efficiency of the program controlling the reading process. As a rule of thumb, 8½" x 11" pages should be scanned at approximately 10 to 20 per minute.

DETERMINING SPEED

When determining the through-put rates of scanning equipment, one must differentiate between the rated speed, as indicated by the manufacturer, and the actual speed, which can be achieved on the equipment. For example, a page reader which is rated at 500 characters per second can only achieve this speed if it can read a line 50 inches wide at 10 characters to the inch, without advancing to another line. Since most equipment will not read a horizontal line of more than 11 inches, we can readily see that there is quite a difference between rated and actual speed as it relates to the de facto reading of characters per second.

Most OCR equipment manufacturers offer controllers starting at 4K computer memory and staying within the range of 4K to 8K. Some are stand-alone units; others are interfaced with a small or medium size computer. Almost all are programmable, rather than plugboard type. Much of the system's efficiency will depend on how well an operation is programmed. The sophistication or the degree of programming that is required must be considered similar to that of programming any other standard computer.

SOFTWARE

Software is available and in several instances, depending on the manufacturer, is quite good. However, due to its generalized nature, it is not geared either for speed or to handle the exception. The fact that good software is available is significant since there are few who can program the stand-alone reader. Because of this scarcity, it is difficult to retain the people who have learned to program an OCR device. Consequently, if software cannot always do the job, another option might be to look into contract or service bureau programming.

Scanners are built to read a multiplicity of fonts as well as to read numeric handprinting. The more capabilities a piece of equipment offers the more expensive it is. The font used most often is the Standard American Font USASI (upper case only). This font was developed by qualified specialists representing printers, users and manufacturers and approved by the Bureau of Standards for Government use. It is considered a stylized font since each character is uniquely different, and can be easily recognized by scanning equipment. Most of the scanning equipment manufactured recently does have the capacity to read this font.

SINGLE FONT VERSUS MULTI-FONT

Other fonts, including lower case characters, are available which may or may not be considered stylized. The important thing is that practically any font can be read by scanning equipment if the manufacturer wishes to incorporate it into the equipment. Single font readers, especially those recognizing numerics only, may be considered more accurate since the recognition unit need only be concerned with distinguishing between the characters of a particular font. In other words, the fewer the characters to be recognized the more accurate the recognition should be. In addition, these readers normally read only upper case characters, prepared on typewriters or printers, using a one-time carbon ribbon rather than a fabric ribbon. All of these factors tend to increase the accuracy of data acceptance.

A true multi-font environment is quite different. The equipment must be engineered to recognize many fonts of both upper and lower case prepared on a multitude of typewriters, imprinters and printers with various quality ribbons. Naturally the quality of imprinted data will not be as good as that prepared for a single font reader. Consequently, because of the complexity caused by the number of fonts and quality of the imprinted data, a multi-font reader must be engineered with much more capability and flexibility than a single font reader. Of course, the user must pay for this added capability.

The potential user must determine the full scope of his scanning operation before deciding whether to use single or multi-font and which type of equipment to obtain. The following factors must be evaluated carefully: (1) controlled or non-controlled input; (2) volumes; (3) urgency of scheduling; (4) number of terminals (typewriters or imprinters); (5) location of terminal (central, remote, in or out-of-doors); (6) training of personnel; and (7) the cost of the individual terminals and scanning equipment. Only when these and other questions have been answered can a decision on equipment be made.

For a controlled type scanning operation (typing and proofreading in lieu of key punching and key verifying) single font equipment will be both more accurate and economical. Where source capture is the goal, a multi-font reader will probably be the answer, depending on the number of terminals involved. It is entirely possible that it may be cheaper to purchase or rent typewriters and acquire a less costly single font reader than to obtain a more expensive multi-font reader and use existing typewriters. In addition, it is unlikely that all of your present typewriters will be acceptable. The quality of the typewriter and its particular character set will determine its acceptability. All of these factors must be weighed carefully to determine what will improve an operation and still save money.

HANDPRINTING

The capability to read handprinted numerics has been available as an option with OCR equipment for several years. It does work, but has not received the users' acceptance originally anticipated by the manufacturers. The constraints placed upon the individual doing the handprinting are too exacting. The individual is required to record his numerics in a confined area and must be attentive to such things as closing all the characters, staying within the confines of the box, and keeping the characters as basic as possible. No curlicues or flairs are acceptable and the type of pencil used must be the one specified by each manufacturer; keeping the pencil properly sharpened is also necessary in order to achieve the best results.

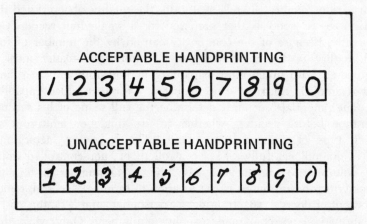

7.1

Because non-acceptable characters are easily discernible by the human eye there is a real problem. It is extremely difficult to discipline personnel, who are not directly under your control, to correct printing habits which they have developed over many years. Especially, when the information they are recoding can be read. A check digit approach, with reconstruction of a rejected character, could be a valuable systems tool in this type of operation. Unfortunately, this obviates the real purpose of a check digit which is to check not to generate data.

Numeric handprinting has had its greatest success when it is either required very rarely and the individual has been provided with a guide to follow, or where there is a definite incentive for the individual to record these numbers as carefully as possible. In the former case the individual is asked to do something rarely and it is different. Since it requires limited effort, the person will enjoy doing it and will be careful. In the latter case, if a salesman is recording data which will be used to compute his commission payments, he may not enjoy printing continually like a first grader, but he will certainly heed all the instructions. Either an incentive motivation or strict discipline is a must in order to insure a continued successful handprinting operation.

APPLICATIONS

OCR can be applied in lieu of a keying operation, such as key punching, and as a means of capturing data at the source. Type scanning or type read, as it is also known, requires a great deal of attention in order to compare favorably and even surpass other keying operations. In fact, for the typist to operate as fast as a key punch operator in a batch processing mode, she should use continuous feed forms and have the typewriter equipped with a numeric cluster similar to the one on a key punch machine. The continuous forms are necessary so that the typist will not lose time inserting a new page and then lining-up on the first typing position. Cut forms, in a batch processing production mode, are certain to decrease the output rate by at least 10-20%.

The numeric cluster is also of equal importance to compete favorably with a key punch operation. More than 50% (probably closer to 75%) of the data encoded for input are numeric. Consequently, if the majority of the data is then recorded by using the top line of a typewriter, the slowest typing line, it is impossible to achieve satisfactory production speeds for type scanning without using a numeric cluster. The numeric cluster normally appears on the right section of the keyboard and is easily operated with one hand.

Where the actual pay-off comes is, not in the operator's speed since this depends much more on the efficiency and willingness of the operator than on the equipment, but in the speed obtained through system short cuts. For example, type scanning is faster than key punching for transactions which require multiple card input since the typist is not limited to an 80 column card and therefore need not repeat the same control information, etc. on many cards. Card handling is also eliminated.

COMPARING SALARIES

From a cost stand-point, salaries for type scanning are less than those for key punching, both on the typist versus key punch operator level as well as on the proofreader versus key verifier level. Although some companies pay their typists as much as key punch operators, few, if any, will pay proofreaders as much as key verifiers. In a large operation this becomes meaningful, especially if we can see a difference in monthly salaries between a proofreader and a verifier in the area of $100.00 per month, and between a typist and key punch operator in the area of $50.00 per month. Advantages of type scanning are:

- Typists are more available than key punch operators.
- Not limited to 80 columns per transaction.
- Ease of correction. Typist sees what she is typing and can make corrections easily by the use of a correction symbol, without retyping.
- Scanner editing and reformatting.
- Errors can be disclosed immediately during scanning operation.
- Nothing is written to tape unless the entire transaction is accepted. This is extremely helpful on input that would have required multi-card input if key punched.
- Typist types the information in the best sequence for operator ease and production . . . Scanner re-sequences information for computer programs.

The disadvantages are:

- Back-up. Since all of the information is funnelled through one piece of equipment, urgent schedules could present a problem if the equipment is malfunctioning.
- Forms. The printing of proper OCR forms can be a problem if the OCR specifications are not met. It is possible that a particular printing firm does not have either the equipment or the know-how to print good OCR forms and the user must be aware of this. Of course, this problem can be greatly reduced by using a firm which has had solid experience in this field.

Type scanning is just another means of data entry, although it is not, as often quoted, 20-50% faster than key punching or key taping. If implemented properly, it is as accurate, as fast, and less costly. From a cost standpoint, a type scanning operation should not be initiated unless there is a minimum of 25 typists. Of course, as the typing pool increases the cost per transaction decreases. A complement of approximately 50 typists is within the capacity of one page reader and should provide optimum savings. If proofreading is an integral part of the system, a ratio of one proofreader to every two typists should be considered. The actual ratio will vary depending on the complexity of the data proofread. The ratio between typists and proof-readers narrows as the document becomes more difficult. Obviously, the reverse is also true.

Source data collection is the real pay-off area in scanning. Approximately 75% of the cost in data entry is operator cost and only 25% equipment cost. Source data collection is based on the principle that data should be recorded in its entirety only once. Often the same data are recorded, in certain instances, as many as five times. An example of this is where two organizations exchange data. Organization "A" types the data and sends them to organization "B." Organization "A" then key-punches and key verifies the same data, using a copy of the form; organization "B" does likewise. The more normal case is where data are typed and then key punched and key verified within the same organization for a total of three recordings of the same data.

Capturing data at the source is then predominately geared to reducing operator or labor costs by decreasing the number of people involved in the data collection system. As a by-product, accuracy is also increased since the more we automate, the more accurate the operation becomes.

Problems exist with any system, especially when the data required are prepared at a source over whose personnel there is little or no control. However, the rewards are plentiful and the effort worthwhile.

The reject rates for this type of system must also be evaluated carefully. A high reject rate of even 50% or more may still indicate an economical system when it is weighed against a total keying operation. Volumes would be the key factor in determining whether half a loaf is better than none.

CONCLUSION

In conclusion OCR offers a new flexibility for reducing input cost and problems. It is not the panacea for all problems, but rather another improved method of collecting data. The efforts expended in the development and implementation of an OCR system will be commensurate with the rewards obtainable.

DATA COLLECTION:
DISCUSSION QUESTIONS

1. What is source data automation? What characteristics must the data collection process have before source data automation becomes feasible? Why?
2. Should source data automation systems be used only for large-volume, standardized applications? Why or why not?
3. What impact is source data automation likely to have on costs, performance times, and integrated operation for other system functions (for example, data communication, data organization and storage, data processing, and information retrieval and display)?
4. For what kinds of applications are buffered keypunches likely to be preferred to conventional keypunches? Why?
5. In view of the fact that key-to-tape equipment costs two to three times as much as a card punch, how can its use be justified? For what types of applications is key-to-tape equipment most likely to replace card keypunches? Why?
6. What benefits and limitations do key-to-disk devices (shared-processor systems) have in relation to card keypunches? For what kinds of applications are key-to-disk systems best suited? Why?
7. What advantages do optical scanners have over card keypunches as a method of data collection? Why has optical scanning not been more widely used? What improvements in optical scanners are needed to encourage more widespread adoption?
8. The presence of what general conditions will make it desirable to shift from card keypunch operations to some form of keypunch replacement? What conversion problems must be overcome to make such a change effective?
9. For what types of applications are teletypewriters and touch-tone telephones best suited as data entry devices? What are the limitations of these two devices for data collection purposes?
10. What type of data collection device is most likely to be selected

in each of the following cases (explain fully your reasons for each choice)?

a. Large volume of standardized transactions with high potential for errors and strict accuracy requirements must be handled.

b. Source documents must be in both human- and machine-readable form with requirement for rapid access to stored data.

c. Small volumes of variable-format transactions of a highly strategic nature are collected at a number of outlying, remote locations.

d. Close control over and careful monitoring of data is considered essential for data collection application involving production and order status data captured at widely distributed points throughout an industrial factory.

e. Department with small, irregular batches of data to be collected must minimize equipment costs and utilize surplus labor fully from existing manpower pool.

DATA COLLECTION: BIBLIOGRAPHY

"A Survey of the Character Recognition Field," "Data Collection Systems," and "Source Data Automation: Techniques and Equipment," *Auerbach Standard EDP Reports*, 1967.

Anderson, P. L., "Optical Character Recognition: A Survey," *Datamation*, July 1969, pp. 43–48. See also "Source Data Conversion and Automation," *Ideas for Management*, 1968, pp. 114–119, and "OCR Enters the Practical Stage," *Datamation*, December 1, 1971, pp. 22–27 (or condensed in *Data Processing Digest*, January 1972, pp. 27–28), by the same author.

Aronson, R. L., "New Encoding Methods Spark New Card, Badge, Ticket Uses," *Control Engineering*, October 1969, pp. 88–94.

Auerbach on Data Collection Systems, June 1972, and *Auerbach on Optical Character Recognition*, December 1971.

Axner, David H., "Keyboard to Magnetic Tape—The Iconoclast," *Data Processing*, Part I, September 1968, pp. 50–54; Part II, October 1968, pp. 36–42.

Bauch, James H., "Cut Input Costs with Key-to-Tape Devices," and Barry M. Harder, "Key-Disk Systems Speed Mainframe Processing Off-Line," *Computer Decisions*, May 1971, pp. 36–39, 42–47.

Bauldreau, J., "Mark Reading," *Datamation*, October 1, 1970, pp. 34–38.

Bennett, Edward M., "Data Entry through Distributed Data Processing," *Journal of Systems Management*, September 1969, pp. 30–31.

Bieser, Albert H., "Key-to-Tape and Key-to-Disk Systems," *Modern Data*, December 1971, pp. 32–40. See also John A. Murphy, "Key-to-Tape Data Entry," in same issue, pp. 37–38.

"Cash Drawers That Talk Computer Business," *Business Week*, August 29, 1970, pp. 66–67.

Chu, Albert L. C., "The Plodding Progress of OCR," *Business Automation*, March 1970, pp. 48–55, and "Key-to-Tape: K. O. for the Keypunch?," *Business Automation*, June 1970, pp. 52–59.

Collette, R. P., "Evaluating Key to Disk Systems," *Data Processing,* June 1971, pp. 35–39.

Craft, R. C., "Making Marks Where They Count with Optical Systems," *Computer Decisions,* May 1973, pp. 42–43.

Data Capture Supplement, *Computerworld,* October 28, 1971.

"Data Entry," *Data Systems,* May–June 1971, pp. C1–C15. See also "At the Source," *Data Systems,* May–June 1971, p. 44 (condensed in *Data Processing Digest,* July 1971, pp. 38–39).

"Data Entry Techniques," *Australian Computer Journal,* November 1970, pp. 146–155 (condensed in *Data Processing Digest,* March 1970, pp. 12–13). See also L. Feidelman and G. B. Berstein, "Advances in Data Entry," and P. H. Dorn, "Whither Data Entry?," *Datamation,* March 1973, pp. 44–48, 49–51.

Datapro 70, "How to Select Data Entry Devices," August 1970, and "All About Optical Readers," November 1972.

DeParis, Joe, "The Merits of Mark Reading," *Data Processing,* January 1966, pp. 38–39.

Drattell, Alan, "OCR: Management's New Speed Reading Technique," *Management Review,* March 1968, pp. 65–67 (condensed from *Business Automation,* January 1968). See also Arnold Keller, "OCR Update," *Business Automation,* February 1969, pp. 36–41.

Eisdorfer, Alfred, "A Study of Optical Character Recognition," *Journal of Systems Management,* November 1970, pp. 19–22.

Featheringham, Richard D., "Optical Scanning: Some Principles and Applications," *Journal of Business Education,* November 1969, pp. 58–60.

Feidelman, Lawrence A., and Katz, Jacob L., "Scanning the Optical Scanners," *Data Processing,* October 1967, pp. 34–38. See also "Source Data Automation: Optical Character Recognition," *Modern Data,* November 1970, pp. 56–57.

Feidelman, Lawrence A., "A Primer on Source Data Automation," *Data Processing,* September 1969, pp. 26–29, 32–36. See also "SDA: The Concept and the Equipment," and "SDA: A More Precise Definition," *Modern Data,* April 1970, pp. 84–86, and August 1970, pp. 37–40, by the same author.

Feidelman, Lawrence A., "Keeping the Keypunch Alive," *Modern Data,* October 1971, pp. 28–29. See also J. A. Murphy, "Punched Card Equipment," *Modern Data,* January 1972, pp. 52–56.

Feidelman, Lawrence A., "Keyboard-to-Tape Data Entry Devices," *Modern Data,* July 1970, pp. 50–52. See also "Keyboard-to-Tape Equipment Economics," *Modern Data,* Part 1, September 1970, pp. 52–53, and Part 2, October 1970, pp. 52–54, by the same author.

Feidelman, Lawrence A., "Point-of-Sale Data Collection Systems," *Modern Data*, December 1970, pp. 42–43. See also "Source Data Automation: Optical Readers," November 1970, pp. 56–57.

Ferrara, Raymond, and Nolan, Richard L., "New Look at Computer Data Entry," *Journal of Systems Management*, February 1973, pp. 24–33.

Gabrill, Wilson F., "Data Collection Is Almost Error Free," *Industrial Engineering*, May 1972, pp. 12–16.

Gebremedhin, Elinor, "Optical Character Recognition—Performance up, Prices down," *Data Processing*, June 1970, pp. 42–51.

Gray, Peter J., "Optical Readers and OCR," *Modern Data*, January 1971, pp. 66–82.

Greenblatt, Stanley, "Delete Delays and Dollars with Direct Data Entry," *Infosystems*, September 1972, pp. 20–25.

Hillegass, J. R., and Melick, Lowell F., "A Survey of Data Collection Systems," *Data Processing*, June 1967, pp. 50–56.

Hradowy, E. J., "Keypunch or Key-to-Tape: What Are the Differences?," *Canadian Chartered Accountant*, September 1970, pp. 175–179.

"Improvements in Data Entry," *EDP Analyzer*, Parts I and II, September 1971 and October 1971.

Jackson, Scott, "Data Recorders: Still Best Data Entry for Many Applications," *Data Management*, December 1972, pp. 24–27.

Joss, John, "Three Keys to Data Input: Punch, Tape, Disc," *Data Systems News*, November 1970, pp. 29–30 (also summarized in *Data Processing Digest*, February 1971, pp. 11–13).

Karski, Robert, "Point-of-Sale Data Collection," *Data Processing*, August 1970, pp. 43–46. See also David Hammac, "An Economical Electronic Point-of-Sale Updating System," *Proceedings: ACM Meeting, 1966*, pp. 183–189.

McGuire, W. H., "How Optical Character Recognition Can Eliminate the Input Bottleneck," *Data Processing Annual*, Vol. XII, 1967, pp. 241–246.

McRainey, J. H., "Source Data Automation," *Automation*, October 1967, pp. 87–97.

Melick, Lowell F., "Make Your Mark—An Incisive Look at Optical Mark Readers," *Data Processing*, January 1969, pp. 42–46, 54, 56.

"Optical Scanning Finally Starts to Pay Off," *Business Week*, December 27, 1969, pp. 55–56. See also "Optical Readers Turn a Fresh Page," *Business Week*, October 9, 1965, pp. 185–188, and G. F.

O'Leary, "Optical Reader Speeds Data Entry," *Best's Review,* March 1972, pp. 82–83.

"Optical Scanning: It's on the Move," *EDP Analyzer,* June 1969.

Oram, Derek, "Optical Character Recognition," *Computer Design,* February 1969, pp. 48–53.

Philipson, H. L., "Optical Character Recognition: The Input Answer," *Data Processing Annual,* Vol. X, 1966, pp. 119–130.

Prenting, Theodore O., "Input Devices for Manufacturing Systems," *Systems & Procedures Journal,* July–August 1966, pp. 42–47.

Price, Dennis G., "Whither Keypunch?," *Datamation,* June 1967, pp. 32–34.

Rabinow, Jacob, "Whither OCR?," *Datamation,* July 1969, pp. 38–42.

Reagan, F. H., "Should OCR Be Your Data Input Medium?," *Computer Decisions,* June 1971, pp. 19–23.

Schwab, Bernhard, and Sitter, Robert, "Economic Aspects of Computer Input-Output Equipment," *Financial Executive,* September 1969, pp. 75–87.

Seaborn, True, "How Union Carbide Kicked the Keypunch Habit," *Infosystems,* August 1972, pp. 26–29.

"Significant Cost Savings Possible in Data Preparation," *Lybrand Ross Newsletter,* March 1971. See also "Keypunch Operation Study Focuses on Potential for Higher Productivity," *Lybrand Ross Newsletter,* May 1972.

Smith, William A., "Nature and Detection of Errors in Production Data Collection," *AFIPS, Joint Spring Computer Conference Proceedings,* Vol. 30, 1967, pp. 425–428. See also articles by same author in *Journal of Industrial Engineering,* Part I, December 1967, pp. 703–707; and Part II, January 1968, pp. 24–31.

"Survey Reveals Toughest OCR Forms Problems," *Computer Digest,* September 1971, pp. 1–2.

Synderman, Martin, "Data Verification: A Third Generation Technique," *Journal of Data Management,* November 1969, pp. 28–31.

"Technology Profile Update: Keyboard-to-Tape Input Systems," *Modern Data,* December 1969, pp. 68–77.

"Workable Ways to Cut Input Costs," *Administrative Management,* August 1971, pp. 56–67. See also "EDP Input: The Six Choices," *Administrative Management,* April 1971, pp. 40–46.

PART II

DATA COMMUNICATIONS: KEY SYSTEM COMPONENTS AND DESIGN CONSIDERATIONS

A data communications system links terminal devices, transmission channels, and one or more computers to provide on-line data flow between single stations or through multipoint connections between several stations, as "An Introduction to Data Communications" (*Arthur Young Journal*) points out. The basic elements of a communications system include terminals (general or special purpose, intelligent or slave), modems (which convert signals from conventional input-output units into a form the transmission channels will accept), transmission channels (low speed, medium speed, and high speed), and a central processor. Most communications system applications are data collection/distribution systems, on-line processing systems, or message-switching systems. The benefits of communications systems include information timeliness, centralized data bases, and lower clerical costs. Major limitations of such systems center on cost, lack of trained personnel, and data security.

In designing data communications systems, Applebaum stresses that consideration should be given to selection of a computer, a front-end processor, software, communications equipment, and terminals. The distribution patterns of most systems can be broken down into point to point, one to many points, many points to one, and many points to many points for analysis. Key information characteristics include volume, message urgency, coding, and accuracy required. Considerable attention is paid to error detection and correction. The systems designer can choose from dial-up, WATS, and private-line services. Programming packages available from major hardware suppliers facilitate telecommunications programming. Careful matching of central computer and communications processors is needed for best overall system results. The most common data communications applications are data collection/distribution, message switching, inquiry/response, and time-sharing. As the number of options available increases, the design of data processing/communications systems becomes more complex.

Data communications systems are designed to transfer digital data between two or more terminals in a reliable manner. Fundamental classes of data communications applications include data collection, data distribution, inquiry processing, computer load balancing, computer time-sharing, and message switching. Information flow requirements that must be considered in designing a data communications system include data source numbers and location, information volumes, message intervals, data entry and receipt forms, delays allowed and penalties, and reliability requirements. Problem areas include volume estimates, traffic overloads, balancing storage, processing and transmission capacities and speeds, reliability and backup requirements, economical error detection and correction techniques, communication processor programming requirements, training programs, and capability for system expansion. System components include terminals, input/output control units, error control units, synchronization units, and modulation-demodulation units. Communication facilities can operate in the simplex, half-duplex, or full duplex modes, may be divided into narrow-band, voice-band, or broad-band classes, and are available as leased or public switched service.[1]

Long-distance transmission of data generally requires modems to encode data in a form acceptable to the transmission channel and to decode the encoded data at the receiving end. Modems can be classified as serial by bit or parallel by bit in terms of transmission format, or as asynchronous or synchronous in terms of transmitter timing. The types of modulation techniques commonly used in data transmission include amplitude modulation, phase modulation, frequency modulation, and frequency shift modulation. The selection of a modulation scheme depends on such factors as circuit complexity, required bandwidth, required transmission quality, and tolerance to transmission irregularities. Faster transmission speeds, increased accuracy, and more economical operation should become possible with the widespread adoption of pulse-code modulation by the switched-data transmission networks and from other improvements made in voice-grade channels.[2]

The most frequently used communication networks are of telegraph and voice-grade quality. Dial-up services such as TWX or TELEX are used with telegraph-grade channels and are best suited for customers with widespread, low-volume traffic requirements. Long-

[1] See F. H. Reagan, "Data Communications—What It's All About," *Data Processing*, April 1966, pp. 20–26, 66–67, for a more complete discussion of these points.
[2] See for example, A. Turczyn and T. Jeng, "Data Communications: An Overview of Line and Modem Capabilities," *Data Processing*, March 1970, pp. 16–20.

distance or direct-distance dialing is used with telephone-grade channels by customers who wish to send a low volume over a wide area.
WATS service can best be used with ordinary telephone lines by
customers who have widespread volumes of substantial outgoing traffic. Private-line telephone and telegraph-grade circuits can be either
point to point or multipoint and are best suited for customers with
large traffic volumes concentrated between a few points. TELPAK is
a private-line service designed to fulfill requirements for large capacity
communication facilities between specific points and may be employed
as a single wideband channel or subdivided into a number of lower-
quality channels.[3]

Real-time processing of data requires direct transmission of data
from remote locations to a central processing unit and generation of
responses in a time interval suitable to the operational requirements
of the system. Effective operation of a communications-oriented data
processing system requires careful consideration of system response
times, data volumes and distribution, equipment speeds and costs,
error control and reliability, and communications control techniques.
Simulation of system traffic on a computer is often helpful in indicating bottlenecks, time lags, and other system problems that can be
resolved before full-scale system operation occurs.[4]

The development of a computer-based management information
system requires consideration of the computer, communications facilities, and terminals to be used as an integrated entity, as Murphy
points out. Remote terminals, communication-line facilities, and computer facilities should be selected so as to optimize total system response times, operating costs, and capacity utilization rather than separate segments. The computer facility itself should be evaluated in
terms of file storage capacity, response time requirements, adequacy
of programming, and availability of backup facilities. A communications-based management information system can reduce clerical effort, minimize errors, improve two-way communication, and reduce
transaction-handling time. Successful implementation of such a system will require the unequivocal support of top management.[5]

[3] See John F. Macri, "Communication-Oriented Computer Systems," *Computers
and Automation*, May 1966, pp. 14–15, for a more complete description of data
communication services available.
[4] These factors and problems are discussed more fully in Herb Ranzinger, "Communications Planning for Data Systems," *Automation*, March 1966, pp. 80–82.
[5] The practical aspects of the development of computer-based management information systems are discussed by E. Murphy, "A Guide to an Economically Successful Communications-Based MIS," *Journal of Data Management*, February
1968, pp. 20–25.

For many organizations the most effective type of management information system includes an integrated, on-line retrievable data base, inbound and outbound communication capabilities, response times compatible with user needs, and essential business data stored and processed in such a manner that they meet management's information needs effectively. In selecting remote terminals, the user must give adequate attention to hardware, software, and human considerations, particularly as they affect the operation of the central processing unit. The choice of line facilities requires consideration of switched versus dedicated facilities, costs, availability, and reliability. In designing the data communications portion of the system, the user must evaluate such factors as transmission speeds, error control, flexibility, and data security.[6]

Solem and Buchanan [7] emphasize the wide variety of sizes, shapes, and price ranges available to terminal users. In selecting a terminal, consideration should be given to such factors as end-use, requirements for batch or on-line, direct access or both, need for hard copy versus soft copy, lease versus purchase, transmission speed required, physical requirements, and reliability. After the field has been narrowed down to the most likely contenders, the units remaining should be evaluated in terms of their compatibility with present computer systems, manufacturer's reliability and service record, tape input feature availability, editing capability, output desired, and performance during on-site tests. At some point in the future, the ideal terminal may exist with color graphic display, optional hard copy, quick and simple service and repairs, and sufficient core storage to contain simple programs. Until then, the user will have to settle for terminals with some but not all of these features.

As Lavoie points out, intelligent ("smart") terminals perform some storage and processing tasks for the central processor, thereby reducing communications costs, removing input-output bottlenecks, and permitting system expansion without acquiring a larger central processor. Intelligent terminals include buffered terminals, remote batch terminals, and minicomputers. Intelligent remote batch terminals can accommodate a wide variety of central processors and computer peripherals in an interleaved mode. Programmable buffered terminals are not very intelligent but are user oriented and make data

[6] See D. J. Dantine, "Communication Needs of the User for Management Information Systems," *AFIPS, Proceedings—Fall Joint Computer Conference,* 1966, pp. 403–411.

[7] See Helen Solem and Evanne Buchanan, "You and Your Resident Computer Terminal," *Business Management,* 1970, for a more detailed discussion of terminal selection factors.

entry easier. Minicomputers are an essential element of many hierarchial computer systems. CRT display terminals and OCR machines with expanded capabilities for independent operation can qualify as intelligent terminals.

A trend toward the development and use of hierarchial systems in the future is foreseen by several authorities. Such systems will contain large central processors, capable of handling several billion instructions a second, that are linked to smaller units. Huge networks based on distributed intelligence will use decentralized processors and intelligent terminals arranged in a heirarchial order. With a network of intelligent terminals, several widely distributed processors, and a large central processor connected via data transmission lines, any user can access data from any point in the network. Although such networks are not now being used, satellite processors under the control of a larger central processor are currently controlling production processes. Expansion of the hierarchial structure to other functional areas can be expected in the future.

In recent years, as Hobbs declares,[8] internal storage and memory costs have decreased rapidly, mass memory costs have decreased at a slower rate, and communications costs have remained fairly constant. It is possible to place all computation and processing capabilities in terminals or all processing and computation capabilities in the central processor. Communication, reliability, and processor costs are the key factors in the preceding decision. Processing capabilities are placed in terminals primarily to minimize communications costs. If smart terminals are used, the central processor should have mass storage, expensive or infrequently used peripherals, and large-scale computing capabilities.

Smart terminals may include a small computer, CRT, keyboard, graphic input device, printer, and communication modem. The most common applications for a typical smart terminal with graphic capabilities would be in data entry and conventional accounting applications. In the future, smart terminals with stand-alone capabilities are likely to be developed.

Marvin underscores the importance of cost considerations in choosing between smart and dumb terminals. Time-sharing users are generally concerned with hardware lease or buy costs, terminal connect costs, and communication-line costs. The ability of the smart terminal to store and manipulate data at the local site permits reduction

[8] See L. C. Hobbs, "The Rationale for Smart Terminals," *Computer*, November–December, 1971, pp. 33–35.

of terminal connect and telephone usage time and costs. With smart terminals, time-sharing installations not only can reduce communications costs but can also serve more users and charge lower rates per user.

8.

AN INTRODUCTION TO DATA COMMUNICATIONS

By Bernard E. Brooks

Editor's Note: Reprinted, by permission, from THE ARTHUR YOUNG JOURNAL, Autumn 1970. Copyright © 1970 by Arthur Young and Company.

Just as management was beginning to feel comfortable with, if not thoroughly bilingual in, the language of EDP, a whole new vocabulary of strange and unfamiliar terms—"modems," "data rates," "slave terminals," "sub-voice channels," "front-end systems," and the like—has been thrust upon it by the growing use of data communications systems in business. It is the purpose of this brief article to introduce the reader who has some understanding of EDP but little or no knowledge of, or experience with, data communications to the language and basic concepts of this relatively new but increasingly important area of business data processing.

To begin at the beginning: A data communications system may be defined as any system which links together terminal devices, transmission channels, and a computer in order to provide on-line data flow. This definition includes systems involving a point-to-point connection between single stations and those with multipoint connections between several stations (Fig. 8.1).

"On-line" systems have several features that distinguish them from other data-processing systems. Some of these features are as follows:

- Source data can be entered into an on-line system directly via ter-

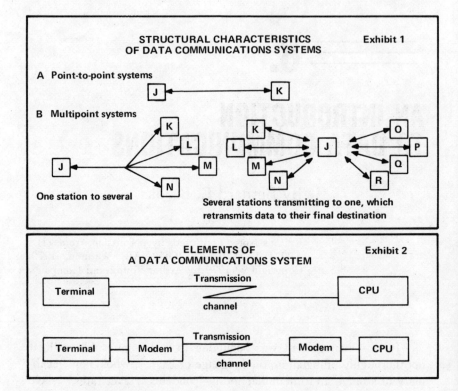

8.1   STRUCTURAL CHARACTERISTICS OF DATA COMMUNICATIONS SYSTEMS

minals, thus eliminating the need to convert such data to machine-readable form prior to processing. This feature is essential in systems which must receive and process information and produce a response within a very short time interval (typically, seconds or fractions of a second). A familiar example is an airline reservations system.

• The nature of the processing program that is being executed by an on-line system at any point in time is determined largely by the nature of the activity occurring at the terminal sites, rather than by a pre-determined job-stream at the computer site. In other words, the problem-solving programs for a specific type of transaction are initialed upon input of the related transaction. By contrast, in a data processing system which is not on line, the execution of a program follows a pre-defined order established by a job scheduler or operator at the computer site.

• The input of transactions at the terminals is independent of the application program. In an on-line system, terminals are under the control of special programs; in a standard data-processing system the application program itself initiates the input of transactions. In most on-line systems, terminal devices may input single transactions for processing; in a standard data-processing system, items are usually batched for input according to processing routines.

ELEMENTS OF A COMMUNICATIONS SYSTEM

The basic elements of a data communications system are terminals, modems transmission channels, and one or more central processing units.

Terminals

Terminals are the devices used to enter ("input") data into and/or extract ("output") data from the central processing unit. They may be special-purpose or general-purpose in nature. Special-purpose terminals are designed for one particular type of application—e.g., a bank teller terminal, a stock market inquiry device, or a traffic sensor that measures the movement of automobiles through an intersection. General-purpose terminals are designed to be used in a variety of applications and include typewriter terminals, cathode-ray tube (CRT) devices, and paper tape transmitters and receivers.

Terminals are also referred to as "intelligent" or "slave." Intelligent terminals have elementary logic and computing capability. Under program control they can perform editing, formatting, and arithmetic functions, thus relieving the central processor of certain transaction-processing tasks. Slave terminals are devices capable only of input and output, with no arithmetic or logic capability.

Modems

Terminals and computers generate DC signals, which are not suitable for direct transmission over great distances. Where such transmission is necessary they are usually converted to the type of signal that can be carried over telephone channels at an alternating frequency. This conversion is accomplished by the use of "modems."

A modem is a device that varies the characteristic of the signal being transmitted to superimpose the data signal on the carrier frequency of the transmission channels—a process known as *modu*lation. On the reception side of the channel, the modem separates the data signal from the carrier frequency to make the data compatible with the receiving device. This process is called *demod*ulation. A modem is required at each end of the line to accommodate the modulation/demodulation processes.

There are several types of modems available. The most common are the data sets supplied by the Bell System and acoustic couplers supplied by various venders of terminal devices.

For the most part, a modem is designed to permit a single one-way transmission at a specific transmission speed at any given point in time. In recent years, however, some suppliers of modems have designed devices that allow the simultaneous transmission of more than one type of data, at more than one speed, via a single modem at each end of the line.

Transmission Channels

Transmission channels are the paths through which the information flow occurs. Channels are usually classified according to the maximum rate at which data can move through them without error. This capacity, or "data rate," is commonly measured in bits per second. Three speed ranges may be used to classify transmission capacity: low-speed, medium-speed, and high-speed.

Low-speed transmission channels are usually capable of transmitting 50 to 300 bits per second (bps). They are commonly referred to as "teleprinter grade," "narrow band," or "sub-voice" channels. Such channels are used primarily for the transmission of teletype signals.

Medium-speed channels are capable of data rates of 600 to 5,000 bps. These channels operate in the same frequency as channels which permit normal telephone conversation, and are therefore referred to as "voice-grade" channels. This type of channel facility accommodates CRT transmission, high-speed paper tape transmission, and high-speed on-line printer devices.

High-speed channels allow transmission in excess of 5,000 bps. This range of transmission capability is commonly referred to as "broad band." Such channels are used to send data via facsimile and to transmit television-type information, and they are also used for transmitting data from magnetic tape to magnetic tape and from computer to computer.

Central Processors

In the data communications environment, the central processing unit (CPU) acts as both problem solver and terminal. In addition to executing problem-solving programs, the CPU may act as an interface between another computer and transmission channels. A CPU which functions in this manner is called a "front-end" system. Front-end systems are employed to receive data from a variety of terminals using varying speeds and codes, the data being converted to a common code and common speed and transferred to a different computer which contains the problem-solving application program. In addition to code and speed conversion, the front-end system may perform re-formatting, editing, or other functions as dictated by the total system design.

The computer acts as a terminal when it receives data and transfers the data to the problem-solving application program within the same CPU.

In most cases a computer requires additional hardware and special software to permit it to operate in the data communications environment. This additional hardware—the "communications interface," as it is called—allows the CPU to recognize, receive, and transfer characters between the communication lines and the processor's memory. The transfer of such characters, the checking for errors, and the validation of messages are all accomplished under the control of the special communications software.

TYPES OF COMMUNICATIONS SYSTEMS

Applications of computer-oriented communications systems are many and varied, and depend to a large extent on the nature of the industry that employs the system. Most such applications, however, tend to fall into one of three basic categories: (1) data collection/data distribution systems, (2) on-line processing systems, and (3) message switching systems.

Data Collection/Data Distribution

Data collection involves the on-line transmission of information from one or more remote terminals to the computer, where the information is stored ("collected") for subsequent processing. Data distribution involves the transmission of data previously processed by the computer to one or more remote terminals.

The process of data collection and data distribution can be considered uni-directional communication, since there is basically no problem-solving interaction between the terminal and the computer. During the transmission of the data to and/or from the computer, there is no processing of the data beyond that which is required to accomplish correct transmission and reception. The data processing (e.g., file update) occurs separately in time from the data transmission.

On-line Processing

On-line processing systems allow data to be input via the terminals and immediately processed. This requires that accessible master files be maintained using storage media which will provide rapid access to records.

On-line processing systems are usually designed for real-time update, inquiry response, and/or timesharing applications:

• A *real-time update system* involves the input of transactions via terminals, with the computer initiating a file update as the result of receiving each transaction. An example of a real-time update system is an on-line savings bank application. This type of system allows the direct entry, via terminals, of savings account deposit and withdrawal data.

• An *inquiry response system* permits the input of queries via the terminals, with the computer retrieving from the files the information that satisfies the inquiry criteria and transmitting a response to the terminal. An example of an inquiry response system is an electronic stock quotation system.

• A *timesharing system* is one in which a number of terminals are connected to a computer and the independent (and usually unrelated) users of the terminals input and execute their applications as though each of them had sole access to the computer.

Message Switching

This type of system employs a computer which receives messages from various remote stations, analyzes these messages, and transmits each message to its ultimate destination. A computer-controlled message-switching system is capable of converting the transmission code of an input message to a different code when required by the receiving terminal. In addition, such systems will temporarily store, or automatically redirect, messages that cannot be sent to a certain terminal, due to its being inoperative or having an excessive amount of messages waiting.

BENEFITS OF COMMUNICATIONS SYSTEMS

No one set of benefits, of course, applies to every data communications system. In general, however, such systems tend to offer the following advantages:

• *Timeliness of information.* On-line data communication is extremely fast. It will facilitate a file update that is very close in time to the occurrence of the transaction—e.g., as an item is removed from inventory, the information can be transmitted and create an instantaneous adjustment of inventory records in the CPU. This increased timeliness of information permits more effective management control of the resources and activities of an organization.

• *Centralization of data bases.* Data communications systems permit those organizations with multiple locations to maintain current information in a single location available for rapid access by all locations. Such systems permit faster and more economical reactions to changes in the policies and procedures that affect an organization by allowing such changes to be made in a central location. All users of the system can be provided immediately and simultaneously with the changed information, thus avoiding duplication of files and preventing the possibility of different locations being exposed to different versions of the same data.

• *Other advantages.* Clerical labor costs may be reduced by eliminating the need for human intervention between the original recording of the transaction and its processing. In addition, a data communications system can eliminate or significantly reduce the need to maintain a separate data-processing capability at multiple locations.

LIMITATIONS OF COMMUNICATIONS SYSTEMS

Data communications systems also have certain limitations or disadvantages, including the following:

• *Cost.* The cost of the necessary additions to the CPU, transmission lines, and terminals involved in a data communications system, plus the cost of the additional programming needed in the communications environment, may well exceed the cost of a multiple-batch data-processing system.

• *Development and maintenance personnel.* Personnel with experience in designing, implementing, and maintaining communications systems may not be readily available, since a higher-level programmer/ analyst is usually required for a communications system than for a typical batch system.

• *Data security*. Since files can be accessed and updated from multiple locations, the potential for exposure of file information to unauthorized persons is increased. This may be true even in those systems where elaborate security controls are designed into the system.

SUMMARY

In the future we can expect to see increasing use of, and interest in, data communications systems. Such systems are nearly always faster and are often more efficient than more traditional methods of information handling. At the same time they tend to be more complex, more expensive, and more difficult to implement successfully. Even more than ordinary data-processing systems, they call for careful, knowledgeable planning from the feasibility stage to the implementation stage.

9.

WHAT DOES IT TAKE TO GO ON-LINE?

Telecommunications Can Get the Right Data to the Right Place at the Right Time

By Stanley Applebaum

Editor's Note: From COMPUTER DECISIONS, January 1970, pp. 21–25. Reprinted by permission of the publisher, COMPUTER DECISIONS, and author.

No matter where you look in the data processing field today, telecommunications is definitely "in." Third generation systems emphasize the ability of computers to switch from task to task and to handle multitudes of peripherals and terminals. This fact, coupled with business demands for up-to-the-minute information, leads to communications as a natural extension.

Although business is applying computers to more and more communications tasks, progress is hampered by a scarcity of expertise in telecommunications. We are far from the time when communications systems can be easily installed. After years of effort and problems today's user still faces many unknown problems and minor crises until the major bugs are removed. Since qualified teleprocessing personnel are hard to come by, it's wise to be informed on some of the common considerations and decisions that you as a communications planner may have to face.

Data Distribution Patterns

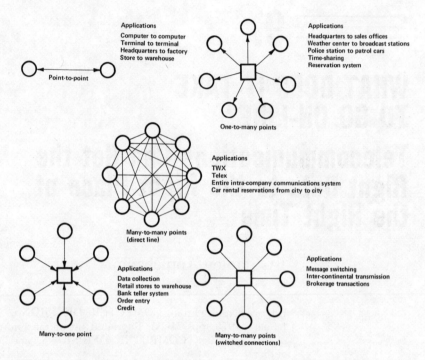

9.1   DATA DISTRIBUTION PATTERNS

In designing a data communications system you'll need a computer, a possible front-end computer or concentrator, software, communications equipment, terminals and, most important, a great deal of thoughtful planning.

First off, the distribution of your company's internal information flow must be analyzed. Most systems can be broken into four basic patterns—point-to-point, one to many points, many points to one, and many points to many points.

The simplest arrangement is point to point, where perhaps one office is communicating with its warehouse or one computer is communicating with another. This type of flow would use either a conventional dial-up service or a private line if many calls are made to any great distance. The one to many point system exists when a central office disseminates information to many locations and is the one initiating the calls. A typical example would be a regional office calling each of its sub-offices to gather sales data. The many to one point situation would exist if several locations call into a computer for information such as in time-sharing or a reservation service.

The many to many points case is the most complex. This can occur in three ways:

1. Each location is connected to another by a direct line;
2. All points go through a central switch; or
3. All locations are connected by a party line so that a message sent is received at every location, or else a call directing code can activate only the equipment located at the intended receiving station.

In each of these basic distribution patterns, the volume of information to be handled is a deciding factor. Therefore, in choosing the arrangement that best suits your company's needs, you must consider four characteristics of the information to be communicated or moved: message volume expected, urgency of the message, coding, and the accuracy required.

Volume: To calculate expected message volume, allow at least a month to make measurements of the present system's traffic. You should come up with a daily average message volume including traffic to and from every point in the system. For example, if you have three regional offices reporting to one central office, actually sit down and count the number of messages received from each one plus the responses to them. Then take several sample messages and figure out the average number of characters in each one. If an office transmits three sales orders at a time, all three constitute the total message length.

Once you have the average message length and volume, you can then calculate your total transmission time. Assume you are going to use Teletypes with a 10 character per second speed. If your average message had 2,000 characters, the average transmission time would be 200 characters. This time, plus time for dialing and connecting, multiplied by the average number of messages per day will give you total transmission time.

Since most systems work with humans, there is always some part of the day that is busier than others. To calculate peak hour traffic, take the average daily transmission time and multiply it by the busy hour load which is 17% in an average 8-hour day. Now you have the figure for system usage in the busiest hour. Your system must anticipate peak volume periods.

Urgency: The number of circuits and transmission speeds are greatly dependent on the urgency of the information. For example, in a real-time system such as airline reservations, the customer is waiting anxiously for a response. If sales offices are sending the head office sales forecasts for next month, it doesn't matter if the transmission takes five minutes or ten. Real time systems users don't like to get busy signals. It is important to have enough circuits to avoid busy signals for the most part.

Language: Still another consideration is the language of the information. While there are over fifty different codes existent for the transfer of information, five are commonly used for communications. These are 5-level Baudot code; 6-level BCD (Binary Coded Decimal); 6-level Teletypesetter code; 7-level Field Data code; and 7-level ASCII. The code you choose depends on the terminals and computers you pick.

Accuracy: Finally, the accuracy of the information must be weighed. Errors can occur in the terminal equipment, the transmission line, and in human operations. Studies of conventional dial-up telephone service show that about 70 per cent of calls would have an error rate of one in every 10 million characters. Technical ability to provide almost complete accuracy is available, but cost is usually the controlling factor.

THE COMMUNICATIONS CHANNEL: ERRORS COMMON

The computer manager is accustomed to outages from time to time. These are not as bad for him as conditions of erroneous output. The communications man faces an opposite set of priorities, since for him conditions of telephone service outages are very serious and even more important than occasional noise on the line. Therefore alternative routes must be available such as backup equipment and means for both the detection and correction of errors.

Telephone noise is the major error source in most systems. It originates within the telephone switching equipment and can sometimes be heard on the line as clicks. Its effect is to prevent the receiving end from detecting a bit correctly sent from the transmitting end. To some extent, communications can be viewed as transportation —there are risks in the voyage.

Parity schemes are used to detect errors when they occur. Some codes are designed to detect the presence of errors but more elaborate codes can actually identify what the error was, and even correct one or more errors in the most elaborate cases. The more elaborate the parity scheme, the less likely that double or multiple transformations of bits will produce acceptable codes. Thus, false acceptance of bad data at the receiving end can be brought to a low probability. Elaborate parity schemes reduce line efficiency since time is lost in sending redundant bits.

						b_7 →	0	0	0	0	1	1	1	1
						b_6 →	0	0	1	1	0	0	1	1
						b_5 →	0	1	0	1	0	1	0	1
Bits	b_4	b_3	b_2	b_1	Col.→ Row ↓	0	1	2	3	4	5	6	7
	0	0	0	0	0	NUL	DLE	SP	0	@	P	\	p
	0	0	0	1	1	SOH	DC1	!	1	A	Q	a	q
	0	0	1	0	2	STX	DC2	"	2	B	R	b	r
	0	0	1	1	3	ETX	DC3	#	3	C	S	c	s
	0	1	0	0	4	EOT	DC4	$	4	D	T	d	t
	0	1	0	1	5	ENQ	NAK	%	5	E	U	e	u
	0	1	1	0	6	ACK	SYN	&	6	F	V	f	v
	0	1	1	1	7	BEL	ETB	'	7	G	W	g	w
	1	0	0	0	8	BS	CAN	(	8	H	X	h	x
	1	0	0	1	9	HT	EM	)	9	I	Y	i	y
	1	0	1	0	10	LF	SUB	*	:	J	Z	j	z
	1	0	1	1	11	VT	ESC	+	;	K	[	k	{
	1	1	0	0	12	FF	FS	.	<	L	\	l	|
	1	1	0	1	13	CR	GS	–	=	M	]	m	}
	1	1	1	0	14	SO	RS	■	>	N	∧	n	–
	1	1	1	1	15	SI	US	/	?	O	_	o	DEL

9.2 ASCII CODING CHART. EACH CHARACTER IS REPRESENTED BY SEVEN BITS.

During the growth of data communications many different codes and parity schemes were implemented but people found a problem in that data from one set could not easily be converted into another set. Users became unhappy and some way out of the mess was sought. The current ASCII (American Standard Code for Information Interchange) grew out of a difficult series of compromises between the many systems of codes. ASCII uses seven bits for information plus one for parity. 128 (2^7) elements or characters can be represented by ASCII. However, for IBM 360 systems, the nine bit EBCDIC code gives a universe of 256 (2^8) elements. ASCII is more than just a code set, however. It is also a discipline for the communication of data. There are procedures in this discipline that allow non-ASCII codes to be communicated. By using those procedures, the EBCDIC code can be transmitted on channels designed for ASCII.

Once the requirements and objectives have been set for a data communications system, the next step is getting the necessary equip-

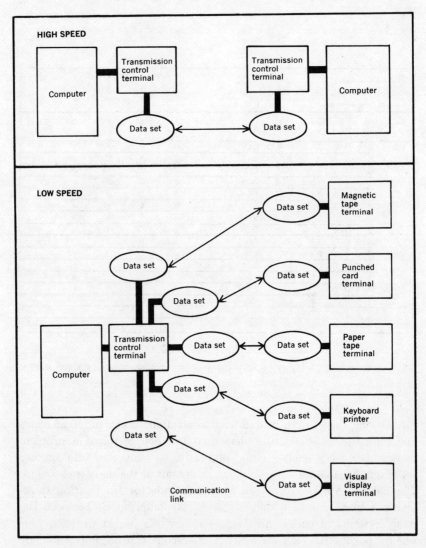

9.3 COMMUNICATIONS CAN LINK ONE COMPUTER TO ANOTHER OR A VARIETY OF TERMINALS TO A COMPUTER

ment. A variety of terminals can be selected. Transmission may be in the form of punched cards, punched paper tape, magnetic tape, visual display, or keyboard. The nature of the application determines the type of terminal or computer to be used. A vital part of any telecommunications system is of course the telephone equipment.

The common carriers—telephone companies, Western Union, and private microwave networks offer the user a variety of choices. The telephone company offers about five basic choices as to which type of communications service to employ. Most data is communicated over regular dial-up or voice grade lines. The heavier data communicators can also choose to have a private line, WATS service for high volume long distance calls, Telpak for large volume point-to-point transmission, and teleprinter exchange service such as Telex or TWX.

HOW DO YOU CHOOSE?

Since the common carrier tariffs for phone service and data sets vary from state to state and system to system and no handbook of the various choices is readily available, your best bet is to contact your local telephone company and request that a data communications consultant be assigned to you. Before you enmesh yourself with a strangling network, let him help you choose the system best suited to your needs. Then, armed with a head full of transmission speeds, message volumes, and locations, open yourself to proposals from terminal manufacturers and modem makers. Your systems analysts can work with their systems analysts to achieve a workable solution.

Dial-up

Terminals transmitting over voice lines have a data set attached to them. Both the sender and receiver have a data set which converts electrical signals from the machine into tones suitable for telephone transmission. A data set is also known as a modem (modulator-demodulator). Since early 1969 manufacturers other than the telephone company have been allowed by the FCC to attach modems to the telephone switched network. The telephone company calls its data sets Data-phones and has 400 different models available. They vary in speed and bandwidth, ranging from 300 bits per second speed for voiceband up to 4,800 bits per second for wideband services. The costs range from $10 to $200 just for the set.

How much will it cost to use Data-phone service? Using the

switched network, dial-up system the rates are the same as for regular
voice calls, varying from state to state. The actual cost of communications is a function of usage and the number of stations. The usage
cost takes into account the speed of transmission, the number of
calls, the holding time, and the grade of service. The number of stations takes into account distance from one to another and how they
are clustered. Also to be considered are the common carrier's tariffs
or rates. The cost of the physical data set increases as transmission
speeds increase. For example, the 202 Data-phone with a speed of
1,200 bits per second rents for $40 per month while the 201 Data-
phone rents for $80 a month with a speed of 2,000 bits per second.

Wats

Savings can sometimes be made in telephone line costs by employing WATS (Wide Area Telephone Service). These tariffs are
calculated for the geographic area being served, with the country divided into six bands for each user. The service provides either outward or inward calling. For outward, the central station must initiate
all calls (remember the one to many point arrangement?). With inward WATS the remote stations initiate the calls. There is a provision
in the inward tariff that allows the telephone company to increase the
number of inward WATS lines a user employs if the demand from the
remote stations results in a large number of busy signals. A typical
WATS tariff is the one for band 6, which allows unlimited calls
through the nation for $2,250 per month.

Private Line

Private line voice service provides circuits for the exclusive use
of a particular subscriber. These services may be used for voice or
data transmission. A private line can be set up on a two-point or multipoint basis. You would get a private line if you make many calls to
the same place. Charges are based upon mileage and the number of
stations on the network.

Telpak

Telpak is a private line service that is suitable for large volume
point-to-point systems. The capacities can be arranged to constitute a
group of voice channels suitable for use with voice or data or a group
of channels for use with teleprinter equipment. It can also be used as
a single large channel for highspeed data services such as magnetic

tape, computer memory and facsimile transmission. For example, one Telpak "C" channel, which is the equivalent of 60 voice grade channels, can be used for high speed transmission at a speed of 15,000 characters per second. Telpak "A", "B", and "D" are equivalent to 12, 24 and 240 voice channels. Channel capacities similar to that of Telpak are also available with privately owned microwave systems.

SOFTWARE COMES IN HANDY

You are not just at the mercy of the common carriers when it comes to help in setting up communications systems. Various computer manufacturers, such as IBM, RCA, Honeywell and Univac, have communications software available to make it easier to program for telecommunications. These programming packages come along with operating system software, usually as part of the bargain. Unbundling may change this.

Packages such as IBM's BTAM (Basic Telecommunications Access Method) ease the burden by providing a means for generating the necessary communications coding during the running of an operating system. All the programmer has to do is define the communications system through a series of declarative statements which contain the terminal addresses and parameters. BTAM builds the links and tables that control the operation of the teleprocessing. In effect, the remote terminals become part of the input/output system of the central processor and are accessed just as other input-output devices. The programmer does not have to write assembly level statements but he must understand the role of these terminals and the flow of data created by the BTAM code. A variety of options are offered such as the creation of a polling list and the generation of an error report. Polling refers to the surveying of each terminal to check if it wishes to send a message.

BTAM also performs a buffer management function for the programmer by allocating buffer cells to incoming messages and keeping track of the buffers in use and available. Buffering refers to temporarily storing data between device-to-device transmission to make up for speed or time differentials. The programmer may choose dynamic buffering to conserve more space. Only the amount of buffer memory necessary is used, with more available as needed. Core assigned to buffering is varied automatically according to the number of lines to be serviced and the number of buffer cells simultaneously in use.

QTAM (Queued Telecommunications Access Method) is another IBM package which adds features to the BTAM function to allow it to handle messages from output to input. QTAM assigns priorities to all messages that are buffered and arranges them in queues for output to other communications lines or for output to processing systems. It appears to have been written for the message switching application (one terminal talks to another via a central switch computer such as the IBM 2703 or GE Datanet 30) and is somewhat difficult to use for other applications.

Honeywell provides a similar package for its 200 line. The communications I/O package operates with Operating System-Mod 1 to provide macros that will connect and disconnect terminals, perform translations, and check and correct errors.

RCA offers a program like BTAM and QTAM on its Spectra 70 series. The Multichannel Communications System (MCS) performs dynamic or fixed buffering, error handling, logging, code translation and polling. A supervisor section of the program resides in 20k bytes and responds to all communications interrupts. One advantage claimed by RCA is that MCS will handle uncontrolled lines in addition to polled lines (a feature not included in QTAM). This means that with MCS a terminal does not have to be polled but can send data at any time.

DO I NEED A FRONT-END?

Theoretically the communications channel is merely a reservoir of data as is a tape drive and you can program for it in the same way. However, the fact that the terminal is physically remote from the computer creates a qualitative difference that calls for different techniques. What you can do is use another computer for the communications channel. In this case, the communications signalling is handled by a "front-end" processor and the main computer can be more closely programmed as though the communications channel was a virtual tape drive.

The front end processor is generally one of the "mini-computers" such as the PDP-8 or Honeywell 516. These are generally twelve or sixteen bit machines with a limited number of peripherals on them. Sometimes the front-end is specially designed for communications such as the GE Datanet-30 or IBM 7740. In some cases, the communications input is written onto a disk which then serves as the interface between the front-end and the central computer. For the applications programmer, there is no communications environment to deal with—he simply gets his data from the disk whenever the mini-computer indicates that some input has accumulated.

In other cases the front-end is connected to a selector channel and treated as another peripheral. One of the difficulties is that selector channels are not identical from one installation to another. Engineering of the interface has become an important problem for the front-end manufacturer. He often finds that his interface will not operate properly because the selector channel has some unforeseen engineering change incorporated in it.

Data communications has grown greatly in the last few years. Applications can be grouped into four general categories: data collection/distribution, message switching, inquiry/response and time-sharing.

The data collection/distribution system is one in which information flows in two directions at different times during the cycle. An example is an order processing system such as the one Lever Brothers Co. uses. Orders are delivered to Lever sales offices each day. The orders are punched into paper tape and transmitted by a Digitronics D-505 over the public telephone network. When the station is called by headquarters (one-to-many point arrangement) the tape is transmitted to a magnetic tape station in New York.

Lever warehouses receive data on paper tape terminals. These tapes are converted into hard copy shipping orders for picking the goods.

Message switching is one of the original data communication applications. Many businesses use this type of system, especially airlines. In a typical application, Teletype equipment is installed at many remote stations. The network consists of private lines with many stations on one line. The messages are collected in the message switching computer and the addresses analyzed for queuing them to the proper output line.

Inquiry/response systems are very common in the securities industry. A data bank is created with detailed information on many different items. Calls made from many locations are seeking short responses to specific questions. The price of stocks is typical.

Time-sharing is the seemingly simultaneous use of a computer by several users. Communications links the many users with the central computer. Communications problems have been a major Achilles heel in many such services.

As with any new computer installation, designing and implementing a teleprocessing system even with programming packages, standard codes, and powerful computers is no easy task. You must work with the computer manufacturer's systems people and the common carrier's communications consultants to achieve a workable solution. As the data communications field matures, the number of options grows also. While a few years ago there were just a few data sets to choose from, the modern business sees new entrants all the time, as does the terminal manufacturing business. The decisions grow more and more cumbersome. Therefore it is wise to at least know the language when you take the plunge.

USEFUL COMMUNICATIONS LITERATURE

Data Communications in Business by E. C. Gentle Jr. is a very helpful introductory book put out by AT&T. Copies may be ordered for $2 from Publishers Service Co., Room 600, 75 Varick St., N.Y., N.Y. 10013.

Policy Issues Presented by the Interdependence of Computer and Communications Services and *Digests of the Responses to the FCC Computer Inquiry* by Stanford Research Institute may be ordered for $3 each from the Clearinghouse for Federal Scientific and Technical Information, Springfield, Va. 22151. The two volumes cover current topics in communications as seen by various industries. Many useful charts and tables are included. Report Nos. are PB183612 and PB183613 respectively.

Data Communications Concepts and Communications Facilities is a short manual offered by IBM. The *IBM System/360 OS BTAM* and *QTAM* manuals which get into the nitty-gritty of communications software can also be obtained from your local IBM sales office.

DATA COMMUNICATIONS GLOSSARY

ASCII — American Standard Code for Information Interchange. An eight bit character code.

Bandwidth — The difference expressed in cycles per second, between the highest and lowest frequencies of a band.

Baud — A unit of signaling speed. The speed in bauds is equal to the number of bits per second.

Baudot Code — A transmission code with five bits per character, used in standard teletypewriter transmission.

Buffer — A storage device used to compensate for a difference in rate of flow of data or time of occurrence of events, when transmitting data from one device to another.

Central Office — The place where communications common carriers terminate the customer lines and locate the equipment which interconnects those lines.

Channel — A path for electrical transmission between two or more points. Also called a circuit, facility, line, link or path.

Coding — Conversion of a communications signal into a form for transmission or processing.

Concentrator — A device used to feed the signals from several data terminals into a single transmission line for input to a computer and vice versa.

Connect time — The total time required to establish a connection between two points.

Data Access Arrangement — Provides a protective connecting arrangement as the interface between a customer-provided modem and the switched network.

Data-phone — A trademark of American Telephone & Telegraph Co. to identify the data sets made and supplied for use in the transmission of data over the regular telephone network.

Data set — The complete interface unit supplied by the carrier, including a network control and signalling unit, a modem, and devices to protect the network from signals that might interfere with other users.

ESS — Electronic Switching System—the successor to present electromechanical switching system used in telephone exchanges.

Full Duplex — Simultaneous two-way transmission.

Half Duplex — Alternate, one-way-at-a-time, independent transmission.

Holding time — The length of time a communication channel is in use for each transmission. Includes both message time and operating time.

Hz — Hertz, internationally used term for cycles per second.

Interface — A common boundary, for example, physical connection between two systems or devices.

Message switching — The switching techniques of receiving a message, storing it until a suitable outgoing circuit and station are available, and then retransmitting it toward its destination.

Modem — A modulator/demodulator that transforms a typical two-level (binary) computer signal into a signal suited to the telephone network, for example, converting a two-level signal into a two-frequency sequence of signals.

Multiplexing — The division of a transmission facility into two or more channels.

Narrow band — A relative term used to denote a communication channel through less than voice-grade.

Parallel transmission — Method of information transfer in which all bits of a character are sent simultaneously. Contrast with serial transmission.

Polling — A centrally controlled method of calling a number of points to permit them to transmit information.

Response time — The amount of time elapsed between generation of an inquiry at a terminal and receipt of a response at that same terminal. Includes: transmission time to computer, processing time at computer, and transmission time back to terminal.

Simplex channel — One-way channel.

Switched network — The network that provides switched telephone service to the public. This term is used interchangeably with public switched network and switched message network.

Teleprocessing — A form of information handling in which a data processing system utilizes communication facilities.

Telpak — A service offered by communications carriers for the leasing of wide band channels between two or more points.

Tie line — A private line communication channel of the type provided by communications common carriers for linking two or more points together.

Voice grade channel — A channel suitable for transmission of speech, digital or analog data, or facsimile, generally with a frequency range of about 300 to 3000 cycles per second.

Wideband — A bandwidth greater than a voiceband.

≡ 10.

A GUIDE TO AN ECONOMICALLY SUCCESSFUL COMMUNICATIONS-BASED MIS

By E. Murphy

Editor's Note: From DATA MANAGEMENT, February 1968, pp. 20–25, published by Data Processing Management Association, 505 Busse Highway, Park Ridge, Illinois 60068.

In a large far-flung corporation with many field offices, there is the ever-increasing complexity of managing, operating, and expanding the business. It becomes more difficult to know what is going on in all facets of the company, to improve efficiency, to find out quickly when you have a problem and how to correct it promptly, to discover quickly when a new idea is working well so that you can take advantage of it and, in general, to continue to maintain tight management control without creating unnecessary impedances.

A number of small-loan finance companies are engaged in pioneering efforts to overcome these problems through a communications-oriented management-information system.

What does such a system consist of? What are its overwhelming advantages? What does the businessman have to know about computers, communication facilities and terminals? What are the implications of a system of this type?

This article intends to address these questions in a clear-cut manner that will make sense to the businessman. Today, the businessman is often exposed to the lip-service and romance of "real time," "management information systems," "timesharing," etc. *What is often hidden or not mentioned in this technical array are simple answers to important questions relating to the business itself.* The answers presented here are based on experience to date with the application of communications-based management-information system to finance companies. These answers are not intended to be complete, but instead they will indicate a frame of reference for considering a communications-based management information system.

WHAT IS A COMMUNICATIONS-BASED MANAGEMENT-INFORMATION SYSTEM?

Terminal equipment in the various branch offices records basic transactions as they occur. This information is received by the home-office computer from telegraph or teletype lines which connect the terminals to the computer. The computer obtains the proper file associated with the transactions, makes necessary calculations to update the file and, if necessary, replies to the terminal at the originating branch.

The following example illustrates a communications-based management information system in action: A customer makes a payment on a loan at one of the branch locations. The branch employee records this transaction using the terminal. Necessary data for this transaction is quickly forwarded to the computer which will obtain the customer's file. The computer reduces the principal of the loan, taking into account items such as interest, late charges, etc. It then replies to the terminal by posting the customer's ledger card or by notifying the branch employee of some error (wrong account number) or problem (late charge due). All of this has occurred within minutes, with a minimum of effort on the part of the branch employee. In addition, the home-office records are up-to-date and available for input to computer runs which can reveal the over-all status of the business on a daily or even more frequent basis.

WHAT ABOUT COMPUTERS, COMMUNICATION FACILITIES AND TERMINALS?

Most businessmen today are aware of computers and know that remote terminals can be linked to computers by communication facilities such as telegraph or telephone lines. However, a communications-based management information system is not an isolated application. It will be the foundation of the business if installed, and therefore is worthy of careful study. Some of the important considerations that should be examined are described below in three categories: computers, communication facilities, and terminals. These three parts of the system interact with each other and they must be understood and evaluated with reference to the system objectives.

Computers

In a communications-based system, the selection of the right computer and its peripheral equipment will require the evaluation of many factors. One place to start this evaluation is to examine the adequacy of the computer facility in terms of (1) file storage, and (2) the capability of the computer complex to meet response-time objectives. In the finance company application, the computer must have access to all customer records, including inactive accounts. In addition, there will be other file requirements, some of which pertain to the system itself such as the storing of programs, which may be called upon by the computer to perform certain processing operations. Response time has a great deal to do with the computing facility performance, such as core-memory size, internal processing speeds, the time required to access files, and so forth. Response time can be defined as the allowable length of time from message entry at the terminal to message reply at the same terminal. It may be decided, for example, that a one-minute response is necessary because a customer is waiting at the counter to complete his transaction; therefore, the amount of time for the message to get to the computer, the time required for the computer to accept the message, to access the customer's file, to process the message, to formulate a reply, and to transmit this reply back to the terminal must be within the response time objectives.

Since there are many terminals in the system and the computer will be receiving many messages all at the same time, meeting the response-time criteria becomes a complex problem which can influence the size of core memory that the computer must have, the organization of files to achieve the best access speeds, and so on. To evaluate these questions, the various types of transactions have to be defined. The number of characters that each transaction will consist of, and the volumes of these transactions, especially for peak periods, must also be defined.

Programming considerations are extremely important from several aspects; one aspect is cost. If the computer manufacturer supplies adequate systems programs, or programs necessary to make the system operate, then the main cost will be that of writing application programs. It should be noted that the systems programs can influence the performance of the system. In addition to the cost of writing programs, the question of having these programs completed on time must also be addressed. Both cost and availability of programs will be dependent upon how much the system is expected to do, the availability of programming skills, and the man-years of effort involved.

Some other computer considerations will be the backup facilities and execution procedures in the event of equipment failure. Consideration should be given to having the computer monitor its own performance, such as keeping track of errors and their origins, so that an effective maintenance plan can be carried out. The possible use of multiprogramming techniques which enable a computer to handle several unrelated applications at once should be evaluated only after it is determined that the terminals can be serviced and sufficient additional capacity exists.

Communication Facilities

In addition to selecting the type of communication facilities that will meet the system objectives, one of the principal considerations is to optimize the cost of these facilities. There are a number of variables that can affect cost in this area. Network layout is one of them. This is the physical arrangement of communication lines and terminals. Having a number of terminals share the use of one communication line will tend to reduce communication cost, provided the response times can still be met. Computer programs have been used to optimize network layouts and to indicate the cost of these layouts based on tariffs filed by common carriers with the Federal Government.

In some cases, additional terminal cost can reduce the monthly cost of the communication facility. For example, terminal buffering that permits the composition of messages without tying up the communications line will make that line available to other terminals on the same line; thus a larger number of buffered rather than unbuffered terminals could utilize a single line facility. This in turn would tend to reduce the number of lines required.

In some cases, remote line concentrators can be used to reduce communication costs. While these remote concentrators can be expensive, they sometimes pay for themselves in reducing monthly communications costs. Usually these concentrators will receive a number of low-speed communication lines at a particular geographical point and transmit the information received from these lines over a single high-speed line to the computer facility.

The type of "line control" used by the terminal and computer can also influence how efficiently the communication line is used. "Line control" is the language that the computer and terminal use in order to talk to each other. This line control can generate "turn-around time" on the communication line which can cause a considerable reduction in the rate of useful data that is transmitted. This area should be evaluated by competent technical people.

Terminal Considerations

In a large terminal system it is not unusual for the cost of the terminals to exceed the cost of the central computer configuration. In addition to cost, there are other considerations.

First of all, all of the transactions that the terminal will handle must be defined in as much detail as possible. This will include such things as identification of input and output data, message lengths, forms requirements, etc. Frequency of transactions must also be defined because both terminal capability and system design are dependent on this information. From this definition, the functional capability that the terminal must have can be established. Then, a terminal can be selected or designed that has a minimum of unwanted function and cost.

Another very important consideration is "who will use the terminal." Because of the obvious importance of the terminal to the successful operation of the system, human factors must be carefully evaluated. The skill level of the terminal operator will dictate the amount of complexity the terminal operation can have. Operator turnover must be considered with relation to the training necessary to use the terminal. Location of lights and switches, the choice of terminology used in labeling, and the number of physical operations necessary are examples of things that contribute to the simplicity or complexity of terminal operation. In some cases, it may be desirable for the computer to issue a series of printouts on the terminal which will instruct the operator in performing a transaction. However, this method will add to the programming complexity and may decrease the communication-line efficiency due to the large number of characters being transmitted.

Error correction procedures at the terminal is another important consideration and, ideally, these should be relatively simple. For example, correcting a paper tape may be awkward and time consuming. In most cases, it is desirable to stop errors at their point of origin rather than compound them inside the system.

Terminal packaging should be considered in connection with physical installation requirements and the physical environment in which the terminals will be located. The wrong packaging, for example, could generate high cost in terms of remodeling branch offices to accommodate the terminal.

The terminal design is also influenced by the system requirements such as response time that was mentioned before. Buffering and transmission speed are examples of items in this category that should be evaluated.

WHAT ARE THE ADVANTAGES OF A COMMUNICATIONS-BASED MANAGEMENT INFORMATION SYSTEM?

Generally, many of the advantages of both centralization and decentralization can be achieved by a single system. Using a finance company as a model, these advantages are examined at branch and home-office levels.

Branch Office

The objective of a communications-based management information system at the branch level is reduced operations. The terminal and system designs are important in realizing this objective because they bring about:

Less Reporting. With each transaction captured by the home-office computer, it is not necessary for branch personnel to summarize the transactions for periodic reports to the home office. The computer can accomplish this more accurately and much sooner.

Less Transaction Time. Through the use of a properly designed terminal, the elapsed time of each transaction should be less than with previous methods. For example, a large percentage of new loans are renewals, and in most of these renewal situations, the computer has sufficient information about the applicant to prepare most of the loan form with minimum effort by the branch employee.

Less Clerical Effort. Because branch office personnel have access to a computer through their terminal, there is little or no need to perform calculations or consult rate tables. Even cash balancing at the end of the day is simplified with assistance from the computer and terminal. The terminal maintains a journal of all transactions, and the computer keeps a cash balance and a duplicate record of each transaction.

Reduction in Office Equipment. Again, with access to a computer, the need for adding machines, etc., is minimal.

Improved Branch Management. The computer can issue daily branch operating statements through the terminal. Policy or procedure changes can be issued to all branches immediately. Branch managers can be effectively measured and informed when they are not meeting objectives such as handling delinquencies.

Error Reduction. With the computer handling much of the clerical load and with simplicity in handling transactions in the branch, errors can be greatly reduced. Furthermore, most errors generated in the branch can be caught and rejected by the computer with notification to the branch to correct the error. For example, the branch sends an account number and payment amount to the computer. If the payment amount is wrong, the computer detects the error and notifies the branch immediately.

More Customer Time. Reduced operations permit more customer time. Thus, a branch may be able to handle more accounts without more employees, or the same number of accounts with fewer employees. Since most finance companies prefer small geographic areas for each branch, it may be possible to open new branches by redistributing employees from existing branches.

The branch manager will have more time available to pursue delinquent accounts or to solicit new customers. The terminal automatically tells him, or other branch personnel, that a customer presently in the office should be solicited for a new loan up to a certain amount. The terminal can even tell the employee how much the customer's payments would be.

Inquiries. The branch manager who needs an answer to a question can make an inquiry of the system through the terminal; in fact, he can communicate with another branch through the system. He may wish to do this because he is receiving a payment from a customer on vacation (an opportune time to solicit if the customer's record is good!).

Home Office

The principal advantage of a communications-based management information system from the home-office point-of-view is improved control of the business. With all the basic information contained in the computer, exception reports or special analysis can be of significance in managing the business. Some examples are

Timely Decisions. Statistics can be generated to suggest the best geographic locations for expansion based on account activity by area.

Quick Status Report. Current status of the business is available on an up-to-the-minute basis. Decisions involving investment or expenditures can be viewed in this light.

Prompt Correction. Management action can be taken to correct problem situations immediately. A branch with too many delinquent accounts can be brought to management attention. The amount of money to be floated through banks can be more accurately defined, based on up-to-the-minute branch experience.

Management by Exception. Example: The computer reports an unusual increase in the number of loan applications at a particular branch during the day. Management investigates immediately and finds that an economic problem in the branch's area has caused this surge in applications. This may be an opportunity or a risk for the company, and management could issue special ground rules for accepting applications in that branch.

Elimination of Recreating Data. The terminal system makes it unnecessary to keypunch incoming mail from the branches and the subsequent processing for computer input.

Elimination of Peak-Period Volume Reports. With everything on a current basis, month-end closings are minimized. Management by exception techniques makes it unnecessary for management to pour over voluminous reports.

Instant Communications. Policy or procedural changes can be sent to all branches. Even management recognition of service anniversaries can be accomplished with the help of the computer.

Interdepartmental Benefits. Other facets of the business can derive important advantages from this system. Sales promotion can look at computer statistics concerning the number of customers brought in by radio, television, newspapers, etc., and capitalize on this experience. Insurance may decide to write policies at the home-office rather than in the branch. These loan policies could be written and mailed the same day the loan was made at the branch. Auditors can examine branch records at the homeoffice and travel to branches on an exception basis.

WHAT ARE THE IMPLICATIONS OF A COMMUNICATIONS-BASED MANAGEMENT INFORMATION SYSTEM?

It should be clear at this point that even the decision to investigate a communications-based management information system can involve time and effort of competent technical and management people. This effort can be wasted unless top management support is clear at the very beginning. At the completion of the investigation effort, a proposal representing a multimillion dollar investment will in all probability require approval from the president and the board of directors; thus, top management support in the beginning is an obvious necessity.

The effort involved will amount to examination of present procedures, collection of data for system design purposes, collection of the facts necessary for economic justification, and so forth. A proposed plan for implementation, including costs, schedules and necessary personnel skills, will also be required.

There is another reason why top management support will be necessary. A system of this type, if installed, could dictate changes to the organizational structure of the company. As these changes become apparent to those involved, the possibility exists that internal politics can develop. For this reason, top management should make it clear that it supports the system investigation in order to avoid possible distortion of the facts necessary to make a decision for or against implementation.

The facts presented above are not intended to discourage the investigation of a communications-based management information system; rather, the intent is to give management some insight into some of the facts it will need to make an intelligent decision. To assist management in this respect, the services of a competent equipment manufacturer—one that has the know-how and ability to implement and maintain such a system will be invaluable.

However, management must face the issues squarely. Despite the investment implications and the effort that will be required, it is becoming increasingly clear that the future competitive standing of a business may well ride on the decisions it makes today with regard to a system of this type. If a competitor decides to install a system of this type and a wait-and-see attitude develops to see how the competitor makes out, the time advantage the competitor would have may be extremely difficult to overcome later. Management must recognize that communications-based management information systems are becoming a reality, offering unprecedented breakthroughs in control and management of a business.

═══ 11.

TERMINALS ARE GETTING SMARTER

By Francis J. Lavoie

Editor's Note: Reprinted from MACHINE DESIGN, January 13, 1972. Copyright, 1972, by Penton Publishing Company, Cleveland, Ohio.

WHEN IS A TERMINAL NOT A TERMINAL?

The dividing line is somewhat fuzzy between a simple terminal/ central processor system, and a hierarchical computer system. In the latter, the "terminal" functions as a true stand-alone, general-purpose machine, communicating with one or more larger central processors only when its own capabilities are exceeded.

A spokesman for a large computer-research firm said recently that hierarchical systems will be the trend in this decade. He foresees a linked system, with, as its "center," a huge super-scale central processor capable of handling a billion instructions per second, Such huge networks will be based on "distributed intelligence," and will make use of decentralized processors and intelligent terminals arranged in a hierarchical procession. All the elements in the network will be connected by data-communications networks. With this multi-tiered arrangement, made up of intelligent terminals, several widely distributed processors, and a single large central processor, each user can access data from any other terminal or decentralized processor, as well as the central processor.

Today, such vast hierarchical systems are only a dream. But the concept is already being used, albeit on a much smaller scale. Typical examples are found in the control of manufacturing processes, where a number of satellite processors (often minicomputers) control each process or station under the overall control of a central processor. In many such systems, still another level of hierarchy digests data from several supervisory computers. This provides management with information on the entire plant operation.

According to a recent survey, the intelligent-terminal market is probably the fastest-growing segment of the computer industry. In the first six months of 1971, the number of installations grew by about 32%, from 7,000 to well over 9,000.

Intelligent terminals (also called smart terminals) are a recent phenomenon—so recent, in fact, that there is as yet no universally agreed on definition of what they are. There is even a hierarchy of intelligence; some terminals are considered just barely smart enough to qualify.

In very basic terms, an intelligent terminal is one that can do for itself some of the tasks that ordinarily fall to the central processor or host computer (or, in some cases, the operator). For example, it can do at least limited processing on incoming data before sending it along to the CPU (central processing unit). This can include reducing the data, changing its forms, or otherwise manipulating it. In addition, some IT's can take over certain transmitting and control functions. Many of them can store partially reduced data and send it to the CPU at a convenient time, so that they do not tie up the computer unnecessarily.

The intelligent terminal can take many forms. There are CPU-controlled buffered terminals, remote batch terminals, and minicomputers used as terminals. In addition, some CRT and character-recognition terminals qualify.

Most observers rate the future bright for intelligent terminals. Some experts feel that before long, all terminals will be capable of some degree of intelligence. This will be especially likely to come about when inexpensive, powerful microprocessors are developed to replace minicomputers in those applications where the mini is still too expensive.

Why the Surge of Interest?

There are several reasons why IT's have aroused considerable interest, all of them tied to the more efficient utilization of the main processor.

Some experts feel that the most important advantage of IT's is that they reduce communications costs. In fact, they go so far as to say that unless such costs are a factor, there is little advantage to having intelligence in a terminal.

Although not everyone agrees with such an absolute statement, there is no question that communications costs, both direct and indirect, are a major consideration. Some costs are obvious—for example, the raw cost of transmitting data over leased lines. Other costs are less easily pinpointed. For example, a large-scale computer can process a great deal of information very quickly. But if it is asked to do much low-level computational work, a bottleneck can easily develop because of the excessive data that must be shuffled back and forth between the "dumb" terminal and the central processor. This can lead to excessive queueing, resulting in loss of user time.

When the central processor is being used for a number of different jobs, or where it is being used to full capacity during working hours, the buffering capabilities of some intelligent terminals can be very important. Since the IT operates to varying degrees like a free-standing computer, it can preprocess the data and store it until the CPU is ready, perhaps during off hours. Where the terminal is so powerful as to be in effect a computer system in its own right, it can operate in a hierarchical mode, calling on the central processor only when its own capacity has been exceeded.

Because the more powerful IT's operate like small computer systems, and relieve the central processor of so many chores, they provide a convenient, and relatively painless, way of expanding a data-processing system without the need for a larger central processor. In many cases, it isn't even necessary to increase the programming staff. Just about anyone can program the average terminal, freeing high-level programmers for the more demanding requirements of the central computer.

As might be expected, dissenting voices have been heard. Intelligent terminals are, naturally, primarily oriented to large-scale central computers. Some observers feel that the current excitement over IT's constitutes a smokescreen that obscures the fact that in many cases, small, dedicated stand-alone computers may be a better choice.

What's On the Market?

Over half of the intelligent terminals now in use are of the remote-batch type. These units are located at some distance from the central processors, and handle data in "chunks," as opposed to those terminals which operate in an immediate, "interactive" mode. Similar terminals are available for use in the time-sharing mode, and some can operate in both the batch and interactive modes.

As is the case with other IT's, remote-batch terminals can't always be rigidly defined in terms of intelligence. They range in capability from older units, which provide only "on-location" card reading or printing to minicomputer-based systems that are in fact small computer/peripheral systems.

One of the greatest advantages of the remote batch intelligent terminal is that, unlike the hard-wired terminal, it can easily be programmed to be compatible with a wide variety of central processors. This means that a terminal can accommodate a number of central processors of different makes, by the use of software that simulates the terminal that each computer is designed for. An additional advantage is that the terminal can keep up with advances in central processors and peripheral equipment; before the advent of the intelligent terminal, the user who wished to upgrade to a better central processor often found that all his terminals were outdated. The same held true if he decided to switch to a different manufacturer.

The basic remote-batch IT consists of a linked system comprising a processor section, which provides both logic and control functions, and a card reader and printer. The processor does the "computing," and also provides communication with the central processor and the various peripherals attached to the system. The card reader and printer provide input and output.

Remote-batch IT's are often far more sophisticated than such a basic system. They may include magnetic-tape stations, paper-tape punches and readers, CRT displays, plotters, and extra printers, all under IT control. Often, all that's necessary to add peripherals is to plug in special device-controller boards into existing connectors, providing the necessary interface.

Because remote-batch IT's generally incorporate a minicomputer, or the equivalent, they can also function as stand-alone general-purpose computers. Thus, much preliminary calculating, checking, program debugging, and other low-level work can be done without tying up the large central processor. Basic memory can usually be expanded, in some cases up to 64K. All that's needed is to plug in one or more modular circuit boards. To further enhance the terminal's stand-alone capabilities, some manufacturers have developed comprehensive software packages for use by the terminal in the stand-alone general-purpose mode.

One of the more important advantages of the remote-batch IT is its ability to operate in a multileaving mode. This enables the terminal to handle a number of peripherals simultaneously, so that, say, CRT's, printers, and plotters can output data, perhaps at different locations, at the same time. This multileaving capability provides shorter turnaround time, makes for better use of available terminal time, and reduces communications costs.

As remote-batch terminals have become more intelligent, they have also become more reliable and easier to maintain. Circuits are often mounted on boards that are easily removed and replaced in the field. In line with the trend in other data-processing equipment, LSI and MSI have received increasing use, leading to substantial reductions in terminal system prices.

Programmable Buffered Terminals. PBT's appear to be the hottest current item on the intelligent-terminal market. As the name implies, these devices can be programmed to do certain (albeit restricted) kinds of data processing, and can store data for transmission to the central processor at a convenient time. Although not high on the intelligence scale, they do ease the data-entry chore, both for the central processor and, because they are highly operator-oriented, for the user.

Essentially, the programmable buffered terminal is a form-handling device, often serving to lead the operator through the steps necessary to prepare source documents for transmission to the central processor. It also does editing, formatting, error detection, and other similar functions. It generally uses preprinted documents for data entry. Although it can do some logical and computational work, these capabilities are limited. The user can tailor the terminal's operation to his own application.

PBT's, unlike many other intelligent terminals, are controlled by the central processor. Without it, they are of very limited use; but connected to the cpu, they go a long way to automating the input function. Unlike some other IT's, they are not computers in their own right.

Most PBT's have limitations that make them unsuitable for use as remote intelligent batch terminals. One, for example, can't be programmed except through the central processor, requiring an experienced programmer. In addition, input/output equipment includes only a typewriter and a card reader/punch. Only one keyboard can be tied to the terminal. Another terminal can function as a guide for the operator in filling forms, and also serves as a communications processor. However, it has a very small memory and it, too, is restricted in the number of peripherals it can accommodate.

The Computer. The computer itself is without doubt the most powerful and intelligent terminal. Although the minicomputer comes to mind for such applications, in fact small and medium-size computers have been used as IT's for a long time; such systems are often classified as hierarchical. Today, most such systems use the minicomputer.

The mini can function in varying degrees of intelligence. A minimum configuration (with perhaps 1K memory) might be called on to do only low-level "housekeeping" tasks, such as formatting. But this minimum mini can be upgraded easily, by the addition of more memory and, if needed, a variety of peripherals. Thus, it can quickly become a powerful preprocessor in a hierarchical system.

Many mini-based remote batch terminals are in effect nothing more than an integrated system of mini and associated peripherals. It's quite possible for the user to build a similar (although possibly less flexible) system by starting with a mini and adding peripherals. The major difference is that the RBT was designed as a unit to do its job and comes complete with the necessary software.

There are those who feel that the microprocessor will eventually replace the built-in minicomputer in intelligent-terminal systems, especially as "computers on a chip" become plentiful and inexpensive.

There is some evidence to support this prediction. Microprocessors are in effect small computers. In fact, they are often known as functional, or task-oriented, computers. They can be designed to do a specific job, thus eliminating the possibility of extra charges for interfacing, software, and packaging, that might be needed with the mini.

However, the microprocessor has limitations. Although it can do just about any computational or data-handling task that the mini is capable of, it is limited to about 250 program steps. It is not generally suitable where frequent programming changes must be made.

Eventually, the best compromise may turn out to be a combination of minicomputer and one or more microprocessors.

CRT Display Terminals. CRT display terminals have become

more intelligent, not surprising in light of the growing use of graphics in data processing of all kinds. They can be used by themselves, or they can serve to control a variety of peripherals. A number are fully programmable, some of them coming complete with their own minicomputer.

Typically, the programmable CRT will have a basic memory capacity of 4K words or less, expandable in modules to, in some cases, more than 64K words. In some machines, the memory is read-only; hard-wired programming is necessary. But there is usually a considerable amount of memory in these machines, so that versatility isn't seriously impaired. One recently introduced machine, for example, offers 48K words of hard-wired memory, but also makes available another 16K of random-access memory.

Despite their increased capabilities, CRT's are getting smaller, thanks to high-density electronics. One new offering has all its logic, file registers, and program and memory registers on a single chip. This means that the entire processor can be placed inside a standard-size keyboard/CRT terminal.

Optical character-recognition machines. Optical character-recognition machines, although not yet widely used except in certain business applications, are thought by many to be the wave of the future in mass data input. But to win wide acceptance, the OCR terminal must have some intelligence, especially if it is to function efficiently in relatively low-volume applications.

Because of the nature of the job they do, OCR terminals already can be classified as intelligent. From raw, "people-oriented" input, in one of several forms, they reduce data to a form directly acceptable to the computer. But to be truly effective as input media, they must also be able to control other peripherals, such as printers. And, say the experts, the price must come down.

Like other types of intelligent terminals, OCR machines can function either independently, under their own control, or they can depend on the central processor for their intelligence.

═══ 12.

SMART VS. DUMB TERMINALS: COST CONSIDERATIONS

By Cloyd E. Marvin

Editor's Note: From MODERN DATA, August 1970, pp. 76–78. Reprinted by permission of the publisher, Modern Data Services, Inc., and author.

The basic elements of cost to the time-sharing user are a combination of hardware lease or buy costs, connect costs of the terminal, and communication costs usually associated with the use of a telephone line. There may be costs associated with the use of the computer CPU, but for the sake of clarity, we shall assume that cost to be constant for the various systems in question.

A typical time-sharing system is shown in Fig. 12.1. The system

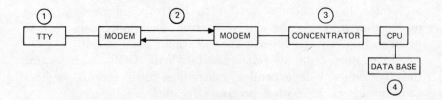

12.1 TYPICAL TIME-SHARING SYSTEM

is composed of a teleprinter connected to some means of tying that machine to a CPU at a remote time-sharing service center. The time-sharing center will have a concentrator to allow multiple terminal access to the CPU and will have a data base for the use of the subscribers. This data base may be dedicated to a specific terminal user or it may be shared by several users. The use of the data base is an additional cost option of the time-sharing service.

The elements of cost break down as follows: *Terminal lease costs*—Typically a TTY terminal will lease for about $80-$90 per mo. with an acoustic coupler. This is approximately $4 per day for a 20-day month. *Telephone line costs*—Assuming that a local telephone connection is available, usage costs are typically $4 per hour of connect time. This assumes that the telephone call is completed and the connection is continuous for the entire hour. *Connect Time* —This is the hourly charge made by the time-sharing service, and is approximately $12 per hour assuming multiple access to a powerful CPU such as a Univac 1108. *File Storage*—It is assumed that a constant amount of storage will be used by the various systems and the storage charge will drop out as a constant.

One can now plot a simple chart of expense versus usage as shown in Fig. 12.2.

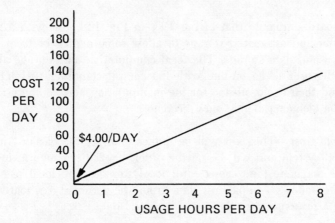

12.2 TTY TERMINAL COSTS

From Fig. 12.2 we see that the fixed elements of cost (i.e. terminal lease) determine the zero hour intersection of the curve and that the variable elements of cost (connect time and telephone charges) quickly outrace the terminal charge. The specific fixed and variable costs can be adjusted for any specific system, but the general character of the graph will remain constant.

Midway between the "dumb" terminal and a truly "smart" terminal is a type of system composed of a keyboard, a CRT with some rudimentary formatting ability, and a magnetic tape cassette for pooling entered form data. These systems, such as the Viatron System 21, are primarily designed for data entry and retrieval applications, not for computation or file manipulation. Thus they do not fit into any of the curves in this article.

The "smart" terminal system includes both local computation and storage equipment (Fig. 12.3). A typical installation consists of

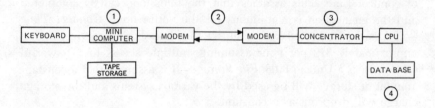

12.3 "SMART" TERMINAL COST ELEMENTS

a keyboard similar to that of the TTY in Fig. 12.1, but with a mini-computer and associated storage to allow some degree of local computation and data storage. The local computation and storage ability allow the user to go on-line with the central computer to fetch old data and then to go off-line for file manipulation and computation.

The elements of cost now become:

Terminal Costs—This cost will be higher than for the earlier "dumb" terminal system and will be on the order of $250 per month, including the magnetic tape cassette for local storage. The local use of a computer allows compacting data from the terminal keyboard and storing a response from the system's central data base.

Telephone Line Costs—The same rates will apply, but the amount of connect time will vary with the specific application. A family of curves will reflect various degrees of compacting available due to limiting the telephone use to high-speed computer-to-computer communication.

Connect Time—This cost will be reduced by the same degree and will be charged at the same rate as in the first example.

File Storage—Same as before for an equivalent amount of data. The

The elements of cost now yield Fig. 12.4.

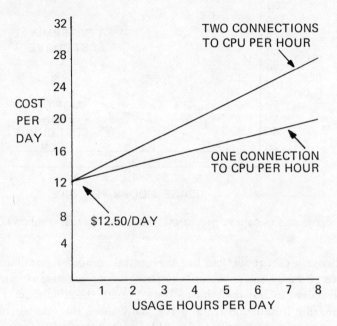

12.4 "SMART" TERMINAL COSTS

The interesting effect here is one of reducing the most costly elements of time-shared usage: the terminal connect time and the telephone usage time. The reduction of these cost elements results from the ability of the "smart" terminal to store and manipulate data at the local site. The local computer can cut down on its access to the CPU because communication is done at high computer speeds and not at typewriter speeds. The slope of the curve in Fig. 12.4 will be shifted up or down depending on the particular application and the skill of the user, but a typical curve could be seen as the slope resulting from one (3-minute) connection per hour to the CPU. The connect time using this slope is certainly a conservative estimate and could go as low as one connect per day if the local memory were sufficiently large to hold nearly a day's activity and the user could organize his use of the CPU for minimum access.

One can see from Fig. 12.5 that if the use of the system exceeds approximately 45 minutes per day, the subscriber begins to save money by using the more expensive terminal. Not only does the user

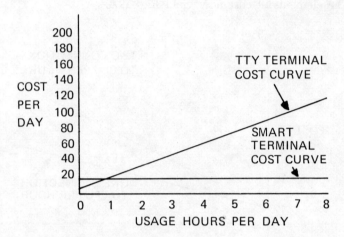

12.5   COMPARISON OF TTY TERMINAL COSTS VS. "SMART" TERMINAL COSTS

experience a cost reduction, but the central computer installation can now serve many more subscribers than before because of the high-speed access to the data base. With "smart" terminals, an existing time-sharing installation could serve many times the number of users as were previously served and could amortize the CPU costs over a broader base. This would serve to lower the hourly connect rates even further. This simple use of the "smart" terminal as an initial data concentrator also duplicates the current trend in time-sharing companies to use small computers as concentrators between towns to minimize telephone line costs.

DATA COMMUNICATIONS: DISCUSSION QUESTIONS

1. How can data communications facilities be used to improve the performance of such functions as data collection, data processing, and information retrieval and display? What role does data communications play in performing such functions as time-sharing, message switching, and inquiry processing?
2. What effect will such factors as expected peak loads, average message lengths, reliability, response-time requirements, and a need for convenience and flexibility in the location and operation of data entry devices have on the design of data collection and transmission systems?
3. What are the common types of data transmission/communication terminals available? What types of terminals would most likely be used with telegraph channels, common carrier telephone lines, private telephone grade channels, wideband channels? Why?
4. For what types of applications is each of the following types of services best suited: Direct Distance Dialing, TWX or TELEX, WATS, DATAPHONE, and TELPAK? Consider such factors as data sources and distribution points, data volumes, message intervals, delay penalties, and reliability and accuracy requirements.
5. What are the most important benefits of a communications-based management information system? What problems must be overcome in developing such a system?
6. What effect will the processing speeds, storage capacity, software requirements, and mode of operation (that is, continuous or batch processing) of the central processing unit have on the choice of data transmission terminals, channels, and services for a communications-based management information system?
7. How is it possible to optimize total system response times, minimize operating costs, maximize capacity utilization, minimize errors, and maintain system reliability at high levels in selecting remote terminals, communication-line facilities, and computer fa-

cilities for use in a computer-based management information system? Explain fully.

8. What types of terminals, transmission channels, and data communications services are most likely to be used in each of the following cases?

    a. A large number of short messages are to be sent to a wide area of the country at frequent intervals.

    b. A large volume of variable-length messages are to be transmitted between two specific points with peak loads occurring at infrequent intervals.

    c. Load balancing is to be accomplished between two central processing centers located several hundred miles apart and large volumes of data must be transmitted in short periods of time.

    d. Approximately thirty users at remote locations are to be connected to a central processing system for purposes of inquiry processing and solving short problems.

    e. Small amounts of payroll, billing, and inventory data are to be transmitted to a central service center for batch processing and report preparation.

9. How is it possible to distinguish between a "smart" and a "dumb" terminal? What conditions must be present to justify the higher cost and complexity of a smart terminal?

10. How do communications (that is, front-end) processors differ from ordinary central processing units? In view of the higher hardware and software costs entailed, why would such units be included in a communications-based computer system? Explain fully.

DATA COMMUNICATIONS: BIBLIOGRAPHY

"A Communications Revolution," special issue of *Science & Technology*, April 1968. See especially "A Communications Revolution," pp. 14–20; "The Computer as a Communication Device," pp. 21–25; "Network," pp. 45–50, and "Challenge in Transmission," pp. 54–62.

"An Introduction to Data Communications," *Arthur Young Journal*, Autumn 1970, pp. 35–37.

Applebaum, Stanley, "What Does It Take to Go On-Line?," *Computer Decisions*, January 1970, pp. 20–24.

Aronson, R. L., "What's Happening to Data Communications," *Control Engineering*, November 1969, pp. 107–111.

Auerbach Guide to Data Communications, 1970; *Auerbach Guide to Intelligent Terminals*.

Ayen, Esin, "Data Transmission Equipment," *Electronics Products Magazine*, August 21, 1972, pp. 104–111.

Barstow, J. N., "The Terminal That Thinks for Itself," *Computer Decisions*, January 1973, pp. 10–13.

Carne, E. Bryan, "Telecommunications: Its Impact on Business," *Harvard Business Review*, July–August 1972, pp. 125–133.

"Communications Systems Modeling," *Modern Data*, November 1972, pp. 34–36.

Computing Terminals, F. D. Sherwood, editor, *Infotech* (distributed by *Datamation*), 1971. See also *Computer Networks*, I. St. J. Hugo, editor, *Infotech*, 1971.

Croft, J. C., "Applying Data Terminals," *Automation*, November 1970, pp. 66–70.

"Current Status of Data Communications," *EDP Analyzer*, March 1969, and "Future Trends in Data Communications," *EDP Analyzer*, April 1969.

Dantine, D. J., "Communications Needs of the User for Management

Information Systems," *AFIPS, Proceedings—Fall Joint Computer Conference,* 1966, pp. 403–411.

"Data Communications: How Do You Use It? What Does It Cost? What's in the Future?," *Business Automation,* October 1971, pp. 22–38.

"Data Networks Spread across the U.S.," *Administrative Management,* February 1970, pp. 22–25. See also "Data Networks Are a Vital Link for Industry," *Iron Age,* September 21, 1972, pp. 53–54.

Datapro 70, "All about Data Communications Facilities," August 1971; "All about Communication Processors," January 1973; "How to Analyze Your Data Communications Needs," July 1971.

Davenport, William P., "Efficiency and Error Control in Data Communications," *Data Processing,* Part I, August 1966, pp. 34–40, Part II, September 1966, pp. 30–35. See also "Planning a Data Communications System," *Journal of Data Management,* February 1969, pp. 18–25, by the same author.

Deal, Richard L., and Wood, P. C., "Data Communications: Putting It All Together," *Datamation,* December 1972, pp. 72–80.

Dean, Robert F., "Communications-Oriented Systems of the Seventies," *Ideas for Management,* 1968, pp. 182–190.

Dolkos, Paul J., "Multiplexing: Communications Cost-Cutter," *Data Processing,* June 1970, pp. 34–40.

Doll, Dixon, "Planning Effective Data Communications Systems," *Data Processing,* November 1970, pp. 27–30.

Fruitman, M., "Cost of Communications," *Canadian Chartered Accountant,* March 1970, pp. 191–193.

Gourley, David E., "Data Communications: Initial Planning," *Datamation,* October 1972, pp. 59–64, and N. R. Dyes, "Planning a Data Communications System," *Datamation,* November 1972, pp. 74–81.

Hersch, Paul E., "Data Communications," *IEEE Spectrum,* February 1971, pp. 47–60.

Hobbs, L. C., "The Rationale for Smart Terminals," *Computer,* November–December 1971, pp. 33–35.

Holt, Arthur W., "Smart Terminals," *Datamation,* October 15, 1970, pp. 51–57.

"Intelligent Terminals," *EDP Analyzer,* April 1972.

Kaufman, Felix, "Data Systems That Cross Company Boundaries," *Harvard Business Review,* January–February 1966.

Laska, Richard M., "Portable Terminals: You Can Take It with You When You Go," *Computer Decisions,* September 1970, pp. 8–13.

Lavoie, Francis J., "Terminals Are Getting Smarter," *Machine Design,* January 13, 1972, pp. 109–113.

Marvin, Cloyd E., "Smart vs .Dumb Terminals: Cost Considerations," *Modern Data,* August 1970, pp. 76–78.

Menkhaus, Edward J., "The Ways and Means of Moving Data," *Business Automation,* March 1967, pp. 30–37. See also "Terminals: Pipeline to Computer Power," *Business Automation,* May 1970, pp. 48–55, 68.

Murphy, E., "A Guide to an Economically Successful Communications-Based MIS," *Journal of Data Management,* February 1968, pp. 20–25.

Nisenoff, "Design of Distributed Communications System—A Case Study," *AFIPS, Fall Joint Computer Conference Proceedings,* 1969, pp. 637–653.

O'Brien, B. V., "Why Data Terminals?," *Automation,* May 1972, pp. 46–51.

Parke, N. G., III, "Systems of Computers: Dispersal of Computing Power," *Data Management,* January 1973, pp. 14–20.

Perkowitz, Sandra, "Telecommunications Control Programs," *Modern Data,* October 1971, pp. 32–35.

"Planning a Data Communications System," *Modern Data,* Part I, "Basic Concepts," April 1970, pp. 134–141; Part II, "Common Carrier Facilities," May 1970, pp. 76–81, and June 1970, pp. 62–69; Part III, "Data Communications Terminals," August 1970, pp. 68–73.

Poppel, Harvey L., "Managing Telecommunications," *Business Horizons,* August 1969, pp. 37–44.

"Programmable Terminals," *Data Processing,* February 1971, pp. 27–35. See also R. L. Deal, "Programmable Communications Processors," and J. A. Murphy, "Programmable Communications Processors: Front-End Selections," *Modern Data,* July 1972, pp. 30–36, 38–45.

Ranzinger, Herb, "Communications Planning for Data Systems," *Automation,* March 1966, pp. 80–82.

Reagan, F. H., "Data Communications—What It's All About," *Data Processing,* April 1966, pp. 20–26, 66–67. See also "A Manager's Guide to Phone and Data Services," *Computer Decisions,* October 1971, pp. 20–23.

"Selecting Remote Terminals," *EDP Analyzer,* February 1969; "Software Factors for Remote Terminals," *EDP Analyzer,* May 1969; and "Developments in Data Transmission," *EDP Analyzer,* March 1973.

Simms, R. L., "Trends in Computer/Communications Systems," *Computers and Automation*, May 1968, pp. 27–29. See also J. F. Macri, "Communication-Oriented Computer Systems," *Computers and Automation*, May 1966, pp. 14–15.

Solem, Helen, and Buchanan, Evanne, "You and Your Resident Computer Terminal," *Business Management*, 1970.

"The Terminal Take-Over," *Business Automation*, Part 1, March 1972, pp. 22–28, and Part 2, April 1972, pp. 26–28, 60.

Theis, D. J., "Communications Processors," *Datamation*, August 1972, pp. 31–44. See also F. H. Reagan and J. B. Totaro, "Take the Data Communications Load off Your System," *Computer Decisions*, February 1972, pp. 30–36.

Theis, D. J., and Hobbs, L. C., "Trends in Remote Batch Terminals," *Datamation*, September 1, 1971, pp. 20–26.

Turczyn, A., and Jeng, T., "Data Communications: An Overview of Line and Modem Capabilities," *Data Processing*, March 1970, pp. 16–20.

Turnblade, Richard C., "The Case for Dedicated Computers," *Data Processing*, May 1971, pp. 41–44.

Wallace, Robert E., "Data Communications," *Computers and Automation*, May 1967, pp. 16–20.

"Why Ma Bell Chops Up the Signals," *Business Week*, January 13, 1968, pp. 82–84.

Young, Neal F., "Distributed Computer Systems," *Automation*, October 1969, pp. 89–93.

Zakarian, Z. V., "The Mad, Mad World of Data Communications," *Infosystems*, August 1972, pp. 18–21. See also K. W. Ford, "About Communications Processors," *Infosystems*, February 1973, pp. 46–47, 88–89.

PART III.
DATA ORGANIZATION AND STORAGE

IV.
DATA ORGANIZATION
AND STORAGE

All data organizational methods, as Dodd points out, are built upon three basic types of organization: sequential, random, and list. Sequential organization permits rapid access to records stored in a logical sequence but presents difficulties in updating individual records and in retrieving records out of sequence. Random organization permits fast access to individual data items or records but may require complex hardware and software, may create overflow problems, and may involve the use of large unwieldy directories. When random organization is used, records may be accessed directly (the programmer or the hardware supplies the address at program execution time, by dictionary lookup—both the key and direct address being stored in a directory—or by using calculation methods in which the record key is converted directly to an address). List organizations use pointers to divorce the logical and physical organization and may take the form of simple list, inverted list, or ring structures.

Cost and space requirements for pointers must be weighed against the advantages of storage and retrieval when considering the use of list organizations. Media space management is essential when records are stored in random fashion to ensure that storage space is utilized efficiently. Sequential and direct-access media should be matched with the appropriate form of data organization according to application characteristics. The greatest shortcoming of today's storage systems may be a failure to provide adequate capability for handling random and list structures.

Ward emphasizes that the development of an adequate data base for a typical organization will normally require gradual changes in operating procedures, improvements in hardware and software currently available, and active top management support during the implementation process. Since low-cost, high-speed, and large capacity direct-access storage devices are not yet available, the systems designer must settle for something less than an idealized data base. The manner in which the file is used must determine how a file is to be organized or an unacceptable increase in inquiry response time may result. The designer should also start with the processing problem and develop the software requirements needed to solve the problem rather than try to adapt processing procedures to existing software packages. Transaction-oriented (random) processing should not normally be used for high-volume input applications since requirements for storage space and processing time will often be excessive, resulting in system bottlenecks. Finally, cost per inquiry figures for various information applications will aid the systems designer in deciding if shorter response times are economically justified.

The systems designer seeks to select a method of file organization and appropriate storage media so that storage capacity will be utilized efficiently, computer processing time will be kept low, and storage and processing costs will be minimized. Physical sequential methods (in which an entire file is arranged in ascending or descending sequence), indexed sequential methods (where records can be retrieved in logical key sequence or individually), and random organization methods (in which neither records nor transactions are arranged in any logical sequence) can be used with direct-access storage devices. Physical sequential organization is preferable when fast access to and updating of an entire file is necessary, whereas indexed sequential organization is often desirable when both logical sequential processing and retrieval of individual records are required for the same file. Random organization is best for files with relatively small numbers of transactions that must be processed rapidly and individually without sorting or batching and that must be available to respond to inquiries on a demand basis.

Direct-access storage devices can be used to increase the speed and reduce the costs of processing data for many applications, but generally have smaller storage capacities, higher storage costs, and higher programming costs than serial access devices. In addition, efforts to obtain media with larger storage capacities and lower storage costs will generally result in slower access times and higher processing costs. The choice between serial and direct-access storage devices or from among direct-access media depends greatly on the programming, storage, and processing costs involved in handling a given set of applications, on file activity rates, and on the extent to which fast response times are required to meet inquiries on demand.

Thorn points out that computer systems today are characterized by faster processing speeds and larger storage capacities. Memories used by computer systems can be divided into five classes: main memory, cache or buffer storage, registers, logical storage, control storage, and bulk storage. With the exception of local and control storage, a hierarchy of storage components can be found in many systems. Differences in speed, capacity, and volatility have led to the emergence of the storage hierarchy. In essence, the most frequently or recently accessed information segments are placed in storage components with the fastest access times. Less frequently needed information is located in slower-access storage. As storage requirements expand and the need for higher computer performance through faster access times becomes more evident, the storage hierarchy should come into much wider use.

Magnetic tape, drum, or disk memories are highly versatile and widely used, provide permanent storage of large amounts of data, and serve as input/output units, as Meyer explains. Drums are principally used as high-speed extensions to core memory, while disks serve as main memory extensions, input-output media, or main on-line memory banks. Magnetic tapes are most widely used as input and output from other on-line media. In selecting a secondary storage medium, the user should weigh systems cost against system performance, including reliability, expandability, and flexibility.

Lobel and Farina emphasize that in selecting secondary storage devices, consideration must be given to estimated transaction volumes and sizes, file sizes and accesses, processing frequency, and other scheduling problems. New problems of data storage and new data organization schemes are emerging to go along with today's more costly, more complex, and larger systems.

Secondary storage is not an integral part of the processor but is directly connected to and controlled by it. Secondary storage devices include drums, disks, magnetic cards, and magnetic tape. They generally are slower in transfer rates and less costly than primary storage devices such as thin films, magnetic cores, or plated wire memories. Frequency of updating required, speed with which data must be accessed, capability for expansion, and compatibility with data transmission equipment are factors that largely determine which kind of secondary storage device is most suitable for a given system.

As *Infosystems* (September 1972) points out,[1] virtual storage promises to help increase the potential of an organization's programming staff. Available address space is no longer limited by real processor size. The operating system manages the job of transferring data and instructions into and out of the system in such a way that wasted

[1] See "How IBM Talks about Virtual Storage," *Infosystems*, October 1972, pp. 26–28.

space and unused resources are minimized. The CPU, real storage, and auxiliary storage of a system are used in such a manner that the system appears to have real storage of considerable size. System Control Programming dynamically allocates real storage to active programs according to their changing requirements. The run time for any given program depends on the program structure, programming systems used, system configuration, input data being processed, and real storage demands of other programs being processed at the same time.

Virtual storage technology makes it possible to run one or more programs dynamically even though total program size exceeds main storage capacity (according to the article in *Computer Digest*). Only the active sections of a program are stored in main memory; the other portions reside in direct-access storage until needed. Programs are divided into pages and segments that can be easily transferred back and forth between main memory and secondary (page) memory as needed. Virtual storage provides flexibility of operations that can aid an organization in making more effective use of its computer hardware, software, and personnel resources. In particular, large-scale applications can be developed and implemented faster and more effectively just as day-to-day operations are facilitated by virtual storage use.

═══ 13.

ELEMENTS OF DATA MANAGEMENT SYSTEMS

By George G. Dodd

Editor's Note: From COMPUTING SURVEYS, June 1969, pp. 117–133. Copyright 1969 by the Association for Computing Machinery, Inc. Reprinted by permission of the publisher, the Association for Computing Machinery, Inc., and author.

INTRODUCTION

Data management problems are what the Internal Revenue Service has when it receives 65 million income tax returns every April 15. They are encountered by librarians in cataloging the 17,000 new books published annually, as well as by library users in trying to locate one of them. Business management personnel have them in reviewing the daily, weekly, and monthly reports that arrive from every department in the plant, or every plant in the company. Even computers have them in compiling code for symbolic language programs.

A number of data management systems have been described during the past few years [2, 3, 5, 15, 21, 22], all of which store, retrieve, and update data. A number of seemingly different data organization schemes to support these and other data management systems have also evolved; Figure 13.1 shows a few of their names.

These data organizational methods are utilized for two reasons. The demands of the users who are storing, updating, and retrieving data differ. In some situations, such as information retrieval systems, data must be retrieved rapidly but updating of existing data can proceed at a slower pace. In other situations, such as the real-time re-

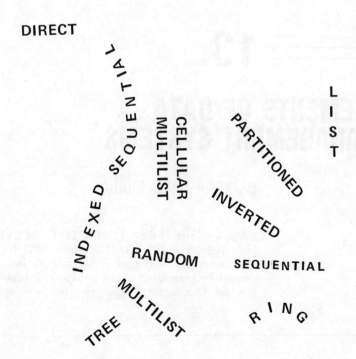

13.1 DATA ORGANIZATION SCHEMES

cording of missile test data, it is necessary to store rapidly large volumes of data which are retrieved later at a slower pace. Each type of demand may call for a different data organization which will satisfy the requirements of the application and at the same time keep overhead at a minimum. Another reason for the existence of more than one data organization is that the characteristics of the media on which the data is stored are not always compatible with the demands of the application. Different data organizations are therefore used to bridge the gap between the logical user requirements and the physical realities of storage media and computer hardware.

It is convenient to note that all data organizational methods are built up from three basic organizations: sequential, random, and list. We begin by describing and comparing the basic organizations and then demonstrating how they are used as foundation blocks to build the more complex data organizations. As a result of this discussion it will become apparent why the more complex data organizations are often desirable. Then there is a description of the characteristics of the media on which data is stored and an examination of the capabilities of the programming languages available for implementing data management systems.

DEFINITIONS

A few terms are defined here for clarity. These correspond to the USASI Standard COBOL [17] definitions.

Data management systems deal with elementary data items, records, and files. Each piece of raw information the system stores, retrieves, and processes is called an *elementary data item*. In general, several elementary data items are used to describe something stored by a data management system.

A collection of such elementary data items is called a *record*. If the system were to store information about an employee, the employee record would contain the name, city, occupation, and age of each person recorded in the system, as shown in Figure 13.2. The

ELEMENTARY DATA ITEMS   **VALUE**

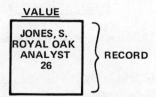

13.2   EXAMPLE OF ELEMENTARY DATA ITEMS IN A RECORD

grouping of data items into records is desirable, since for each item processed by the system there is a certain amount of hardware and software overhead. Collecting the items together into records reduces the overhead on a per item basis. A record may contain only one elementary data item in cases where it is desirable to deal with each datum individually.

For bookkeeping purposes records are collected into logical units called *files*. Often each file corresponds to the storage medium on which it is recorded. However, it is possible to store several files on one medium, e.g. disk.

The arrangement and interrelation of records in a file form a *data structure*. Different data structures are used depending upon the operations to be performed on a file.

To put this in proper perspective, a data management system deals with records in a file. These records contain information, called elementary data items, which are the object of processing.

SEQUENTIAL ORGANIZATION

Perhaps the best known data organization is the sequential organization, wherein records are stored in positions relative to other records according to a specified sequence. To order the records in a sequence, one common attribute of the records is chosen. When it is a data item within the record, the attribute selected to order the records in the file is called a *key*. By selecting a different key for a file and sorting on the basis of that key, the sequence of the records in the file may change. Figure 13.3 shows a sequential organization

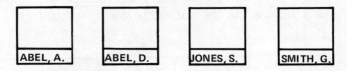

13.3   SEQUENTIAL ORGANIZATION

in which the name data item of each record is used as the key for ordering the file. Records may be stored without keys; this occurs when records are stored in order of their arrival into the system, in which case each record is positioned sequentially following the preceding record. In both cases the logical order of records in the file and the physical order of records on the recording medium is the same.

A sequentially organized file may be composed of records of different types, but the records are grouped into a file because they have a common functional purpose. The entries in a telephone directory are an example of a sequential organization in which the key for sequencing is the surname data item of the record.

The advantage of sequential organization is fast access per relationship during retrieval. If the access mechanism is positioned to retrieve a particular record, such as the "Jones" record in Figure 13.3, it can rapidly access the next record in the data structure according to the relationship which was established when the data was stored, in this case, alphabetical order. Where the records are stored in sequence on a direct access medium (e.g. disk or drum) or in high speed memory, a binary search is possible. The data is sampled in the middle, eliminating half the cases in one comparison; the remaining half is then sampled in its middle and the process repeated until a sequential search of a small portion of the file is possible and it is established that the desired record is or is not present.

The advantage of being able to rapidly access the next record becomes a disadvantage when a file is to be searched until a record having a particular key value is encountered. Here the first record is examined; if the key is not correct, the next record is examined and the process continued until the correct record is found.

Updating values in a record stored in a sequential organization is also difficult. Should the new record be shorter or longer than the original record, adjacent records in the file may be destroyed or become inaccessible to the hardware when the record is rewritten. Updating of blocked records, which are described in the "Storage Media" section, is impossible unless the entire block is rewritten. For these reasons a file having sequential organization is usually updated by copying records from one file to another, making updates to the records as needed. It becomes expensive to update one record in a sequentially organized file; usually updating occurs only when a number of records are to be altered.

It is difficult to insert new records into or remove old records from a sequentially organized file. The insertion process requires that already stored records be pushed apart to make room for a new record, resulting in the copying of the entire file. The converse is true for removing records, in which case existing records are pushed together. New records can be added out of sequence to the end of the file, however, and sorted into the proper sequence at a subsequent updating of the file. List organizations, which are described later, provide an easier insertion/removal facility and avoid the copy problems of sequential organization.

It is often desirable to store and retrieve records using more than one key. A case in point might be a record of a personnel file which is to be stored and accessed either by the name or the occupation of the person the record describes. This is most easily accomplished by storing the data in duplicate files so that the first file is searched if the first key is known and the second file is searched if the second key is known. This duplication, however, uses twice the storage space and doubles the maintenance cost, since records to be updated must be accessed and changed in both files.

In summary, sequential organization allows rapid access of the next record in the file but offers difficulties in updating a file and retrieving records out of sequence. To overcome this disadvantage, a second data management technique has been developed; it is called random organization.

RANDOM ORGANIZATION

In random data organization, records are stored and retrieved on the basis of a predictable relationship between the key of the record and the direct address of the location where the record is stored. The address is used when the record is stored and used again when the record is retrieved. Figure 13.4 shows the record with the key "Jones,

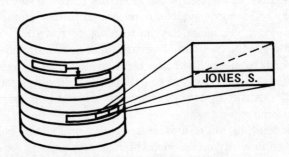

13.4 RANDOM ORGANIZATION

S." being stored in a particular position on a direct access medium. Since the relationship between the key and the address of the record is very important for dealing with randomly organized data, let us examine the three methods for accessing records on direct access media [15]: direct address, dictionary look-up, and calculation.

Direct address. In the simplest form, the direct address is known by the programmer and is supplied at storage and retrieval times. The hardware then uses this address to access the record on the storage medium.

Dictionary look-up. Figure 13.5 illustrates the dictionary look-up and calculation methods by which a record's direct address is obtained prior to storage or retrieval. When the dictionary method is used, both the record's key and its direct address are stored in the dictionary as shown in the upper part of Figure 13.5. When a record is stored or retrieved, the key is found in the dictionary and the cor-

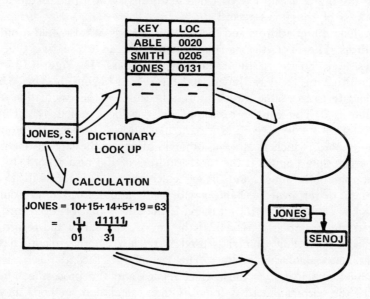

13.5 DICTIONARY LOOK-UP AND CALCULATION METHODS TO OBTAIN A RECORD'S DIRECT ADDRESS

responding direct address is used. For example, the key "Jones" is compared with the dictionary and the direct address 0131 is found. The direct address 0131 is then used to store or retrieve the record.

The use of a dictionary insures that each record has a unique address. However, to do this the dictionary must be large enough to include all potential direct addresses and it may occupy as much space as the data itself. Also, the step-by-step sequential search of a dictionary may offset the gains offered by having unique record addresses. If the dictionaries are very large, they are often accessed with a binary search, or they may have a tree organization (to be described later) to reduce search time.

Calculation. The calculation method [9, 12] involves converting the key of the record into a direct address, which is not necessarily unique. In Figure 13.5 a simple calculation method is used. Each letter of the key is replaced by a number—J by the number 10 (because J is the 10th letter of the alphabet), O by 15, N by 14, E by 5, and S by 19. These numbers are added and the result is converted to a binary number, whose rightmost 5 bits form two octal digits which are the rightmost 2 digits of the address, with the remaining bits forming the digits in the left part of the address. The result is the direct address of the Jones record.

The direct address and dictionary methods always yield a unique address. However, the calculation method can cause two different keys to calculate to the same direct address. In Figure 13.5 the record having the key "Jones" and the record having the key "Senoj" calculate to the same direct address because of the calculation algorithm used. This causes "overflow" and may be handled by putting a pointer in the first record at a particular address to point to the overflow record, which is at some other location on the storage medium. The overflow pointer is the direct address of the next record. In this example, both "Jones" and "Senoj" calculate to the address 0131. The storage or retrieval mechanism will access address 0131 and examine the key of the record stored there. If the key is that of the record desired, the record is retrieved. If the key is not that of the record desired, the overflow pointer is used to retrieve another record having the same calculation address. The key of this second record is examined to see if it is the correct record and the process continued until the correct record is found. Other calculation methods may be used to reduce the occurrence of overflow and to produce a more uniform distribution of records in the storage medium.

Feldman [7] introduces the concept of calculation with multiple keys. In his file structure all records and all elementary data items have names. Both the record name and the elementary data item name are used as keys in the calculation algorithm. To store and retrieve a "name" data item in a "personnel" record the keys NAME and PERSONNEL would be used to calculate the direct address at which the value of the name is stored. This technique has been expanded and generalized in the TRAMP system [21].

The advantage of using random organization is that any record can be retrieved by a single access. Other records in the file do not have to be accessed and their keys examined, as in the sequential method, when trying to retrieve a particular record. Individual records can be stored, retrieved, and updated without affecting other records on the storage media. However, all records are generally of a uniform length. This requirement is sometimes imposed by the way hardware addresses reference the storage media and also permits easier handling of overflow records.

Random organizations are used most often in conjunction with direct access storage media, and the direct address of a record corresponds to a hardware address on the storage media. Although random organization does allow for rapid access of a particular record with a known key, it is not suited for rapidly accessing a number of records. This limitation is imposed by the time taken by the hardware access mechanism to locate a record. Other difficulties are (1) handling the overflow problem when calculation is used for obtaining the direct address, and (2) manipulating large and unwieldy dictionaries when dictionary look-up is used.

LIST ORGANIZATION

The use of pointers to handle the overflow problem in a random organization suggests a third form of data organization, called the list organization. There are three main types of list organization: simple list, inverted list, and ring. The basic concept of a list is that pointers are used to divorce the logical organization from the physical organization. In a sequential organization the next logical record is also the next physical record. However, by including with each record a pointer to the next logical record, the logical and physical arrangement can be completely different. A *pointer* may be anything which will allow the accessing mechanism to locate a record. If the records are stored on direct access media, it is the direct address of the record; if the records are in core memory it is the core address of the record.

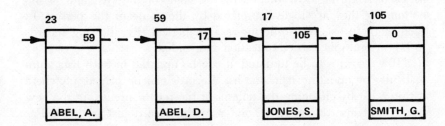

13.6 SIMPLE LIST STRUCTURE

Simple List Structure

Figure 13.6 is an example of a simple list in which four records are stored in a logically sequential order. They are not, however, in the same physical order. The first record is at location 23, the second record at location 59, and the third and fourth records at locations 17 and 105, respectively. The logically sequential organization is obtained by using pointers. Initially, there is a pointer to the first record. The first record contains a pointer, 59, to the second record, which contains a pointer, 17, to the third record, and so forth through the list. The last record in the list is designated by a special symbol, in this case, 0.

Since any data item in a record may be treated as a key, many lists can pass through a single record. Figure 13.7 shows several

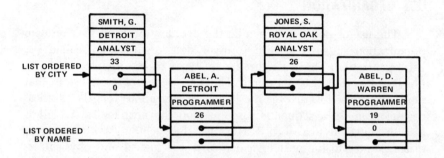

13.7   TWO LISTS PASSING THROUGH A RECORD

records. Each record contains four elementary data items: name, city, occupation, age. Each record is also a member of two lists. In the top list records are logically related by the name of the city, and in the bottom list they are logically related by the name of the person. In each of these lists, the ordering is alphabetical. By allowing records to be on multiple lists, duplication is avoided.

If a record is to be updated, it can be updated in both lists automatically by updating it in one list. Records can be placed anywhere within a list by changing the pointer of the record preceding the new record and inserting a new pointer in the record just inserted. For example, if a record were to be inserted between the "Jones" and the "Smith" records in Figure 13.6, the pointer in the Jones record would be set to point to the new record, and the new record would be given the pointer value 105, which then points to the Smith record. The removal of a record from a list requires changing the pointer in the preceding record to point to the record following the one being deleted. When a record participates in a single list, deletion is not difficult, because the record is initially accessed from the preceding record. However, if a record is a member of several lists, it becomes more difficult to find the preceding records of all the lists, and extra pointers must be stored so that the preceding as well as the next record of the list may be found.

With large files the lists themselves tend to be long, and extended searches may be required if the list length is not controlled in some way. Where the list length is not restricted, there is only one starting point for each list. Where the list length is restricted, the effect is to create sublists, each of which has its own starting point. This reduces the search at the expense of maintaining an expanded index of starting points. Figure 13.8 shows a partially inverted file in which the

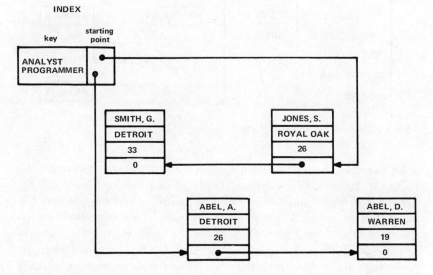

13.8 PARTIALLY INVERTED LIST

occupation datum of each record has been put into an index. Each entry in the index has a starting point to the list of records having the same value as the key in the index; Jones and Smith are "analysts" and Abel and Abel are "programmers." Observe that the occupation data item has been removed from each record and resides in one place in the index at the expense of adding a pointer to each record. If the pointer is smaller than the replaced data field, the record occupies less space.

Inverted List Structure

When the restriction on list length is taken to its ultimate conclusion, the list length is restricted to 1, and each key appears in the in-

dex. The index thus points directly to the record sought and no
pointers are required. The list has now become inverted. Figure 13.9

INDEX

key	pointer
ANALYST	105, 17
PROGRAMMER	23, 59
19	59
26	23, 17
33	105
DETROIT	23, 105
ROYAL OAK	17
WARREN	59

105
SMITH, G

17
JONES, S

23
ABEL, A

59
ABEL, D

13.9   INVERTED LIST STRUCTURE

is an example of an inverted list. Here all pointers are kept with the
index. If, for example, all the records having the key "analyst" are
desired, the word "analyst" is found in the index and the pointers 105
and 17 are obtained. These point to the actual data records shown on
the right side of the figure. By keeping the pointers with the index, a
request for information can be obtained by first manipulating the
pointers in the index. Once the correct data pointers are found, they
are used to retrieve the data from the file. For example, let us assume
that a data request for information on all the analysts who live in
Royal Oak is received. The "analyst" entry in the index shows that
records having pointers 105 and 17 satisfy this requirement. An examination of the "Royal Oak" entry in the index shows that the record having a pointer of value 17 satisfies this requirement. By comparing the entries under these two indices, it is concluded that only the
record having the pointer 17 satisfies the initial request. An access of
the file is then made and the record having the name "Jones" is retrieved. By keeping the pointers with the index it is possible to process a request without having to go to the file. For instance, let us
process the request to retrieve the names of the programmers living
in Royal Oak. The "programmer" entry in the index shows that pointers
23 and 59 are relevant, while the "Royal Oak" index entry shows that
the pointer 17 is relevant. Comparing these two lists of pointers leads

to the conclusion that there is no information in the file on programmers who live in Royal Oak and the access to the file never takes place.

The inverted list organization makes available every data item as a key. Such an organization requires a dictionary of all data values in the system containing the addresses of all locations where those values occur. The dictionary can be as large as or larger than the data itself. The virtue of such a system is that it allows access to all data with equal ease. Consequently, it is more suitable for situations where the data retrieval requirements are less predictable, for example, decision-making and planning functions, than it is for specific processing functions. Although the inverted list approach lends itself to easy retrieval, storing and updating data is more difficult, because of the maintenance of the large dictionaries. It is best to combine an inverted list organization with either a sequential or random organization. In this way records are inverted on only one or two keys rather than all the keys. Dictionaries become smaller and it is still possible to access all records in the file.

Ring Structure

Rings are an extension of a list organization. In Figures 13.6, 13.7, and 13.8 it is noted that the end of the list is designated by a 0 value for the last pointer. In a ring the last record points back to the first record of the ring and a special symbol is kept in the first record to designate that this is the first, or the starting point of the ring, as shown in Figure 13.10. It is possible to follow the ring to find any record, such as the preceding record, the next record, or the starting record of the ring. Figure 13.11(a) shows how

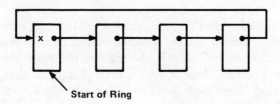

Start of Ring

13.10 RING STRUCTURE

multiple rings can pass through a record. The primary ring goes from left to right; however, a second ring going from right to left also connects each record. It is therefore possible to pick up the following or

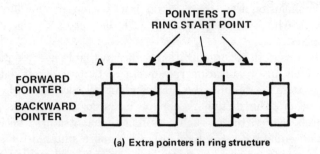

(a) Extra pointers in ring structure

13.11a EXTRA POINTERS IN RING STRUCTURE

preceding record by obtaining and using the appropriate pointer.
Extra pointers can also be stored in each record to point to the starting point of the ring. The CORAL structure [18] shown in Figure
13.11(b) makes use of a ring structure in which each record points

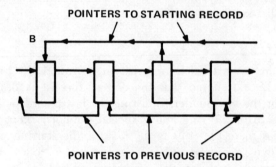

(b) CORAL ring structure

13.11b CORAL RING STRUCTURE

to the next record in the ring. All records of the ring except for the
starting record have a second pointer, which either points to the
starting record or is used as a backward pointer. Back pointers point
to the closest previous element with a back pointer, so that they form
a complete ring. Since rings are most often processed in the forward
direction, alternation of the less useful back pointers and starting record pointers retains the advantages of both of these less useful pointers
in half the space.

The ring structure proves to be very powerful, as it provides a
facility to retrieve and process all the records in any one ring while
branching off at any or each of the records to retrieve and process

other records which are logically related. Such records would also be stored in a ring structure and in turn permit the same facility; this nesting is carried through to any level required by the logical relationships in the data. These more complicated ring organizations form what is called a *hierarchical storage organization*.

The need for a hierarchical storage can be illustrated by examining the data structure in Figure 13.9, where the records are accessed after processing the pointers in an index. Assume that a record is re-

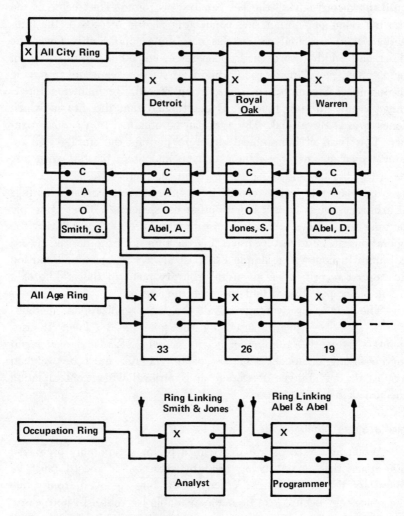

13.12   HIERARCHICAL STRUCTURE

trieved by the key "analyst." Once the record is found, however, it is not possible to obtain anything from the record except the name. The age of the individual and the city in which he lives are kept in the index, and the record keeps no pointers from it back to the index entries containing this other vital information. The file can be restructured into a hierarchical organization, as shown in Figure 13.12, so that related information can be obtained. The new structure is used in the following manner. Assume that information on all records having the key "analyst" is desired. The "occupation" ring is first searched until the record having the key "analyst" is found. This record is the starting point of another ring connecting all the records of the individuals who are analysts, in this case Jones and Smith. Once the Jones and Smith records have been retrieved, other information can be obtained by following the C ring to its starting point and retrieving the name of the city from the starting record. By following the C ring passing through Jones, it is determined that the city in which Jones lives is Royal Oak. The ages can be obtained in a similar manner. This form of hierarchical structure permits the storage and retrieval mechanisms of a data management system to start with any record in the file and move up or down the hierarchy.

It is easier to insert records into and remove records from rings at arbitrary points than it is with other list structures. This is possible because the adjacent records whose pointers are modified during the operation can be found by traversing the ring until the desired record is found. In contrast, a simple list must always be examined starting at the first record, since given an arbitrary point in the middle of a list it is not possible to find the preceding record.

The prime disadvantage of all the list organizational methods is the space overhead caused by the pointers. In inverted lists, pointers reduce the number of occurrences of a key and may result in the saving of space. The cost of the pointer must be weighed against the advantages of storage and retrieval when contemplating the use of list organizations.

Media Space Management

When new records are stored in a list or a randomly organized file, space that is not being used by some other record must be found for the new records. When records are removed from a file the space they occupy can be made available for reuse. In both cases, a space management mechanism is invoked for keeping track of all the space in the storage medium. Several factors govern the operation of this mechanism:

(1) The new record should be located so that minimum access time is needed to retrieve it. For example, overflow records in a random organization on a disk should be placed so that the disk arms will not have to move to locate the next overflow record. Records in a multilist file (which is described below) should be so located in pages that the crossing of page boundaries while searching a list is minimized.

(2) If records are of variable size, space for them should be allocated in such a way that the storage medium won't be fragmented into small pieces of free space that are unusable for future space requests.

(3) The compacting of pieces of free space into larger blocks should take place at intervals frequent enough so that large blocks of space will be available for reuse (thus helping to reduce the problem of fragmentation). At the same time, it should be recognized that there is an overhead associated with compacting space, which should be kept to a minimum.

Meeting these three criteria can present a nasty problem when dealing with random and list organizations.

A number of strategies have evolved to deal with space management. Lisp [12, 20] sequentially allocates all the space on the storage medium. When none is left a "garbage collection" routine looks around and claims all discarded space for reallocation. Other techniques [10, 14, 18, 19, 23] dynamically reclaim space occupied by deleted records. If properly handled, space management is not a serious problem. However, it does present a small overhead when storing and deleting records in both random and list organizations.

EXAMINATION OF COMPLEX STRUCTURES

Now that sequential, random, and list methods of data organization have been considered, let us look at some of the more exotic data management techniques shown in Figure 13.1 and see how they can be implemented by the use of sequential, random, and list data structures.

Multilist File

Figure 13.13 depicts the organization of a multilist file. In this file a sequential index contains the key values by which records are

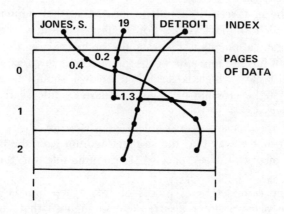

13.13 MULTILIST FILE

indexed. Associated with each key value is a pointer to the list of records having that key value. Records are stored in fixed-size blocks called *cells* or *pages*. They are addressed by a page number and a record number within the page: the record identifier 0,4 references the fourth record in page 0, and the record identifier 1,3 references the third record in page 1.

The grouping of records into pages is an important concept used in storing list structures on direct access media. Rather than using a record's direct address as a value in a pointer, a page number and record number are specified. The page number is used as a direct address to retrieve the page and the record number is used to locate the record within the page. In this way a group of records can be retrieved at one time and the access time per record is reduced. Saving is achieved only if a number of records in the page are desired —it is inefficient to retrieve an entire page to process only one record. In using a multilist file it is therefore preferable to store related records within a common page. To eliminate unnecessary accessing of pages, it may be desirable to limit list length so that all the records on a list fit in a single page.

In summary, a multilist file consists of a sequentially organized index with each index entry pointing to a list of records. Records in the file are blocked into logical units called pages. An entire page is accessed when a record is stored, updated, or retrieved.

Cellular Multilist File

When working with the multilist file, quite often several pages are accessed to retrieve a record. A data organization that limits lists so that they do not cross page boundaries is shown in Figure 13.14. This is called a cellular multilist because each list is contained in one and only one cell (page). This structure is processed in a manner similar to that used for a fully inverted list: the values of the indices are retrieved and only those pages containing record lists satisfying all the search criteria are retrieved. In Figure 13.14 the index is

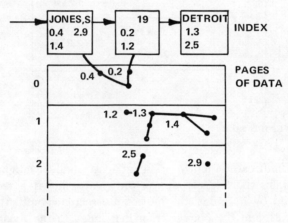

13.14 CELLULAR MULTILIST FILE

organized as a list, while in Figure 13.13 it is organized in a sequential fashion. This is only to demonstrate that either type of index organization is possible. In the cellular multilist the list length is restricted so as to fit within a page; if the list length is limited to 1, the file becomes inverted, as shown in Figure 13.15.

While the multilist file is simpler to program and update, the retrieval time is longer than that encountered with the inverted list or the cellular multilist. The longer times are caused by excessive page retrievals encountered while following a list from page to page in pursuit of a particular record.

Indexed Sequential File

An indexed sequential file organization is shown in Figure 13.16. This file has the property that records can be accessed either by the use of indices or in a sequential fashion. In the top part of the

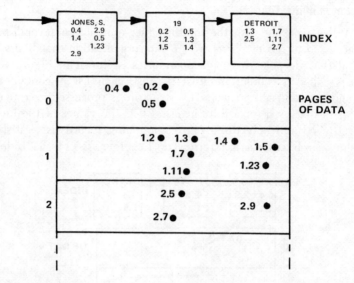

13.15   INVERTED FILE

figure the indices are shown as being sequentially contiguous. Each index contains the address of a record in the file. If a record is to be retrieved by its index, the indices are searched until the desired key is found, and the pointer from that index to the record is used as a direct address to retrieve the record. The records are also stored on the storage media in a sequential fashion, permitting the records to be accessed in a sequential order.

Indices in an indexed sequential file are often oriented to the characteristics of the storage media. In some systems there is a cylinder index as well as a track index for each data item stored in the file [9].

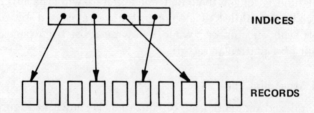

13.16   INDEXED SEQUENTIAL FILE

Tree Organization

A tree data organization is one in which several levels of indices are used. The index on the first level points to a collection of indices on a second level. One of these second-level indices is used to find a collection of indices on a third level, and so forth, until the actual data value has been found at the bottom of one particular branch on this tree. Figure 13.17 is an example of a multilevel dic-

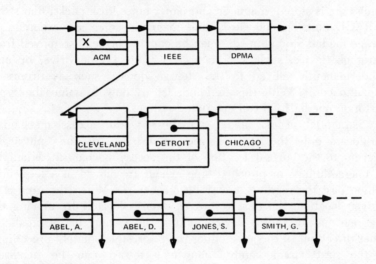

13.17 TREE STRUCTURE

tionary having a tree organization. In this figure the indices on the various levels are organized in lists. If the record identified by "ACM.DETROIT.JONES" is desired, the following actions take place. The first list is searched until a record having the key value "ACM" is found. From this record a pointer to the second-level index list is obtained. The records on the second-level list are sequentially examined until the key "DETROIT" is found, and the pointer in the "DETROIT" record is used to access the index list on the third level. The keys of the records on this level are searched until the record having the key "JONES" is found. In this record is the direct address of the record identified by "ACM.DETROIT. JONES." Of course, the indices can be organized sequentially as well as in a list.

The tree organization is conveniently used in maintaining large dictionaries. Portions of the dictionary can be added, deleted, or changed without disturbing the rest of the organization.

STORAGE MEDIA

It is important to clearly distinguish between storage devices and storage media. *Storage devices* are the hardware units, such as tape units, disk drives, and data cell drives, that participate in the storing and retrieving of data. *Storage media* are the material on which data is stored; magnetic and paper tapes, disk packs, film strips in RACE units, punch cards, and magnetic cores are examples of storage media. Storage media may be capable of being removed from a storage device, such as a tape reel from a tape drive, or may be permanently affixed to the storage device, such as drums or magnetic cores. With this in mind, let us now examine the types of storage media found in computer systems.

Sequential access media are those whose access mechanism can locate only the next or prior record, i.e. the one physically adjacent to the current location of the access mechanism. Examples are magnetic tape or punched tape, which are moved in a sequential fashion past the reading or writing mechanism. When the tape is at a given location, the next record of data is located by moving the tape one position. Some devices permit the reading of the media in either direction. In this case either the prior (immediately preceding) or the next (immediately following) record can be accessed. Sequential access devices excel in reading or writing the next record on the medium being used in the device and are used most often with sequential files.

Direct access media are those in which a hardware address is used to position the access mechanism. This address is used when data is written onto the media and again when it is retrieved. Core memory is an obvious example of a direct access medium, since every

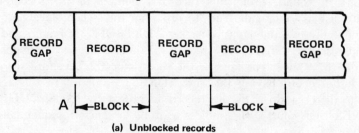

(a) Unblocked records

13.18a   UNBLOCKED RECORDS

location in the memory has an address. Magnetic disks and drums are also considered to be direct access devices, since each part of the recording surface can be addressed. However, once the access mechanism has positioned itself at an address, data is read or written in a sequential manner onto a track of recording medium passing beneath the access mechanism. Direct access devices excel in locating a particular data record having a known address. They are also used to retrieve a page of records in the multilist organization, where the page number corresponds to the address of the page on the direct access medium.

Figure 13.18(a) illustrates the physical appearance of data which has been recorded onto any storage medium except magnetic core. The record gaps are placed on the storage medium by the hardware. They are used to separate the areas on the tracks and to permit certain equipment functions to take place as the gap moves past the access mechanism of the device. Within each block of recorded data is one record of data, which may be of any length. It is often advantageous to group several data records into one block, as shown in Figure 13.18(b) Blocking improves the speed with which records

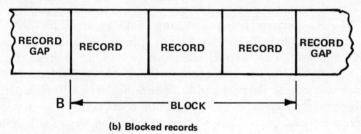

(b) Blocked records

13.18b   BLOCKED RECORDS

may be read or written because the overhead involved in locating a block is distributed over the access and use of all records within the block. It also saves record gap space, since the gaps between records within a block are eliminated.

LANGUAGE FACILITIES FOR PROGRAMMING DATA MANAGEMENT SYSTEMS

There are many programming languages exclusively aimed at handling a particular type of data organization. The common programming languages, such as PL/I, FORTRAN, and COBOL, all have mechanisms for dealing with sequentially organized files. By means of the READ statement the next record is retrieved, and the WRITE statement stores a record in the next location in a sequentially organized file. In FORTRAN the file can be backspaced by the BACKSPACE statement and returned to its starting point by the REWIND statement. PL/I and COBOL do not have a backspace statement; by means of the CLOSE statement the file is returned to its starting point.

List languages, such as LISP[12] and IPL-V[14], were initially developed for experimentation in the more mathematical and scientific areas of computing, such as heuristic processes, general problem-solvers, self-organizing machines, and automata theory. They were not aimed at data management, and while they handle lists very well, they are cumbersome in the handling of the underlying data. Primitive machine-level-type operations are used for arithmetic and it is not easy to manipulate and test data in expressions. In some implementations the programmer must be concerned with moving the lists to and from high speed memory if the size of the lists is greater than the memory. PL/I provides a pointer capability, enabling the programmer to dynamically allocate space for a record and to store pointers between records, thus creating his own list and ring structures. Records are stored in an area (similar to a page), and areas can be read from and written on external storage media using the PL/I input/output facilities. Although PL/I requires the maintenance of pointers and the performance of all input/output by the programmer, it is very useful for constructing new types of list organizations. SLIP[23] is a list processing language for handling two-way ring structures and exists as a set of subroutines callable from FORTRAN.

Perhaps the least often provided feature of all programming languages is the ability to handle random data organizations. The COBOL language provides some rudimentary statements, which are not fully implemented by any manufacturer. PL/I has a class of statements to READ, WRITE, and REWRITE records on direct access media. However, these statements are limited to work within the provisions of the OS/360 job control language and do not let the programmer have access to all the capabilities of the physical hardware.

There are two languages which permit the programmer to organize his data in a ring structure. APL [6] consists of six statements which have been added to the PL/I language, and IDS [1] has a similar number of statements, which have been added to the

COBOL language. These languages conduct ring operations on the same high level as array operations are conducted in FORTRAN and PL/I. They permit the programmer to define the ring relationships between data records, to create new data records within the data set, to insert data records on rings, and to search rings to find data records having particular data values, without having to become involved in the mechanics of pointer manipulation. After the records have been retrieved, the data values may be modified or used in any arithmetic calculation. Complementary statements for removing records from rings and deleting records from the file are also provided. Both these systems work in the paging environment handled automatically by the system; so the data base and the associated ring structures can be much larger than the high speed memory itself. Since these languages are supersets of PL/I and COBOL, they also suffer from the restrictions of their host languages. The concept, however, is one that could be added to any language.

There is no one language that is best suited for programming all data management systems. Data management systems have been programmed in assembly language and JOVIAL, as well as the other languages described above. Only a study of the language facilities, the types of hardware to be used, the types of input queries and the way they will be submitted to the system, the capabilities of the storage media, and the compiler efficiencies will dictate which language to use for programming a particular data management system.

SUMMARY

There has been a brief discussion of the purposes of data management systems. A description of the primitive data management techniques—sequential, random, and list—has been given. Sequential data organizations have matching physical and logical storage requirements, permitting rapid access of the next logical record in the file. Random data organizations are characterized by rapid access of data based on a key indicating the location of the data on the storage media. List organizations divorce logical relationships from the physical storage mechanisms by means of pointers, permitting data records to efficiently take part in multiple-relationship files.

The mechanics of how more complicated structures can be built using the primitive data organizations has been considered. Rings, inverted lists, trees, hierarchical, and other types of data structures have been explained. Storage media were discussed and it was observed that sequential access media are suited for sequential organization, while direct access media are used for random organizations and list organizations. Programming languages to deal with data management systems were examined and it was concluded that no one language can handle the universe of problems satisfactorily.

Because of the large number of references available on the subject, only a few of the more prominent ones have been cited. Reference 3 contains an excellent bibliography on file organization with 97 entries, which can be consulted for further information. Knuth[11] presents an advanced text for the serious student containing exercises and solutions on file organization and space management techniques. Lefkovitz [24] describes several types of file organizations, including the multilist organizations, along with dictionary designs, storage and timing formulations.

ACKNOWLEDGMENTS

The author would like to acknowledge the help given by John T. Murray, who listened to the initial oral presentation of this paper and suggested how it could be made into a tutorial. Michael J. Mithen, who produced the figures in this paper, should also be commended. Special credit is due to Tax A. Metaxides, whose contributions to the COBOL Data Base Task Group Report [4] on extensions to the COBOL language were used to help formulate the initial paper.

REFERENCES

[1] Bachman, C. W., and Williams, S. B. A general-purpose programming system for random access memories. Proc. AFIPS 1964 Fall Joint Comput. Conf., Vol. 26, Pt. 1, Spartan Books, Washington, D.C., pp. 411–422.

[2] Bleier, R. E. Treating hierarchical data structures in the SDC time-shared data management system (TDMS). Proc. 1967 ACM Nat. Conf., Thompson Book Co., Washington, D.C., pp. 41–49.

[3] Climenson, W. D. File organization and search techniques. In *Annual Review of Information Science and Technology, Vol. 1,* C. Cuadra (Ed.), Wiley, New York, 1966, pp. 107–135.

[4] Data Base Report. Doc. No. PB177682, Clearinghouse, U. S. Dep. of Commerce, Springfield, Va., 1968.

[5] Dixon, P. J., and Sable, J. DM-1–a generalized data management system. Proc. AFIPS 1967 Spring Joint Comput. Conf., Vol. 30, Thompson Book Co., Washington, D.C., pp. 185–198.

[6] Dodd, G. G. APL—a language for associative data handling in PL/I. Proc. AFIPS 1966 Fall Joint Comput. Conf., Vol. 29, Spartan Books, Washington, D.C., pp. 677–684.

[7] Feldman, J. A. Aspects of associative processing. Rep.-TN-1965-13, MIT Lincoln Laboratories, Lexington, Mass., Apr. 1965.

[8] Hobbs, L. C. Review and survey of mass memories. Proc. AFIPS 1963 Fall Joint Comput. Conf., Vol. 24, Spartan Books, Washington, D.C., pp. 295–310.

[9] Introduction to IBM/360 direct access storage devices and organization methods. C20-1649, IBM Corp., White Plains, N.Y., 1966.

[10] Knowlton, K. A fast storage allocator. *Comm. ACM 8*, 10 (Oct. 1965), 623–625.

[11] Knuth, D. E. *The Art of Computer Programming, Vol. 1.* Addison-Wesley, Reading, Mass., 1968.

[12] McCarthy, J., et al. LISP 1.5 Programmers Manual. MIT Press, Cambridge, Mass., 1962.

[13] Morris, R. Scatter storage techniques. *Comm. ACM 11*, 1 (Jan. 1968), 38–44.

[14] Newell, A. *Information Processing Language-V Manual.* Prentice-Hall, Englewood Cliffs, N.J., 1961.

[15] Peterson, W. W. Addressing for random-access storage. *IBM J. Res. Develop. 1*, 2 (Apr. 1957), 130–146.

[16] Postley, J. A. The Mark IV system. *Datamation 14*, 1 (Jan. 1968), 28–30.

[17] Proposed USA Standard COBOL. ACM SIC-PLAN Notices 2, 4 (Apr. 1967).

[18] Roberts, L. G. Graphical communication and control languages. In *Second Congress on Information System Sciences*, Spartan Books, Washington, D.C., 1964.

[19] Ross, D. T. The AED free store package. *Comm. ACM 10*, 8 (Aug. 1967), 481–492.

[20] Schorr, H., and Waite, W. M. An efficient machine-independent procedure for garbage collection in various list structures. *Comm. ACM 10*, 8 (Aug. 1967), 501–506.

[21] Ash, W. L., and Sibley, E. H. TRAMP: An interpretive associative processor with deductive capabilities. Proc. 1968 ACM Nat. Conf., P-68, Brandon/Systems Press, Inc., Princeton, N.J., pp. 143–156.

[22] Sundeen, D. H. General purpose software. *Datamation 14*, 1 (Jan. 1968), 22–27.

[23] Weizenbaum, J. Symmetric list processor. *Comm. ACM 6*, 9 (Sept. 1963), 524–544.

[24] Lefkovitz, D. *File Structures for On-Line Systems.* Spartan Books, New York, 1969.

14.

PRACTICAL DATA BASE DESIGN

By D. S. Ward

Editor's Note: From CONTROL ENGINEERING, May 1968, pp. 83–86. Reprinted by permission of the publisher, CONTROL ENGINEERING, and author.

To management, the idealized version of a computer-based information system is a magical system of which it can ask any question about the minutest detail of company operations and get an immediate answer. To the system designer, as keen as anyone to see these dreams become a reality, the system represents a vast computing complex with multibillion-character mass-storage files, accessed by a multiprogramming central processor supplying a multichannel communications network to give management the split-second response it would like. But the hardware for such systems is not available at a cost that most companies can justify, so there has been no real need to worry about exactly how these systems will be implemented. There is a vague feeling, shared by management and the system designers, that when the hardware is available there will be some kind of complete software package to handle the whole job.

DATA BASE DESIGN CHANGES PRESENT OPERATIONS

But a management information system cannot be developed overnight, nor can it be made operational simply by purchasing (or getting free) a "software package." The key ingredient of these systems is the data base—it can take months, if not years, to establish this. Data-base design involves a complete analysis of present operations, often requiring major changes in traditional operating procedures.

Developing a data base is an evolutionary process with the end objective being the "idealized data base." This is an information file that contains all the necessary data about all facets of a company's operations and from which information can be extracted instantaneously in any form desired in response to inquiries in any format.

HARDWARE IS NOT AVAILABLE

There are no really idealized data-base systems in operation today, although there are many examples of partial systems. An airline reservation system is typical. In these, one segment of an airline's business—filling seats—is handled on an instant-response basis but, so far, the many other factors in running an airline have not been integrated into a total information system.

The hardware available today, particularly for file storage, is not suitable for the idealized data-base concept, in spite of the wide range of random access storage devices that are currently available on the market (see CtE, March 1968, page 65).

To implement such an idealized system would require an enormous memory device into which data could be shoveled without too much regard for its eventual use. Access times would have to be extremely short since, almost invariably, it would take several accesses to the file to obtain even the smallest amount of data. So that the data could be retrieved in any form, multiple indexing and chaining would have to be used; this takes up a lot of memory besides that needed for the data. So the cost of such a memory must be very low. But let's face it: Low cost and high access speeds are not features of today's on-line random access file devices.

A comparison of the three common ways of storing data illustrates the high cost of on-line random access storage. Assume a company has to store one billion characters of data. If this data is stored on conventional sequential magnetic tape about 100 tape reels are needed (assuming each reel is filled to only half its capacity). The cost of tape is about $3,000. Three tape drives included in the system bring the total cost for the tape approach to just under $50,000.

The next step upward in performance is to use disc packs. One billion characters of storage in this medium costs about $110,000 ($40,000 for the disc packs and $70,000 for the drives). Moving up to the ultimate—complete on-line random access storage—ups the price tag to about $500,000 for disc files with a one-billion character capacity. From the above figures the table below can be constructed, indicating the relative costs of the three approaches. Note that the important difference between the on-line and off-line approaches is the response speed of the overall system.

File mode	File type	Relative cost
Off-line	Sequential tape	X
Off-line	Random (disc pack)	2X
On-line	Random (fixed disc)	10X

The "X" in the above table includes a factor for the cost of tape-drive units. The figures on which the table is based are order-of-magnitude costs rather than costs that are completely accurate to the very last dollar and cent.

The ratio of 10, relating cost of sequential tape storage to fixed disc, applies only to the cost of the physical storage media. Other factors increase the ratio still further. For example, communications equipment for entering and receiving data generally costs more than the card reader and printer used in a tape system. And the programs and operating systems for handling data in a communications environment are more complex and require a more powerful central processor than that required for tape-oriented, batch processing systems.

FILE USE MUST DETERMINE ORGANIZATION

An important attribute of the idealized data base is that information can be retrieved from it in any form desired by the users of the information system. But the way in which the file is to be used must determine how the file is organized. Otherwise the response time for an answer to any inquiry, no matter how simple, will be drastically increased.

To illustrate this, consider the case where a production control file is organized in such a way that all data relating to a particular part is grouped together in random access storage as shown in the table below:

123–2354	Part number
XYZ	Description
34	Stock location
140	Quantity
123–2355	Part number
ABC	Description
29	Stock location
120	Quantity
123–2356	Part number
PQR	Description
64	Stock location
3500	Quantity
124–2356	Part number
DEF	Description
25	Stock location
240	Quantity

With this file organization, given a part number it is easy, through an indexing or randomizing process, to retrieve all the data for the part. But if production control wants to know how many parts are in stock location 25 the entire file must be scanned to find the answer.

If the file were designed differently, however, the answer could be found after scanning only a portion of the file. The organizations could be as shown in the table:

Part number subfile	123–2354	Part number	1
	123–2355	address	2
	123–2356		3
	124–2356		4
Description subfile	XYZ	Description	1
	ABC	address	2
	PQR		3
	DEF		4

	34	Location 1
Location	29	address 2
subfile	64	3
	25	4
	140	Quantity 1
Quantity	120	address 2
subfile	3500	3
	240	4

To retrieve data on the number of parts in location 25 involves only two searches, first the location subfile to get the address in the quantity subfile and, second, the quantity subfile to get the quantity. While this scheme works well for the type of inquiry for which it was designed, it is not efficient if complete data on any part is required because a separate access has to be made for each field in the record. Thus the data base engineer must know in what form the data is required so he can organize his files efficiently.

SOFTWARE PACKAGES CAN BE DANGEROUS

There are many file organization techniques available to the data base designer. Some of them are supported extensively by manufacturers' software. But, the designer should start with the problem and then work back to the techniques which will provide the solution. Maybe a manufacturer's package does not provide the whole solution but it can be used in part. Too often there is a tendency to say that because a particular package is available it must be used. Packages are available from computer manufacturers for nearly every major industry and are being increasingly accepted by users because of the shortages of experienced computer personnel. The principal area of concern in using software packages is that it puts the user in the dangerous position of having a solution and looking for a problem.

A typical answer to the above objections to the idealized data base is that the cost of random access storage is falling rapidly and soon everyone will have as much as he can use at a price he can afford. Although costs will certainly come down, it is doubtful if the drop will be so dramatic as to outweigh the increase in the amount of data people will want to store. And, in a period where all computer manufacturers are committed to, and have delivered, considerable quantities of conventional random access equipment, it is doubtful if any revolutionary mass storage will be developed which will offer considerable reductions in both access time and cost.

TRANSACTION-ORIENTED PROCESSING, A MEMORY HOG

It seems only realistic to plan that the data base must be fitted into the available hardware parameters. These parameters—far from preventing implementation—only call for an objective analysis of a company's requirements before designing the system. Available hardware dictates that off-line files are a vital, perhaps, a predominant, part of a management information system and that a real need must be proved before data is retained in on-line storage. Batch processing is going to continue as a major input to many files. Certainly, transaction-oriented processing particularly for inquiries, is going to increase in volume. But, transaction-oriented processing particularly is prodigious in its use of computer and file access time. Unless a dramatic decrease in access time is assumed, it is not practical to change high value input applications into transaction mode jobs currently being done by batch processing techniques. Either the computer system would simply run out of time, or extra equipment would be needed to do the job, which could be justified only by a valid, overall advantage in processing that way.

MUST KNOW COST-PER-INQUIRY

There will always be opposition to the concept of using off-line files. Everyone likes to think he needs information right now. It is the responsibility of the data-base designer to examine each type of information request and have the requester prove his need. The designer should be able to calculate the cost of each type of information request in terms of a fixed cost for the equipment associated with maintaining the data base and a cost-per-inquiry.

From an analysis of a given situation in a company, the data-base designer can make a rough classification for response-time ranges:

Class 1.   Less than 1 min
Class 2.   1 min to 1 hr
Class 3.   1 hr to 24 hr
Class 4.   Over 24 hr

Against these classifications it is then possible to approximately indicate the computer configurations and characteristics as shown in Fig. 14-1. The minimum configuration costs are shown in the graph associated with the table in the box. These are ballpark figures which include allowances for a "reasonable" quantity of peripheral equipment, machine features, and so on. The size of the data base was assumed to be in the ¼ to 1 billion character range. It is apparent that cost climbs very rapidly as responses are required in shorter and shorter time intervals.

MANAGEMENT MUST SUPPORT PROJECT

The management of a company intending to make use of a data base system—and all indications are that this will include an increasingly large number of organizations—must support the effort in three ways: 1) by making clear to the system designers the management objectives; 2) by supporting the effort with the people and time resources needed to implement such an important undertaking; 3) by being prepared to change some of its methods to use the new tool and information services available to it. This may require a considerable re-education.

As stated earlier, a data-base system cannot be implemented overnight. By following a phased plan some of the pain of implementation can be reduced. The plan embraces a five-phase transition from conventional processing to full, data-base oriented processing.

Phase 1: Get the current batch processing jobs cleaned up, using third generation hardware.
Phase 2: Initiate inquiry processing in the simplest way possible: for example, by extracting data from standard files and by laying it out on random access. This gives experience the easy way with a minimum of programming and hardware expense.

Fast response needs complex equipment

Class	Response speed	Computer: Major characteristics	Operating characteristics
1.	< 1 min	Large core, on-line mass storage, communications environment.	Time shared or devoted.
2.	1 min to 1 hr	Large core, on-line plus off-line mass storage, communications.	Time shared.
3.	1 hr to 24 hr	Medium core, off-line mass storage.	Batch processing.
4.	> 24 hr	Small core, off-line sequential.	Batch processing.

14.1 FAST RESPONSE NEEDS COMPLEX EQUIPMENT

Phase 3: Introduce conversational techniques between the computer and the inquiry station and allow for the input of transactions which are then batch processed in the normal way.

Phase 4: Establish full data-base files. This is where the full hardware complement comes in. The batch process files can become back-up files.

Phase 5: Expand to intercomputer processing where appropriate and build the management reporting and inquiry system.

With the proper approach, a practical data-base system could be designed and implemented starting now. A company having such a system will be able to secure significant advantages from the new information resources available to it and can begin to exploit the real potential inherent in a mechanized information system.

15.

COMPUTER STORAGE AND MEMORY DEVICES

By Caryl A. Thorn

Editor's Note: From ELECTRONICS WORLD, October 1970, pp. 40–42. Reprinted by permission of the publication, ELECTRONICS WORLD, and the publisher, Ziff-Davis Publishing Company.

Progress in the digital-computer industry during the past 20 years can be measured in various ways. For example, the number of computers in existence has grown from a few in the 1950's to nearly 50,000 in the U.S. today. One can also speak of the increased speed at which operations are performed by computers, noting that solid-state computers today are in some cases several thousand times faster than the vacuum-tube machines of the early '50's.

Another indication of progress is the increased amount of storage used by computer systems. The internal, addressable main storage available on computers has increased from approximately 10^5 bits in the early 1950's to more than 36 million bits today. On-line external, non-addressable bulk storage (e.g., single disc or drum) has increased from 10^6 bits to more than 10^9 bits during the past decade.

These few examples illustrate the significance of storage in the computer system. In this article, various types of storage and their uses are discussed.

While some uses of storage within a computing system are well known (for example, main memory and bulk storage), many other uses exist within the computer (See Table 15.1).

Table 15.1.   Types of storage and memories, and characteristics

Use Charac.	Registers	Local Storage	Control Storage	Cache Memory	Main Memory	Bulk Storage
Access Time (sec.)	$2\text{-}50\text{x}10^{-9}$	$50\text{-}200\text{x}10^{-9}$	$.1\text{-}.5\text{x}10^{-6}$	$20\text{-}100\text{x}10^{-9}$	$.5\text{-}5\text{x}10^{-6}$	.02-several
Transfer Rate (bits/sec.)	—	—	—	$.1\text{-}3\text{x}10^{9}$	$2\text{-}100\text{x}10^{6}$	$.5\text{-}50\text{x}10^{6}$
Capacity (bits)	50-1000	100-10,000	$1\text{-}10\text{x}10^{3}$	$10\text{-}200\text{x}10^{3}$	$.04\text{-}100\text{x}10^{6}$	$10^{7}\text{-}5\text{x}10^{10}$
Bits per Access	6-72	6-72	30-100	6-72	6-500	6-25
Readability	Yes	Yes	Yes	Yes	Yes	Yes
Writability	Yes	Yes	Not necessarily	Yes	Yes	Yes
Volatility	Acceptable	Acceptable	Acceptable if writable	Acceptable	Often acceptable	No

1. *Main Memory.* Main memory storage is the one most commonly referred to in a computing system. Its function is to hold programs and data which are awaiting processing or have just been processed by the central processing unit (CPU).

Typically, a program occupies upwards of 10^{14} bits of storage. Associated with this program may be a variable amount on which the program works.

When the quantity of data is small, it may be loaded into main memory along with the program. When the quantity is large, it is common to load segments of the data (perhaps from bulk storage) into main memory as needed by the program. Since a program will occasionally have to wait for needed data to be transferred from bulk storage to main memory, it is obvious that initially loading all the data into main memory along with the program will allow that program to be completed more quickly. The performance of a computing system can thus be generally improved by providing a large-capacity main memory.

The need for a large-capacity main memory is also evidenced by applications which require that several programs "time-share" the computer. By time-sharing, we refer to the interleaved use of the computer by multiple programs, each of which is in the process of being executed. One implication of such time-sharing is that main memory must generally hold several programs and several sets of data. It is not unusual to find the main memory capacity requirements for such an application specifying many million bits.

Since main memory must generally be accessed for each instruction in a program, as well as for each piece of data to be processed, the speed of main memory is one of the most critical factors in determining the speed of the computer. Accordingly, various schemes have been devised to reduce the impact on computer performance of a main memory speed, which is slow in comparison with the CPU. One such scheme involves use of *cache* or buffer storage.

2. *Cache Storage.* Cache or buffer storage, when used in a computer system, is interposed between the main memory and the CPU (Fig. 15.1). Although smaller in capacity than main memory, cache storage is usually ten to twelve times faster than main memory.

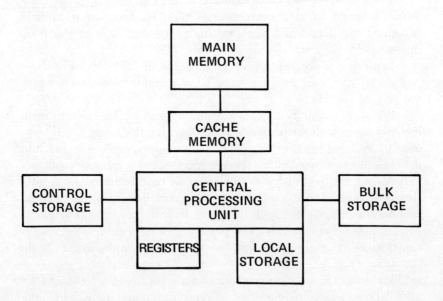

15.1 VARIOUS MEMORY FUNCTIONS OR FUNCTIONS THAT ARE ASSOCIATED WITH THE CENTRAL PROCESSING UNIT OF COMPUTER

The value of cache storage becomes apparent when it is observed that accesses to main memory are not evenly distributed across all of main memory. In a typical data-processing application, a large number of accesses are made to one area of memory, and then a large number of accesses are made to another part of memory. Performance improvement is accomplished by loading into the cache a portion of main memory the first time a location in that portion of memory is accessed. Thereafter, successive accesses to locations in that same portion will not have to go to main memory but need only go to cache storage with its much shorter access time. When accesses are made to different portion of memory, that new portion of memory is loaded into the cache. Portions no longer being accessed are eventually replaced, once main memory has been updated.

3. *Registers*. Another means of avoiding degradation resulting from a slow main memory is the use of registers in the CPU. These registers usually have a relatively small capacity (3-16 registers with 32-64 bits per register) and are very quickly accessed. By placing frequently accessed information or intermediate results in these registers, accessing of main storage can be avoided.

Other registers, not directly accessible by programs, may be used by the CPU to hold addresses, transient data, instructions, or control information. Since these registers are involved in the execution of instructions, the highest possible speed is essential.

4. *Local Storage*. In many data-processing situations it is convenient to have available to the CPU some non-program accessible storage facility which can be used for storing control information and data where accessibility is not as critical as that of the information stored in registers. Local storage can be provided for this purpose. Operations with external devices (card readers, printers, tapes, communications equipment, etc.) frequently require control information which is appropriately kept in local storage. Data being transferred to or from such devices may also be buffered in local storage so that accesses to main storage are required only when a full memory width is needed.

Some CPU's also use local storage for the retention of "checkpoint" information to be used in the event of an error. By periodically collecting and saving information pertaining to the state of the CPU, the CPU can, upon the detection of an error, perform a check-point restart, *i.e.*, restore the CPU to its earlier state and re-do the operations which encountered the error.

5. *Control Storage*. A number of CPU's have been designed to

use a technique called "microprogramming." The microprogramming technique is generally used when lower cost is desired and reduced speed can be tolerated. As a by-product, greater functional flexibility can usually be obtained. Microprogramming involves control of the individual gates and logic blocks of the hardware by means of very rudimentary, hardware-oriented instructions. The microprogram is stored in a *control storage* which is not accessible to the program. Since the microprogram determines how the CPU operates, it must always be present in the CPU and is not alterable. For this reason the control store is usually "read-only."

6. *Bulk Storage.* Long-term storage of information (*e.g.*, programs, data) is provided for by bulk storage. Bulk storage is usually in the form of discs, tapes, and drums and has as its major requirement a massive storage capacity. Bulk storage is also referred to as "secondary storage" (main memory is called "primary storage"), since data and programs stored there cannot be directly operated upon by the CPU. Information to be executed or processed must be loaded into main storage from bulk storage.

Bulk storage is used for three purposes: unprocessed input information; processed output information; and information for long-term storage. Input information is loaded into bulk storage from an input device such as a card reader. Output information may be placed in bulk storage prior to transfer of this information to an output device such as a printer. Information for long-term storage is simply data retained for some future use; for example, payroll records or inventory data.

Bulk storage is often spoken of as being "on line" or "off line" storage. On-line storage allows information to be accessed by the computer and transferred to main memory without outside intervention. An example of on-line storage would be a drum which always remains connected to the system. Off-line storage is not accessible without outside assistance. Any bulk-storage device with removable media (such as magnetic tapes) would thus provide off-line storage. While the amount of information which can be stored off-line is thus limited, on-line storage capacity is finite, although generally very large.

Categories of storage uses and their essential characteristics, as discussed above, are summarized in Table 15.1. With reference to the information contained in the table, several features are noteworthy.

There is, for example, an exception to the need for writability in the case of control storage. This is true because the control storage component contains information which should never need changing.

There is also a difference in the number of bits (or widths) involved in each access. The width for control storage depends upon the hardware makeup of the CPU, the number of registers, and the number of conditions which need to be tested. Main memory width is large so that transfer rate can be high. Since accesses to main memory are often sequential (particularly when cache memory is used), accessing many contiguous bits is practical. Bulk storage transfer width is often constrained by cabling considerations.

HIERARCHY OF STORAGE

Implicit in Table 15.1 is a hierarchy of storage among the generalized storage components (all but local and control storage). There is, for example, a progression of access times from 2 nanoseconds to several seconds; capacity goes from 50 to 5×10^{10} bits. There is also a trend in the volatility from registers, where the loss of information is acceptable, to bulk storage, where the loss of information is quite intolerable. These three characteristics: speed, capacity, and volatility are benchmarks of a storage hierarchy. The concept of storage hierarchy is not new, but only lately has it been exploited in computer system design. The general idea is to place the most recently accessed segments of information in that storage component which is most quickly accessed. When it is possible to anticipate the need for certain information, that information can also be transferred to a storage component with quicker access. Infrequently used information is generally kept in slow-access storage.

A rather extensive storage hierarchy is shown in Fig. 15.2. To illustrate how such a hierarchy might be used, we can consider the following application. In a typical business situation, their quarterly reports would be stored on a reel of magnetic tape conveniently kept in the tape library. The executive program, supervising all other programs running in the computer, would be located in main memory, with portions of the executive program residing at times in a cache, or in a slow-access storage component.

During the past 15 years magnetic technology has occupied a dominant place in computer storage. This is true because magnetic technology is applicable to a very broad range of uses: from bulk storage to high-speed main memories.

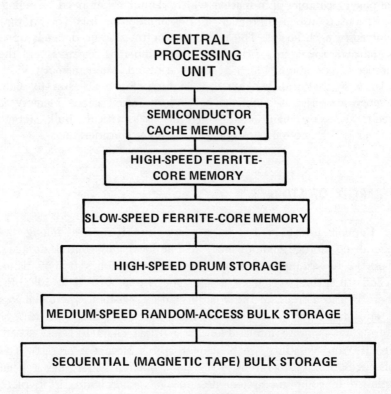

15.2 ARRANGEMENT OF STORAGE ELEMENTS INTO A HIERARCHY

In the bulk-storage area, magnetic applications have largely taken the form of ferric-oxide coated discs, drums, and Mylar tape. Other magnetic devices have also been designed; for example, semi-rigid cards or strips. Information is recorded onto, and read from, these devices by passing the oxide-coated medium near a recording and/or reading head which produces minute magnetized spots on the medium or detects spots already recorded. The material technology, in conjunction with precise read/write head alignments, have made possible recording densities up to 3000 bits per linear inch.

The application of magnetic technology in the main memory area is typically represented by ferrite cores and thin films. While reading and recording in bulk-storage magnetic devices is accomplished by media motion, cores and thin films are stationary when accessed. Information is accessed by means of conductors passing through, near, or around the core or thin film. When the conductors are energized, the magnetic-polarity state of the core or thin film can be sensed or changed.

In an effort to obtain greater speed, various semiconductor devices are now being used in mass-storage operations. While the speed attainable for semiconductor devices is more than ten times greater than for cores, the greater cost and volatility of semiconductors have restricted their application. New fabricating techniques, however, are reducing the cost factor, thus a comparable cost for the two techniques can be expected. The accompanying requirements for non-volatility that each memory element constant draw current is a limiting factor for semiconductor storage. Millions of bits of storage in a semiconductor device implies densely packaged components which may require large power consumption and special cooling systems.

A general summary of the various types of storage devices discussed is shown in Table 15.2. Typical applications of storage devices in computers are shown in Table 15.3.

Table 15.2.　Various devices that are employed for the storage or memory function.

Type *Characteristic*	*Ferrite* *Core*	*Thin* *Film*	*Semi-* *conductor*	*Optical*
Access Time (seconds)	$.2\text{-}5\text{x}10^{-6}$	$70\text{-}300\text{x}10^{-9}$	$20\text{-}700\text{x}10^{-9}$	$\sim 100\text{x}10^{-9}$
Cycle Time (seconds)	$.5\text{-}10\text{x}10^{-6}$	$100\text{-}600\text{x}10^{-4}$	$50\text{-}1000\text{x}10^{-9}$	$\sim 200\text{x}10^{-9}$
Cost (cents/bit)	1-4	.5-3	1-10	—
Volatile	Generally no	Generally no	Yes	No
Readable	Yes	Yes	Yes	Yes
Writable	Yes	Yes	Yes	No
Density (bits/in)	—	1000-10,000	1000-10,000	1000-10,000

Type Characteristic	Movable-Head Mag. Drum, Disc	Fixed-Head Mag. Drum, Disc	Magnetic Tape
Access Time (seconds)	$50\text{-}500\text{x}10^{-3}$	$8\text{-}25\text{x}10^{-3}$	—
Transfer Rate (bits/sec)	$.5\text{-}4\text{x}10^6$	$1\text{-}30\text{x}10^6$	$.05\text{-}3\text{x}10^6$
Typical Capacity (bits)	$5\text{-}5000\text{x}10^6$	$5\text{-}300\text{x}10^6$	$2\text{x}10^8$
Cost (cents/bits)	.0025-.1	.001-1	$2\text{x}10^{-5}$
Volatile	No	No	No
Readable and Writable	Yes	Yes	Yes
Removable	Generally yes	No	Yes
Density (bits/in)	600-1500	500-3000	200-1600

Table 15.3.   Here is where the various devices are applied to the different storage and memory portions of computer.

Use Type	Registers	Local Storage	Control Storage	Cache Memory	Main Memory	Bulk Storage
Ferrite Core	Generally not used	Used if fast cores and/or slow CPU	Used if fast cores and/or slow CPU	Generally not used	Yes	Generally too expensive
Thin Film	Generally not used	Suitable	Suitable	Suitable	Yes	Generally too expensive
Semi-conductor	Yes	Suitable	Suitable	Suitable	Suitable but somewhat expensive	Generally too expensive
Movable-Head Mag. Drum, Disc	No	No	No	No	No	Yes
Fixed-Head Mag. Drum, Disc	No	No	No	No	Rarely used now	Yes
Magnetic Tape	No	No	No	No	No	Yes

FUTURE TRENDS

Simple extrapolation of storage trends of the past several years indicates that storage-capacity requirements will continue to rise, both in terms of main memory or bulk storage. To manage expected increases in storage capacity, there will be growing use of the storage hierarchy, including a widening range of storage devices.

Attainment of higher computer performance will continue to demand storage devices with even shorter access times. Semiconductor devices seem to be one answer to this requirement, with continued improvement of existing semiconductor devices claiming an attention at least equal to that of cores.

It is likely that developments in storage systems over the next several years will emphasize the organization of the storage, and the information in storage, rather than the technology of the storage devices. However, when different ways of organizing memories are required, new technologies are often necessary and these new technologies will certainly be developed.

=== 16.

MAGNETIC TAPE, DRUM, DISC MEMORIES

By Henry T. Meyer

Editor's Note: From ELECTRONICS WORLD, October 1970, pp. 40–43. Reprinted by permission of the publication, ELECTRONICS WORLD, and the publisher, Ziff-Davis Publishing Company.

Tape, drum, and disc devices are used to record information passed to them by data-processing equipment and, at a later time, reproduce that data, passing it back to any data-processing equipment that requests it. Data is passed back and forth between the storage devices and source or destination equipment in discrete form (as binary information digits, or bits). Information bits are usually collected into eight-bit "bytes"; the various bit patterns in an eight-bit byte are each representative of a specific number, letter, character, or symbol.

Each of the three magnetic devices contains a moving medium capable of being magnetized. This is moved, with respect to record/reproduce heads, allowing data to be recorded in or reproduced from various data tracks. The width of a data track is determined by the characteristics of the head which is, in turn, determined by the speed of the medium, the nature of the medium, and the density at which data is recorded.

The magnetizable material on tape, drum, and disc provides for the "permanent" recording of data. Data, once written, must either be erased or overwritten; it is not lost when power is turned off. Each head can record in one or more tracks. If a head is fixed, it can only record in one track. If the head is movable, it can record in as many tracks as there are head positions. Devices which have one head for each track are commonly referred to as "head-per-track" devices while all others are called "movable-head" devices.

Each type of device is available in models which permit removal of the medium. Magnetic tape is the most common removable medium; discs may also be removable; drums and discs in a head-per-track arrangement, are the least commonly removable medium.

Tape, drum, and disc are all used as extensions of the main memory of a computer; they are also used to provide input to and receive output from either a computer's main memory or its extension. Sequentially oriented data is most often stored on reels of magnetic tape; randomly oriented data is usually stored on discs or drums.

PHYSICAL CHARACTERISTICS

Fig. 16.1 shows the three magnetic memory systems described in this article. Magnetic tape is usually cut into strips which are wound on reels. Reel diameters vary from 1 to 10.5 inches; with tape lengths varying from 50 to 3600 feet. Tape thicknesses vary from 0.0005 inch to upwards of 0.002 inch; while tape widths vary from .150 inch to upwards of 2 inches. The most common configuration is a 0.5-inch-wide, .002-inch-thick, 2400-foot-long ANSI-compatible computer-grade tape. This .5-inch tape is typically recorded using a head assembly which contains either seven or nine heads; thus, typical .5-inch tape contains either seven or nine data tracks (actually, in both cases, one track is used for error detection). Several devices, which contain tape loops to which heads are transported on a carriage, exist, but these have not had general acceptance.

Drums are rotatable metal cylinders from 6 to 48 inches long, which are magnetically coated over their curved surface. Head-per-track drums contain fixed heads which are usually mounted in the drum housing. Each head records a single circular track. Movable-head drums contain positionable assemblies of heads; this arrangement results in as many tracks per head as there are head positions. In most cases, drums are not a replaceable device; however, there have been cases of small replaceable drum memories.

Discs are rotatable metal platters, varying in diameter from 6 to 48 inches, which are either magnetically coated or electrolytically plated on both faces. More than one disc can be stacked on a single shaft. Discs can be mounted so that they rotate in a horizontal or vertical plane. Both head-per track and movable-head disc devices

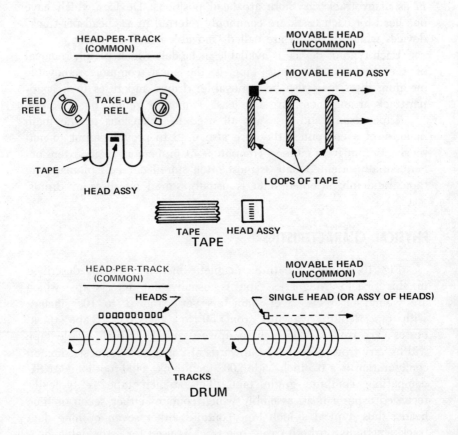

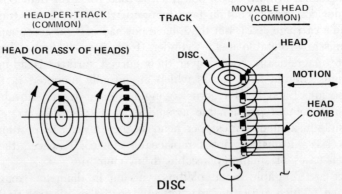

16.1 PHYSICAL ARRANGEMENT USED IN TAPE, DRUM, AND DISC

are readily available. Head-per-track devices are usually rotated in a vertical plane while movable-head devices usually rotate in a horizontal plane. The medium in movable-head devices can usually be removed, while in the fixed-head (head-per-track) device it cannot.

A look at Fig. 16.2 shows that the average random-access times

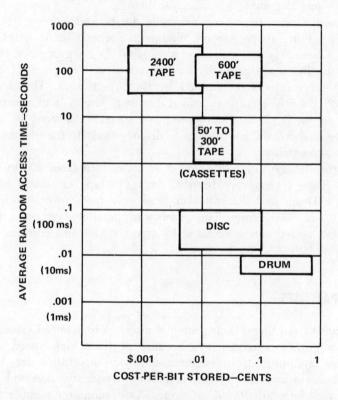

16.2 ACCESS TIME VERSUS COST OF THE THREE MEMORY TYPES

for standard 2400-foot tape are quite slow. Even at top magnetic tape speeds of 200 in/s, average random-access time is almost a minute. Speeds from 37 to 200 in/s and costs from $3000 to $60,000 were used to make the 2400-foot tape estimations. Tape devices, using 600 feet of tape on a seven-inch reel, lower average random-access time at the expense of cost-per-bit stored. Still, this access time is hardly suitable for random access, even on slow-speed data processing equipment. Tape devices using 50- to 300-foot cassettes begin to approach acceptability, *i.e.,* 1 to 10 seconds. This is achievable because of fast-search capabilities which are not generally used on standard tapes.

Drums generally have average random-access times in the 8 to 10 ms range, which is faster than their disc equivalents. Disc average random-access times generally run from 17 to 100+ ms. It is possible to build disc memories with access times of less than 10 ms, although these are just beginning to come into being.

Transfer rate (between a magnetic device and a using station) is measured in bits-per-second, characters-per-second, or bytes-per-second. Characters are generally considered to be groupings of six bits, while bytes are generally considered to be groupings of eight bits. Transfer rate is determined by three factors: 1. The density at which data is recorded (called packing density and measured in bits-per-inch), 2. medium movement speed (measured in in/s) for tape and r/min for disc and drum), and 3. the number of parallel data paths.

Typically, the range of packing densities runs from 200 to 4000 bits/in. Tape speeds vary from 1⅞ in/s (in tape cassettes) up to 200 in/s. Drum and disc rotation rates vary from several hundred r/min up to 6000 r/min. The number of parallel data paths from tape, disc, and drums is dictated by systems uses and costs as well as by standards.

PRINCIPAL USES

Drums have found their principal usage as high-speed extensions to a computer's core memory. Because of their high speed, such items as system-control programs, address directories for large random-access storage devices, and other frequently accessed programs and data, are stored on drums. One computer manufacturer uses drums as a mass memory.

Discs have come into much more widespread use than drums. They have been used as extensions to computer main memories like drums; they have been used as an input/output medium like tape; and they have also been accepted as main element of an on-line data memory bank. Small discs are being used in minicomputers where they are employed as fast-access concentrators for data to be subsequently stored on other media.

Magnetic tape devices, although at times used in an on-line mode, are increasingly being used as input and output from other on-line media. Magnetic tape is lower-cost medium than discs or drums. A reel of tape costs approximately $30 while a disc pack costs about $500. Tape is readily replaceable and easily transported. Other advantages include user acceptance over a long period of time, established recording and data-format standards, and lower device cost per bit than either drum or disc.

The two foremost limitations are its non-adaptability to random accessing and its resistance to selective updating. Data must be accessed sequentially and updated sequentially. The comparative market size and projections for the three memory systems described are shown in Table 16.1.

Table 16.1. Approximate past, present, and future markets for magnetic memories.

	1960	1965	1970	1975
Total Computer Systems	$800 Million	$2.5 Billion	$7.2 Billion	$14.6 Billion
Tape	75 Million	270 Million	810 Million	1.3 Billion
Drum	15 Million	50 Million	110 Million	150 Million
Disc	55 Million	155 Million	890 Million	1.7 Billion
Total: Tape, Drum and Disc	$145 Million	$475 Million	$1.810 Billion	$3.15 Billion

TRANSPORTING & RECORDING

Tape is usually driven by capstan-like wheels which are brought into contact with the non-record side of tape using direct friction, enhanced by vacuum or positive air, or friction enhanced by other rollers which "pinch" the tape against the drive rollers. Since the speed at which tape is either reeled or unreeled varies with the amount of tape wound on the reel at a given time, and since no irregular resistance can be presented to the drive system, the reeling system must include a means for "buffering" the tape before it reaches the drive roller. This buffering is usually accomplished by using columns which have vacuum applied through the bottom or, in the case of lower-speed units, by using flexible arms. The buffering agents contain sensors which servo-control the speed of the reel motors thus maintaining constant lengths of tape in the buffer for each reel. See Fig. 16.3A. The tape is guided during the

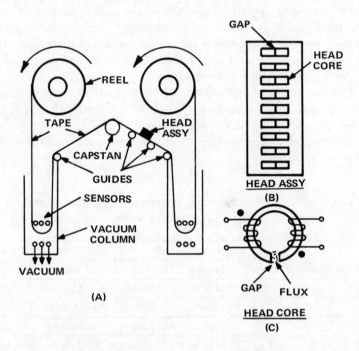

16.3   (A) TAPE TRANSPORT, (B) NEED ASSEMBLY, (C) CORE

time that it is wound on either reel by means of precision-tooled, double-edged tape guides.

In magnetic drum devices, drive is applied to the drum *via* an axle which passes through its axis. Record/reproduce heads record and reproduce data as the drum surface passes adjacent to them. Thus, when accessing particular items of data, there may be a rotational delay (called latency time) of as much as a complete revolution.

In the case of magnetic discs, one or more discs are mounted on a single shaft in parallel planes. Data is recorded in concentric tracks, usually in bit-serial form, and usually on both faces of each disc. Most discs have literally hundreds of tracks per surface. When two or more discs are ganged on the same shaft, similarly located concentric tracks (one per face) are said to constitute a cylinder. The majority of drives in existence today are disc-pack drives. They are characterized by one movable head per face, mounted on a common actuator, as opposed to other movable-head discs which, like movable-head drums, have multiple heads per face. Movable-head discs are usually operated so as to minimize the effects of head-movement time. This is done by orienting the storage of data to a cylinder (*i.e.*, storing it sequentially in long contiguous blocks of data like magnetic tape). This limits access time to latency time (typically 12.5 milliseconds in disc-pack drives).

The recording and reproducing process involves a magnetic pattern, the intensity of which is controlled by the intensity of the current passing through the recording head as well as the ability of the magnetic material to retain the flux pattern induced by the recording current. Fig. 16.3B shows a nine-head record/reproduce assembly; a head within that assembly is shown in Fig. 16.3C. When current is passed through the left winding, the core is magnetized in one direction and a directional flux pattern is established at the head gap. The flux thus produced affects a magnetic medium passed through it. The effect is to unidirectionally magnetize the medium in the area where the flux is felt. When current in the left core winding is cut off and current is started in the right core winding, the head core is magnetized in the opposite direction: this results in flux reversal in the head gap. At flux reversal time, there is a heavy concentration of flux in the core gap which results in a heavy concentration of flux in the magnetic medium. The concentration of flux in the magnetic medium is considered a "bit" of information—considered a binary bit because it has two states: it either exists or it does not.

The reproduction process is primarily sensitive to the rate of change in the recorded medium. The reproduced signal then tends to be the time derivative of the record signal. The signal which emerges from the reproduce head must then be integrated in order to reconstruct the recorded signal. The integration usually takes place in electronics that are located in the magnetic storage device or its controller. This process usually includes compensation for distortion introduced by the variables in recording, the medium, and reproducing.

The methods used to give bits of data coded significance are generally separated into non-return-to-zero (NRZ) and phase-coded methods (PE). In NRZ, the medium is either magnetized in one direction or the other of flux saturation. In the straight NRZ method of recording (Fig. 16.4), a flux transition indicates a change in bit significance; in a modified version called NRZI (for "inverted"), flux transitions are considered to be 1 bits; the lack of flux transition is thought of as 0 bits. Included in the recording methods shown is

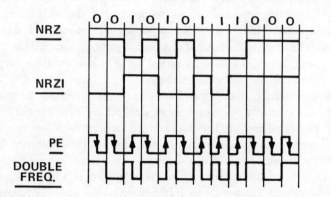

16.4   VARIOUS METHODS OF RECORDING INFORMATION BITS

the phase-encoded method of recording (PE), where downward transitions are 0 bits, upward transitions are 1 bits. Whereas NRZI is preferred over NRZ because, in NRZI, each flux transition is indicative of a 1-bit, PE is preferred over both because at least one flux transition is assured per bit period. However, PE could require up to twice as many transitions to store the same amount of data as NRZ. Double-frequency recording is still another method. It includes one flux change for a 0 and two flux changes for a 1; direction is not important. Thus, the method chosen to record data can affect the "format" of that data.

The physical disposition of bits written on a medium also affects the format of data. This is primarily evidenced by the location of tracks and the arrangement of control data in those tracks. Location of the tracks, width of the tracks, and the arrangement of data within the tracks is related to the way in which a computer system wishes to use the medium, coupled with the often over-riding constraints of compatibility.

Magnetic tape recording usually involves magnetic tape in direct contact with the record/reproduce transducer. At high speeds, however, an air bearing begins to form between the tape and the head. Disc heads, in almost all cases, "fly" at heights of 100 micro-inches or less above the rotating discs. These heads fly on an air bearing through which recording on the disc surface takes place. A few manufacturers have had limited success with contact-recorded discs; but even in those cases, the degree of contact was minimized. There is usually an adjustable gap between drum heads and drum surface. Thus, the heads do not actually "fly" over the drum surface, in most cases. One manufacturer, who uses a movable-head, mass-memory type of drum, flies heads over the rotated drum surface just as over the disc surfaces.

All magnetic-type media are sensitive to contaminants. such as dust and small particles of dirt. Contaminants cause misreads called "drop-outs" in many cases and, in some cases, can result in crashes between a flying head and its associated rotating medium. For this reason, environmental control of cleanliness is very important.

Magnetic media differ in the methods used to bond oxide coatings to metal or polyester backings. They also differ more dramatically in whether they are "coated" or "plated." Magnetic tape is, for the most part, a coated medium. Disc-packs are also a "coated" medium. Some disc-packs are spray-coated; others are centrifugally spin-coated. The coating is a composition of iron-oxide particles. Fixed discs are often plated; using a nickel-cobalt composition. Plated discs generally have a thinner magnetic medium than coated discs, thus affording higher resolution with less signal strength, more uniform surface flatness, and the capacity for storing higher packing densities than coated discs.

SELECTION OF MEMORY

The end user of tape, disc, and drum devices is the person referred to in most companies as a Data Processing Manager. DP managers, along with the systems analysts, programmers, computer operators, and key-punch operators who work for them, comprise the team which puts a DP system to work. A DP manager buys tape, disc, and drum devices in either of two situations: as part of a new or replacement system or as add-ons or replacements for an existing system.

Most users of DP systems rent their equipment rather than buy it. Hence, these users want to rent the latest equipment available and turn in any previous generation equipment they may have. An end user who is shopping for a new system will find that all system manufacturers offer a line of tape and disc (or drum) equipment. He will find that whether he chooses disc or drum, he will still be advised to back-up his on-line files on reels of magnetic tape.

The user should strive for system balance, that is, he should seek a blend of performance and capacity which adequately meets the needs of present and planned uses for the equipment. He should

weigh systems prices against systems performance, including reliability, expandability, and flexibility.

In applications where accesses are random and transaction turnaround is critical, the user will likely end up seeking devices with
very low average random-access time. When discs or drums are
operationally loaded and unloaded using magnetic tapes, tape transfer
rates which approach those of disc or drum become important.

Compatibility is an important consideration when more than
one system is involved. This is especially true when disc packs or
tape reels are to be interchanged between systems.

FUTURE OF MAGNETIC MEMORIES

Table 16.1 shows how magnetic tape device sales, estimated
at $810 million in 1970, are expected to grow to $1.3 billion during
1975. This represents a 60-percent increase or an average growth rate
of 12 percent a year. During this time period, systems sales are
expected to increase to about 100 percent, or an average of 20 percent
a year. Tape-device sales, as a percentage of systems sales, is expected
to decrease from 11.2 percent in 1970 to 8.9 percent in 1975. This
is primarily attributable to inroads expected to be made by disc-pack
drives. These inroads might be even more significant if it were not
for the impact on the punch-card and punch-tape markets being made
by small reel-type magnetic tape units and magnetic tape cassettes.

Table 16.1 also shows how magnetic drum sales, estimated at
$110 million in 1970, are expected to grow to $150 million during
1975. This minimal growth, averaging only 5.3 percent a year, is
in contrast to a corresponding system growth of 20 percent a year.
Drum sales, which were 1.5 percent of systems sales in 1970, will drop
to only one percent of systems sales in 1975. The relatively poor
showing for drums is attributable to inroads made by head-per-track
discs on one side and by bulk core on the other.

Table 16.1 shows disc sales estimated at $890 million in 1970
rising to $1.7 billion by 1975. This represents a 90 percent increase
—an average of 18 percent a year. The disc figures include both
head-per-track disc and disc-pack drives. Head-per-track drives are
expected to increase from $70 million in 1970 to $150 million in
1975. This represents an increase of 114 percent or an average of 22.8
percent a year. The increase is attributable to use of the head-per-
track disc as a memory extension, i.e., as systems memory, as well
as the increased use of head-per-track file in data banks where

access time is critical (banking, airline reservations, time-sharing, etc.). Disc-pack sales will increase from $820 million in 1970 to $1.55 billion in 1975—89 percent over a 5-year period—an average increase of 17.8 percent a year.

Large tape systems will require high-speed tape units (200 in/s and higher) with high packing densities (3200 bits/in is reportedly the next step in terms of industry standards). Automatic-loading features and other automatic methods aimed at reducing operator involvement will gain in popularity.

The upper end of medium tape systems will use the same high-speed tape units as large systems; the lower end medium systems will use the low-speed tape units also used by small systems. Most of the medium systems will use manually operated tape units in the 75 to 150 in/s speed category. Their popularity will be attributable to price and reliability.

Small systems will use reel-type tape units varying in speed from 12½ to 75 in/s; reel sizes of approximately 7, 8, and 10½ inches will be used. Small systems will also use cartridge-type tape units varying in speed from 1⅞ to 10 in/s. The *Philips*-type cassette will be a popular type of cartridge in this market area.

Magnetic tape will also find use in the mass-memory field. Mass memories ("trillion-bit stores") are being developed, using video recording techniques and ultra-high packing densities. When used as a mass memory, a tape device loses its systems orientation and becomes an archival storage area which could be accessed by small, medium, or large systems.

Drums will be used on large, medium, and small systems as high-speed memory extension in situations where systems designers choose drum over head-per-track disc. Small drums will find limited use as data concentrators on minicomputers; large drums as mass memories.

Discs will be used in a wide range of systems applications. They will be used in small, medium, and large systems: there will be both fixed- and removable-medium applications. Fixed-medium disc drives will be used as memory extension and as fast-access data banks in applications which demand low access times and predominantly random accessing of data. Removable medium drives will be used when the application contains several data bases, each used at a different time or when the application dictates the intersystem exchange of media. Generally speaking, the prevalence of (and frequency of performing the interchange) disc packs, varies inversely with systems size. As systems get large, packs are less frequently removed but as systems get smaller, packs are often removed.

═══ 17.

SELECTING COMPUTER MEMORY DEVICES

By Jerome Lobel
and Mario V. Farina

Editor's Note: Reprinted from AUTOMATION, October 1970, pp. 66–70. Copyright 1970 by the Penton Publishing Company, Cleveland, Ohio.

Anyone who has served on a computer selection committee or taken part in a system feasibility study knows that reason does not always prevail. Computer decisions frequently are politically biased. Temperament and personal prejudice often affect decisions. The best solutions generally are reached by resolutely weighing current practices and trends against proven operating and growth capabilities of a system. Here, however, participants often become frustrated.

Usually, not enough is known or can be established about the potential uses of the system being selected. More often, little can be foreseen about how subsequent breakthroughs in computer design or techniques may affect the correctness of the decision. In the selection of auxiliary memory, fortunately, logic will usually win over pride and prejudice. This is true because the greatest hurdle has already been cleared with the selection of computer make.

Nevertheless, the considerations that influence the selection of auxiliary memories for a computer cannot be minimized. The technological and economic criteria surrounding such decisions must necessarily begin with prevailing methods of processing or storing data. Speculation about the nature of future data processing requirements and the development of new devices is essential. But, it is inadvisable to commit too many resources to the unknown or unproven.

The most careful scrutiny must be applied to what is known about present and future requirements. The better we understand detailed requirements, as well as state-of-the-art, the more intelligent and lasting will the final decision be.

SIGNIFICANCE OF AUXILIARY STORAGE

In the early days of the computer, selection of secondary storage devices was mainly for noncommunications-oriented systems. These systems were typically uni-programming (one program run at a time). The data was processed mostly in a batch/serial mode.

Advent of random access processing added only a slight complication to the selection process. Only a few different types of random access devices were on the market, and data communications-oriented systems were much more limited in scope and complexity.

Selection techniques generally were limited to an estimate of future transaction volumes and sizes, file sizes and accesses, processing frequency, and related scheduling problems. Communications often required only the addition of an analysis of peak loads and carrier or line availability. Technical feasibility was ascertained with some unknown degree of confidence, and hardware components were ordered accordingly.

With rare exceptions, no matter how well the system applications were planned in advance, the growth of a system always seemed to be underestimated. Usually, the system worked satisfactorily until it ran out of capacity; then upgrading would occur until limits had again been reached. Next, a larger system would be ordered and the process begun all over again.

Today's environment is not too different, except for three important factors. *First,* users are not satisfied with cost experience for their previous system nor, in many cases, with the operating results of the implemented system. *Second,* many of the information systems on the drawing boards today are much larger than existing ones. *Third,* the complexity of today's new systems has greatly increased.

With the added system complexity come new problems of data storage, and new ways of organizing data are coming into prominence. General Electric's Integrated Data Store (IDS) is one example. Functional application files are totally integrated into a single data base. Records stored in this manner provide for complete updating of all data affected by a single transaction. All records are up-dated in phase whereas, in conventional files, transactions are re-quired to be processed once for each file updating.

IDS makes it possible for application packages to answer ques-tions, such as where a part is used or what parts are used in an as-sembly. For example, suppose an organization's inventory file is re-corded on disc. Knowing the assembly number, a user can obtain a breakdown of all the parts in that assembly; or knowing a part num-ber, he can obtain a list of all the assemblies using that part.

Because modern systems require complex interactions between main and auxiliary memory storage, the auxiliary storage devices have become very important system components and must be se-lected with utmost care. It is clear that superior techniques for their selection are needed.

CLASSES AND TYPES OF SECONDARY STORAGE

Three classes of storage, Fig. 17.1, are normally associated with electronic data processing:

1. Internal or primary storage holds the programs being executed and the data involved in processing. Internal storage consists of elec-tronic components and is characterized by relatively high access speed and high cost. Recent product offerings such as extended memories provide the advantages of high-speed, on-line storage capacity at re-duced cost. Magnetic core store is the most commonly used class of internal storage. Other types in use are thin films, magnetic rod, and plated wire devices. Work is also being done on the development of internal storage based upon laser and cryogenic technologies.

2. Secondary storage is not an integral part of the processor, but is directly connected to the processor and controlled by it. Data is read from secondary storage into internal storage for processing. Secondary storage devices include drum, disc, magnetic card, and magnetic tape peripherals. Secondary or auxiliary storage is charac-terized by lower speed and less cost than primary storage.

3. External storage is separate from the data processing device itself. Examples of external storage media include removable disc packs, magnetic tape, punched cards, and paper tape.

Four types of secondary storage devices are in common use: magnetic tape, magnetic drum, magnetic disc, and magnetic cards and strips.

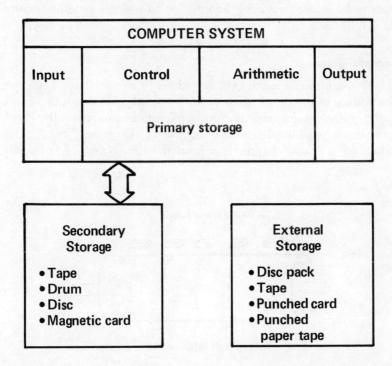

17.1 BLOCK DIAGRAM DISPLAYS THE RELATIONSHIP OF THREE CLASSES OF STORAGE FOR A COMPUTER SYSTEM. PRIMARY STORAGE IS LOCATED INSIDE THE COMPUTER PROCESSOR, WHEREAS SECONDARY AND EXTERNAL STORAGE ARE BOTH LOCATED OUTSIDE THE COMPUTER SYSTEM.

Magnetic Tape

Magnetic computer tape is similar to that used in tape recorders. It is a plastic material, coated on one side with a metallic oxide on which data may be recorded in the form of magnetized spots. The spots are recorded in a series of parallel channels running the length of the tape. Typically, there are seven such channels, but nine-channel tape is also being used. The tape on one reel may be up to 2,400 feet in length.

Magnetic tape is said to have a high data density because a large number of characters may be recorded in a small amount of space. Typical densities are 200, 556, 800, and 1,600 characters per inch. Several magnetic tapes can be mounted on tape handlers and be on-line to a computer system at the same time. It is not unusual for 16 tapes to be in use providing information to a single program or storing results from it.

Magnetic Drum

This device is a metal cylinder which rotates at about 3,600 rpm. The surface of the drum is coated with a special ferrous oxide. Tracks on the surface are capable of storing information magnetically. Read/ write heads positioned near the surface of the drum "write" information on or "read" information from the drum, *Fig.* 17.2. Usually,

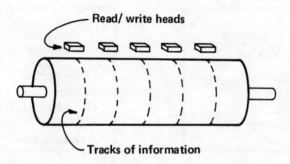

17.2   AS A MAGNETIC DRUM STORAGE UNIT ROTATES, READ/WRITE HEADS DEPOSIT OR EXTRACT INFORMATION ON OR FROM THE SURFACE OF THE DRUM ALONG SPECIFIC INFORMATION PATHS CALLED "TRACKS."

each track on the drum has its own read/write head. If an information system uses a drum at all, the number used is generally limited to one or two.

Magnetic Disc

A disc storage is a thin metal platter ranging from 14 inches to two feet in diameter. The surfaces of the disc are coated with a ferrous oxide and information is recorded magnetically in concentric tracks on both sides. Movable arms, containing read/write heads, traverse the surface of the disc as it rotates, writing information thereon or reading information from it, *Fig.* 17.3.

Usually a number of discs, as many as 16, are grouped and mounted on a single spindle of a disc drive to form the disc unit. In

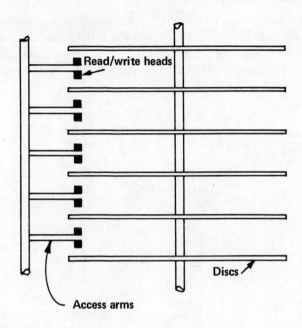

Read/write heads

Discs

Access arms

17.3 CROSS-SECTIONAL SCHEMATIC SHOWS HOW READ-WRITE HEADS SCAN THE DATA TRACKS OF STACKED STORAGE DISCS. AS MANY AS 16 DISCS CAN BE MOUNTED ON A SINGLE DISC DRIVE SPINDLE.

general, each disc surface has its own movable arm, with each arm holding one or more heads. The most recent offerings provide a read/write head for each track. Most units operating today with large-diameter discs use permanent disc arrangements, while units utilizing the smaller-diameter discs often provide for the removal and replacement of groups of discs. Groups of replaceable discs of this kind are called disc packs.

Storage capacity of a single disc pack currently ranges upward to more than 29-million characters, which is the capacity of an 11-inch disc pack. Several removable disc units may be on-line at the same time. A lineup of eight removable disc units will store more than 230-million characters. This comprises a typical high-level disc subsystem. Today, most information systems users are employing removable disc packs because of the virtually unlimited storage capacity such files permit when planning for possible future expansion.

Magnetic Cards or Strips

These devices are rectangular plastic cards or strips upon which information can be magnetically recorded. The cards or strips are stored in small bins until the information system requires their use, *Fig.* 17.4. When needed, the card or strip is withdrawn mechanically

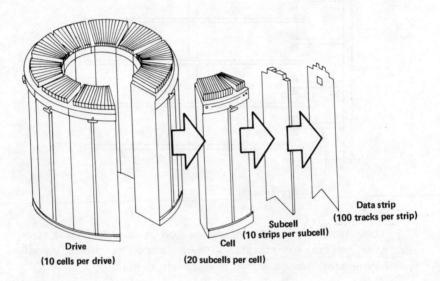

Drive
(10 cells per drive)

Cell
(20 subcells per cell)

Subcell
(10 strips per subcell)

Data strip
(100 tracks per strip)

17.4 AN EXAMPLE OF MAGNETIC STRIP STORAGE UNIT IS THE DATA CELL, MANUFACTURED BY IBM. EACH UNIT HAS A CAPACITY OF 400 MILLION CHARACTERS OR BYTES. EIGHT SUCH UNITS MAY BE STORED ON-LINE, PROVIDING A TOTAL STORAGE CAPACITY OF OVER 3 BILLION CHARACTERS.

from the storage bin and wrapped around a rotating drum. Read/ write heads either record information on or read information from the card or strip.

The primary uses, typical capacities, access speeds, transfer rates, and costs of these four secondary memory devices are compared in TABLE 17.1. The figures given are only representative, since prices of individual devices made by different manufacturers will vary. For more accurate figures, the reader should refer to the specification sheets of the devices being considered.

Table 17.1—Comparing Secondary Storage Devices

Device	Principal Use	Typical Capacities	Typical Access Time		Typical Transfer Rates	Cost Per Stored Character
			Head Positioning	Rotational Delay		
Tape	Files for batched serial processing.	200 million characters	5 ms (time required to traverse ¾ inch Inter-Record Gap @ 150 inch/sec.)	NIL	120,000 characters/sec	Very Low
Drum	Computer software.	4 million characters	NIL	8.6 ms	1,200,000 characters/sec	Very High
Disc	Files for random processing.	29 million characters	75 ms (NIL where each track has read/write head)	12.5 ms	156,000 characters/sec	High
Magnetic Strip	Files for batched serial processing or random processing for inquiries.	400 million characters	175-375 ms See Note 1.	25 ms	55,000 characters/sec	Low

Note: No strip on drum: 175 ms; restore strip to storage and select new strip for drum: 375 ms.
GLOSSARY:

Access Time: The time required to locate information in main or auxiliary memory storage.

ms: Millisecond (1/1,000 sec).

Rotational Delay: The average amount of time it takes for information located on drum or disk to arrive under the R/W head.

Transfer Rate: The rate that information is transferred from auxiliary memory storage to main storage.

NIL: essentially zero.

SELECTION CRITERIA

The first question a user invariably asks himself when selecting secondary storage devices is, "How often and with what speed do the records in my files have to be accessed?" Where files need to be updated only once a day or even less, magnetic tape is an almost ideal secondary storage device. Tape is inexpensive, adequately reliable, and convenient to handle.

Where files must be updated more frequently than once a day, or even immediately, one or more kinds of random access devices must be selected. The ultimate choice depends on how frequently updating must be done. A magnetic drum provides the fastest access speeds and transfer rates, but is the most expensive. Disc storage is less expensive, but access speeds and transfer rates are slower than those of drum storage. Magnetic cards or strips provide the least expensive form of random access, but they are the slowest of the devices in access speed and in transfer rate.

As already mentioned, several manufacturers have recently introduced magnetic disc units with read/write heads for every data track. Access time is reduced, since no arms need be moved. Access time is therefore determined by the rotational speeds of the discs. On an average, the time required to reach the needed data is one-half the time required for the disc to make one complete revolution. The fastest discs provide transfer rates of over 500,000 characters per second, thus, narrowing the gap between drum and disc rates.

The crux of the problem in hardware selection is being able to analyze present requirements, making trade-offs between what is desired and what is actually required and can be afforded. Immediate file updating, for example, is not always required. Often, satisfactory results can be obtained with devices that require low transfer rates. Thus, the second question to be answered is, "What trade-offs can I make between what I would like to have and what I can afford?" Of course, selections must be made within the framework of what the manufacturer makes available. Not all manufacturers, for example, offer magnetic cards or strips.

A "counter" application is an example where access time is critical. A person waiting at an airlines counter doesn't want to wait very long to find out whether reservations can be made for him. Disc storage should probably be used for all such applications, including credit checks, bank balance updating, stock-on-hand inquiries, and the like.

Many applications do not require such rapid access. For example, it is not necessary to process payroll information at the end of each day. Discs need not be used to store master file information: Magnetic tapes offer a more practical medium. Often a user will find that certain files, intended for random access, need not be on-line at all times. While not actually being used for processing, files can be economically stored on magnetic tape or in disc packs.

Experts estimate that about 70 percent of the computer systems installed in the 1970's will include some form of data communications, principally remote data transmission to and from a computer center. This means that particular emphasis will be placed on the selection of auxiliary storage devices designed to serve in this environment. The third question to be answered is really a dual one: "Will my auxiliary storage devices serve my requirements, not only for the present, but also for a reasonable period in the future?" Also: "If changes are ultimately required, are data devices available which will enable me to expand my auxiliary memory or increase access speed without extensive reconfiguration?"

Once the basic information needs of a given application have been identified, the next most important factors in selecting secondary storage equipment are information scheduling and response requirements. Outdated information can be worse than no information at all. Current and immediately accessible information may be a luxury that the organization cannot afford. By precisely identifying both the basic information needs and realistic user response requirements, a much clearer picture is presented of both software (programming) and hardware (computer equipment and peripheral devices) requirements. The direction of future growth also becomes more evident.

In the data communications environment, identification of the required on-line secondary storage devices becomes a major factor upon which many other system features will evolve—features such as the computer operating system, file management system, and internal (core memory) and external storage.

The object of any analysis for the selection of the proper secondary storage devices is to relate the response requirements of a particular data system to the capabilities of different secondary storage devices. By knowing what information must be on-line to the computer at a particular time for update, processing, or retrieval purposes, the general specifications of the devices that *probably* should be ordered can be identified. It is necessary to use the word "probably" since other factors will have a significant bearing on the particular equipment that will actually be ordered. Factors such as file size requirements, purchase or rental costs, manufacture delivery capabilities, and software support must all be carefully considered.

USER-ORIENTATION

In the final analysis, the type and amount of auxiliary storage required for an information system depends on user applications. User response or information scheduling requirements must be related to the computer selection decision, including the major peripheral devices required. A further need is to apply those analytical techniques that will permit anticipating probable future system usage: usage that most assuredly will occur when the user becomes familiar with the advantages of the new computer and communications-oriented information system.

18.

IBM ADDS VIRTUAL STORAGE TECHNOLOGY

Editor's Note: From COMPUTER DIGEST, September 1972, pp. 1–3. Reprinted by permission of the publisher, COMPUTER DIGEST.

IBM has finally introduced its System/370 virtual storage system. This represents a major redirection of System/370 technology, designed to make it easier and more economical for users to develop new applications.

Virtual memory (IBM prefers to call it virtual storage) can increase the productivity of programmers by freeing them from much time-consuming and routine work. In addition, it enables a System/370 to process more jobs concurrently, adding new flexibility for user operations.

To provide virtual storage for System/370, IBM announced new system control programming and circuitry, and two new computers—System/370 Models 158 and 168.

Virtual storage links as much as 16 million bytes, or characters, of direct access storage to a computer's main storage through a combination of circuitry and programming. This fully automated resource allows programmers, computer operators and other users to work with their computer as if it had up to 16 million bytes of main storage—even though the computer's real main storage may be only a fraction of that capacity.

Basic to the implementation of virtual storage is a machine facility called dynamic address translation, which is available now with System/370 Models 135 and 145. It will be standard on the Models 158 and 168, and may be ordered for already purchased Models 155 and 165.

New versions of IBM's Disk Operating System (DOS) and Operating System (OS) interact with the dynamic address translation unit, automatically transferring programs and data between main storage and the direct access device in an operation that is transparent to the user.

Essentially, virtual storage is a means of managing a computer's main storage dynamically so that a program—or more than one in a multiprogramming environment—can be run on a computer even though total program size exceeds main storage capacity.

In conventional computer operations, programs being executed generally must be in main storage in their entirety, even though large sections of each program are idle for lengthy periods of time, tying up vital main storage space.

With virtual storage, only the active sections of each program need occupy main storage; the rest of each program can be stored automatically on the direct access device. Main storage space is automatically allocated to meet the changing demands of each program as it is being executed.

EXTRA FREEDOM FOR USER

The new flexibility provided by virtual storage can help a computer user's staff to make more productive use of their time both in carrying out existing data processing applications and in developing new ones. Special, high-priority jobs, for example, can be run immediately, without disrupting operations. A sales analysis program could be processed to provide a "rush" report for management—even though main storage is filled to capacity with regularly scheduled applications, such as payroll or inventory control programs.

Instead of stopping one of these programs to make room, a computer operator enters the rush job immediately. Main storage space required for processing is provided by removal of inactive portions of the other programs.

Accommodating the rush job could add to the total running time of the regular programs. Typically, the additional time would have no significant effect upon the departments served by the programs.

The operation of computer terminals—located across the hall or across the country from a central System/370—can be scheduled for longer periods of time each day without impacting the computer center's own batch operations.

An insurance company, for example, might have its agency offices linked to its central computer by means of television-like terminals. Agents use such a system for various applications, such as inquiry into customer policies, entering prospect information and receiving data for the tailoring of special proposals. Without virtual storage, a major portion of main storage would have to be dedicated to handle each application program segment—even though usage of some occurs infrequently. Dedication of this "teleprocessing partition" would prevent the running of all batch jobs during the period the terminals are in use. Typically, therefore, terminal activity is scheduled during normal business hours, with batch operations, such as the processing of premium-due files, scheduled for the second shift.

By dynamically allocating main storage to meet the computing needs of the moment, a System/370 with virtual storage could allow the coexistence of both batch and all teleprocessing operations during the entire period the computer is in operation, automatically taking advantage of low application usage periods to allow batch processing.

Virtual storage also helps a data processing center make more effective use of system resources. At a multi-computer installation, a small system with virtual storage could be used to back up a larger computer during periods of higher-than-normal data processing activity. In addition, selection of job combinations can be made easier. For example, a payroll program with many input-output operations is ideally suited to run concurrently with a simulation program that requires a great deal of computation. Even though the two programs may exceed main storage size limitations, virtual storage allows them to be run concurrently.

Besides providing increased flexibility in day-to-day operations, virtual storage enables the user to develop and implement large-scale applications earlier and more smoothly.

A programmer writing an application program can spend less time coping with main storage size limitations; he no longer has to create special techniques to "telescope" the program into a limited amount of storage. Allowed to concentrate on the application itself, he can produce new programs more quickly and—equally as important—can alter and expand programs more easily because of the straightforward manner in which they can be written.

Program testing and debugging—an important part of application development—can be expedited because virtual storage allows a System/370 to accommodate program test runs on an immediate basis, despite main storage size limitations. This reduces a programmer's nonproductive waiting time to a minimum.

Virtual storage could shave months from the implementation of a new application by allowing it to be run on a smaller computer before the higher-performance computer targeted for the application is even installed.

For example, a manufacturing company many be developing a plant floor communications system for a System/370 Model 158. The application can first be installed on a Model 135 which, with virtual storage, could handle the same storage requirements as the Model 158, but at slower processing speeds and longer response times. Using the Model 135, the plant can test, alter and prove out the system and then install it with little or no change upon the arrival of the Model 158.

HOW VIRTUAL STORAGE WORKS

When programs are placed in virtual storage, they are automatically divided into small sections called pages. For ease of addressing, these pages are assigned to larger groups called segments. Initially, a page must occupy real storage—the computer's main storage—but as real storage space becomes needed elsewhere, the page is transferred to external page storage on the direct access device. When required again by an operating data processing job, one or more pages are automatically copied back into real storage. The ongoing transfer of pages between real storage and external page storage is termed demand paging.

Demand paging can take place because all instructions and data are referenced by their virtual storage addresses—regardless of whether, at a given time, they occupy real storage.

When an instruction or a data record is referenced by a program, the system's dynamic address translation facility automatically breaks the virtual storage address into segment number, page number within segment, and the position of the instruction or record with regard to the beginning of the page.

Segment tables and page tables maintained by the system control programming indicate whether the needed page is already in real storage. If this is the case, execution of the program continues. If the page does not exist in real storage, then paging takes place under supervision of the system control programming.

To speed program execution, the dynamic address translation facility contains a translation lookaside buffer, which holds the addresses of previously referenced pages located in real storage. If the real storage location of a referenced page is found in this manner, a search of segment and page tables is not required.

The system control programming and circuitry automatically monitor page usage in main storage to identify inactive pages. These are paged out, when necessary, to meet demands for main storage space. If a page has been changed during the run of a program, it is written over the former version that exists on external page storage. If a page has not been changed, no actual transfer of data need take place. This helps keep paging time to a minimum.

Monitoring of paging activity also helps prevent programs from being reduced below their optimum real storage space—the minimum real storage they need to perform efficiently. Thus, if too much paging activity takes place, the system control program will free additional real storage space by temporarily deactivating the lowest priority program. This helps ensure that actual processing of programs is not impacted by abnormal paging rates.

Although System/370 virtual storage ranges up to 16 million bytes, DOS/VS and OS/VS users can use smaller capacities to meet individual requirements.

DOS/VS, OS/VS1 and OS/VS2 all automatically divide virtual storage into segments of 65,000 bytes each. OS/VS2, designed for larger data processing jobs, divides programs and data into pages of 4,000 bytes each. DOS/VS and OS/VS1, in order to meet requirements of smaller programs and applications, work with page sizes of 2,000 bytes each.

DATA ORGANIZATION AND STORAGE: DISCUSSION QUESTIONS

1. What are the characteristics of sequential file organization, indexed sequential organization, and random file organization? For what types of applications would indexed sequential organization be preferred over physical sequential organization? Random organization over indexed and physical sequential organization? Explain fully.
2. What effect will the selection of the indicated storage media and file organization methods have on average access times, storage capacity requirements, cost per character stored, processing times and costs, and software development costs?
   a. A large, very active file using sequential organization (that is, indexed sequential) is stored on magnetic tape and individual records must be accessed periodically to answer information inquiries.
   b. A small, active file organized randomly (that is, key transformation) is stored on magnetic disks.
   c. A large file is divided into two segments. The most active segment is organized randomly and is stored on magnetic drums, whereas the less active portion is stored on magnetic cards in sequential fashion. Periodically, the complete file is dumped onto magnetic tape for updating.
   d. A large, integrated data base is organized sequentially by functional areas (for example, finance, production, engineering, and marketing), is stored on magnetic cores, is updated on a batch basis, and is referenced periodically by diverse users seeking answers to information inquiries.
   e. A large payroll file, organized sequentially, is stored on magnetic disks, and is updated once weekly in serial form. It is seldom necessary to access individual records in the file.
3. How do magnetic tapes, magnetic disks, magnetic drums, and magnetic cards differ in terms of physical characteristics? Name

one application for which each type of storage medium is best suited.

4. Distinguish between serial access and direct-access media. Since direct-access media are generally more costly and require more complex and expensive software than serial access media, what circumstances must be present to justify the use of direct-access media?

5. Distinguish between direct addressing, key transformation, and indexing. What problems are likely to occur in updating and accessing files using key transformation methods? Indexing methods? How can these problems be overcome?

6. Explain the nature of randomizing and indexing methods for file entry. How do they differ in terms of cost, storage-space utilization, average access times for individual data records, processing time, convenience, and flexibility to meet changing requirements?

7. What are the major benefits and limitations of magnetic cores, thin films, and integrated circuits as main memory for a computer system? For what kinds of applications is each type of medium best suited?

8. What are the prospects for widescale use of magnetic cores, planar thin films, plated wire devices, and integrated circuits in mass memories during the coming decade? What are the major barriers to more widespread use of thin films and integrated circuits? How might these problems be overcome or minimized?

9. What are the major types of holographic memories? How likely is the adoption of holographic memory devices for use in main memories during the near future? In mass, on-line memories? Why?

10. Explain how the systems designer can resolve each of the following conflicts in systems design of a direct-access file system:
    a. Ease of access versus file security.
    b. Fast response time and flexibility of file access versus low processing and storage costs.
    c. Minimizing data redundancy versus reducing response times.
    d. Ease of file modification versus minimizing storage requirements and system complexity.
    e. Simplicity of programming requirements versus ease of file access and fast response to information inquiries.

11. What problems of file security and protection are unique to direct-access storage use? How can these problems be resolved or at least minimized?

12. What effect will the number of records involved (that is, size of

file), average record lengths, file activity ratios, and frequency of file reference have on the choice of a file organization method, of storage media, and methods of processing data? Is it really possible to maximize the utilization of a minimum of equipment while minimizing programming effort and operating costs in designing random- or direct-access files? Explain fully.

13. Explain how virtual storage differs from conventional storage operation. What effect will virtual storage use be likely to have on the following?

a. Utilization of storage space.

b. Simultaneous processing of programs of different lengths and/ or priorities.

c. Expansion of hardware (CPU) capacity or leasing of additional computer time.

d. Project assignments to in-house programmers.

e. Hiring of new programmers or purchase of contract programming services.

DATA ORGANIZATION AND STORAGE: BIBLIOGRAPHY

"A New Focus for the Hologram," *Dun's Review*, August 1970, pp. 59–61.

Auerbach Guide to Key-to-Storage Equipment, 1972; *Guide to IBM Plug Compatible Discs and Tapes*, 1972; and *Guide to IBM Compatible Memories*, 1972.

Bailey, S. J., "Putting Memories to Work On-Line," *Control Engineering*, February 1970, pp. 126–134.

Bauchman, Charles W., "The Evolution of Storage Structures," *ACM Communications*, July 1972, pp. 628–634.

Benner, Frank H., "On Designing Generalized File Records for Management Information Systems," *AFIPS, Proceedings of Fall Joint Computer Conference*, 1967, pp. 291–303.

Bleier, Robert E., "Treating Hierarchiac Data Structures in the SOC Time-Shared Data Management Systems," *Proceedings of the ACM 22 No. National Conference*, 1967, pp. 41–49.

Bradley, W. P., "Managers' Guide to Virtual Memory," *Journal of Systems Management*, Part I, January 1973, pp. 8–11; Part II, February 1973, pp. 20–23.

Brown, David W., and Burkhardt, James L., "The Computer Memory Market," *Computers and Automation*, January 1969, pp. 17–26.

Bryant, J. H., and Semple, Parlan, Jr., "GIS and File Management," *Proceedings ACM National Meeting*, 1966, pp. 97–107.

"Bubble Memories Start Taking Shape," *Business Week*, November 21, 1970, pp. 26–27. See also "The Poor Man's Magnetic Bubble Memory," *Business Week*, April 29, 1972, p. 80.

Buchholz, Werner, "File Organization and Addressing," *IBM Systems Journal*, June 1963, pp. 86–111.

Climenson, W. Douglas, "File Organization and Search Techniques," *Annual Review of Information Science and Technology*, John Wiley and Sons, 1966, pp. 107–135.

Datapro 70, "All about add-on main memories;" and "All about disk and drum storage," August 1972.

DeParis, Joseph R., "Random Access," *Data Processing*, February 1965, pp. 30–31.

Dodd, George G., "Elements of Data Management Systems," *Computing Surveys*, June 1969, pp. 117–133.

Elson, Benjamin M., "Semiconductor Memories Evolve," *Aviation Week & Space Technology*, June 15, 1970, pp. 30–40.

Eppstein, Anthoney D., "The Technology of Disk Data Storage," *Data Processing*, September 1968, pp. 26–30.

"4096-Bit Mos Ram Latest to Challenge CORE," *Electronic News*, Dec. 4, 1972, p. 26. See also "Computer-Memory Technology Takes a Bigger Byte," *Iron Age*, August 10, 1972, p. 43.

Gould, William C., "File Organizations on Mass Storage," pp. 123–127; and Dennis S. Werd, "Mass Storage File Design," pp. 111–120, *Data Processing Annual*, Vol. XII, 1967 DPMA Conference Proceedings.

Graham, Robert F., "Semiconductor Memories; Evolution or Revolution," *Datamation*, June 1969, pp. 99–104.

Henry, W. R., "Hierarchial Structure for Data Management," *IBM Systems Journal* no. 1, 1969, pp. 2–15. See also E. J. Hauch, "Hierarchical Data Files Cut Storage Requirements," *Data Processing*, June 1971, pp. 22–28.

Hoagland, A. S., "Mass Storage—Past, Present, and Future," *Fall Joint Computer Conf. Proceedings*, 1972, pp. 985–991.

Ver Hoef, Edward W., "Design of a Multi-Level File Management System, *Proceedings ACM National Meeting*, 1966, pp. 75–86.

"How Can Steel Use Virtual Storage in Its Computers," *Iron Age*, August 31, 1972. p. 39. See also "New Computer System Cut Big Jobs Down to Size," *Chemical Week*, Nov. 1, 1972, pp. 45–46.

"How IBM Talks about Virtual Storage," *Infosystems*, October 1972, pp. 26–28.

"IBM Adds Virtual Storage Technology" *Computer Digest*, September 1972, pp. 1–3. See also, "Virtual Memory Considered Boon to Most Users," *Electronic News*, Monday, December 4, 1972, pp. 14, 30, 33.

Kaimann, Richard A., "Entry to the File: Randomize or Index," *Data Processing*, Part I, December 1966, pp. 18–21, Part II, December 1968, pp. 24–27.

Kaimann, Richard A., "Random Accessing for Large Tape Files," *Data Processing*, February 1969, pp. 22–23.

Kitzmiller, Don, "Is There a Cassette in Your Computer's Future?," *Journal of Data Management*, June 1970, pp. 28–32.

Koehler, H. Frederick, "An Impartial Look at Semiconductors," *Data-*

mation, July 15, 1971, pp. 42–46. See also "Large Scale Integration in Electronics," *Scientific American* (F. G. Heath).

Lachter, Lewis E., "Mag Tape or Disc?," *Administrative Management,* December 1971, pp. 68–69.

Lapidus, Gerald, "The Domain of Magnetic Bubbles," *IEEE Spectrum,* September 1972, pp. 58–62. See also A. H. Bobeck and H. E. D. Scovil, "Magnetic Bubbles," *Scientific American,* June 1971, pp. 78–90.

Lee, Robert M., "Selecting Storage Devices for Large, Random-Access, Data Storage Systems," *Computer Design,* February 1970, pp. 59–63.

Lobel, Jerome, and Farina, M. V., "Selecting Computer Memory Devices," *Automation,* October 1970, pp. 66–70.

Mayne, David, "What's Next in Memories," *Datamation,* February 1968, pp. 30–32.

McGee, W. C., "Generalized File Processing" *Annual Review in Automatic Programming,* Vol. 5, Pergamon Press, 1968.

Meyer, Henry T., "Magnetic Tape, Drum, Disc Memories"; and Caryl A. Thorn, "Computer Storage and Memory Devices," *Electronics World,* October 1970, pp. 40–43, 37–39.

Miner, Robert A., "Digital/Graphic Record Access," *Modern Data,* January 1970, pp. 66–70. See also, "Filing by Television Provides Speed and Flexibility," *Best's Review,* October 1971, pp. 84–88.

"More From Less With Virtual Memory," *Administrative Management,* January 1973, pp. 25–27.

Murphy, William J., and Murphy, John A., "Magnetic Tape Systems" *Modern Data,* Part I, Cassettes, Cartridge, and Small Tape Transports"; Part II, "IBM Compatible Transports," August 1971; and Part III, "IBM Plug-to-Plug Compatible Tape Transports," September 1971.

Patton, P. C., "Trends in Data Organization and Access Methods," *Computer,* November/December 1970, pp. 19–24.

"Random Access Storage: A State of the Art Approach," and "Magnetic Tape Recording: A State of the Art Report," Auerbach Standard EDP Reports, 1968.

Seitz, Hans A., "New Approaches to Direct Access Computer Files, *Ideas for Management,* Systems and Procedures Association, 1967, pp. 64–76.

Sussenguth, E. H., "An Evaluation of Storage Allocation Schemes," *Information Storage and Retrieval,* AD-287-945, September 1962, Federal Scientific and Technical Information, Springfield, Virginia.

"Technology Profile: Disk and Drum Drives," *Modern Data,* January, February, and March 1971.

"The Great Memory Debate—Semiconductors, Plated Wire, and Cores," *Computerworld,* Parts I, II, and III, August 5, 12, and 19, 1970.

"The Laser May Be Ready for the Big Time," *Business Week,* September 18, 1971 pp. 54–58. See also "The Little Colossus of Holography," *Business Week,* September 11, 1971, pp. 122–123.

Trimble, George R., "Building the File Structure for a Direct Access System," *Data Processing, Proceedings of the 1966 DPMA Conference,* Vol. XI, pp. 359–375. See also "Information Retrieval for Internal Reporting," *Ideas for Management,* 1968, pp. 19–28, by the same author.

"Virtual Storage-Key to Enhanced Application Development," Special Issue, *IBM Data Processor,* September 1972. See also series of articles on Virtual Storage in *Datamation,* 1973, pp. 48–60.

"Virtual Storage—New Dimensions in Problem Solving," *IBM Computing Report in Science and Engineering,* Summer 1972, pp. 2–3. See also "Paging, Programming, and Real Storage Management" (same issue).

Walter, Cloy J., Walter, A. B., and Bohl, M. J., "Setting Characteristics for Fourth Generation Computer Systems: Part III—LSI," *Computer Design,* October 1968, pp. 48–55.

Ward, D. S., "Practical Data Base Design," *Control Engineering,* May 1968, pp. 83–86.

Weitzman, Coy, "Optical Technologies for Future Computer Systems," *Computer Design,* April 1970, pp. 169–175.

"Why Cores Could Become Just a Memory," *Business Week,* December 26, 1970, pp. 60–61. See also, "An Integrated Circuit That Is Catching Up," *Business Week,* April 25, 1970, pp. 134–136.

PART IV.

DATA BASE MANAGEMENT: AN EMERGING FUNCTION

A trend toward more integrated file structures has resulted in the grouping together of all data items relevant to the management and operations section of a using organization. The emerging data base concept requires placing all relevant data in one file in a consistent and standardized manner, eliminating unnecessary duplication and file handling, and providing selective inquiry and extraction capabilities designed to meet a wide variety of information requests. A data bank is a specialized data base implying record selectivity and compatibility, standardized data formats, provision for growth of files, and validity of data bank deposits (that is, accuracy, completeness, reliability, and relevance). It is particularly important that new files created conform to data base standards and that a machine-readable index or bibliography be available for ease of reference to stored data.

The data base concept, based on the use of integrated file structures and random-access storage devices, permits more comprehensive, timely information services to be provided to computer users as well as economies in the design and operation of computer systems. Data base systems allow coordination of files of basic data to serve many users, reduce data duplication, produce system economies through common data organization and access, and allow files to be updated continuously or on a batch basis as desired. Planning a data bank or specialized data base requires consideration of the scope, composition, and priority of data; hardware and software requirements for maintaining the data base; storage media to be used; file organization schemes to be employed; allowances for growth of records or data sets; and the best possible methods for entering data into and retrieving information from the data base.

Johnson spells out the basic concept of a data base as a central reservoir of information in which each data element is recorded only once. The data base management system (DBMS) is computer software that associates logical relationships of data elements without regard to physical organization, assigns data to physical storage locations, and handles information retrieval requirements. A DBMS increases flexibility of information use and reduces programming requirements as compared to conventional approaches. Data dictionaries and query languages further enhance the utility of the data base and the use of a centralized data base administrator can simplify and facilitate the solution of information-related problems.

According to Cohen, the data base system includes the data base, queries and query programs, file organization, and data management. The data base is composed of records that contain content, index, and structure data. Query programs permit the user to ask questions and obtain responses from the data base by means of a user-oriented language. Appropriate file organizations permit key value search of the data base in a fast and efficient manner. The essential data management functions performed by the system include record storage, record retrieval, and space management. Design of the data base requires consideration of content, retrieval methods, interfile relationships, and storage structures, as well as an analysis of user service requirements. In addition, total data volumes must be broken down into subunits that can be handled in an independent manner for purposes of record design, volume and activity analysis, file design, and data management specification.

Schussel points out that there has been a widespread shift from storing functional files containing duplicate data in separate locations toward placing each item of data used only once in a common data base. Software packages called data management systems (DMS) perform many functions the programmer was formerly responsible for and supply information in a more accessible, easier to retrieve form. More programs are available for use at one time with a DMS and faster responses to information inquiries are frequently possible. Lack of familiarity with DMS capabilities, heavy investments in tape systems, and gigantic data files have inhibited the development of data base systems by many organizations.

Key characteristics of a data base include common data definitions, on-line access capability, effective data administration, and maintenance of security procedures. The data base approach saves programming time, improves storage efficiency, and permits economic use of one-time decision-making programs. Problems encountered with data base use include lack of trained personnel, creation of a need for larger memory banks, greater complexity of reruns, and the difficulty of getting total management commitment. Successful data base implementation approaches have generally been characterized by a team approach, logical data organization, emphasis on real information needs rather than present system production, dictionary development, data administration control, and phased implementation.

Shugar uses the development of the Western Electric Corporate Data Pool (CDP) as an example of how the common data base approach can eliminate redundancy in capturing, converting, and storing data. The development of standard data languages and logically related integrated data structures helped insure company-wide compatibility of data (permitting transfer of data between local data bases) and lower physical storage requirements. Basic components of the CDP include record sets, files, and fields. Collections of data components called Named Data Segments support each information system function. The CDP provides a reference point for development of separate compatible data bases throughout the organization in a manner capable of supporting an integrated information system.

Generalized data management systems, which store, retrieve, and update data files, are now available. Such systems have emerged from a need to obtain more information from current data base files, to utilize mass random-access storage devices and software systems more effectively, and to reduce programming bottlenecks arising from long lead times for new applications. Different data organizations are used to bridge the gap between logical user requirements and the physical realities of storage media and computer hardware. These systems are built around easy-to-use management languages for describing information files and processing requests as well as functionally organized software tools that automatically handle complex information access to highly structured data bases. File description is separated from file processing, thereby facilitating the process of adding, deleting, modifying, or updating file elements. System functions include data definition and organization, file creation and maintenance, processing, retrieval/display, and statistical collection.

Data base management systems are needed to provide control of data structures, comprehensive languages for data manipulation, adequate execution performance, and system integrity, as Schubert points out. A data base permits two or more applications to share a common data source. The basic elements of a data base are physical storage structure, data and control information, and logical relationships among stored data. Physical storage structures include blocks of information called pages and areas containing a given number of pages. Data base contents include data elements, data records, and record occurrences. Logical data relationships are exemplified by sets that establish owner-member links by use of pointers. A schema is a complete description of all data base elements and a subschema is a logical subset that names only elements accessed by specific programs. Separation of data base descriptions from access programs and requirements for access by multiple applications have created the need for new, and extension of existing, programming languages. Data description and manipulation languages have emerged to meet this need. Self-contained systems and data base administration are two other important offshoots of data base management systems.

Ward emphasizes that major new developments encompass hierarchial file utilization of mass storage, listing techniques using multiple indexes to access files, and storage of data description information in the data base. Response time, data maintenance requirements, and space utilization are key factors in developing file structures. Content retrieval structures, multiple indexing, inverted list files, and stored file descriptions are innovations that can be incorporated into data base management systems. Data description languages are used to specify the structure, logical contents, format, and file-access methods for a given application. Data management languages are concerned with retrieval and reporting functions. The principal advantages of data base systems over conventional approaches to file organization include faster response time, comprehensiveness, and flexibility. The ultimate result is to improve communication between the user and the data base.

19.

MANAGING INFORMATION

By William G. Johnson

Editor's Note: From MANAGEMENT CONTROLS,
June 1972, pp. 118–121. Reprinted by permission
of the publisher, Peat, Marwick, Mitchell and Co.,
and author.

Gut feelings still form the basis for many business decisions, but no rational business executive today would deny the impact that information, or the lack of it, has on his decision-making and the general well-being of his company. Pertinent and current information about customers, employees, operating costs, and all the other elements that must be dealt with in running a business, form the basis for better management decisions and healthier companies. Disregarding other relevant factors for the sake of argument, it follows that those businesses that provide their executives with meaningful information at the time and place needed, should be more successful than those that do not.

Indeed, although qualitatively different from the traditional assets, information should be recognized as an important business asset. And just as cash, inventories and other assets need to be properly managed, business information also needs to be managed.

Using inventory management as an analogy may help to clarify what is meant by managing information. As with inventories, information of the right variety and type should be stored and made available for use in the proper locations and at the required times and frequencies. Again like inventories, too much information is costly and too little is equally damaging. Information also must be made secure and not available to unauthorized persons or vulnerable to physical loss through fire, flood, and power loss.

Unlike inventories, howevei, information can be physically managed and controlled *directly* by computers. Important developments in recent years have advanced the state of the art in information management by computers. To appreciate these new developments let us first gain a perspective on the way in which information is presently organized in many businesses.

In most companies, information is structured along functional organizational lines of responsibility: The controller has his information files, sales has its own files, production its own, and similarly with personnel and other functions. This arrangement is prevalent not only in manual processing but also in electronic data processing, and even when a single computer center services the entire company. Thus, computer programs are often designed to use dedicated information files—payroll programs use employee payroll master files, inventory programs use inventory master files, etc.

These types of information files receive only limited usage. The information content of these files is generally not available to others who may also need the same information—although perhaps for different purposes and at different times—suitably reclassified or differently formatted. Often attendant upon data processing in this traditional mode are confusion, redundancy, and proliferation of data. Multiple records of the same data elements—employee and customer names and addresses, payroll, sales and production data, etc.—result in higher processing costs and still do not make information accessible to all those who can use it to advantage at the time needed or in a usable form.

The original systems approach in dealing with this problem was to integrate two or more computer application files, such as payroll and personnel, into one physical file to be drawn upon by multiple users. This was a step in the right direction but quite limited because of the rigid organization of data imposed by a single physical file. Moreover, to reorganize the file through sorting, merging, etc., was to reduce the advantage of a physically integrated file approach and was often self-defeating. Any change, addition or deletion of information elements to the file called for by one user requires changes to all the application programs of all the users of that file. This created either huge program maintenance problems—and thus was frequently not done—or a severe constraint on the users' freedom to change the contents of their files when necessary.

The hardware tools necessary for improving information management have been available for many years. The development of direct access computer storage devices with mass storage capacities, remote terminal devices and data communications, removes the physical constraints of distances and the logistical problems of collecting and disseminating data to multiple users regardless of their locations. However, the systems approach and software development have lagged behind until the recent development of a new approach to information management—the data base concept.

A data base can be viewed as a central reservoir of information in which an element of business data is recorded and stored only once. From that single source, information is made accessible in varying desired output formats and classifications—and associated with any other logically relevant information stored in the same manner—to any user with an established need to know, at the time needed. It is in fact a practical concept, and significant progress in its use has clearly been made by sophisticated users of computers.

Essential to the data base concept is a data base management system (DBMS). A DBMS is computer software which handles the physical storage and retrieval of information in a data base. It also has the important capability of associating any logical relationships of data elements (for example, employee names are logically associated with job skill classifications, hourly pay rates, co-workers, department supervisors, etc.) regardless of the physical organization or location of the individual data elements in the data base. Hence, all the different logical relationships of data elements required by multiple users' applications can be accommodated from one data source without changing the physical organization of the data in the data base. Further, new data elements can be added and old ones deleted without affecting all the application programs that use the same data base. This greatly increases flexibility and reduces program maintenance costs considerably. With a DBMS, the user (and his representative programmer) need not be concerned with the physical location organization and procedure for accessing information needed for his particular purpose. This is the purpose of the DBMS. Users then can concentrate on their own business information problems without undue concern with the technical data processing problems of information storage and retrieval. The gap between the business information requirements of the user and the technical complexities of data processing is greatly narrowed.

Available software for this type of system varies considerably in functional capabilities, operating efficiency, stage of development, and degree of time-tested usage, and any selection should be made very carefully. Some user organizations have developed their own DBMS with varying degrees of success, but in most cases the cost to a user of developing his own DBMS system would be prohibitive and far exceed the cost of one obtained from an outside source.

Two important peripheral developments which complement and further increase the utility of the data base approach are the data dictionary and a query language. As the name implies, the data dictionary provides company-wide standards for data names and definitions which are used by both users and programmers to communicate with each other as well as with the computer through a programming language. The query language provides a way for users to directly request and obtain data from a data base through a remote terminal, without the need for a special program written by a professional programmer.

Implicit in the use of a data base approach to managing information are new functional responsibilities and organizational changes. Where before, systems people and programmers developed their own file organizations, a data base administrator now has centralized responsibility for overall control, design, and organization of data in the data base. This greatly simplifies programming and testing and allows application programmers more time to devote to solving users' basic information-related problems rather than to the complexities of data organization, storage and retrieval.

This perspective on information management is not being advanced as a panacea for all companies and for all information-processing problems. We are discussing what is fundamentally simply one tool that can provide greater flexibility and capability. Problems of computer capacity, running time and costs must still be measured and evaluated, and pros and cons must be weighed in the light of the special circumstances surrounding each company, but the data base concept is a very important development and one that must be given consideration. Within the next few years, most companies with computers will be utilizing it in some form to better organize and manage information.

═══ 20.

DATA BASE CONSIDERATIONS AND IMPLEMENTATION TECHNIQUES

By Leo J. Cohen

Editor's Note: From DATA MANAGEMENT, September 1972, pp. 40–45, published by Data Processing Management Association, 505 Busse Highway, Park Ridge, Illinois 60068.

In dealing effectively with a new and complex technology, especially one as extensive as the data base technology, it is necessary to provide a coherent dissection into major elements which can then be treated as disciplines in their own right. It is with such an objective in mind that the data base question can be looked at from the system point of view: that is, as a data base system.

The four major elements of the data base system are the data base itself, queries and their query programs, file organization, and the data management functions. The data base is the repository of all data of interest to the user of the system. The queries, in their form in the computer as query programs, represent the users in the system and create its actions. File organization is necessary to expedite operations, while the data management functions represent the set of all operative programs in the data base system necessary for storage, retrieval and space management.

Figure 20.1 is a schematic diagram depicting the general relationships that must exist between these four elements for a functioning data base system. The query program is the source of reference action in the system; user programs create queries in some program-oriented, or "access method," language which are then delivered to the programs of the data management function. The particular programs

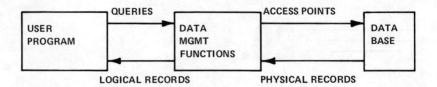

20.1 THE DATA BASE SYSTEM

charged with the responsibility for handling queries and translating them into access points are then executed.

The access points are specific physical locations in the device that stores the data base; that is, the query is the formal user program expression of its data requirements. The access point is the corresponding position of the required data in the data base. The net result of reference to the data base by the data system is a physical record. This is returned to those data management functions which are designed to separate the physical record into its logical components for delivery to the user program. Finally, file organization within the data base system provides for expedient retrieval of specific data, or the retrieval of generally related data, given specific characteristics or attributes of that data.

THE DATA BASE

The data base represents the set of all information in the data format that is of interest to the system's users. However, the data base is a passive element of the data base system. Like the encyclopedia it is a highly structured collection of data that must be addressed or referenced to be useful. The essential element of the data base is the record which can be described, physically, as a set of contiguous locations on its storage device and, logically, as a set of sub units (sometimes referred to as fields). Thus, a record is made up of a number of fields. These fields may be fixed in length or variable in length, or the record organization may be such as to exclude fields from the record for which there is no data. Whatever the record structure, there are three general categories of data that appear within a record: These are content, index data, and structure data.

Content is the information of the data base problem. Index data distinguishes one record, or several records, from all others in the data base. For example, in an employee field we may designate the employee number as index data to distinguish all the data in its associated record from all other records in the data base, since employee number is generally a unique identifier for the employee that it represents. However, a city name might also be considered as index data in a record. In this case a particular city name, rather than serving to uniquely designate a single record, might determine a group of records. These records are of course associated by having the given city name in common. Structure data provides the means for expressing relationships among information that is represented in the record as content. That is, structure data in one record both guarantees the existence and designates the location of other records which are associated according to some criteria. Structure data represents the pointers, or links, or chains, that become the basis for building relationships among the records of the data base.

Thus, the record is a collection of data that has been given a certain, definitive format in terms of its fields. The data in the fields of the record represents the content, index data, and structure data, with the latter two categories serving the functional purposes of record reference and retrieval.

QUERIES, KEYS & KEY VALUES

Query programs provide the means for creating references to the data base. The query program, in fact, is intermediate between the human user of the system and the data base. As such, the needs of the human user require some translation in order to result in the query program. Figure 20.2 is an expression of the relationship of the human user to the data base via the query program.

First, there is a user oriented language by means of which the query is expressed to the system. This generally requires some translation, and the result is the specification of a set of programs for loading and execution. These are the query programs, and in the course of their execution they will create the necessary references which are structured according to the design of the data management functions that will translate these queries into points of access in the data base. The result of system operation is first the physical and then the logical record, as discussed earlier. It is these selected data elements of the logical record that are returned to the query program, which must then formulate a response to the human user and deliver it to him.

Query languages vary from high degrees of English language

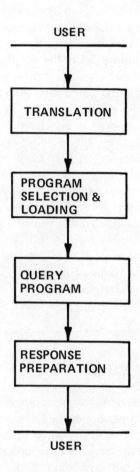

20.2   QUERY PROGRAM

orientation to compiler and assembly languages. The problem of translating an English-like query expression into a specification of the required programs is much akin to the problem of compilation. This is
precisely its nature when the data base system is closely associated
with a programming language such as COBOL. COBOL becomes the
query language for the user, and the COBOL compiler becomes the
mechanism by means of which the query programs are prepared for
execution in the data base system.

The preparation of responses to the human user from the data
delivered by the data base system can vary from program-created re-

ports, to reports derived from RPG. Where a programming language such as COBOL is employed as the query language, RPG usually is involved in report preparation. Where special languages of reference have been designed for the user, there is often a special report preparation language as well.

With regard to the program selection and loading functions that provide the query programs for execution, it is generally necessary that a query be prepared and operated in the context of an operating system. For economic reasons, parallel access by a multiplicity of queries is a necessity to the financial viability of a large scale data base system, therefore, an operating system is fundamental to its operation. Thus, the program selection and loading functions are properly functions of the operating systems. The associated allocation and program-to-program reference functions, which deliver the query data to the required data management programs, are in the province of the operating system as well.

Whatever the reference language, the query programs resulting from the translation of this user reference must accomplish four basic functions. The key and key values of the query must be identified. A key may be considered the name of a field within a record of the data base. A key value is a specific data value which a record must possess in this key field to satisfy the query. For example, the EMPLOYEE NUMBER field might be specified as the key, while the employee number 50154 would be a particular key value. Thus, a query involving the EMPLOYEE NUMBER field and the given employee number as the explicit key-value pair, causes the data management functions to seek among those records with an EMPLOYEE NUMBER field for the specific record having the key value indicated. Thus, if queries are to be expressed in terms of key and key value pairs, it is the function of the query program to identify them to the data management routines of the data base system.

Very often a query specifies two or more conditions to be satisfied simultaneously. An example, "find all employees with more than 10 years experience as machinists, living in Newark." There are three key-key value pairs involved in this query. The keys are EXPERIENCE, CITY, and JOB, while the respective key values are "more than 10 years," "Newark," and "machinists." The records to be delivered to the query program as a consequence of this reference must simultaneously satisfy all of the stated conditions, referred to as a query conjunction. Query disjunctions, in which an OR relationship is expressed between key-key value pairs are also possible. More complex relationships can be built up from combined conjunctions and disjunctions to form the full conditions of a query. These may have the general form of Boolean functions, and it is explicitly the responsibility of the query program to formulate and identify these Boolean relationships on its key and key value pairs.

Very often a query has a complex structure that takes the form of a hierarchy. That is, the first step of the reference might result in records that contain data out of which the key-key value pairs for the next step of the reference are determined. Thus, the use of the search facility of the data management system must be employed in an ordered sequence dependent upon previous data delivered by the data base to the query program. Another function of the query program is to order the utilization of the search facility of the data management functions so as to satisfy the structural properties of the query.

Several records usually result from a reference to the data base. So that the records will be delivered in some sequence to the query program, this sequence must be specified by the query program along with the processing to be applied to each record. This processing, of course, results in the response that is prepared for the user of the system.

FILE ORGANIZATION

In any data base having field names that may serve as keys for user's queries it is clearly possible to find all records satisfying even the most complex of Boolean conditions on a large number of key-key value pairs. By the simple brute force technique of repetitive search of the data base, all query conditions can be satisfied and the requisite records delivered as a result.

A data base system, however, has at least implicit association with timeliness, which in turn suggests searching efficiency. The achievement of such searching efficiencies is the role of the file organization in the data base system. Figure 20.3 is a schematic diagram

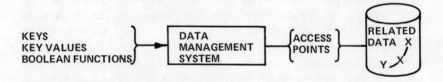

20.3 THE ROLE OF FILE ORGANIZATION

suggesting this role. Queries that come to the data management system have the form of keys and key values that are related in the form of Boolean functions. These key-key value pairs are transformed into access points, which in turn lead to specific physical locations in the data storage device. Each physical location contains a record of the data base, and is our first reference to it for this query. Suppose, however, that we were seeking to satisfy query conjunctions that were based on, say, the CITY key and the JOB key of the record. Suppose further that we had organized the records of our file so that via structure data all records having a common key value for the CITY key and a common key value for the JOB key were linked together to form respective lists. We would initially locate the first record with the CITY key equal to NEWARK, and then search down the associated list until we found all records for which the JOB key had the value MACHINIST.

There are many types of file organization, with that of the above example being known as a "partially inverted" list. These organizations vary in degrees of generality from the simple list organizations and various types of multi-list and inverted list, to rings and networks. In each case there are explicit motives and payoffs for the particular file organization chosen. It should be noted however, that in every case the purpose is to implement retrieval functions with efficiencies that can be associated with the particular retrieval requirements. In fact, in somewhat different terms, file organization is one of the bases for designating that a subset of the total data of the data base be treated as a file.

In this example there is an employee file, a history file, and a special indexing file leading from the history file back to the employee file. A condition for locating employee records in the employee file may be such that a specific form of file organization is required. The employee file may indeed point to records of the history file. In fact, the natural utilization of this approach is to associate an employee history record with the current employee record in his employee file via structure data in the employee record. However, our requirements for retrieving records in the history file may indeed vary to the extent that the organization of this file must be implicitly different from the organization of the employee file. Furthermore, if we are able, as the example suggests, to go through an indexing file that leads us back to other employee records as a function of a particular historical reference, this indexing file must be specifically organized to search a large table. Thus, the table becomes its own separate file with its own specific organization.

DATA MANAGEMENT FUNCTIONS

The preceding elements of the data base system are passive, or, as in the case of file organization, are essentially conceptual. Data management functions, however, represent all of the actions taken by the system in order to translate from query specification to access point, to develop the logic of the file organization, and to retrieve specified records from the data base for delivery to the user. Three general types of functions in the set of functions associated with data management are required: record storage, record retrieval, and space management.

There are only three ways to accomplish physical storage of a record. The first is sequentially, the second randomly, and the third with an arbitrary, but not random, distribution. Records are sequentially placed in their physical device when they have been sorted on the basis of the values of specified data, usually index data, and then placed into the device in this order. Records are placed at random when their position in the device is determined by a randomizing function. This is a mathematical function which transforms the value of a specified key into a position in the data base device. The quality of the randomizing is of course determined according to statistical principles of randomness testing, or uniformity of record distribution over the allocated storage space. The third and final method for physical record storage is into arbitrary positions of the storage device, however, not according to the dictates of a randomizing function. Such storage positions are generally selected at the convenience of the system and are generally employed where variable length records are in use. In such a case, a list of memory "holes" is maintained by the system. Record storage space is then allocated from this list based on criteria associated with the size of the storage space required by the records.

Record retrieval falls into three major categories usually referred to as indexing techniques: spatial indexing, calculated indexing, and tabular indexing. Generally they correspond to the three types of record storage described earlier.

Any indexing technique that makes use of sorted order among a set of sequenced records is said to be a spatial indexing technique. The characteristic example of spatial indexing is binary searching. Calculated indexing is the retrieval oriented terminology used synonymously with randomizing, or placement oriented. Thus, the calculated indexing functions like the randomizing function maps given key values into positions in the storage space of the data base. Tabular indexing, as its name suggests, is a tabulation of record positions in the storage space and contains structure data, or pointers, leading from the table to the records themselves.

These three indexing techniques may be used in various combinations, and it may be said that any particular indexing technique is some concatenation of these three.

The programs required to operate these indexing techniques are considered to be part of the data management functions. Data management also must contain programs for operation of the file organization developed for the files. Thus, if a specific file is referenced having a partially inverted structure, it is necessary for the data management functions to supply the required programs for stepping from record to record, and for making the necessary evaluations suited to determining whether a record is to be delivered to the user, or passed by in continuation of the search.

When records are placed either sequentially or arbitrarily, it is necessary to supply data management functions designed to maintain physical organization within the storage device. In sequential placement, new records must be organized at least logically to satisfy the sequencing requirements. At some point, of course, it may become necessary to reorganize the entire file in its storage space so that the physical sequential property of the file is preserved.

In the case of arbitrarily placed records it is necessary for data management functions to keep track of the available storage space. That is, the data management functions must develop a storage map if its storage functions are to be properly carried out.

For variable length records, the introduction and deletion of such records leaves variable length holes throughout the storage area. This will ultimately lead to fragmentation, i.e., areas too small to serve for storage and as a consequence cause the data management function to reorganize the records currently in storage.

DESIGN QUESTIONS

The organization, design and implementation of a data base system begins with questions concerned with the problem toward which the implemented system is to be oriented. For discussion purposes, this can be related to four general questions that must be successfully answered if the data base system is to be achieved.

What information must be stored? That is, what content must

appear in the records of the data base. This involves further questions associated with the services that the data base system is to supply.

How will this information be retrieved in response to queries? How will these retrieval requests be formulated, or more generally, what will be the structure of the query language.

The third question is related to cross references that must exist between the information in the various files of the data base. This is the structure data that will appear in the records and which, by its presence, will implement the file organizations designed for particular files.

Finally, we must ask how this information should be stored. We must design our records in terms of fields, determining lengths for these fields, whether or not they will be variable, and their order within the record.

The net result of the analysis of these design questions will be a clear cut approach to the system's design. We will determine the total data of the problem, break this data into subsets which are to be treated as individual files, organize these files, determine the data to appear in each of their records, specify the query language and consequently the nature of the query programs required for making reference to the data. Finally, with these results in hand, we are able to give consideration to the necessary routines for implementing these elements of the data management functions of our data base system. We turn now to a more detailed investigation of the data gathering process.

SERVICE ANALYSIS

An effective formal mechanism for determining the data of a data base system problem is by means of the so-called service analysis. In simplest terms this means determining what services the data base system will perform for its clients. In closer analysis, however, this also means determining who the customers are. For the purpose of discussion, we can divide the clients of the data base system into three groups. These are the customers of the business, the management of the business, and the computer system itself. For each of these we may assume that the data base system will supply certain services.

In asking the service questions, client-category by client-category, we might relate them to three other questions fundamental to the data gathering process. What data objects are available to the clients? What functions must the data base system perform on them? And what are the information availability requirements? Let us consider these questions in the light of a simple example.

Suppose that our data base system is to serve as the operational element in an inventory control environment for a warehousing function. The data base system must manage data concerned with the inventory of items in stock, and inventory of orders from customers. It must also provide information to management concerning not only financial questions regarding the customers, but information regarding the inventory as well. We begin with the customer services.

The data object of explicit interest to the customer is the order. That is, the customer is represented in the data base system by his current orders, and in our service analysis we may discover that the functions to be supplied on these data objects are order verification, history by shipping date, order cancellation, and order receipt. Let us further suppose that our analysis of customer services shows that verification, and the histories by ordering and shipping dates, are questions from customers which are to be answered by the system over the telephone. The information availability requirements for these services represented by the data objects and the functions on them are relatively stringent. We may assume for this example that functions associated with order cancellation create information whose availability requirement would be less than, say 24 hours, and similarly for the receipt of a new order.

Suppose management requires individual financial data on each of its customers, a customer listing in alphabetical order, and a listing in order of decreasing outstandings. We might also assume that an inventory cost summary on currently ordered items of the inventory is also required, as well as a periodic update of the inventory itself in manual or printed form.

The first of these management services involves financial data objects and, depending on the format of the report to management, will imply functions that must be carried out on these data objects. Customer listings in alphabetical order, and in order of decreasing outstandings already implies not only the data object involved but also the nature of the functions to be carried out. We may presume in each of these cases that management's requirements for the availability of this information is, say one hour from request.

For the inventory cost summary on current order items, we are involved with data objects that can join both items on order and the total value of these items. The availability requirements for this information by management might be taken as forty-eight hours.

If a printed listing of the inventory is required in update format, the data object involved is the inventory item, and the listing function is implied. It only remains to determine management's availability requirement for the updated inventory.

If the system is to carry out the various services and functions implied by the analysis thus far, it very likely will require certain specific data to make these operations feasible. For example, we might identify as the data objects for system services, new customers and additional orders for current customers. The data items are customers and orders, and the information availability requirements might be taken as overnight, thereby making them compatible with other general updating processes for the inventory file. A third system service might be associated with the purging of received orders. In this case the data objects are orders; and date of receipt, and the availability requirements might be thirty days.

FILE DETERMINATION

The purpose of the general service analysis is to determine the total data, or information of the problem.

This total volume of data now must be viewed with the objective of splitting it into smaller sub-units that can be handled relatively independently of each other. Suppose that from the total data of our problem certain subsets appear to be associated with a high frequency of reference. This situation calls for determining independent data subsets.

Another criterion might be common functions required on respective data objects. For example, where a certain collection of the total data is to receive logically sequential processing, with the sequencing based on specified keys and their key values. It becomes an especially strong criterion where the data objects so associated have a roughly equivalent frequency of access as well.

The third criterion for segregating the totality of data to be associated with a data base might be referred to as probability of modification. That is, if the data base system provides for a data edit mode, special techniques very likely involving particular file organizations will have to be established for its efficient execution. Data objects with such requirements in common then may well be considered as candidates for conjoining into associated data sets within the data base.

The purpose of organizing or splitting the total data of the problem along lines described above is to determine subsets of this data that may then be considered as the basis for the organization of files. These subsets can be treated relatively independently, and consequently their file organizations, as logical structures, can be independently designed as well. If there is to be interaction, or interrelationship between data elements of such independent files, it can be achieved by means of structure data within the respective records that point across the file boundaries to the associated records.

Analysis of the data base problem in system terms provides us with an organization of the subject into four major topics which can then be considered more or less independently. In the design process however, there is a point at which independent considerations must conjoin to produce an implementable result. This requires that the data of the problem be carefully developed along the lines commensurate with the system design process. It is toward this objective that the service analysis has been organized. With this accomplished we can then view the design process as a set of six explicit steps which must be taken to achieve the final result.

Step 1—Data Splitting

Given the total information of the problem, or rather the set of data that represents this information, it is necessary to separate it into subsets which can be dealt with more or less independently. Each of these subsets of the total data can then be given consideration as an independent file of the data base, with specific data in the records and specific structure for them.

Step 2—Record Design

For each of the data subsets determined in step one, we must now consider the question of record design—in essence, determining the format of content to appear in the record and deciding on the modes of indexing so as to establish the index data that must be present. Finally, inter-relationships between content will decide what structure data must be included.

Step 3—Volume Analysis

Once the record design has been completed, estimates must be made of individual record sizes and then of expected file sizes. For fixed length records, the question reduces to total number of records expected in the file. For variable length records, estimates of field length and total number of fields must be made as well. The physical distribution of the number of records in each file must then be taken into account, since each of the distribution methods will generally require that some amount of excess storage capacity be made available for the file in order to satisfy space management requirements. The net result will then be an estimate of the storage requirements for each file, and of the total requirements for all files. From these estimates it can then be determined whether or not there is sufficient storage capacity in the system. If sizing adjustments have to be made, then attention should be turned to those files having the largest requirement.

Step 4—Activity Analysis

Using the data developed, giving frequency of reference and for determining the information availability requirements, estimates of the total activity for records of each file must be made. Such estimates are in terms of total number of references per unit time, and should be broken down into storage, retrieval, and update categories. It is this activity analysis which is essential to the question of file design.

Step 5—File Design

The choice of file organization is dependent upon record structure, physical distribution of the records in the storage device, and the indexing method employed for making the initial reference. To some degree, the amount of storage space available will influence the file design as well. The critical issue for file design then becomes the efficiency of its performance. This must be established in terms of record storage, record retrieval, and management of the available storage space.

Step 6—Data Management Specification

Once the various conceptual entities of the data base system have been established, it is necessary to develop a specification for the several programs that will implement them. These are the data management functions, and they must accomplish storage, retrieval, and general space management. In addition, they must provide programs for indexing, editing, update, data base security, and data base recovery. In many environments user access to the data base system is via telecommunications packages, and it may then be an important aspect of the data management functions to establish the necessary formal interfaces for data receipt and transmission.

Each of the six design steps outlined above should be considered in the context of the four elements of the data base system. Record design, for example, involves data requirements and should reference the query specification and indexing techniques to be employed. Record design is also concerned with the file organization and with potential data management function design. The same is true for all of the other design steps. The problem of data base system design, although describable in step-by-step analytical form, must be carried out as a set of composite steps taken concurrently—an organized approach to successful implementation.

≡≡ 21.

DATA BASE: A NEW STANDARD FOR INSURANCE EDP

By George Schussel

Editor's Note: From BEST'S REVIEW, PROP-
ERTY/LIABILITY INSURANCE EDITION, October 1972, pp. 26–30, 86–92. Reprinted by permission of the publisher, A. M. Best Co., and author.

A new concept for business data processing is achieving significant acceptance by computer manufacturers and major users of computer systems. This new technique uses standard "data management
systems" (DMS) software packages to implement business data processing on a "data base" (DB).

Current estimates put the number of DMS users at approximately 500 nationally. DMS availability holds promise for reducing
long-term costs of data processing and increasing the capabilities of
the business programmer by automating many of the functions now
performed manually. The data base concept has developed over the
last decade to the point where it can be implemented practically by
most medium- and large-scale users of data processing equipment. The
1960's saw the COBOL programming language emerge as a standard
for business applications; the 1970's will see data base enhancements to
COBOL enabling this new combination to become the standard procedure for implementing business data processing systems.

DB has existed for about five years, but is only today beginning
to gain widespread acceptance by the data processing user community. The DB concept involves software packages (data management
systems—DMS) that remove many of the functions of the business
programmer from his direct control and vest those functions in the

DMS package. The package standardizes all information for the systems application while supplying it to the programmer in a more readily retrievable form.

Historically, business data processing files have been oriented toward storing information on tape. Each application had its own master file containing its own information. This file contained data which typically was repeated on numerous other master files, depending on needs.

The whole DB concept stands in stark contrast to this. It says in effect, "Let us put all our eggs in one basket; instead of storing identical information in different places, we'll put it all in one place and everyone will know where it is and how to get it; it will be on an accessible piece of equipment and we'll control updating."

MORE PROGRAMS AVAILABLE

With DMS processing on a DB, many of the transactions entering the DB will evolve in much the same way as they are currently developed from paper to keypunching and batching. However, other transactions and inquiries will be coming through more immediate on-line techniques such as by local terminals, by communications with other computer systems or remote users, or by computer-assisted instantaneous monitoring of transactions (such as point-of-sale monitoring of the checkout register at a retail store). Located on disc storage and available in thousandths of a second are the programs required to process the input and the master files against which input will be processed. As data enters the computer, the computer analyzes it and decides what program(s) is needed for proper processing. This program is called into the primary memory from the disc and activated. As the program proceeds, it will require certain data off the master file. Although the entire master file exists on discs, typically only a small portion of it is required to prepare printed reports, respond to an inquiry, or be updated. In these cases, only needed pieces of DB information are entered into the primary memory, updated, and returned to the disc.

There are two ways to communicate with other systems. Either the input data is kept in the computer and other application programs are brought in and use the same information; or intermediate storage files—either on the disc or on tape—are created which subsequently serve as the input for updating the other systems.

INSTANT RESPONSES

The output from the data base oriented computer is often similar to current output—exception or general printed output reports. In addition, however, the on-line characteristics provided by the DMS enable some response to queries to be provided directly to teletypewriter or cathode ray tube terminals with only seconds delay between the time the inquiry is initiated and the answer received.

Companies now using time-sharing or interactive man-computer systems already appreciate some of the advantages of the DB approach. These interactive systems permit input and response from inquiry terminals (or through the use of communications) in the same way that DMS do. However, the interactive system is only half the answer, since typically the data required for a particular application requires special loading onto a disc. If it is already there, it is not interfaced with other applications for uniform use and updating by several systems. In other words, the DB approach typically will replace several master file updates with one. The simple on-line interactive computer system still leaves all of the problems of updating files that may use similar information independently.

Recent Developments

The advent of the large-scale disc drive, with its 100 million character capacity in one removable disc pack, was the engineering breakthrough which made practical the DB concept. It is now possible to retain up to several billion characters on line to a computer at any one time, and summon any piece of that information in less than one-tenth of a second.

The concept of a total DB on a direct-access device such as a disc drive is not new. Initial approaches were tried with smaller, slower discs and second generation computers 10 years ago. These approaches were not widely adopted because they didn't use standard programming packages—DMS—which do much of the tedious yet necessary programming housekeeping. These packages sell or lease for a small fraction of the cost of writing such a system.

CHOICE OF SEVERAL

Several DMS packages are available in today's market. The three best known are

• Information Management System (IMS and IMS-II), developed by IBM for its 360 and 370 lines of computers.

• Integrated Data Store (IDS), developed by General Electric —now Honeywell—and now available on the Honeywell 6000 series of equipment.

•TOTAL, marketed by Cincom Systems of Cincinnati and available for several computers, including the RCA Spectra 70 (now UNIVAC) line, the Honeywell 200 series and the IBM 360 and 370 series.

DMS in the Insurance Industry

Until recently the insurance industry lagged significantly behind many other users in adopting DMS for systems developments. Within the last two years, however, many companies have taken the step, acquired a DMS, and have either completed development or are in the process of installing systems using a DMS. Below is a list of some insurance companies currently using data management systems:

Aetna Life & Casualty
Allendale Mutual
Employers of Wausau
Factory Mutual Engineering
Federated Mutual
Home
INA
John Hancock
Liberty Mutual
Massachusetts Blue Cross
Northwestern Mutual Life
Hartford
Travelers

Since DMS have been widely available since about 1968, an interesting question is why only a relatively small number of insurance companies have moved to use these systems. I think the answer is threefold.

The first DMS was IBM's Bill of Material Processor (BOMP). It was not really sold or intended to be a pure DMS for information processing. BOMP provides a parts explosion and has been extensively used in manufacturing industries. It was only after this program was already being widely used that it became obvious that the inherent logic of the system also lent itself to generalized processing of all types of information. Because BOMP was oriented toward manufacturing industries, financial institutions such as insurance companies were late in being exposed to the idea by potential vendors.

The second major reason why insurance users have lagged in developing DMS applications is that most major life and property/liability companies became heavy users of data processing in the early 1960's when tape oriented sequential master files were the computing industry's standard. Having made substantial investments in now outmoded computer systems, these companies naturally have moved slowly and carefully in actively embracing the new random disc file design philosophies.

GIGANTIC DATA FILES

The third reason that insurance companies only recently have begun to move in the DB direction is that the size of insurance information files is typically enormous—substantially larger on average than is true for manufacturing. Extremely large files cause concern because the cost of storing information in on-line discs is much more expensive than using tapes for secondary storage. However, in 1970 with the announcement of the IBM 370 line of computers (and competitive systems such as the Honeywell 6000 series), new large disc files became available with storage capacities three times greater, access time twice as fast, and costs per character stored less than half of the prior-to-1970 standard disc files. This triple combination improvement in disc hardware technology finally made insurance companies, whose need for storage runs in the order of billions of characters of information, sit up and take notice as many applications became truly feasible and economical to implement.

Data Base Characteristics

The first important point in the DB approach is that the corporate DB represents all pertinent information that might be correlated and cross referenced. This totality can be defined in several ways. For example, the operation of a typical insurance company may be split into two parts: the larger is the actual insurance operation, involving premium collection, claim processing and payment, accounting and controls, and administration, including payment of expenses; the smaller segment concerns investing premiums to provide a steady income and capital appreciation. If the operation of these two areas is clearly segregated, there may be no need to correlate investment information with insurance results (except, of course, in the annual statement where all results are gathered—usually manually). In this environment, investment information should dwell in a separate DB.

COMMON DEFINITIONS NEEDED

An important part of creating the DB is that creators and users must agree on a common set of definitions for all information in the DB. This is not as easy as it might seem. Examination of data definitions in almost any medium- to large-scale user of data processing quickly exposes three classic problems:

(1) *Synonyms:* identical items of data called by different names in different applications.

(2) *Alternate Definitions:* different systems using the same name to describe different pieces of data.

(3) *Close Definitions:* two different names used to describe different pieces of data which have such similar definitions that there should be only one name and one definition.

To derive the advantages of DB, the corporate user must be willing to surrender his own definitions in order to live with a common set acceptable to all. The designers first must develop a complete dictionary of definitions; obtain support of the users for these definitions; keep it current, and enforce it for new applications. The dictionary needn't be particularly sophisticated. For example, it doesn't have to be on-line in a computer. It can be nothing more than a loose-leaf binder with all of the data items used listed alphabetically and carefully defined.

The next essential characteristic of the DB is that it resides on a secondary storage device—usually a disc drive. (Primary memory is the very fast, expensive magnetic core or integrated circuits.) The disc drive or other device used for a DB permits quick access to all data. This contrasts with tape or card storage. It could take a computer 150 times longer to locate a piece of data nearer the end of a tape reel than the beginning. It is through this pseudo-random ability to access data that the DMS may retrieve data swiftly and in desired sequence.

ALLOWS ON-LINE ACCESS

Another basic characteristic of the DB is that it can be interrogated by on-line terminals, usually cathode ray tube, TV-like devices. While not all DB systems have this feature, the trend toward DB allows for useful exception reporting, and the most efficient approach to getting this is through the use of inquiry and on-line terminals.

Most of the leaders in DB development and marketing who don't presently have on-line features for their systems have announced or are planning to announce support for on-line and terminal access.

Most DMS may be implemented as extensions to one of the common languages used in business programming. Typically, this language is COBOL, the universal standard language for business. Not all DMS are COBOL extensions, however; a couple have provided a new language as a complete replacement for COBOL. Nonetheless, this approach is not as generally useful or as powerful as the basic COBOL language extended through DMS facilities.

Finally, users from different departments and through different application programs will be using one common DB. This concept has several important implications for the company electing this approach. Two of these—common data definitions and the data element dictionary—have been discussed. A third is the need for a totally new job—the data base administrator.

Data Base Administrator

The DB approach is data or information oriented, as opposed to most current business data processing which is application oriented and treats data as an adjunct to programs implementing that application. Now the definition and creation of the corporate DB is primary while the various application programs are secondary. These programs select needed data and operate against the common total DB. This stresses the importance of information and the way it is created, maintained, defined and handled. Many DB systems benefits result from requirements placed on the systems department for the establishment and maintenance of the total DB.

BROAD RESPONSIBILITIES

The data administrator's job resolves into two broad areas. First is creation of the DB. Until the first run, this may be a full-time job. But even after the first few applications are running, development remains a continuing job as new data elements enter the business stream while old ones are being culled. The second part of the administrator's job is, logically enough, administration. He is responsible for the control and usefulness of the DB and as such has an ongoing administrative responsibility. During the DB creation the administrator must relate with various users to develop his data element dictionary and win concurrence on definitions.

He must also structure relationships among different data within the DB, describing how one piece of information is related to or belongs to another.

SECURITY IMPORTANT

Once the DB is established, the administrator is responsible for maintaining its security, and developing procedures for recovery from disaster. With all corporate information eggs in one basket, it is extremely important to prevent unauthorized or improper access to the DB.

Through DMS tools, statistics on data usage, frequency of access and total volume are readily available. By carefully monitoring these statistics, the administrator can optimize the data locations on different peripheral devices and suggest new definitions or the elimination of unused information. The data base administrator position is of key importance to the data processing department and the entire corporation. Depending upon the organization of the data processing department, he can report either to the manager of all data processing or to the manager of systems design and programming. Any point lower within the systems organization will not give sufficient visibility to the importance of this function.

Advantages of the Data Base Approach

The primary reason for adopting a DB is to realize significant savings in programming and de-bugging time in the development of new business applications. The few studies that have appeared on this subject show that once the DB has been established, implementing comparable programs by comparably trained programmers can be two to four times faster than with the COBOL programmer who must develop his own master files. Since the cost of the hardware in most large data processing departments has dropped below 50% of the EDP budget, and in many cases to 25% of the budget, any approach which saves on labor costs can provide highly persuasive cost justification.

MORE EFFICIENT, PRODUCTIVE

A second important reason is the efficiency in data storage and nonredundancy that result from clustering all data in one file. Also, when the information is in one file it can be more easily updated and accessed, and is therefore more reliable.

The ease of developing new applications once a DB has been perfected is also significant. Probably the hardest part of business data processing is building and maintaining the master files. By removing much of this task from the programmer, the systems shop can use less experienced programmers and become productive more quickly under the DB environment.

One of the DB advantages most apparent to top management is that it enables one-time-only programs for decision-making or operations research to be written economically and processed against data already resident in the corporate DB. Currently, such programs are either impossible to implement or prohibitively costly and time-consuming because they require centralization of numerous tape files. It is, of course, this very sort of one-shot, decision-making information that is one of the most valuable products of a data processing department.

Problems with the Approach

Currently, the first and probably thorniest problem is that DB is considered conceptually advanced and there is a concomitant lack of well-trained people to implement it. Time will overcome this. Training is readily available, from computer manufacturers, software vendors and management firms specializing in executive and technical seminars. Already several hundred applications have been implemented and some knowledgeable people are available.

LARGER MEMORY BANKS

A second DB problem is that we are withdrawing from the programmer functions he once performed and delegating them to the integrated hardware/DMS system. By doing so, we create a need for computers with larger memories and greater processing power. Most DB users have been of a size that can afford powerful computer systems. This will likely remain true until after 1975, when new computer capabilities may depress the overhead cost to a level acceptable to smaller users.

Another problem (and associated opportunity) related to DB is that rarely are a company's existing systems merely converted onto a DB. The enlightened company will use the conversion as a complete redesign springboard for systems to be changed and in so doing develop a more versatile product. For example, it will generate exception reports instead of grinding out massive stacks of paper for inquiry use. One requirement for a redesign is a total commitment in terms of money and time; after all, we're talking about systems that may have had a 10-year genesis. They will not be replaced quickly or easily even with tools such as DB.

Along with the fact that the new system may not be just a simple conversion of the old but, in fact, new and different comes the concomitant problem of inability to use parallel runs—those computer runs which can be computer compared old to new to see if there are errors in the new system. This means that the output from the new DB approach will have to be visually examined, a much more laborious process than is involved in many standard system conversions. While DB technology permits more junior programmers to became more productive sooner, the other side of the coin is the requirement for expertise in systems programmers. These are the people who maintain the computer's operating system, and they are among the most highly skilled and paid data processing professionals. As is the case with operating systems, the introduction of DMS requires comparably skilled systems programmers to maintain data management software, and therefore an additional individual(s) with specialized expertise in this area.

RERUNS MORE COMPLEX

Malfunctions in computer hardware or software during the running of today's typical business applications call for reruns. Normally, the program is rewound to a check point or the beginning, the original master file and transaction file are loaded, and the run is regenerated. Even if a particular master file is destroyed, one can go back to the "father" tape—the original master from which the current master was created—and rerun a couple of times to make the system current. Under the DB approach several programs may be updating and accessing the DB at the same time, and the results of a malfunction in the hardware or software are not so easily cured. The primary technique for recovery in this situation involves continual journaling of transactions against the DB and the use of these lists to restore. Because of the large number of potential interactions, this procedure is more complex and requires more time than would be required under today's most common procedures.

TOTAL COMMITMENT

Finally, top management commitment is essential, initially and throughout the project. In a complete evaluation of the company's systems, quiet errors, previously undiscovered, will almost certainly come to light. Data processing and top management must be prepared to accept these as normal and take necessary steps to eliminate such errors in the new system design. Management commitment is also necessary because unfamiliar definitions may be generated whose use is mandatory to interface with the DB. Unless top management understands the objectives and is committed to the DB approach, one of the problems I have described will almost certainly lead to the premature death of the project.

Characteristics of Successful Companies

Some valuable lessons have been learned by comparing successful and unsuccessful DB approaches. For example, successful users have done the following:

Corporate Committee. A team of middle managers representing all major business functions was formed at the outset, sometimes during and sometimes after the preliminary feasibility study had been conducted by the data processing department. This team defined data and heard appeals regarding conflicts in approaches. *All* DB-related functions were represented on this team.

Logical Organization. The DB structure itself and the list of applications to be programmed against it were organized functionally: marketing, production, engineering, etc. Peculiarities of any individual organization because of specific individuals holding a job at one point in time were not accorded importance.

New Approach to Systems. The corporate committee, in concert with the data processing department, identified the decision-making process in the business and designed the system accordingly. In other words, current systems and their requirements were not accepted as the prototype for the new system. A more detailed investigation into information needs formed the basis for the DB system.

Dictionary Development. Early in the development, the DB data elements were defined and put in dictionary format. Often it was at this stage that the relationship among the data elements was firmed up. The analysis of this data also was structured to eliminate duplication and redundancy and to develop standardization.

Data Administrator Control. A system for data control, usually managed by the data administrator, was set up and implemented before system activation.

Phased Implementation. Finally, a schedule was developed for phased implementation of reports and information out of the DB system. While overall implementation may have been lengthy, products were identified which could be successfully delivered at early points and were made available as soon as possible throughout the development cycle of the new DB system.

Conclusion

Acceptance by the user community based on technical progress in hardware and computer software shows that the concept of DB implementation through DMS will become the standard for implementing business oriented data processing during the 1970's. For management, this means three things:

(1) Start to Investigate Now. Companies with medium to large data processing efforts should begin at once to relate the DB approach to their own information system.

(2) Recognize Importance of Basic Data. If you decide on DB, your data processing department organization will have to be changed to recognize the importance and thereby control the data used by systems. As a result, in addition to emphasizing application programs, the data processing department must search more deeply into the information needs of the firm than it did with past applications.

(3) Obtain Commitment to a Controlled Environment. Top management commitment will be needed to resolve disputes among users. It must be recognized ahead of time that some preferred definitions must be sacrificed to assure commonality in the systems language. These common definitions, in fact, are only one aspect of the more controlled environment of the DB approach. Individual users and "hotshot" programmers will have to surrender some of their specialties. This more controlled environment will provide the standards necessary for more cost effective management information systems.

22.

THE WESTERN ELECTRIC CORPORATE DATA POOL

By Samuel R. Shugar

Editor's Note: From WESTERN ELECTRIC EN-
GINEER, 1971, pp. 52–57. Reprinted by permission
of the publisher, Western Electric Company, and
author.

BACKGROUND—THE WESTERN ELECTRIC INFORMATION SYSTEM

Today's expanding technology is resulting in an explosion of information and an urgent demand for a means by which this information can be controlled and presented for use in the decision-making
processes. Throughout industry, the collection, manipulation, retrieval,
and presentation of information, and the decision-making operations
using this information have resulted in the growth of very large
and complicated information systems.[1] Frequently, this is a de facto
growth situation. In some cases, serious attempts are being made to
provide some order to the establishment and growth of information
systems. The Western Electric Company is among those companies
who are attempting to provide guidelines within which the orderly
growth of information processing can proceed.

Information processing in the Western Electric Company is an
operation involving over 30 major computer centers with more than

[1] One definition of a system is, "A system (information or otherwise) is a collection of elements or functions which are unified or structured in order to achieve
some specific objective." See W. A. Welsh, "Engineering An Information System,"
Western Electric Information System Engineering Document No. 100001. February 14, 1967.

35 satellite centers using approximately 130 computers of various models and manufacturers. A concern for the optimum use of this computer complex, for the most effective interaction between men and machines, caused Western Electric to establish the Information Systems Engineering (ISE) organization in 1965 with a charter to provide a methodology and appropriate aids for the efficient design, development, and utilization of information systems.

The objectives were to develop a set of system design standards and procedures which would:

1. Reduce design and development costs of new information systems.
2. Provide a framework which would:
   (a) Insure that new information systems could be integrated into and be compatible with the total corporate information system,
   (b) Insure the development of systems whose expected life spans are substantially greater than the life spans of present systems,
   (c) Insure the development of flexible systems which would meet the needs of diverse situations and be transferable from one location to another.

ISE began its task by studying the decision-making activities which take place within the company and the data required by these activities in their operation. Then, ISE engineered and defined a series of standard modules or *functions* [2] which in total describe the decision-making activities found in today's man-machine Western Electric Company information system. These functions define mutually exclusive groups of decision-making operations. Each function provides a fixed boundary and a clearly defined interface such that it can be grouped with other functions to completely describe the operations which take place within virtually any information system (regardless of complexity). The functions represent a standard system design language which can enhance user-designer and designer-developer communication and minimize redundant and incomplete design and development effort.

Just as an effective outline assists in the organization and subsequent development of a book, the functions provide guidance in the

[2] A partial list of functions includes *Develop Labor Hours, Analyze Attendance, Compute Payroll, Forecast Requirements, Determine Safety Requirements, Determine Net Requirements, Determine Procedures, Establish Time Values, Determine Physical Design.* About 45 functions have been defined thus far.

description of problem elements within an information system which are solved by the system design. When problems are described and the related information systems are designed in terms of these standard functions, an orderly and somewhat-sequential discipline is afforded the user which minimizes incomplete design and development effort. Perhaps, not all of the operations described by the functions apply to a particular problem being solved. But, the use of the functions provides that no aspect of the problem will have been overlooked. Also, this use of the functions in the design and documentation of information systems makes it easier to identify and understand systems which have been developed, thus reducing the potential for redoing work that cannot be recognized.

In specifying the functions, ISE identified and defined the data components which were required to support the activities contained within the function boundary. The data required by the functions was integrated into a single logical data structure which was named the Western Electric Corporate Data Pool (CDP).

The functions and their associated data provide a set of system design standards, a framework, *within which information systems are to be designed, developed, and implemented.*

In addition to these design standards, the ISE organization developed tools to facilitate the use of the standards in the system design process and to provide for more effective communication between the users, designers and developers of systems. These tools include *Configurator Diagrams,* commonly called *Configurators,* which assist in identifying the functions which are contained within the system being designed; and *Problem Descriptions* which provide detailed documentation on the specific problem which must be solved for each function identified.

This set of design standards and the tools for their use are described and/or referenced in Corporate Instruction 51.204, "Information System Design, Development and Implementation." Collectively, these elements provide an approach (a discipline) and the procedures for designing and developing information systems within an engineered framework called the Western Electric Information System (W.E.I.S.).

The CDP is an integral part of the W.E.I.S. and serves as the single integrated structure for the data which is required to support the activities within the W.E.I.S. The article on the facing page describes the Western Electric CDP, its concepts, development and use.

THE CORPORATE DATA POOL

The Western Electric Corporate Data Pool (CDP) performs an important and critical role in the design, development, and implementation of information systems within the Western Electric Company. The purpose of this paper is to explain what the CDP is, why it exists, and how it is used in the Western Electric Information System (W.E.I.S.—see Background section). But first, some comments on the *common data base* concept are in order.

The common data base is a single repository for all machine readable information which supports the operation of a computer location (data center). As such, it tends to eliminate redundancy in capturing, converting, and storing data. Because of these advantages the current trend in the design of information systems is toward the construction and the use of common data bases. But, problems have arisen in the implementation of common data bases concerning:

1. What data is required.
2. How the data is to be identified and defined.

These problems are being solved in the W.E.I.S. with the development of the CDP and the application of the CDP to the development of information systems.

Figure 22.1 shows the evolution of the common data base concept from the autonomous file period where every application constructed and maintained its own files of data (with attendant redundancies

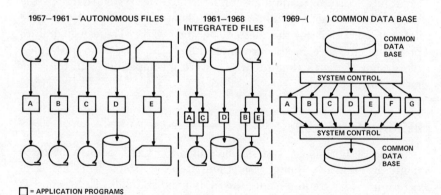

□ = APPLICATION PROGRAMS

22.1   THE EVOLUTION OF THE COMMON DATA BASE CONCEPT FROM THE TIMES WHEN AUTONOMOUS FILES AND INTEGRATED FILES WERE USED

and duplications); through the integrated file period where an attempt was made to have applications share appropriate files; and, finally, to the common data base concept where, through a common data management system (shown as System Control), the system data is made available to authorized users.

The relationship between common data bases and the CDP needs further clarification. The CDP is not designed to be physically implemented as a common data base would be. The major role of the CDP is to provide a standard data language capable of supporting the decision-making activities performed in the company, and to be an integrated structural framework and directory from which local common data bases throughout the company can be developed and physically implemented. The CDP is, therefore, similar to the hardware configurators provided by computer equipment manufacturers. These hardware configurators identify all permissible logical component interconnections. The user who wishes to install a physical system to fulfill his unique requirements selects components from the configurator within the logical constraints specified on the configurator. Similarly, the CDP defines all data components having multi-location (corporate) significance and specifies their logical interrelationships. Using the CDP, common data base developers at each computer location will select the logical subset of data components required to support the decision-making activities at the location and proceed with the physical design and implementation of their common data base.

The common data base concept implies a data management capability to store, manipulate, and retrieve the system data. In the W.E.I.S. the design capabilities for the data management system were determined prior to the design of the CDP. These capabilities provided guidance in the development of the CDP and prevented the design of data structures which were incompatible with the data management system.

DESIGN OF THE CDP

The design of any system, including the CDP, consists of three mutually exclusive, though sometimes iterative, steps. The first is to determine what requirements the system must fulfill. The second is to determine the logical design necessary to meet the requirements. The third is to determine an effective physical design to carry out the logical design. The concern here is for the application of the first two steps to the specification and design of the CDP.

First, it was decided that the CDP would provide a standard data language and a logically related, integrated data structure to support the company's decision-making activities whether performed by man or machine. The CDP was also to contain the data necessary to carry the decision-making processes to their conclusions (e.g., names of personnel for inclusion on paychecks would be required).

ISE viewed the CDP as a directory which should provide:

1. Company-wide compatibility of data by eliminating different names for identical data and specifying the logical relationships among data components.
2. A reduction of the physical storage requirements for data by eliminating redundant storage of identical data.

With an effective data management capability and with local common data bases created within the CDP framework, the user was to gain the ability to capture data at its source while minimizing or eliminating the effort and expense of data re-creation and conversion. Also, the CDP was to provide a foundation for the design of local common data bases. Since the data would be mutually compatible the translation of system data between locations would be eliminated.

The logical design of the CDP entails naming and identifying all the data components to be included in the CDP, in accordance with consistent guidelines. The design also requires that each component's logical context be identified; i.e., how the component relates to other CDP components.

One particular name is used whenever a data component is referenced. Data names are selected to be used by people as they place inquiries on the data base and by programs as they read data from and write data to the data base. This standard data language helps to break down current communication barriers; to eliminate many programs now used to translate data as it passes from one data base to another; and to reduce the redundant storage of identical information within a local common data base.

THE STRUCTURE OF THE CDP

A segmentation arrangement was developed for the CDP to assist in classifying and cataloguing the data required to support the functions. Record sets, files and fields (in the hierarchical sequence) were defined as the basic components of the CDP.

Record sets are the highest level data nodes possible in the CDP. They might be related to today's master files. However, there is a major difference in the approach taken to their definition. Typically, master files are segmented along application or organization lines; e.g., Cost Accounting Master, Production Scheduling Master, or Employee Master. Since each master file is designed to support a specific application within a location, much identical data is stored redundantly at a location. Also, master files defined in this manner are inherently unstable. Organizations change in scope and objectives, and applications, such as payroll, have little consistency in definition. Record sets were designed to be more stable and to be more universally applicable than the typical master files.

Data [3] can be categorized by things; e.g., employees, product items, customers, and production units. These things provide a top level segmentation for the CDP which is quite stable. They also provide consistent guidelines for deciding upon the orientation of lower level data. Personnel and payroll deduction information are, for example, employee oriented while accounting, standard cost and production control data are product item oriented. Approximately 30 such record sets [4] have been defined toward which all lower level data are oriented.

The next component in the hierarchical structure is the file. Files are defined as repeating sets of other data components. Files have unique names across the CDP. By definition, the first component (the primary key) in each repeating set is one which uniquely identifies one set of repeating components from another. Since files are allowed to contain other files, it is possible to construct multi-level structures to reflect complicated data relationships.

Fields are the lowest addressable component of data allowed in the CDP. Although a field usually consists of multiple characters, it may be defined as a single character or even a binary bit if

---

[3] The American National Standards Institute defines data as: ". . . any representation such as *characters* or *analog* quantities to which meaning might be assigned."

This rather generic definition can be further categorized by saying that data is made up of:
1. Symbols to denote "things" (e.g., customers or employees),
2. Symbols to describe attributes of these "things" (e.g., an employee's name, address, and telephone number), and
3. Symbols to relate one "thing" to other "things" (e.g., the organization to which an employee belongs or the facilities located in a customer's place of business).

[4] *Item, Resource Unit, Customer Facility, Employee, Circuit,* and *Organization* are names of some typical record sets.

required. By definition, field names must be unique within a file.

Two other types of components have been defined which can appear anywhere in the logical data hierarchy. The first is a "Component to be Defined Later." Occasionally, in structuring the CDP, the designers are unable to complete the logical structure. They know that, logically, more data belongs in a certain context, but they cannot uniquely define the data at the time. The Component to be Defined Later is used to denote the need for additional data and flag it for later action. Before the CDP construction is complete these special components must be translated into normal fields or files. An example might be "Organization Identification." Should two fields, "Location Identification" and "Organization Number," be used to define the component or should just an unique, arbitrarily assigned number be used.

The second special component is a "Component to be Defined Locally." Again, it is known that additional data is required, but it cannot be defined at the CDP level. This is a component that can only be uniquely defined at the (local) common data base level—since it can take on different meanings depending on the problem involved. An example might be the local "Production Data" required for clocking purposes. This component could consist of several fields including "Product Identification," "Product Quantity," and other related data.

THE INTERACTION OF THE W.E.I.S. FUNCTIONS AND THE CDP

The hierarchical structure of the CDP just described was set out as the objective structure for the CDP. As previously stated, it was first used in defining the data required to support the W.E.I.S. functions. A function can be viewed as a module which is really a data transformer. Data is taken in, operated on, and new or revised data is outputted. In the W.E.I.S. the data going into or out of a function is shown as logically structured collections of data components. Each collection is given an unique name. These collections of data components supporting the functions are called Named Data Segments (NDS).

Each function designer, in defining the function's data requirements, designs the logical structure of the NDS's in a way best suited for the independent operation of the function. The NDS's are defined with minimum regard for physical conditions (e.g., how the data is to be stored or what traffic the users of the data might expect in particular applications). This approach provides the system designer at the locations with the flexibility of using combinations of the W.E.I.S. functions in the design of a system and enables the local common data base designer to determine the optimum physical data base organization to support the particular function mix being implemented at his location.

The function designer or system designer is expected to use the existing version of the CDP as a starting point. He cannot arbitrarily define new components if the CDP already has components which match his need. He has to define the NDS's as logical subsets of the existing CDP. This rule is enforced unless the designer can convince the CDP Review Committee, that a second logical structure including already defined data components is essential.

The data required to support the functions (the NDS's) provides the raw material from which the CDP is built. The formal documentation of each function (a function specification) includes: a formal name and standard reference mnemonic for the NDS; an indication as to whether the NDS is input to or output from the function; the name of the record set to which the components of the NDS belong; and finally, two retrieval parameters for sequencing and bounding the data.

The sequencing parameters are used to arrange the data components of the NDS as they are delivered to the function by the data management system. Consider the following Named Data Segment:

```
–EMPLOYEE  NUMBER
–MALE/FEMALE  CODE
–RATE HISTORY  FILE
    –DATE OF RATE CHANGE
    –RATE
```

It might be desired to deliver sets of data values corresponding to this NDS in employee number ascending sequence with the rate history file in a sequence of oldest rate change first.

The data base will generally contain many sets of data values for each NDS. In the above example, there is one such set of values for each employee. It may be desired that only data values for a subset of employees be retrieved. By properly defining the bounding parameters, the data management system will deliver only those values which pass the qualification test(s); e.g., only data values for female employees who have had a rate increase during the previous month might be desired. All data components used for sequencing and bounding must be included as components of the NDS.

The documentation of each function also contains detailed information about each data component of an NDS, including the standard component name and its unique definition. Also provided are a code specifying what type of component it is (file, field, or one of the special components); codes specifying the origin or destination of the component (e.g., raw data, data from another function, or data for an output report); and an indicator to show the need for a corporate content standard (a reference to the standard, if one is available, is also provided).

STRUCTURING AND DOCUMENTING THE CDP

Figure 22.2 shows the procedure for merging NDS's into the CDP. The CDP Review Committee insists upon the design of an integrated logical data structure. Note the submission of data from sources outside of the ISE organization including:

1. Special company projects for which the decision-making functions have not been completed or which are simply information retrieval systems,
2. Inter-location system input/output messages which contain data components not already defined in the CDP; e.g., a supplier "Ship To" address which is not required for decision-making but must be included on a shipping ticket, and
3. Completed definitions of Components to be Defined Later.

Regardless of the source, the CDP Review Committee is the focal point for design approval. Via the committee and the procedures established to collect new information, the CDP is constantly updated to reflect solutions of current corporate problems.

The documentation for the CDP consists of a current work copy and a formal published version. Since all function design does not proceed at the same pace, an immediate means of documenting the current work copy of the CDP is required by the function designers of I.S.E. This is accomplished by use of magnetic cards on a metal wall. A color coding scheme for the cards is used to denote files, fields, and all other data components. Logical structure is shown by the level of indentedness of the cards on the wall (see Figure 22.3). The formal component names are visible and the component's "used

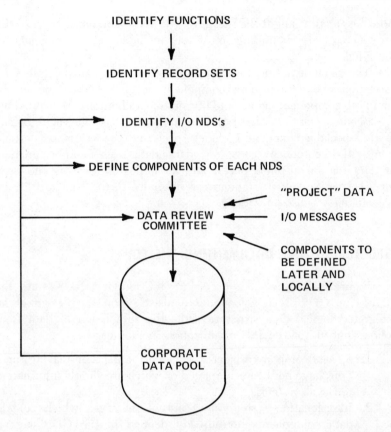

IDENTIFY FUNCTIONS

IDENTIFY RECORD SETS

IDENTIFY I/O NDS's

DEFINE COMPONENTS OF EACH NDS

DATA REVIEW COMMITTEE

"PROJECT" DATA

I/O MESSAGES

COMPONENTS TO BE DEFINED LATER AND LOCALLY

CORPORATE DATA POOL

22.2   THE PROCEDURES FOR INCORPORATING DATA COMPONENTS INTO THE CDP

on" list is documented on a portion of the card. The used on list identifies all NDS's of which the component is a part. This information aids in maintaining the CDP and the associated NDS's.

The CDP Review Committee meets in the room containing the wall display of the CDP. The display provides the committee with the CDP documentation it requires.

The formal documentation is produced mechanically from a CDP/NDS file system. Printouts of NDS's are generated and included as part of the appropriate function specifications. The printout includes all known information about the NDS and its components. In addition, a graphical representation of the NDS structure is provided. This representation, together with the NDS printout, completely documents an NDS.

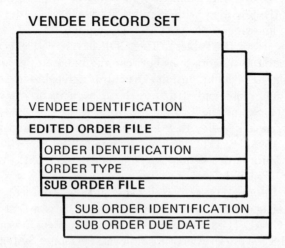

22.3 FILE CARDS ARE ARRANGED ON THE WALL TO DEPICT THE LOGICAL STRUCTURE OF THE CDP. PART OF THE VENDEE RECORD SET IS SHOWN

Similarly, the CDP (by record set) is periodically printed and distributed. In the printout, logical structure is shown by the degree of indentedness of the data components. Component names and their definitions are published along with any applicable data content standards. The list of component used on information is also printed. Included in the CDP documentation is a narrative resumé which describes the contents of each record set to help the reader determine where his area of interest lies.

RESULTS & CONCLUSIONS

Defining the contents of a common data base is not enough. The entire environment in which it exists must be considered if a common data base is to have value in information systems of the future. The Western Electric Information System has addressed this total environment. The Western Electric CDP provides the directory and logical data structure used in developing unique but compatible common data bases which support the design, development and implementation of integrated information systems throughout the company.

At Bell Laboratories in Holmdel an information system is being developed for the mechanized production of engineering information currently provided with equipment specification drawings. The system is known as CAMELOT (Computer Aided Mechanized Engineering Lists Or Tables). The CDP has served effectively as a reference point for negotiations between the Laboratories and Western to determine data definitions and structures agreeable to both parties. The data definitions and structures have been incorporated into the Item Record Set of the CDP.

At Merrimack Valley they have helped to define and are making use of the CAMELOT data incorporated into the CDP as they develop an information system which is an extension of the CAMELOT concept to a manufacturing environment.

Other information system design and development efforts are making similar use of the Western Electric CDP as a central point of reference. GRAD (Graphics Aided Drafting) is such an example.

WEEPS (Western Electric Employee Personnel System) is being developed by the Finance Division for the mechanization of personnel records. The CDP is being used in the design and development stages of WEEPS. When WEEPS is implemented in Headquarters, it will provide a major example of building a common data base using the CDP as a starting point.

Experiences with CAMELOT, GRAD, WEEPS and other systems indicate that the CDP can provide the singular reference point required for the development of unique, but compatible, common data bases throughout the company capable of supporting a corporate integrated information system.

ACKNOWLEDGMENT

The author acknowledges the extensive contributions of Mr. N. W. Nilson, Assistant Manager—Staff-Service Division, East who has provided many of the ideas which are contained in this paper, and the contributions of many members of the Information Systems Engineering organization.

REFERENCES

W. A. Welsh, "Engineering an Information System," *Western Electric ISE Document No. 100001*, February 14, 1967.

N. W. Nilson, "Features and Aspects of the Western Electric Information System," *ISE Document No. 100802*, May 19, 1967

S. R. Shugar, "The Logical Data Base," *Talk given at American Management Association Seminars* of March 12–14, 1969, May 26–28, 1969 and October 29–31, 1969.

Western Electric Information Systems Manual—Corporate Data Pool.

"Creating the Corporate Data Base," *EDP Analyzer,* February, 1970, Vol. 8, No. 2.

23.

BASIC CONCEPTS IN DATA BASE MANAGEMENT SYSTEMS

By Richard F. Schubert

The design and implementation of a data base management system is one of the most elusive and complicated projects in software development. The software graveyard is filled with data base management systems. These systems have all died by abandonment in quiet corners of software shops. Some data base management systems operating today are kept alive only by vendor executive edict and the zeal of marketing representatives. Today, there is a continual emergence of new data base management systems—many of which, like some ancient cities, are built on the rubble of previous devastations.

Data base management is currently a hotly debated subject, filled with controversy, emotion, and covert vendor manipulation. Many users and vendors who are not involved in the debate are nonetheless interested and concerned about the subject.

HOW DID WE GO WRONG?

The Conference on Data Systems Language (CODASYL) was organized in 1959 in response to the need for a common business oriented language (COBOL), designed to be independent of any current or future make or model of computer and which would reduce the cost of program creation, maintenance, transferability, and documentation. COBOL allowed the user to define data and procedures to exactly fulfill the processing requirements of an application. The original COBOL specification assumed serial processing of data, provided by existing magnetic tape technology which is an acceptable approach in many applications.

However, the implementation of more sophisticated business applications combined with the development of disc and drum technology showed the shortcomings of serial methods and emphasized the need for new methods of data storage and retrieval on direct access devices.

The onslaught of third-generation hardware and software in 1964 diverted considerable software resources into development of viable operating systems and language compilers at the expense of data base management system development. The primitive access methods provided by many vendors greatly influence the design, implementation, and performance of many advanced applications. As a result, many applications require additional sort/merge programs, greater data redundancy, and repetitive entry of input data.

Clearly, the need exists for a data base management system to provide: control of data structure, comprehensive language for data manipulation, adequate execution performance, and system integrity.

Note that the basic needs have not changed; only the hardware technology and application requirements have changed. Failure of a system to meet user needs in any of these functions leads to the ultimate abandonment and/or replacement of the system so affected.

A NEW WAY OUT OF THE MORASS

Acceptance of the April '71 report of CODASYL Data Base Task Group (DBTG) by the Programming Languages Committee in May 1971 for inclusion in the COBOL Journal of Development language specifications marked the culmination of six years of effort by many knowledgeable software developers and users to produce a language for the description and manipulation of data stored within a data base. The language specifications for describing a data base are designed to be independent of any programming language.

However, the language specifications for manipulation of data are designed to be used as an extension of existing programming languages. Like any new language specification, the DBTG report needs refinements which can be created only by implementation and use of the language. As it stands, it offers significant advantages over currently available data base management systems. It represents a giant step in the right direction. The subject of data base management systems, data base data description, and data manipulation covers a wide range of topics of varying complexity. However, the basic concepts of a data base management system are not difficult to understand.

This article will briefly describe the philosophy and terminology of the DBTG languages and give examples, wherever appropriate, of B. F. Goodrich Chemical Co.'s implementation experience on IBM hardware. All of the concepts and languages have one thing in common: the data base. It is important, therefore, that a basic understanding of the elements of a data base be obtained. The definitions and descriptions in this article are only an introduction to the subject.

A convenient starting point in the discussion of data base management systems is to describe the concepts and elements of a data base.

DATA BASE CONCEPTS

In its most primitive form, a data base is a centralized collection of all data stored for one or more related applications. Current direct-access hardware technology permits data for many applications to share the same storage device. This in turn makes it possible for two or more applications to use a common, single source of data and thus eliminate the cost and complexity of data redundancy. Once data has been integrated, a need arises for the ability to structure data in a manner which meets the requirements of each application. An application requirement may be to access only a specified portion of data in the data base and thereby remove data required by other applications from view. Furthermore, all applications may not be written in the same programming language. This in turn requires that the data and its description be independent of any programming language.

Data independence and the separation of data description from the restrictions and conventions of any programming language allow centralized data base maintenance, protection, and control over physical aspects of the data base.

A data base then can be viewed as more than an ordinary collection of data for several related applications. The data base must be viewed as a generalized, common, integrated collection of company or installation-owned data which fulfills the data requirements of all applications which access it. In addition, the data within the data base must be structured to model the natural data relationships which exist in a company.

DATA BASE ELEMENTS

The three elements of a data base are: physical storage structure, data and control information contained within a data base, and logical relationships among data stored within the data base.

Terminology and definitions used will be based on the April '71 report of the CODASYL Data Base Task Group and an implementation of a subset of the DBTG specifications produced by B. F. Goodrich Chemical Co. called Integrated Database Management System (IDMS).

PHYSICAL STORAGE STRUCTURE

The physical storage structure of a data base can vary considerably depending on the design of the direct access storage device and the manufacturer of the machine. In this discussion, let us assume that an entire integrated data base is contained in a single disc unit.

The single disc unit contains 44 cylinders (or arm positions). Each cylinder contains 19 tracks (or recording surfaces), each of which has capacity for four 3,156-byte blocks of information. Thus, the physical data base is subdivided into $404 \times 19 \times 4 = 30,704$ contiguous blocks. Each block of information is called a *page* and is the unit of physical data transfer between the data base and main memory of the system. The pages are numbered in consecutive order beginning with the first block in the first track of the first cylinder and ending with the last block of the last track of the last cylinder. The page numbers will range from 0 through 30,703. In this manner, every page has a unique number identifier and occupies a known location within the data base.

An *area* is a named subdivision of a data base consisting of a given number of contiguous pages. The area defined for the BFG online order processing system (TOPSY) and the area for payables, raw material inventory, and engineering stores system (PRESTO) is defined as follows:

EXTENT

Area Name	Low Page	High Page
TOPSY	4000	12999
PRESTO	13000	19000

Thus the 9,000-page TOPSY area begins at page 4,000 and continues to the page numbered 12,999. A user program which requires access to information stored within the TOPSY area must execute a statement which declares the type of data base operations to be executed and whether concurrent access by other independent programs is allowed.

CONTENTS OF A DATA BASE

The smallest unit of named data in a data base is a *data item*. In addition to a name, a data item has other attributes which define its type and length. A data item may be described by

$$\text{CUST-NO} \qquad \text{PICTURE } X(11)$$

where CUST-NO is the name of the data item and the $X(11)$ picture indicates that the length of the item is 11 bytes and may contain any character in the machine's character set. An occurrence of a CUST-NO data item would have a value such as 71320601011.

A *record* is a collection of one or more data items. A record description consists of its name followed by the names and attributes of all data items included within the record. The record named CUSTOMER contains the data items:

$$
\begin{array}{ll}
\text{CUST-NO} & \text{PICTURE } X(11) \\
\text{CUST-NAME} & \text{PICTURE } X(32) \\
\text{CUST-ADDR} & \text{PICTURE } X(32)
\end{array}
$$

where CUST-NO is the identification number assigned to the customer followed by the customer's name (CUST-NAME) and address (CUST-ADDR). Any reference to the CUSTOMER record implies reference to all data items within the record. This description may be considered a model or template for the CUSTOMER record type wherever it appears in the data base.

An *occurence* of a CUSTOMER record type exists when a value for each data item exists within the data base. Three occurrences of the CUSTOMER record appear in Table 23.1.

CUSTOMER

RECORD	CUST-NO	CUST-NAME	CUST-ADDR
Occurrence #1	71320601011	H.Martoyal Inc.	689 Pennington Ave.
Occurrence #2	81182803003	Texoil Inc.	P.O. Box 1608
Occurrence #3	87580701001	Weathering Co.	P.O. Box 310

Table 23.1

The distinction between a record type and a record occurrence is important. Note that any number of CUSTOMER record occurrences may appear in the data base, and each occurrence will contain a string of characters which are defined by the CUST-NO, CUST-NAME, and CUST-ADDR data item description.

Physical placement of records within a data base is controlled by specification of one or more areas in which record occurrences may be stored. In addition, one record type may be stored close to another record type to improve execution performance of the system. Any number of record types may be specified within any given area. Unless otherwise restricted, any number of record occurrences may appear for any given record type, subject to the total physical storage space limitation of the specified area. In addition, an occurrence of any record type specified for an area may be stored in any page in the specified area.

In addition to record occurrences, the data base also contains system information used to control access to each page, provide audit trail information, and inventory available space on each page.

LOGICAL DATA RELATIONSHIPS

The most common and familiar type of data structure exists within a record type. The CUSTOMER record type is an illustration of intrarecord data structure where the CUST-NO, CUST-NAME, and CUST-ADDR data items have an implied logical relationship to each other by their appearance together within the same record. Intrarecord data relationships are largely determined by the data content of the record and the meaning imparted to it by logical procedures within the application program. Intrarecord data structure is an important and useful capability which is essential in all data base applications. The additional provision for a flexible method of establishing relationships between record types is essential to fulfill the complete data structure requirements of an integrated data base.

Logical relationships between two or more record types are established by the *set* mechanism. The set establishes a logical relationship between two or more record types and is, in effect, a building block which allows various data structures to be built.

Fig. 23.1 is a representation of a set occurrence which includes three record occurrences shown by rectangular boxes. A set must have only one record type which functions as *owner* of the set. In addition, a set must have at least one record type which functions as a *member*

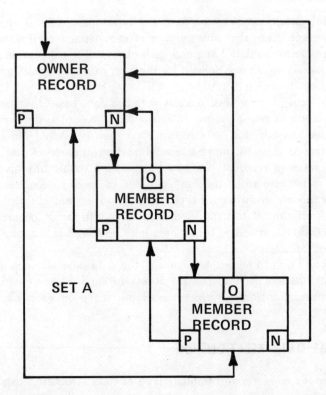

23.1 SET OCCURRENCE WITH NEXT (N), PRIOR (P), AND OWNER (O)
POINTERS

of the set. Fig. 23.1 shows one owner record occurrence and two record occurrences which participate as members. One possible implementation of the set mechanism is to use pointers which are included
with the data as part of each record occurrence. The owner of the
set contains a pointer marked "N" (next) which identifies the first
member record occurrence.

The first member record occurrence also contains a pointer marked
"N," which identifies the second member record occurrence in the
set. Finally, the last record occurrence contains a pointer marked "N"
which identifies the owner record. Taken together, all of the "N"
pointers form a ring structure which is commonly called a chain.
Moreover, the "N" pointers establish a logical chain order in the *next*
direction.

The pointers marked "P" (prior) establish a logical chain order
in the *prior* direction. The owner contains a pointer marked "P" which

identifies the last member record occurrence in the set. The last record contains a pointer marked "P" which identifies its logical predecessor which in turn points to the owner record occurrence. In addition, each member record occurrence may optionally contain a pointer marked "O" which identifies the owner record occurrence. The next and prior chains along with owner pointers are considered as a model or template for all occurrences of the set named "A." Note that a data base may contain any number of owner record occurrences which in turn may have any number of member record occurrences.

Since the set mechanism can be used to build complicated relationships between record types, an abbreviated "shorthand" set notation is needed to simplify the graphical representation of data structure within the data base. Fig. 23.2 shows the owner record type as a

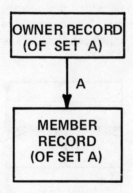

23.2 SET REPRESENTATION

rectangle with an arrow pointing to the rectangle representing all occurrences of the member record type.

The arrow is the shorthand equivalent of all next, prior, and owner pointers shown in Fig. 23.1. The name of the set (A) appears next to the arrow. The general rules for this representation are: The tail of the arrow touches the record type which is the owner of the set; the pointer of the arrow touches the record type which participates as a member of the set.

The set mechanism is a basic building block which can be used to construct complicated data structures. There are four basic rules for the formation of set relationships between record types:

1. Any record type may participate as a member in one or more sets. Fig. 23.3 uses the shorthand set representation described in Fig.

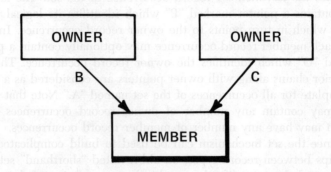

23.2 to show a record type which is a member of two sets, B and C.

2. Any record type may be the owner of one or more sets. Fig. 23.4 uses shorthand set representation to show a record type which

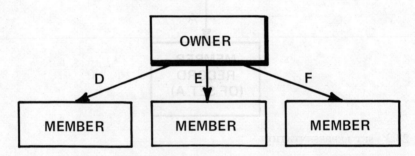

is owner of three sets, D, E, and F.

3. Any record type may participate as a member in any number of sets, and also be owner of one or more other sets. Fig. 23.5 shows a record which participates as a member of set G and also is owner of set H. This is the representation of a hierarchical data structure.

4. A set may have only one record type as its owner but may have one or more record types as members. Fig. 23.6 shows two record types which participate as members of set J.

These four basic rules are used to design data structures which meet the overall requirements of an integrated data base. Fig. 23.7 illustrates the type of data structure which can be described with

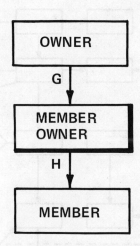

23.5 RECORD TYPE AS MEMBER OF SET G AND OWNER OF SET H

these rules using the shorthand notation described in Fig. 23.2. This structure is a portion of the B. F. Goodrich Chemical Co.'s on-line order entry system called TOPSY.

A complete description of data items included in each of the 34 record types and the structure provided by the 31 set types is beyond the scope of this article. The design of this part of the data base required considerable analyst effort over a six-month period. The objective was to provide an optimum balance between the data structure requirements of all applications which access the data, and execution performance. This structure has allowed the implementation

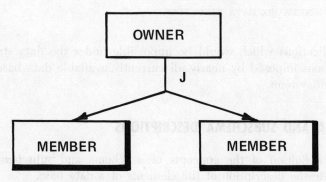

23.6 TWO RECORD TYPES AS MEMBERS OF SET J

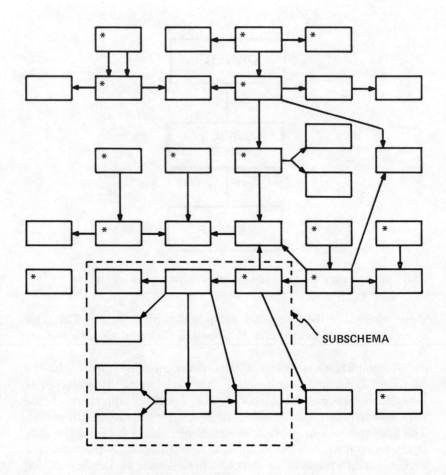

23.7 B.F. GOODRICH CHEMICAL CO. ON-LINE ORDER PROCESSING SYSTEM (TOPSY) NETWORK DATA STRUCTURE

of applications which would be impossible under the data structure restrictions imposed by nearly all currently available data base management systems.

SCHEMA AND SUBSCHEMA DESCRIPTIONS

A definition of the concepts of a schema and subschema will complete the description of the elements of a data base.

A *schema* is a complete description of all elements of a data base.

It includes the names and descriptions of all areas, data items, records, and sets which exist in a data base.

A *subschema* is a logical subset of the schema which names only those areas, data items, records, and sets which are accessed by one or more specific programs. The concept of a subschema is important because it provides a measure of data privacy and programming convenience by "removing from view" all of the other areas, data items, records, and sets not included in a given subschema. A measure of data independence is achieved in that certain changes may be made at the subschema level to provide compatibility with existing programming language conventions. However, a subschema must be a consistent and logical subset of the schema from which it is obtained.

In any data base there is only one schema, but there may be any number of subschemas. The TOPSY data structure in Fig. 23.7 is a large subschema which would not normally be used in its entirety in one processing program. A subschema of more reasonable scope is shown by those record and set types included within the dotted area at the bottom of Fig. 23.7. All records and sets outside the dotted area are removed from view of the program which invokes the subschema shown.

DATA BASE LANGUAGES

The common approach of data description, followed by most programming languages in current use, is to include the data description in the same program as the procedures which access the data. The files are frequently designed to optimize processing for only a few programs. Other programs which require access to the same data frequently require extraction of redundant data and sorting to create a file which is then optimized for processing by a few more programs. Moreover, the data files reflect the data formatting characteristics of the language used to create the file. The use of more than one programming language to access the same data normally requires data conversion from one format to another. The cost of handling ever-increasing volumes of data combined with increasingly complex processing demands have created the urgent need for a method to create and manipulate a data base which is common to all applications but independent of any particular programming language.

The required separation of data base description from the programs which access the data, and the need to provide access by multiple applications, has created the need for new languages and the extension of existing programming languages.

DEVICE MEDIA CONTROL LANGUAGE

The DMCL is a language which is used to assign and control physical space for the data base. It includes the specification of number of cylinders required for the entire data base, page size, number of pages per track, amount of page storage space in main memory, and other physical aspects of control. In the IDMS system, DMCL is handled by Job Control Language statements and generated parameters furnished to the Database Management System before the data base is created.

SCHEMA DATA DESCRIPTION LANGUAGE

The schema DDL is used to name and describe the attributes of all areas, data items, records, and sets included in the data base. The schema DDL compiler processes free-format DDL statements for areas, records, and sets to produce an object schema description of the data base which is stored in a specific area of the data base. This object description is then available to other compilers and processors in the system.

SUBSCHEMA DATA DESCRIPTION LANGUAGE

A separate subschema DDL is required for each processing language which accesses the data base. Each subschema DDL is used to select only those areas, data items, and sets which are required by one or more specific programs. Provisions are made for re-naming of areas, items, records, and sets to conform to the naming conventions of a specific language. The subschema DDL compiler accepts free-format subschema DDL statements and produces an object subschema which controls access to the data base and provides the required data interface during program execution.

The DML is designed to provide data base access capabilities to an existing programming language. As such the DML may be viewed as a language extension which conforms to the syntax of the host language. The schema DDL and DML specifications included in the April

'71 report of the Data Base Task Group are designed for COBOL and as an example for development of subschema DDL's and DML's for other languages.

The DML functions can be grouped into control, retrieval, and modification categories.

Control. Control statements are used to obtain access to an area within the data base. The OPEN statement announces the user's intention to begin processing within one or more specified areas of the data base. When access is established by the data base management system, retrieval or modification statements may be executed. The CLOSE statement announces completion of processing in the specified areas of the data base.

Retrieval. Retrieval statements are primarily concerned with locating data in the data base and making it available to a program. This is where the greatest language flexibility is needed because of the different data access requirements of all applications which process the data. The DBTG language specifications provide a variety of methods for access of record occurrences within a data base:

1. Direct access of any record occurrence in the data base is possible provided that its system-assigned unique identifier is known. This type of access is independent of any set relationships associated with the record.

2. If specified in the schema DDL, a record type may be stored and retrieved based on the value of one or more data items contained within the record. The data base management system uses the data item value to "calculate" (CALC) the position within the data base to store each record occurrence. To retrieve a record occurrence, the user must furnish the value of the specified data item before execution of the retrieval statement. Any number of record types in the schema may be defined with a CALC location mode regardless of the set relationships associated with the record. This capability allows as many entry points into the data base as needed by the applications associated with the data base. The BFG TOPSY subschema illustrated in Fig. 23.7 contains 14 CALC entry points, indicated by asterisks.

3. Record occurrences may be accessed through their participation in one or more set occurrences. Once a record occurrence has been retrieved, the sets in which it participates as either owner or member provide an access path for retrieval of other associated record occurrences. With this capability, an application program can access related data by stepping along the pathways through the data base provided by sets.

4. Records which participate as a member in a set may be speci-

fied as ordered in either ascending or descending sequence based on one or more data items contained within the record. Access of a specific record occurrence in an ordered set is accomplished by furnishing the values of the sort-key data items before execution of the retrieval statement. In addition, a non-ordered set may be automatically searched to find a record occurrence with data item values matching values supplied by the program.

5. All occurrences of any record type may be accessed by a complete scan of an area starting with the first page and ending with the last page in the area. This method of access is independent of any other set relationships or location mode.

Modification. Modification statements result in a change to the contents of the data base. Changes include the addition of new data, modification of existing data by replacement of data item values, or deletion of data which currently exists in the data base. Modification statements are also provided which permit participation of existing record occurrences in specified sets to be established or removed.

SELF-CONTAINED SYSTEMS

A self-contained system provides data base access and data display capabilities through the use of a simplified, high-level language, designed to be used by nonprogrammers. The language provides considerably less flexibility than a language such as COBOL, but is easier to learn and use. Such a language would allow a simplified method of describing the format and content of a report for display on a video terminal or a printer. A simplified method of describing the criteria for selection of data to be used in the output report allows users to quickly and easily obtain the desired information in an acceptable format. These languages are nonprocedural in the sense that the user is not required to specify input/output commands or the precise logical sequence of operations required to produce the desired output.

The simplest and easiest to implement form of a self-contained system is provided by a data base inquiry program written in COBOL using DML statements. After the data base is designed, it is possible to formulate many "canned" reports which are useful to many users. To operate the system, the user must enter a code to select a specific canned report followed by data values required by the inquiry procedure. The procedure then uses the input to access the data base, formats the output report, and transmits the report to a display device. A typical application would allow an accounts payable department employee to enter a code followed by a vendor number and immediately receive a display of information related to unpaid invoices for that vendor.

The need for both self-contained and host (COBOL/DML) languages which provide access to the same data base was clearly recognized by the DBTG. The specifications for the data description and data manipulation languages have provided the necessary solid foundation for the development of many different types of self-contained systems —each designed to fulfill specific user needs.

DATA BASE ADMINISTRATION

The creation of new languages for data description combined with the responsibility to design a common data base which satisfies the data requirements of many applications has created the need for a new function of data administration to augment the functions of systems analysis and programming.

Data base administration is accomplished by one or more technical experts who are knowledgeable in data base design and creation, operation of the data base management system, and the use of one or more data manipulation languages. The data base administrators must also be capable of working well with systems analysts, programmers, and computer operations personnel. The duties of data base administrators are to:

Work with systems analysts to determine application data requirements;

Aid programmers in most effective techniques in the use of DML;

Specify the content and structure of the data base;

Create subschemas as required by applications;

Maintain documentation of the data base schema and document subschemas for programmer and analyst use;

Establish appropriate operating recovery and rollback procedures to preserve the integrity of the data base in the event of either hardware or software failure;

Evaluate data base loading and program performance characteristics to recommend improvements;

Supervise the addition of new areas, data items, record types, and set types to the data base;

Initiate data base restructuring whenever it is needed to provide additional physical space or changes in data structure;

Establish appropriate constraints in the use of DML statements for each subschema.

CONCLUSION

The most significant development in data base management in recent years was the acceptance of the April '71 CODASYL DBTG report by the CODASYL Programming Language Committee. The subschema and data manipulation language specifications are being prepared for final approval and inclusion into the JOD COBOL specifications. A new CODASYL Data Description Language Committee (DDLC) has been formed for development of a common data description language based on the DBTG schema DDL. These important events combined with the experience and insight now being gained through use of early implementations of the DBTG specifications will lead the way out of the current data base morass. This ultimately will be good news for users.

In the author's opinion, the following publications present an excellent overview of data base design, data base management systems, and current opinions on the subject.

1. *Feature Analysis of Generalized Data Base Management Systems*, Association for Computer Machinery, 1133 Avenue of Americas, New York, N. Y. 10036, May 1971, $8.

2. *Report of the Codasyl Data Base Task Group*, ibid, April 1971, $7.

3. "The Debate on Data Base Management," *EDP Analyzer*, Canning Publications Inc. 935 Anza Ave., Vista, Calif. 92083, Vol. 10, No. 3, March 1972, $5.

4. Lyon, John K., *An Introduction to Data Base Design*, John Wiley & Sons, Inc., New York, N.Y., 1971.

24.

DATA BASE TECHNOLOGY

By Dennis S. Ward

Editor's Note: From HONEYWELL COMPUTER JOURNAL, Fall 1969, pp. 15–25. Reprinted courtesy of Honeywell Computer Journal, Honeywell Information Systems Inc.

INTRODUCTION

The Sales Manager of Thrumble Inc. has an information problem. As a preliminary step in determining the marketing strategy for a new thrumble, he needs a detailed analysis of the earlier model by geographic area code and commercial customers. He knows that all the information is available in the computer files and expects to get his analysis within a few days.

On conveying the request to the Data Processing Department, he found that the analysis would require special programming and no programmer would be free for three weeks. When the programmer finally came to discuss the problem, he found that an apparently trivial task was made complex because of the way an old sales analysis system using a tape file had grown in an uncontrolled way to involve a partial disk file. Four programs were eventually required.

When the Sales Manager received the analysis it listed 1,000 different types of thrumbles which his assistant spent two days in summarizing.

The above scene, which could have been played in many companies, illustrates some of the existing problems in EDP technology that have prevented the full realization of the potential of computers in Management Information Systems. Abstracting the problems, we note that, on the one hand, there is a mass of data—the "data base"—

in computer storage media such as tape reels and disk packs. Using existing techniques the data is generally organized, that is, collected into records and files, and sequenced to suit specific applications designed some time in the past. Access to the data is by a key. The choice of key is critical to efficient access and only one key is allowed.

On the other hand, there is the data user, and we are presently concerning ourselves with a special class of data user, the Manager. Management information requirements such as short lead time for preparation of a new report, one-time or irregularly run reports, requests for information from different files, prediction of future needs, all pose problems that are difficult to solve using conventional data processing techniques. For example, going back to the opening scene, one of the major problems evident in the Sales Manager's attempt to

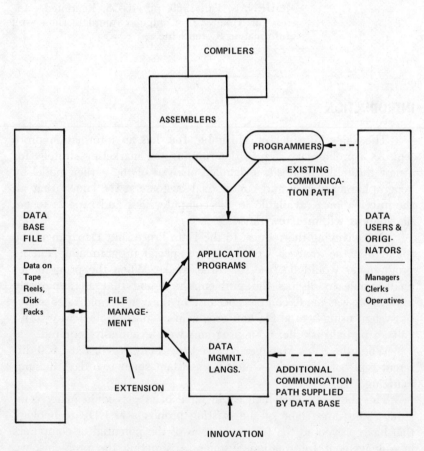

24.1   THE TOTAL DATA MANAGEMENT SYSTEM

access his data base was that of communication. To get the information he required from the Data Base, he had to rely on people whose skills made them scarce. Too often, computer specialists understand the language of the computer but not the language of management. The data base files presented another problem. When it was necessary to alter a file to include another field, a second sales-order file, which would necessarily carry redundant data, was formed because the existing program and files were highly interdependent. Alter the file and you had to alter the program, even though the function of the program had not changed. Another major drawback was the requirement that there be only one key to access the file. This requirement limited the use of the file to the existing application and thus reduced its versatility. Actually, a patched system was built which might eventually break under the strains of new applications.

The innovations brought about by Data Base Systems (DBS) technology tackle these problems. Figure 24.1 shows, in simplified form, the principal components of a generalized DBS. This is using the term in a much wider sense than the purveyors of the packaged "Data Base System" use it. However, it is intended to point out the fact that DBS technology is an extension of existing EDP techniques and not a radical new method—it is an amalgam of software (existing and new), hardware, and people. Specifically, DBS technology has resulted in the addition of one element, the Data Base Language Subsystem, and the considerable extension of another, the File Management System. The remainder of this paper discusses these related developments.

EXTENSIONS IN FILE MANAGEMENT

New File Structures

The major new developments in File Management systems lie in the extension of hierarchical file concepts to mass storage files, the use of list techniques as an aid to accessing files through multiple indexes and the storage of file description information as an integral part of the Data Base. All of these have improved the capability of the Data Base file to model real world data relationships and allow greater data accessibility and use.

Of primary importance in imposing any structure on data files is response time. If response time, defined here as the time between request for access to a data record and data being made available to the end user, were not significant, then data records could be stored completely randomly. Any record could be retrieved (by searching the whole file) with equal efficiency (or inefficiency) regardless of key. However, response time *is* a factor, and data must be organized and structured to permit timely retrieval. We use the word "timely," since what is meant is a response time matched to the *need* rather than necessarily measured in microseconds.

Once a need for timely response is recognized there are other factors that determine file organization. The question of timeliness of response vs. maintenance of the data in the file must be considered. For fast response, management information systems require files oriented for *content retrieval*. Ordinary data processing systems, in which files are optimized for maintenance and updating do not normally provide the necessary timeliness.[1] File structures designed for content retrieval provide fast response to inquiries but are slow to update (as will be seen later). Another consideration is space utilization, which in some structures can be traded against response time.

Hierarchical File Structures

One technique used to economize in space utilization is hierarchical file organization, whereby information common to many data records is stored once and linked to the many records it belongs to. Hierarchical file organizations were used before mass storage devices were widely available. Indeed, the hierarchical file concept was the backbone of the tape oriented FACT System.[2] When mass storage file structures were first developed, they tended to ignore hierarchical concepts and to concern themselves solely with "flat" files. Currently, the new file structures are principally concerned with mass storage organizations where redundancy is even less desirable and the hierarchic concept is gaining new strength.

For example, if, in a payroll file, the fields for department number and department name could be stored in a special type of record but logically linked to the employee records for that department, some savings in space could be achieved. In the terminology of today's data base file structures, these department records are spoken of as master records which "own" employee detail records, and the hierarchy is a "two-level" one. In some Data Base Systems on mass storage, ownership is expressed by "chains" or "threaded lists." We will use the

[1] N. Statland, "Design & Implementation of MIS" in Data Processing Proceedings, International Data Processing Conference, Vol. VIII, pp. 211–230, June, 1965.
[2] O. S. Lumb, "Experience of Program Development with FACT," British Society Symposium on Practical Experience With Commercial Autocodes, London, pp. 104, 1964.

second term. A "threaded list" is a list of addresses of records possessing a common characteristic (in this case, that of being owned by a particular department record). The addresses in a threaded list are stored in the data records; that is, each record contains the address of the next record in the list. Threaded lists are the main techniques used in GE's "Integrated Data Store" (IDS).[3][4] Figure 24.2 shows a payroll file set up this way. The record for Department 100 at physical mass storage address 3000 contains the address of the first man record in Department 100—man number 10150 at physical storage address 3020. The address of the second man record in Department 100 is in the first man record and so on. Zero addresses denote that the end of the list has been reached. By using a threaded list, it is possi-

RECORD FORMATS

Department Record
  Dept. #
  Name
  Pointer to First
   Man Record

Employee Record
  Man #
  Pay Code
  Age
  Pointer to Next
   Man Record

Department Records	Employee Records	
3000 / 100 Sales 3020	3020 / 10150 10 37 3030	3040 / 10163 30 29 0000
3005 / 105 Inventory 3025	3025 / 10156 20 30 3045	3045 / 10200 10 34 0000
3010 / 106 Maintenance 3040	3030 / 10160 10 35 3035	3050 / 0000
3015 / 107 Personnel 0000	3035 / 10162 25 22 0000	3055 / 0000

24.2 AN APPLICATION OF THE THREADED LIST TECHNIQUE

[3] "Introduction to Integrated Data Store," General Electric Pub. No. CPB-1048, April, 1965.
[4] C. W. Bachman, "Integrated Data Store," DPMA Quarterly, January, 1965.

ble to become independent of physical mass storage space allocations. If, in Figure 24.2, a fourth man record is to be added to Department 101, that record can be placed in the next available space (addressed as 3050) and logically "connected" to the Department 101 threaded list by placing the address 3050 in the record for man number 10162.

The simple threaded list structure is the basis of the TRUMP On-line savings system file structure. However, if on-line, rapid maintenance of the file structure is vital, an extension is required which allows each record to contain the address of the previous record, as well as the next record on the list. This technique is used extensively in the Bill of Material file structure to express relationships between components and parent assemblies in a product file. Either of these structures can be made into ring structures by allowing the last detail on the list to point back to the Master, instead of having a zero pointer.

Additional Features in Hierarchical Structures

There are three main extensions to the simple two-level hierarchy described above, and any DBS file structure should possess one,

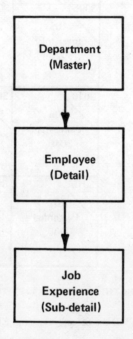

24.3 A THREE-LEVEL HIERARCHICAL FILE STRUCTURE

at least, if it is not to be unduly restrictive. The first of these is to allow a detail record to be a master of subdetails. If a file structure has unlimited capability for levels of details, it is called an n-level hierarchical file structure. A practical example of this would be to allow an employee record in the last example to "own" job experience detail records. The file would then have three levels, shown in simplified form in Figure 24.3.

A second extension is to allow a detail to be owned by two master records. If each of the employees could be assigned to projects, then it might be desirable to set up a second threaded list with the head-of-list address for projects anchored in a project master record as shown in Figure 24.4.

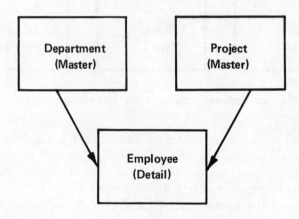

24.4 DETAIL JOINTLY OWNED BY TWO MASTER RECORDS

This file structure again eliminates redundancy by allowing a single data set (employee records) to essentially belong to two files (the department file and the project file) without duplication of data.

A third extension is to allow a "master" to own several different types of "details" (Figure 24.5). Each detail type exists on a distinct list.

The threaded list technique has some disadvantages, notably the uncontrolled way in which the lists expand. Starting at a master record there is no general way of knowing how many details are on the list. This is a serious drawback in on-line retrieval systems.

Considering the file structure in Figure 24.5, an inquiry may

come in asking for the number of employees from Department X
that have worked on Project Y. There are two ways of performing
the retrievals necessary to answer this inquiry:

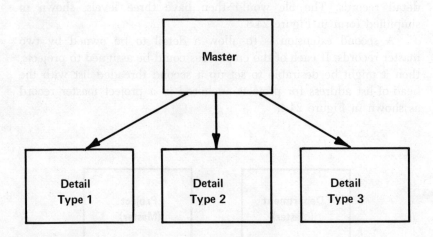

24.5   MASTER RECORD OWNING SEVERAL DETAIL RECORDS

1. Access the master record for Department X and from it follow
the threaded list and retrieve all employee "details" in the Department, one by one. For each employee "detail" access the project
"master" linked to it, and test if it is Project Y.

2. Access the master record for Project Y and from it retrieve
the employee "details" on the project. For each detail, access the
department "master" record linked to it and test if it is Department X.

It would be very helpful to know—for example—that there were
ten employee records in the Department X list and 1,000 in the
Project Y list, in order to select which strategy to use. This information is generally not available from the Data Base File Management
System using threaded lists and—if required—has to be maintained
by the user.

Files Structures for Content Retrieval

For these, and other reasons, some DBS file structures take the
pointer fields out of the records and collect them into lists. This
technique is used in SDC's Time-Shared Data Management System

(TDMS)[5,6] which is an example of a "content structured file system." In systems like this every field appears in an attribute list and the record itself disappears. For example, Figure 24.6 shows a

Index

Employee #	Address
1400	225
1405	250
1410	260
1435	265

Data Record

```
250
     100
     25
     10500
255
     103
     33
     12400
260
     104
     22
     11000
265
     100
     33
     10000
```

DATA RECORD FORMAT
Department #
Age
Base pay

24.6 A PERSONNEL FILE STRUCTURED FOR RECORD RETRIEVAL

record oriented personnel file in which four fields—employee number, department number, age, and base pay—are to be held for each employee.

The only new concept introduced in the figure is that the employee number appears as an "index only" field—that is, it is only contained in the index and not in the data record itself. This may be justifiable for record retrieval if employee number is the only key and, therefore, must be known by the processing program before accessing the file.

Figure 24.7 shows the same file structured for content retrieval.

[5] "A Survey of Generalized Data Management Systems," Codasyl Systems Committee Technical Report.
[6] E. W. Franks, "A Data Management System for Time-Shared File Processing Using a Cross-Index File and Self-Defining Entries," AFIPS Conference Proceedings, Spring Joint Computer Conference, Vol. 28, pp. 79–87, April, 1966.

Employee # List	Department # List
1400	100
1405	103
1410	104
1435	100

Age List	Base Pay List
25	10500
33	12400
22	11000
33	10000

24.7   A CONTENT STRUCTURED FILE

This file structure is designed to answer inquiries, and, particularly, inquiries directed at the content of the old employee records. If a manager wants to know how many employees of age 25 or under are earning $11,000 or more, his question can be answered by collating the "Age" and "Base Pay" lists, coming up with the answer that the third employee in the lists meets these criteria; the employee's number may be found from the "Employee Number" list. Only part of the file was scanned (in a real application, a very small fraction) compared to the necessity of scanning the whole file if a "record oriented" structure was used.

The above is a very simple example of "content" organization and illustrates its advantages in some environments. It should be added that updating this type of file can be very tedious.

Multi-indexing and Inverted List Files

Once structured, a file has to be accessed. The two main stand-bys of the other file structures—randomizing and indexing—are still slugging it out with active proponents on both sides; however, the new techniques which allow a file to be accessed by several keys seem to favor indexing. While it is easy to construct indexes for a given set of records on as many fields as required, it is difficult to construct randomizing methods which allow one record to be accessed by either one of two completely independent key fields. Some Data Base Systems allow many indexes to be constructed against a given file. One Honeywell System allows *any* and, if necessary, *every*, field in a record to be defined at file creation time as an index field. This greatly adds to the accessibility of data and gives the structure the possibility of handling either record or "content-oriented" environments. Furthermore, either a master or a detail record can have indexes set up. The indexes may be of two types —primary or secondary. A primary index contains unique key values (i.e., each key value can appear in one record only). A secondary index (in the form of an "inverted list") can contain nonunique key values (i.e., a key value can occur in many records of the same type). Each key value is followed by a list of addresses of records containing that key value. This file structure differs somewhat from the "content" files discussed previously. For example, the file in

Employee # Index

Emp #	Address
1400	225
1405	250
1410	260
1435	265

Age Index

Age	Addresses
22	260
25	250
33	255 265

Data Records

250	
	100
	25
	10500

255	
	103
	33
	12400

260	
	104
	22
	11000

265	
	100
	33
	10000

24.8 MULTIPLE INDEXED RECORD STRUCTURED FILE

Figure 24.8 is indexed on age (secondary) and employee number (primary).

This structure retains its record characteristics but also allows some improved efficiency in content-oriented inquiries. However, it does require some preknowledge of the type of inquiries most frequently received, so that secondary indexes can be set up.

Stored File Description

Another innovative feature in DBS files is called "stored data descriptions." This is, as will be seen later on, an essential feature, if the file system is to support Data Management Languages. What is meant by the term is that a complete description of the data is stored as a part of the data base itself.[7] This descriptive information may include the following main divisions:

1. Data name information—name of every master and detail record and every field within these records contained in the data base.

2. Data length information—field lengths and record lengths.

3. Data type information—type of fields (e.g., alpha, numeric, etc.).

4. Data validity information—values for any validity checking required.

5. Data structure information—specifications of hierarchic relationships among data records.

6. Data access information—specification of index fields set up to access the data.

In conventional programming, much of this information is contained in every program that processes a file. This contributes to the problems in the opening scene, since any alteration to a part of the file description usually causes alterations in all processing programs. Therefore, rather than alter an existing file a system designer may instead create an additional partially redundant file to serve a new application. With a Data Base System, an alteration can often, although not always, be carried out in the centrally stored file description. Under this method, processing programs make requests for data by name to a central logical file input/output routine. This routine can screen out unnecessary information and give the program only what it requests.

DATA DESCRIPTION LANGUAGE

The function of a Data Description Language is to allow a file designer to specify to the Data Base File Management System the structure, logical contents, format and access methods of a particular

7, 8 Mark IV Reference Manual, Informatics Inc. Publication Doc. #SP69-810-1.

Honeywell
ELECTRONIC DATA PROCESSING

PROJECT _Inventory File Description_ DEPT. NO. _____ PROGRAMMER _____ DATE _____ PAGE ____ OF ____

EASYCODER
CODING FORM

CARD NUMBER	TYPE	LOCATION	OPERATION CODE	OPERANDS
01		SUBFILE		NAME: INVENTORY/PRIMARY KEY NAME: PART-NO
02				PRIMARY KEY SIZE: 9
03				READ SECURITY CODE: 1637/WRITE SECURITY CODE: 1645
04		DETAIL		NAME: STATUS
05		FIELD		NAME: ON-HAND/SIZE: 7
06				NAME: REORDER/SIZE: 7
07		DETAIL		NAME: ORDER/TRAILER
08				NAME: DUE-DATE/SIZE: 6/SECONDARY-INDEX: YES
09		FIELD		NAME: QUANTITY/SIZE: 6

24.9 SAMPLE OF DATA DESCRIPTION LANGUAGE

file in the data base. On the basis of this information, the "stored file descriptions" (referenced earlier) are set up in the data base. In most commercial environments, files will be set up centrally by the EDP department, so the "target user" for this language is a "file manager" who must have detailed technical knowledge of the Data Base System. This contrasts with the users of the data base processing languages, who will normally not be skilled in technical EDP matters. As a result, the format and other considerations relevant to data base processing languages do not necessarily apply to the Data Description Language.

The Data Description Language must be able to express the content and organization of the Data Base file.

In one Honeywell system, a "free form" (defined later) approach has been taken using a keyword technique for identifying statement types. Figure 24.9 gives a sample of this language. The inventory file in the example has a master record containing part number (which is also the primary index key) and two details. Security codes for read and write operations on the file are specified. The first detail has two fields—named ONHAND and REORDER. The second detail —which may be repeated—has three fields, one of which (DUE-DATE) is to be used for a secondary index.

Cards prepared from this form are read by the Directory Maintenance module and the data is stored in the Data Base Directory. This is the first step in setting up the file. Following this a program written in any of the data manipulation languages which can interface with File Management—in this case Easy-coder or COBOL—can load data into the file.

DATA MANAGEMENT LANGUAGES

Functionally, the File Management Subsystem and the techniques discussed in the previous section are only the inner shell of a Data Management System. Externally, there is still the task of communicating with the end-user of the data. Traditionally, this has been done by an intermediary EDP professional who translates the end-users problems into computer programs using assembly or compiler languages. This works in systems involving many people and frequent repetitions of the same pre-defined data input and output. However, where the needs may change or urgent needs for immediate answers arise this method fails. Data Base technology has introduced the concept of a "functionally organized" language. Sometimes known as Data Management Languages (DML's), these systems permit nonprogrammers to communicate directly with files and effectively interface the end-user of the data with the inner shell of File Management and the Data Base. It should be emphasized that these languages do not replace COBOL, Fortran and assembly systems, but do fill an area where they are relatively ineffective.

Data Management Languages are organized around the following classic data processing functions:

1. Data description
2. Data retrieval
3. Report formatting
4. Sorting
5. Data input
6. Update

The first of these functions has already been covered when we were discussing the Data Base Directory and Data Description Language; for the reasons stated there, Honeywell Data Base Systems have taken the approach that Data Description is a general file management problem and not restricted to a specific processing language.

For each of the remaining functions a DML may supply a generalized subprogram which, when primed by parameters, will carry out a specific Data Processing task. The form in which the parameters are input is quite important, since this constitutes the actual language the end-user of the data uses when he communicates with the Data Base. Two basic language types can be identified in today's DML's—"free-form" and "forms-oriented." The free-form adopts a similar format to COBOL and allows the user to write statements which approximate English. The following is an example of a "program" in a free-form DML.

```
FILE IS SALES
IF PRODUCT EQ 100 AND AREA EQ 11
SORT CUSTOMER-NAME
PRINT CUSTOMER-NAME, QUANTITY, VALUE.
```

The advantage of this approach is that the "program" is self-explanatory, at least when kept simple.

It is apparent in this example that the functions are called by particular keywords. The word "IF" calls the retrieval function and the following words specify parameters. This example is a very simple one. In practice DML's generally allow quite complex "IF" statements, possibly involving computed fields on the right hand side of the condition and many levels of logic.

The main disadvantage of the "free-form" approach is the necessity for a manual to detail the rules of the language syntax.

Figure 24.10 shows a simple retrieval request form filled in to

RETRIEVAL REQUEST FORM

Retrieval #: 1234   Date: 2/2/69
File: Sales   Name: A. N. Inquirer

Field Name 1	Condition	Value	Connector	Report Fields
Product	=	100	&	Customer Name
Area	=	11		Quantity
				Value

24.10   SAMPLE RETRIEVAL REQUEST USING A FORMS ORIENTED DML

execute the same problem as in the "free-form" example. The heading information gives identification and reference numbers for the inquiry and specifies the file name. The latter must correspond to the name of a file described to the File Management System through the Data Description Language and loaded with actual data by conventionally written programs or using the Update function of a DML. Each line on the form indicates a criterion for the retrieval with a logical connector to the next line. In the last column are written the report specifications.

The major differences between the "free-form" and the "forms-oriented" DML are at the user interface. Both can perform the same function. In the case of the free-form, the question of the grammar of the language and format is more open and it is usually necessary for a reference manual to be supplied. Ideally, the forms used in the "forms-oriented" approach should be self-teaching. If there is to be a rough rule-of-thumb, a regular user may get along better with the free-form approach because he will, through use, get to know the grammar of the language. Certainly, senior technical people—especially if used to FORTRAN—seem to like the "free form." An intermittent user, on the other hand, may be better served by a "structured" or forms-oriented language since it will, by its format, remind him of the legal ways of formulating inquiries. While more often used for batch processing, the "structured" approach can also be used with terminals of the CRT type. It is much less suitable for terminals like the TTY35.

Current experience indicates that the "forms" approach is most acceptable in a commercial environment, whereas some federal government agencies have indicated a preference for the "free-form" approach. In terms of use, the leading exponents of the two approaches are Informatic's Mark IV system—the "forms" approach,[8] and IBM's Formatted File System [9]—the "free-form" approach.

Either or both of two operating modes—on-line and batch—may be handled by the DML. Of course, the nontechnically oriented manager is not directly interested in whether a Data Base System permits batch or on-line inquiry but he is interested in the capabilities of the total system to get him an answer when he wants it. To this end, it is worth summarizing three principal characteristics of Data Management Systems:

1. Response time—a batch DML implies a longer turnaround on inquiries, possibly up to 24 hours. An on-line DML can give a manager instant access to files. In many cases, a 24-hour turnaround is what is needed. Generally, technical people are the ones who may profitably use an on-line DML. Note also that the cost per inquiry of an on-line DML system is significantly higher.

2. Comprehensiveness—an on-line DML can generally access only part of the Data Base of a company—that part that is on on-line disk storage. Since cost of on-line storage is higher than tape, it is probable that most companies will have a significant part of their Data Base on tape for a long time to come.

3. Flexibility—most Batch DML's have superior facilities in areas such as report formatting. Also, on-line DML's are often restricted to handling inquiry functions only. There are obvious dangers to allowing on-line updating of data using the very flexible approach contained in a DML.

The various functional elements of a DML must be logically connected to form a complete system. Figure 24.11 illustrates in block form the main interactions involved in processing an inquiry in batch mode. The sort in this figure may be omitted if the sequence of the retrieved data is the same as the report. Further processing may also be permitted on the intermediate retrieval file to allow merging of retrieved records or distribution of the records among several reports.

The retrieval function in a DML has an application in the update operation, in addition to supplying input to the report function. One

[9] National Military Command System Support Center, Program Design Approach, System 360/50 Formatted File System, No. SPM 1-67, January, 1967.

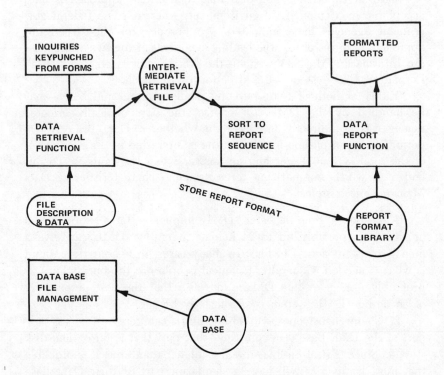

24.11

type of update operation allowed in a DML is the retrieval of a record followed by modification of the record contents and rewriting into the Data Base. Another type of update involves a transaction file which has to be passed against a section of the Data Base file and used to update it. In this case, the DML uses a description of the transaction file, a set of parameters specifying matching conditions between transaction file items and Data Base records and action specifications detailing the update actions in the event of a match, high compare or low compare. In both cases, the retrieval function is used to obtain the desired records and place them in core storage for updating.

The report function has the task of formatting and summarizing the data obtained from the Data Base by the Retrieval function. Among the facilities desirable are the following:

1. Heading and footing creation, lines-per-page and page numbering control, field spacing and field editing options.

2. Totalling, subtotalling and field suppression on control breaks.

3. Various special functions such as counting number of items, averaging fields.

4. Resequencing data records through the Sort function. This may be carried out by taking the intermediate file produced by retrieval and performing several sorts on different keys. Finally, the reports are produced.

Cataloguing

It is very desirable that the DML allow for the storage and subsequent referencing of functional parameter sets. The more complicated report formats can be stored centrally and called out as required—possibly to report on several differing retrieval statements. This technique can effectively be used to create a language for a specific application area or for a terminal with restricted capabilities. For example, suppose a medical-user wishes to set up a specialized retrieval system. His technical computer staff could use the DML to set up retrieval and report formats applicable to medical files and processing requirements. These could be referenced in terms which were familiar to the doctors or scientists using the system and called out by them from the central library. Thus, a specialized DML could be built from a general DML.

Default Strategy

At the heart of a successful DML lies a good default strategy. The main purpose of DML's—whether batch or on-line—is to speed responses to data inquiries. This purpose is not met if the system fails to process an inquiry because of relatively minor errors in formulating the inquiry. Therefore, a well designed DML should be prepared to replace erroneous or omitted parameters (detected during initial analysis) with reasonable default values and to produce a response to the inquiry if at all possible. Of course, there have to be some exceptions to this—for example, a faulty retrieval parameter could result in a large file being completely "retrieved" and passed for report formatting resulting in wastage of computer time. In general, default strategy can be most fully used in the Report functional area. At the other extreme, it should be least used—if at all—in the update function.

SUMMARY

Data Base Systems technology involves both extensions of existing EDP practices and some innovations. The two main improvements are more flexible file management systems and user oriented languages. The former permit a more accurate modeling of real-world data relationships with speedier and more flexible access to the data records and contribute to program/file independence. The latter facilitate communication between the end-user of the data —the Manager—and the Data Base files by reducing the dependency on a human interpreter.

BIBLIOGRAPHY

1. F. H. Benner, "On Designing Generalized File Records for Management Information Systems," AFIPS Conference Proceedings. Fall Joint Computer Conference, Vol. 31, pp. 290–305, Nov., 1967.
2. D. J. Dantine, "Communications Needs of the User for Management Information Systems," AFIPS Conference Proceedings, Fall Joint Computer Conference, Vol. 29, pp. 403–413, Nov., 1966.
3. W. R. Henry, "Hierarchical Structure of Data Management," IBM Systems Journal, Vol. 8, No. 1, pp. 2–16, 1969.
4. A. S. Hoagland, "Mass Storage Revisited," AFIPS Conference Proceedings, Fall Joint Computer Conference, Vol. 31, pp. 255–261, Nov., 1967.
5. D. Lefkovitz, "File Structures for On-Line Systems," New York, Spartan Books, 1969.
6. C. A. Meyers, "The Impact of Computers on Management," Cambridge, Mass., MIT Press, 1967, 310 pp.
7. E. Morenoff and J. B. McLean, "Inter-program Communications, Program String Structures and Buffer Files," AFIPS Conference Proceedings, Spring Joint Computer Conference, Vol. 30, pp. 175–185, April, 1967.
8. J. A. Postley, "File Management Application Programs," DPMA Quarterly, Vol. 2, No. 4, pp. 20–28, July, 1966.

DATA BASE MANAGEMENT: AN EMERGING FUNCTION: DISCUSSION QUESTIONS

1. How does the data base concept of organization differ from conventional file organization methods (for example, with respect to logical and physical organization and storage of data, access times and methods, file updating, and servicing of user information requests)?

2. What major advantages does the data base approach have over separate, functionally organized files? At what point does further integration of files become undesirable in developing a data base?

3. What factors should be considered in planning the size, scope, organization, and control of a data base? Should the data base be designed around available data or should new data sources, formats, and so on, be developed to meet user information requirements? Should data base design be dictated by computer hardware and software or vice versa? Why?

4. What effect is the development of an integrated data base likely to have on programming requirements, storage space utilization, ease and speed of access to stored information, method of processing data, choice of file organization schemes, manner in which information is retrieved and displayed, storage and processing costs and complexity, and file security?

5. Why have generalized data management systems been developed in view of the extensive investment of time, effort, and money required for their development? What are the common characteristics of such systems?

6. Why are data descriptions normally maintained separately from access programs when a data base management system is utilized? What problems are likely to arise from such an arrangement?

7. Why is a data base administrator necessary in many data base management systems? What functions does the data base administrator normally perform?

8. How do data description languages differ from data manipulation

languages in the data base management system? What are the major limitations of such languages? How can these limitations be overcome?

9. How do systems software and application packaged programs differ in terms of functions performed? What problems are likely to be encountered in expanding a packaged program into a complete data management system? What approaches are likely to minimize the problems involved?

10. What effect will in-house software development time and costs, availability of programming resources, amount of modification of packaged program required to fit internal needs, demands of other projects on programming staff, past performance of package supplier, and quoted package price be likely to have on the selection of a packaged program from an outside source for a specific application?

DATA BASE MANAGEMENT: AN EMERGING FUNCTION: BIBLIOGRAPHY

Amending, George W., "Computer Software: The Evolution within the Revolution," *Rand Corporation Reports*, 1967, pp. 1–14.

"Application Packages Revisited," *EDP Analyzer*, July 1971.

Angell, Thomas, and Randell, Theron M., "Generalized Data Management Systems," *Computer Group News*, November 1969, pp. 6–12.

Belanger, L. R., "The Evaluation of Software Packages," *Canadian Chartered Accountant*, December 1972, pp. 57–58.

Bleier, Robert E., "Treating Hierarchical Data Structures in the SDC Time-Shared Data Management System (TDMS)," *Proceedings ACM National Meeting*, 1967, pp. 41–49.

Bleier, Robert E., "The Time-Shared Data Management System: A New Approach to Data Management," *Data Processing*, Vol. XIII, *Proceedings of 1968 DPMA Conference*, pp. 57–67.

Burice, Duane, "Purchasing Packaged Software—A Customer's Point of View," *Computers and Automation*, February 1969, pp. 19–22.

Byrnes, Carolyn J., and Steig, Donald B. "File Management Systems: A Current Summary," *Datamation*, November 1969, pp. 138–142.

Cahill, John J., "A Dictionary/Directory Method for Building a Common MIS Data Base," *Journal of Systems Management*, November 1970, pp. 23–29.

Codasyl Systems Committee, "Introduction to Feature Analysis of Generalized Data Base Management Systems," *Communications of the ACM*, May 1971, pp. 308–318.

Cohen, Leo J., "Data Base Management in a Multi-Access Environment," *Computer*, November/December 1971, pp. 36–46.

Collmeyer, Arthur J., "Data Base Management in a Multi-Access Environment," *Computer*, November/December 1971, pp. 36–46.

Computer Decisions, series of articles on buying proprietary software, February 1971.

Cooke, M. J., "The Data Base Revolution," *Systems and Procedures Journal*, March–April 1968, pp. 20–22.

Coulouris, G. F., Evans, J.M., and Mitchell, R. W., "Toward Content-Addressing in Data Bases," *The Computer Journal*, Vol. 15, No. 2, pp. 95–98.

Coupe, Richard J. "Applying Data Base Management to Production Scheduling and Control," *Automation*, August 1972, pp. 32–37.

Cowles, C. C., "Software Package Overview," *Modern Data*, October 1971, pp. 50–53.

"Creating the Corporate Data Base," *EDP Analyzer*, February 1970; "Organizing the Corporate Data Base," *EDP Analyzer*, March 1970; "Processing the Corporate Data Base," *EDP Analyzer*, April 1970; and "Data Security in the CDB," *EDP Analyzer*, May 1970.

Crutcher, William C., "Common Creation and Ownership of Massive Data Banks," *Computers and Automation*, May 1969, pp. 24–26.

"Data Base Systems a Mistake for Many," *Administrative Management*, 1972.

"Data Management: File Organization," *EDP Analyzer*, December, 1967.

"Data Management: Functions," *EDP Analyzer*, January 1968.

"Data Management Systems: Generating Whole File Updating and Reporting Programs," *Data Processing Digest*, January 1972, pp. 1–15.

"Data Structures and Accessing in Data Base Systems," *IBM Systems Journal*, No. 1, 1973.

DeLonge, David, "Dawning of the Age of Data Banks," *Computer Decisions*, March 1970, pp. 21–24.

Dixon, P. J., and Sable, J., "DM-1—A Generalized Data Management System," *AFIPS, Proceedings of Spring Joint Computer Conference*, 1967, pp. 185–198.

Dodd, George G., "Elements of Data Management Systems," *Computing Surveys, ACM*, June 1969, Vol. 1, No. 2, pp. 117–133.

Doebler, Paul D., "The Data Bank: What Is It and How Would You Operate It?," *Computer Digest*, August 1969, pp. 5–8.

Ficarra, Anthony M., "Data Base Systems Design," *Ideas for Management*, 1970, pp. 74–83.

Frank, Francis A., "Software Services: An Outside Outlook," *Business Automation*, November 1969, pp. 55–61.

Fried, Louis, "Shopping for Commercial Software," *Data Processing*, August 1970, pp. 37–39. See also Thomas L. Newberry, "Software

Purchase or Lease—The Squeeze Is On," *Data Processing,* June 1970, pp. 29–31.

Fry, J. P., et al., "Data Management System Survey," MITRE Corporation for Defense Communications Agency, January 1969. U.S. Commerce Clearinghouse, Springfield, Virginia, AD-684-707. See also "Managing Data Is the Key to MIS," *Computer Decisions,* January 1971, pp. 6–10.

Galley, Thomas A., "An Approach to Data Base Design," *Journal of Systems Management,* February 1969, pp. 26–28.

Harrell, Clayton, "Maintaining a Healthy Data Base," *Business Automation,* February 1972, pp. 16–18.

Head, Robert B., "The Packaged Program," *Data Processing Digest,* April 1968, pp. 1–12. See also, "Software Package Acquisition," *Datamation,* October 1968, pp. 22–27; "Software Packages: Make or Buy," *Ideas for Management,* 1968, pp. 123–125, and series in *Journal of Systems Management:* "Part 1: Purchasing a Package," February 1969, pp. 32–33; "Part 2: Software Packages—Make or Buy," August 1969, pp. 36–37, and "Part 3: Protecting Packaged Programs," October 1969, pp. 40–41.

Henry, W. R., "Hierarchial Structure for Data Management," *IBM Systems Journal,* No. 1, 1969, pp. 2–15.

Hutchinson, Jack, "Packaged Software—What's Ahead for the Insurance Industry," *Best's Review,* Property/Liability Edition, October 1972, pp. 88–95.

Johnson, W. G., "Managing Information," *Management Controls,* June 1972, pp. 118–121.

Jones, Malcolm M., and McLean, Ephraim R., "Management Problems in Large-Scale Software Development Projects," *Industrial Management Review,* Spring 1970, pp. 1–15.

Kanter, Jerome, "The Ubiquitous Data Base Concept," *Data Processing,* May 1967, pp. 28–33.

Kay, Ronald H., "The Management and Organization of Large-Scale Software Development Projects," *AFIPS, Spring Joint Computer Conference,* 1969, pp. 425–433.

"Key Issues in Data Base Management are Non-Technical," *Computer Digest,* June 1972, pp. 1–2.

Kircher, Paul, "Breakthrough in Management Information Systems," *Journal of Data Management,* February 1969, pp. 28–31.

Kreger, Alan, and Nathanson, Janet, "The Tribulations and Triumphs of GIS," *Datamation,* October 15, 1971, pp. 20–25. See also S. A. Holland, "The Remote Inquiry of Data Bases," *Datamation,* November 15, 1970, pp. 54–59, 62.

Liu, H., "A File Management System for a Large Corporate Information System Data Bank," *AFIPS, Proceedings of 1968 Fall Joint Computer Conference,* pp. 145–156.

Mastromano, Frank M., "A Data Base Concept," *Management Accounting,* October 1970, pp. 15–18.

McIntosh, Stuart, and Griffel, David, "Data Management for a Penny a Byte," *Computer Decisions,* May 1973, pp. 35–41.

McElroy, David C., "The Series Data Management System," *Datamation,* April 1970, pp. 131–139.

McLaughlin, Richard A., "Building a Data Base," *Datamation,* July 1972, pp. 51–55.

Milano, James V., "Modular Method of Structuring MIS," *Journal of Data Management,* February 1970, pp. 18–23.

Minker, Jack, and Sable, Jerome, "File Organization and Data Management," *Annual Review of Information Science and Technology,* John Wiley & Sons, 1967, pp. 123–160. See also "Data Management Systems: A Survey," paper presented at the national TIMS Conference, October 1–4, 1969, in Atlanta, Georgia.

Minker, Jack, "Generalized Data Management Systems—Some Perspectives," University of Maryland, Computer Science Center Technical Report 69–101, December 1969.

Nesse, Arthur C., "A User Looks at Software," *Datamation,* October 1968, pp. 48–51. See also "Software Packages: Users Speak Out," pp. 40–47.

"New Common Data Base System," *Modern Data,* April 1970, pp. 102–103.

Nicholson, Charles H., "Building Data Banks for Multiple Uses," *Systems & Procedures Journal,* May–June 1968, 13–22.

"Off the Shelf Software Market Requires Knowledgeable Buyer," *Journal of Data Management,* September 1969, pp. 55–56. See also "Viewing the Software Industry," *Journal of Data Management,* November 1969, pp. 22–24.

Olle, T. William, "Generalized Data Base Systems," a paper presented at the Joint TIMS/ORSA Meeting, San Francisco, California, May 1–3, 1968.

Olle, T. William, "MIS; Data Bases," *Datamation,* November 15, 1970, pp. 47–50.

Pan, George S., "The Characterization of Data Management Systems," *Data Management,* June 1971, pp. 18–23.

Patterson, A. C., "A Data Base Management System," *ACM Conference Proceedings,* 1972, pp. 197–208.

Patton, P. C., "Trends in Data Organization and Access Methods," *Computer,* November/December 1971, pp. 19–24.

Podolsky, J. L., "An Unconventional Approach to Systems Design," *Business Automation,* May 1970, pp. 62–65.

Postley, John A. "The Mark IV System," *Datamation,* January 1968, pp. 28–30. See also "Status of Computer Software," *Bankers Monthly Magazine,* August 15, 1968, pp. 22–25.

"Proceedings of the Second Symposium on Computer-Centered Data Base Systems," *SDC Magazine,* November 1965, pp. 1–24.

Raynolds, Carl H., "Software Development and Its Costs," *Computers & Automation,* February 1967.

Rulle, Thomas A., "Understanding the Software Package Market," *Data Processing,* July 1970, pp. 35–38.

Schubert, Richard F., "Basic Concepts in Data Base Management Systems," *Datamation,* July 1972, pp. 42–49.

Schussel, George, "Data Base: A New Standard for Insurance EDP," *Best's Review,* Property/Liability Insurance Edition, October 1972, pp. 26–30, 86–92.

Schussel, George, "Business EDP Moves to Data Bases," *Business Horizons,* December 1972, pp. 73–84.

Shugar, Samuel R., "The Western Electric Corporate Data Pool," *Western Electric Engineer,* 1971, pp. 52–57.

"Software Forum: Make or Buy?," *Modern Data,* January 1970, p. 56.

Stevens, William B., "The Concept of the Data Analysis and Control Catalog," *Computers and Automation,* April 1968, pp. 40–42.

"Structuring the Data Base for Management Information Systems," *Journal of Systems Management,* January 1969, pp. 9–11.

Steig, Donald B. "File Management Systems Revisited," *Datamation,* October 1972, pp. 48–51. See also Larry Welke, "A Review of File Management Systems, pp. 52–58, in the same issue.

Stross, C. G. M., "Operation of a Disc Data Base," *Computer Journal,* Vol. 15, No. 4, pp. 290–297.

"The Data Administrator Function," *EDP Analyzer,* November 1972.

Treanor, Richard G., "Data Management Fact and Fiction," *Data Base,* Spring/Summer 1971, pp. 17–24 (condensed in *Data Processing Digest,* November 1971, pp. 34–35).

"Trends in Data Management," *EDP Analyzer,* Parts 1 and 2, May 1971, and June 1971.

Tyran, Michael R., "Computerized Financial Data Banks: Transition from Conceptual Design to Reality," *Management Accounting,* September 1968, pp. 36–43.

"Using Shared Data Files," *EDP Analyzer,* November 1970.

Vorhaus, Alfred H., "TDMS: A New Approach to Data Management," *Systems & Procedures Journal*, August 1967, pp. 32–35.

Ward, Dennis S., "Data Base Technology," *Honeywell Computer Journal*, Fall 1969, pp. 15–25.

Ward, D. S., "Practical Data Base Design," *Control Engineering*, May 1968, pp. 83–86.

Waters, S. J., "File Design Fallacies," *The Computer Journal*, Vol. 15, No. 1, pp. 1–4.

Ziegler, James T., "The Data Base: What's at the Bottom of It?," from *Computerized Management System for Top Management*, pp. 13–25, a paper presented at the President's Forum, Texas A & M University, March 1968.

PART V

METHODS OF PROCESSING DATA: BATCH VERSUS CONTINUOUS PROCESSING

Data can be processed in batches or on a continuous basis. Batching requires the accumulation, sorting, editing, and preprocessing of a group of transactions to be processed during a given period of time (for example, day, week, month) and the processing of the complete batch at one time. When continuous processing is used, transactions are processed as they occur and data is normally entered into the system through an on-line data collection device directly connected to a computer. Continuous processing permits rapid file updating, fast response to information inquiries, reduced peak-load problems, and a minimum of sorting and merging operations. Batch processing reduces data preparation time and costs, permits efficient file updating in master file order, and provides effective accuracy control through the use of control totals.[1]

One of the problems with off-line, batch-processed systems (that is, input/output devices are not directly connected to the central processing unit) is that program queues may develop and user waiting times may be long. On-line systems using continuous processing permit time-shared operations in which many users have fast, direct access to the central processing unit through remote terminals, turn-around times are fast, and the user retains control over his program at all times. Experimental studies of batch and time-sharing systems seem to indicate that off-line batch programming permits more efficient machine utilization whereas on-line continuous programming provides more effective utilization of human resources.[2] Routine problems requiring many calculations are probably best suited for batch processing, whereas new, complex problems requiring fast feedback and considerable debugging are more adaptable to the time-sharing operating mode. Further research is needed to compare the cost

[1] See John Field and G. N. Stilian, "Economics of On-line versus Offline Systems," *Data Processing for Management,* June 1963, pp. 9–14, for a more complete discussion of these points.
[2] See Harold Sackman, "Online vs. Offline Programming." *Data Processing Digest,* July 1968, pp. 1–14, for a detailed discussion of these experimental studies.

effectiveness of fast batch and time-shared processing, especially since computer costs are declining and manpower costs are increasing.

Many installations have discovered that they must find the best mix between batch and continuous processing for different applications rather than select one method or the other for exclusive use. Continuous or real-time processing is best suited for applications that have high activity rates for a small portion of the file, require fast response times, and/or have data inputs that occur sporadically at irregular intervals. If most of the records in a file are affected by each processing run, if fast response times are unnecessary, and/or data are normally collected or generated in batches, then batch processing is likely to be preferable. Multiprogramming may be used to insure effective equipment utilization and to provide the basis for sharing of computer time, of computer programs, and even of data by many users. Once the proper mix of operating modes has been determined, the systems designer should give careful consideration to methods of improving system effectiveness, controlling system costs, and maintaining system accuracy.

Spiro points out the dangers of assuming that all data processing should be done in a real-time mode. For applications having ordered data and infrequent access requirements, batch processing is very efficient and economical. If more complex random processing is used, it is necessary to have a smooth-functioning operating system to ensure maximum, effective equipment utilization. Random processing can often be justified if only a small portion of a file is affected and/or fast response time is needed. The systems designer should determine whether only computer time or also programming capability and data is to be shared before selecting a special-purpose or commercially available time-sharing service. The conversational mode option should be exercised only if it is really needed.

As Katterjohn points out, both real-time (continuous) and batch processing can be performed by on-line, time-shared facilities. The fundamental distinction seems to be that response time for real-time systems is measured in seconds and for batch systems in hours or days. Batch processing provides slower response, less system redundancy, less costly errors, and better hardware efficiency than real-time systems. In addition, it permits simpler system modification, requires less user education, gives higher system reliability, and provides complete job processing. Real-time processing requires more data storage and complex programs, less operator intervention, and provides faster response than batch-processed systems. It also requires fewer intermediate steps, simpler input preparation, more complex system design, and is more adversely affected by minor errors. The choice between batch and real-time processing is heavily dependent on whether the value of a rapid solution to a processing problem exceeds the additional cost and complexity of a real-time system.

Computer hardware, peripheral equipment, and programming costs for on-line, continuous processing systems are frequently higher than the same costs for off-line, batch-processed systems. The higher costs of such on-line systems must be balanced against the increased user efficiency possible in terms of greater programming output and faster turnaround time. The advent of third-generation computers has reduced the costs of on-line, continuous processing to the point where on-line systems are competitive with conventional, off-line batch-processing systems for many applications. With the cost gap narrowing between on-line and off-line systems, the added user effectiveness frequently gives the on-line system an advantage.

On-line systems, as compared to off-line systems, permit faster response times for both inquiry and update, simpler controls and audit procedures, minimized user scheduling problems, easier revision of procedures due to input/output decoupling, faster correction of errors, and retrieval and modification of individual records without regard to batching considerations. Of particular importance is the separation of updating and reporting processes, thereby permitting changes to be made in input processes, output operations, or data base structures without affecting other system components, and the reduction of the large number of errors that typically occur in batch-processed reports. With good systems design, the processing costs for applications with high file activity rates will be no higher on on-line systems than for batch-processed systems.

Brown and Hawkins define remote-access computing as making hardware and software capabilities of a centralized processing system available to remote locations on a batch or time-shared basis. Such an arrangement helps to improve turnaround time, permits man-machine interaction, and provides easy access to a wide variety of information services. Problems entailed when remote-access computing is utilized include data transmission bottlenecks, lack of compatibility between terminals and central computers, lack of adequate software and other computer resources, and limitations of available programming languages. Coordination and control of the volume, costs, and data security of outside services used by an organization represent cause for concern to its management.

Some consideration should be given to use of in-house facilities versus outside services. Such factors as overall system control, costs, data and file security, and so on, weigh heavily in the final choice. The computer executive should be responsible for providing all computer services to his organization, giving adequate consideration to user needs, cost comparisons of alternatives, implementation problems, and capabilities of inside and outside services. Particular attention should be paid to technological developments in remote-access computing in relation to user needs.

Lybrand and Cooper have found in a recent survey that remote batch processing can provide faster, more reliable, and closer controlled service than standard batch processing. Even users requiring only a few hours of large computer time a month may find remote batch processing economically attractive. Remote batch entry seems to be most desirable in situations where turnaround time is not critical, when all input data is collected at once, when user interaction is not needed, when normal batch requirements are high, when an in-house computer is not needed, and when EDP personnel are frequently absent.

Turnblade stresses that centralized data processing activities can have adverse effects on management flexibility, departmental cooperation, response times, staffing capabilities, and computer costs. Above all, the user has little control over kinds, quantities, and qualities of service provided by a centralized data processing center. Dedicated systems employing a number of small computers linked to each other and to a large computer provide a promising alternative. Such functions as local computer support, data acquisition, data preparation, data base maintenance, off-line analysis, and report generation and dissemination can be divided between centralized and decentralized processing to achieve greater benefits than possible with a single centralized system.

As Haidinger points out, most time-sharing systems employ a central computer, voice-grade telephone lines, communication couplers, and remote terminals. Selection of a time-sharing system should be made on the basis of computer configuration (including file size, addressing methods, memory size, computing speed, and ability to perform background processing), programming language(s) to be utilized, reliability, and cost (that is, of conversion, processing, file storage, and terminal rental). Some consideration should also be given to proper system design and programming standards.

Since computing power rises exponentially as price is increased, large processors and memory units frequently can be shared by a number of users at a cost less than that of operating their own systems.[3] However, increases in computing power per dollar expended must be balanced against high communication costs and system complexity. Time-sharing is most likely to be beneficial for problems requiring small amounts of computation, sizable memories, considerable man-machine or man-to-man interaction, or fast response times. Time-sharing is less advantageous for problems with similar processing times, for problems whose processing can easily be scheduled, for problems with large computation requirements or problems with noncritical response times.

[3] See Bernhard Schwab, "The Economics of Sharing Computers," *Harvard Business Review*, September-October 1968, pp. 61–70, for an excellent discussion of computer system economics.

═══ 25.

PROCESSING METHODS AND THE SYSTEMS DESIGNER

By Bruce E. Spiro

Editor's Note: Reprinted from DATA MANAGE-MENT, September 1968, pp. 22–27, published by Data Processing Management Association, 505 Busse Highway, Park Ridge, Illinois 60068.

Much has been written concerning the development and implementation of real-time systems. The list of references grows each day —and it is impressive—both in quantity and quality. There are few manufacturers or software firms that do not have expertise in real-time; time-sharing; multi-processing; or whatever the current catchword may be. For the data processor few areas hold more interest or challenge. For the manager, or decision maker, living in his world of undefined problems, few areas hold more problems or are more fraught with danger!

There seems to be little attempt to define systems with specific application oriented goals in mind. While this is quite desirable in the areas of research, it can be disastrous in production fields. We can, and should, welcome the experimenter's desire to "climb a mountain—just because it is there." But we should be highly suspicious of those who tell us that we can run our business better from on top of that mountain. Perhaps we can—but before we start the climb let's take a careful look at what we are trying to do and what the cost may be.

As system men we carefully and studiously instruct that the scientific approach is valuable—that facts and information should provide the basis for decision, rather than intuition or hunches. Yet, we have structured our own house in such a manner that decision can be—at best—an educated guess. Many have taken Norbert Wiener's advice to "render unto the computer those things that are the computer's" to mean that all things belong to the computer, and are now in danger of saying that all things should be done in real-time.

DEFINITIONS

Before we look at what a real-time or time-shared system can do, let's try to understand what they are. There seem to be no clear-cut definitions. A "real-time" system is a very personal thing. Time-sharing is very obscure. Even the definitions used (or felt) in connection with batch processing are no longer quite clear.

For the purpose of this discussion we will use the following:

Sequential Process. That type of process that operates from beginning to end in a pre-defined and rigid order, and on data structured in a similar manner.

Random Processing. That type of processing that operates without pre-determined sequence. The significant aspect is that because there is no sequence, all data that might be used during the process must be available at all times.

Batch Process. That type of process that operates on all relevant data at a pre-determined time; usually in large masses and infrequently run. Batch processing may be either sequential or random.

Real-Time Processing. The processing of individual inputs at the time of occurrence, rather than the most favorable time. Highly critical in any real-time process is the necessity for completing action on a specific element of input data (at least to the point that other processing can continue) within a specified response time.

Time Sharing. The use of single systems (not necessarily a single central processor) by many individually dedicated terminals at the same time. These terminals may be directly coupled, but are normally remotely located.

Multi-Programming. The use of a single central processor by more than one operating program at the same time without significant degradation of individual program running time.

Conversational Mode. The direct interaction of man-machine through a dedicated peripheral device that provides for two-way transmission of intelligible information.

These are brief and generalized definitions, certainly not intended to completely stipulate the full scope and meaning of any term. They are included to provide a frame of reference and a point of departure. Most of these definitions deal with tools or techniques that are inherent in any data processing system. Notably—time sharing does not! It is a combination of tools developed to satisfy a specific application. This is included because of its current prominence and the tendency to treat time-sharing and multi-processing as synonymous. A similar term, though not so often heard, is data sharing. This deals with access and modification of the same data by more than one user. Like time sharing, the users may, or may not be remote, and like time sharing—this represents a combination of tools and techniques to achieve a specific purpose. There is much evidence that data sharing may be a most important area for future development.

These are a few of the tools, though by no means all, that are available to the progressive organization. The systems designer must evaluate and choose the best combination to support a specific application. The use of sequential processing can be seen relatively clearly. If input data is ordered and processing is required relatively infrequently, no system can match the efficiency and economy of the sequential process. The use of random processing systems is dependent on the need to relate input transactions to a variety of record information. This can be accomplished by successive sequential runs and perhaps more economically. The trade-off is between the re-ordering of input necessary for a series of sequential runs, and the more complex and time-consuming access scheme needed for randomly placed records.

OPERATING SYSTEM

As the application becomes more complex, it becomes necessary to consider the merits of various systems of operation. To better understand and evaluate proposed systems, let us look first at the operating system itself—what is it? *Basically, it is the function of controlling the capability of equipment.* The system may, or may not, be automated. In many organizations it is purely a manual procedure of setting up and sequencing individual jobs. As the effort becomes more complex and time more critical, this procedure is usually automated to some extent, but the jobs are still of a unique and sequential nature. That is, individual jobs are stacked by relatively slow speed input equipment and made available to an "executive program" that will run each job to completion and then move on to the next without undue delay. In this kind of system there is no reaction to individual input, rather the entire input for a specific run (or job) will be accumulated and then entered so that one straight-through run may be done.

With a well designed executive system, machine capability will be well used, but input response will still be largely on a manual basis. When the time requirement for response to input data becomes critical enough, however, the entire operation must be put in the hands of the machine—for man can no longer react with sufficient speed. It should be stressed that this is not a functional real-time system, it is more in the nature of another tool—an executive and I/O monitor. It can be valuable in any system, real-time or not, but in the true real-time environment it is a necessity. In batch processing the effective monitor has as its goal 100% utilization of equipment; in the real-time process the goal is to provide the maximum capability of equipment when it is needed. A real-time system must be responsive to random inputs—it is necessary, therefore, to insure that processing is accomplished as quickly as possible. The development of this kind of control of equipment is expensive; it is demanding of high caliber talent and of high cost equipment.

There are many uses to which sophisticated monitors have been put, sometimes with great effectiveness—sometimes without. Regardless of how effective these systems have been, they are expensive and difficult. Many highly touted systems have been delayed—some have been in serious trouble. Be that as it may, there are reasonably good, highly sophisticated, monitor systems available, quite capable of use in any application. Without doubt, better ones are on the way.

EVALUATIONS

Now—with an idea of what tools we have and what kinds of systems we can build, let's take a look at how a few of the different systems may best be used.

The sequential process has been with us for some time in automated form. Its application to the problems of business, industry, and government is wide spread and well defined. Perhaps it is somewhat too wide spread because of the direct automation of many punched card applications. When this is done without proper analysis, the result is often a high speed and quite costly punched card system that takes little advantage of the capability available.

The random process is often considered only in conjunction with real-time. This is not necessarily true—random processing should be predicated on the input transaction to file relationship. The conditions under which random processing may be advantageous are determined by the examination of this relationship. When the input, taken as a batch, will affect only a small portion of the file on a one-for-one basis, random processing can be most efficient. When a single input transaction will have effect on numerous file records in different sequences, random access to the file records may be the most effective approach. Notice that the random process introduces the concept of large files maintained externally to the operating program. During a specific process run very few of the records maintained will be accessed. The cost of this type system lies in the difficulty and complexity of accessing a particular record and the additional task of separately maintaining the massive files.

Not to be overlooked is the requirement for production of the system. Sequential processing lends itself well to the type of report that involves the treatment of every record in the file. Random processing is more effective when output requirements involve a selected portion of the file and does not require the processing of all records.

The often maligned batch process is still the most useful of systems. Whether sequential or random, the governing factors involved in the decision to batch or use real-time are concerned with the availability of input data, as related to the time requirement for output. If input data is available in large quantities at infrequent intervals, and there is no requirement for quick reaction to the latest event—the economy and efficiency of the batch process is unquestionable.

RESPONSE TIME

In reality there is one primary point to be considered—that is—response time: The need for quick reaction to the latest, individual, input transaction. Even though input data may arrive at random intervals, it is quite possible to group these inputs at convenient times and process in a batch mode, provided that there is no need for reaction to specific, individual inputs within restrictive time frames. If the output can be regulated to conform to the system, the batch process will prove to be most effective.

When the fast response to individual inputs becomes the overriding consideration, the real-time system is the only answer. There is no doubt that the problems are considerable, and the cost will be high, but if conditions demand, it may be the only way. Process control is an example of the computer's entry into the real-time world. Here, there is no choice, response must be made to individual, random inputs. The process will not wait for the next convenient time to batch all the data acquired. As an event occurs, it must be evaluated, controlled, and if necessary, a concurrent stream of events must be originated. If the computer based system is to function in this field, it must do so in real-time or not at all.

There are many other conditions in which the real-time system can be effective. They have shown their merit in such applications as reservations, critical inventory control, the military command-control systems, and many others. Unfortunately, the real-time system has had an air of glamour and excitement built around it, and because of this, has been pushed into many areas in which it has not been an unqualified success. Often this has not been the fault of the system so much as the system designer. The plain fact is that the real-time system has one great virtue—response—and many, many problems such as greatly increased hardware costs, larger programming and analysis efforts, and more difficult operational problems. If response time is important enough, these problems are endurable, however.

The undeniable desirability of "push-button" response must not be allowed to minimize the problems. Nor should the magnitude of the problems be considered insurmountable if the need is there.

The designer must carefully evaluate the individual situation and determine the best system to satisfy requirements. The information requirements of progressive business and industry are no longer simple and straightforward, if they ever were. The systems supporting them also become more and more complex, and the task of systems design becomes more critical and more difficult. It seems not too long ago that systems design consisted of a few pages of process flow charts— that all facets of design could be covered in a few pages and diagrams. Today the design phase may take many months and several volumes. Obviously this is not always true—in many applications the design problem is a simple one. Investigation may show a combination of requirements and constraints that leave no alternatives and production may get underway without delay. The designer, however, must recognize this and have a reasonable basis for such a decision.

With a clear conception of whether batch, real-time processing, or a combination of the two, will best meet the need, the elements of the system must be put together. There are many check lists designed to insure that no point is overlooked. These should be obtained and consulted frequently throughout the course of development. With no attempt to treat the entire process of system design, let's look at a few points of current interest.

To determine whether or not to utilize a time-sharing system it is wise to look first at what it is you are going to share. Is it computer time? Programming capability? Data? If the only thing you have to gain is computer time, you may be looking in the wrong direction! The small-scale central processors currently available have quite a bit of capability—enough for many applications. Some have higher-level languages and excellent software packages. In many applications they can be put on site for considerably less than it would cost to time-share. Even if the application is large enough to warrant its own time-sharing system—the use of small-scale equipment to satisfy the real-time requirement may prove to be advantageous. When time is the only thing to be shared, the decision is not too difficult. Proper stipulation of the required work load may be related to the cost of time secured in various ways and the most cost effective chosen.

IMPORTANCE OF TIME-SHARING

Examination will show that the sharing of time alone is not necessarily the most important consideration. Programming capability is one of the most attractive features of many time-sharing systems. It could be argued that a comparable amount of effort could produce even better results without the constraints of time-sharing. However, high caliber talent gravitates toward the more challenging fields and, in the case of time-sharing, has produced some highly effective packages in several application areas.

In order to obtain an effective response time to random inputs the designer has two choices—developing a special purpose system or securing a commercially available service. As with any general purpose system the trade off is in the area of too much you don't need and too little of what you do. This must be weighed against the cost of development of exactly what you want, with full awareness of your own organization's capability and the extensive development time required. Considering the pace of development of time-shared systems, the flexibility and sophistication of general purpose time-shared systems should soon be more than adequate for any application in which they may be required.

DATA-SHARING

Coming into more prominence, and surely of great potential, is the sharing of data. In many cases the acquisition of data is the largest problem facing the systems designer. Analysis may show that there are others interested in the same data, either within the organization or externally. Their use of the data may be entirely different, but the base may be similar enough to fulfill both needs. If the inevitable conflicts can be worked out and all constraints satisfied, the best approach may be a data-sharing system—a comprehensive data acquisition and storage system that will make the data available for many different uses and users. This type of effort will have great impact in the fields of management information systems and those efforts that rely on public information.

No matter what form the system, the designer must establish the general structure. He must consider, among other things, how the input/output will be handled and what kind of operating system will be employed. Again, without attempting to treat the full gamut of input-output or operating systems, let's examine a few items of current interest.

MULTI-PROGRAMMING

In operating systems the use of multi-programming is becoming more than an experiment. Many commercial systems have this capability to some extent. There are advantages and disadvantages to its use. On the plus side; response time, equipment utilization, random input expectance, and more precise operational control. On the minus side; high systems overhead, increased costs, increased possibility of systems breakdown. Since the first computer was installed data processing managers have been especially concerned with idle time, and quite rightly so. Multi-programming offers a way to do something about it. The cost is not insignificant, either in equipment expansion or development effort. There seems no other way to utilize input/output time effectively other than to have at least two separate instruction chains prepared to operate as time is available. To do so is not a simple job and will require additional core and a sophisticated monitor system. This kind of operating system will provide much more precise operational control, but because of its complexity and the dependency of the entire operation on it, it will be more critical. To put it simply: you can obtain full equipment utilization and maximum effectiveness, but it will mean larger equipment and higher development costs.

CONVERSATIONAL MODE

There are many ways to handle input/output; each has its good and bad points. Cards, paper tapes, printers, display boards, all have specific uses in which they are unequaled, and they all have limitations. Judging from some of the recent literature what has come to be known as the "conversational mode" is the ultimate weapon. The systems designer must look objectively at such things. The conversational mode is, in reality, a method of preparing input and presenting output of a system. It should be treated as such. No matter where input comes from the system must perform certain checks before it can be accepted and processed. This may be in the form of verification at key punch level, or it may be CRT presentation to the originator. Conversational mode of operation does not eliminate the need for validity checking; it may change the manner of doing it and the location, but it is still done. The systems designer, therefore, must determine where the checking should be done and proceed to include it in the system accordingly.

QUICK ANSWERS TO SMALL QUESTIONS

Conversing with a computer system is primarily a need of the data processor or some one concerned with quick answers to small, well defined questions. The data processor has used the technique for some time in the form of the question and answer type of console operators instructions. Granted that these are quite simple, they convey the interaction of man and machine in the same manner as more sophisticated systems, and for the purpose they serve, are irreplaceable. There are a few guidelines that are useful in determining the need for conversational operation. There should be the definite need for interaction between man and machine. This does not mean only that the man must need the product of the machine; he must need it right now and be willing to delay his action till he gets it. The kind of information required also has a bearing. There is no advantage in providing report-type information in a conversational mode. Report-type information is used to indicate the processing of large masses of data on a relatively regular basis. This kind of data is best obtained as a normal function of the system rather than on demand which is better suited for data needed less frequently.

The conversational mode lends itself well to the response to short, well defined questions (the query type of operation), and the formation of specific questions *when the user does not know exactly what he is after.* The first use is reasonably well defined—the latter is the relatively new application and looks to be very attractive under the proper circumstances. The realistic definition of these circumstances is the job of the systems designer.

SYSTEM DESIGNER'S ROLE

We have discussed the job of the systems designer. To put this job in the proper perspective, let's look at just what it is that the systems designer is called upon to do. In the life cycle of a data system there are four phases. It is first planned, then designed, then produced, and finally operated. Let's look at the first two—planning and designing. Planning is primarily a function of management, involving the recognition of a need and allocation of resources. It is hoped that there will be some data processing knowledge available to management when plans are made to insure that planning goals and objectives are properly stated and within the realm of possibility. Whether or not this is true, the result of planning is to state an objective which the data processing operation is to achieve and the constraints under which this objective is to be attacked.

The problem then becomes one of design. The data systems designer clarifies the objective and translates it to a description of a system, stated in precise and non-ambiguous terms. The job in data systems is much the same as that of any other discipline. The automotive or aircraft designer does not detail each nut and bolt. He must know the function—the strength and weakness of all the parts. He must be completely aware of how they can and should be put together. His job is "to prepare the preliminary sketch" and to do so with art and skill. So too with data—the designer must prepare the preliminary description. The skill with which he does so will play a very large and a very important part in the eventual success or failure of the final product.

═══ 26.

BATCH OR REAL-TIME PROCESSING?

By John M. Katterjohn

Editor's Note: Reprinted from AUTOMATION, August 1971, pp. 61–64. Copyright 1971 by the Penton Publishing Company, Cleveland, Ohio.

Primary objective of an information system is to provide useful information to a user. Simply stated, the information system must provide information to the user when, where, how, and in the amount that he needs it. This objective may be accomplished by using either batch processing or real-time processing in computerized information systems.

A batch processing computer system has the following characteristics:

- Computer input and output rates are controlled.
- After submitting an input, a user can expect his output in hours or days—not seconds or minutes.
- Each job is processed to completion by the computer before a subsequent dependent job is started in processing.
- Batch systems can be on-line and/or time-shared.

In an on-line processing system, input and/or output data are transmitted directly between the user and the computer system. Batch processing systems can be considered on-line if they have a data-transmitting input terminal or a data-receiving printer located near the user but remote from the batch processing computer. Batch processing systems can also be time-shared systems in which multi-job computer processing is interleaved. For example, time-shared batching could be when two or more independent batch jobs are processed concurrently.

In contrast, a real-time processing computer system is *always ready* to render instantaneous service. This type of processing system has the following characteristics:

- Computer input and output rates are random and uncontrolled.
- After submitting an input, a user can expect his output in seconds or minutes.
- Independent, isolated, and random jobs or transactions are processed instantaneously, simultaneously, and continuously.
- Real-time systems are always on-line and time-shared.

In essence, real-time processing consists of on-line and time-sharing capabilities, coupled with a fast user response time. Since batch processing can also be on-line and time-shared, the fundamental distinction between real-time and batch processing is the factor of computer response time. In the context of today's relatively slow input and output rates, real-time generally implies transaction processing—rather than job processing—in order to meet the requirement of minimum computer response time.

Different types of systems applications are oriented toward real-time processing. Let's take a look at some of the more common systems applications.

Data collection systems typically collect information on a real-time basis for subsequent and periodic batch synthesizing and reporting. This type of system is well suited for applications that do not require immediate and fast user response.

Data inquiry systems collect information on either a real-time or a batch basis. However, the contents of the data base are available to the user through real-time terminal devices. This type of system can be used to improve a user's turnaround time in solving problems. The system allows the user's intellectual activity to progress in a more continuous, uninterrupted process than is possible with an intermittent batch processing system.

Process control systems provide computerized environmental control. Control algorithms usually are contained within the computer program, and a relatively small data base is required for making control decisions. Depending on the nature of the application, decision-making is a function of either a computer or a human.

Management information systems (MIS) provide current facts and scientific projections that are needed to remove guesswork from human decision-making. Such systems play a management role in identifying, analyzing, and defining problems; in suggesting courses of action; and in evaluating alternatives.

Several improvements and breakthroughs in computer-related technologies have made real-time computer processing possible:

- Development of larger capacity and more quickly accessible direct access storage devices (DASD).
- Development of less expensive per character storage, both in core form and in DASD.
- Direct linkage of both terminals and computers to telecommunication networks.
- Development of computer hardware multiplexor channels that allow large numbers of terminal devices to be connected to a system.
- Development of advanced programming and software techniques that make computer multi-programming, accessing DASD, communicating with terminals, and processing system interrupts much easier.

In an overall comparison with batch processing systems, real-time processing systems require more complex and expensive hardware and software, are more difficult to implement and maintain, require greater user knowledge of computers, require more computer room sophistication and control, make high system overhead necessary for accurate user accounting, and require greater system reliability. Conversely, batch processing systems are faster, easier, and cheaper to implement and use than real-time systems.

What, then, are the primary considerations today for choosing real-time processing over batch processing? In many cases real-time is the only solution to certain applications. In real-time, the user is attempting to solve problems that require judgment or response from moment to moment rather than from day to day. This time factor can be evaluated by determining how rapidly the value of a solution deteriorates with the passage of time. If it drops to zero or near-zero after only seconds or minutes, then real-time may be justified. The user must then weigh the increased hardware, software, system and program development, communication, and terminal real-time cost factors against the increased overall economic utility of fast response time. Only then should he rule out batch processing in favor of real-time processing.

Now, let us consider some of the specific selection factors that must be considered in selecting between real-time and batch computer processing.

DIFFERENCES BETWEEN REAL-TIME AND BATCH

Software Considerations

System designing and programming are obviously more complex and difficult tasks for real-time than for batch. Both techniques require software scheduling algorithms. However, real-time supervisory programs are perhaps the most complex type of program that can be written for a computer. They are typically much more sophisticated than batch supervisory programs because of the real-time problems associated with randomized and interrelated inputs and outputs.

The complexity of real-time program interaction necessitates greater system documentation than does relatively simpler batch program interaction. Because of the greater complexity and interdependence of real-time programs, closer programmer coordination and teamwork are required for real-time system development than for batch.

Real-time programs must provide a greater degree of self-monitoring and self-logging routines than batch in order to allow for subsequent analysis of the many real-time types of processing that have occurred. Real-time also requires faster program switching than batch, in order to quickly activate the real-time program that is appropriate for processing a particular transaction.

Application program testing is far more difficult for real-time than for batch because of the "almost" infinite number of combinations of real-time events that can occur. Complex input conditions causing real-time system failure can seldom be recreated for analysis. Therefore, the high volume of test data needed to test the many possible real-time event combinations generally must be checked automatically by computer, rather than manually as for low-volume batch testing. Whereas a batch program can usually begin running before remote errors are removed, a real-time program must be thoroughly debugged for it can contain subtle errors that, if undetected, can have disastrous consequences.

Program Storage

Application program maintenance and accessing is a more significant factor in real-time than in batch processing because all of the programs must be ready at all times to process random transactions. The problem is whether to keep the programs in costly core storages or on relatively slow-access direct access storage devices. Both real-time and batch require dynamic allocation of core storage to achieve system flexibility. However, real-time requires it to a greater extent than batch. In addition, real-time requires direct access storage devices which are not always necessary for batch. File costs of maintaining a given volume of data on DASD are much greater than on magnetic tape.

Real-time processing requires an automatic read-write storage protection feature to prevent destroying instructions and data and to make confidential information available only to authorized users. Batch does not necessarily require this automatic feature.

Input Considerations

Input preparation is simpler and more direct under real-time than batch processing. Batch requires intermediate steps between user and computer such as keypunching and verifying, requesting data processing service, job scheduling, manual computer operation and error handling, and output logging and distribution. Real-time eliminates these "middlemen" operations and allows user/computer interaction.

Real-time requires terminal devices and communications links between the user and the computer, whereas batch processing generally does not. Various types of real-time terminal devices are available:

• Keyboard devices resembling typewriters are very popular. However, these devices are very slow input devices when compared to output devices such as high-speed printers.

• Audio-response units resembling telephones are relatively inexpensive input devices and have the advantage of being easily moved and located. However, these devices are also relatively slow input terminals.

• Graphic display cathode-ray tube (CRT) devices are fast, quiet, and easy to operate. They are becoming very popular input terminals, although they are relatively expensive devices.

• Remote batch processors such as minicomputers and programmable controllers are becoming more common with the development of small computer technologies. In addition to controlling remote processes, these units can also be used to communicate with large central processing units (CPUs).

• Central processing units can communicate in real-time with other CPUs.

Operation Considerations

Real-time implies random unpredictability since input and output data enter and leave the system at random and unpredictable time intervals and record lengths. Available programs on DASDs or in a core memory are randomly activated, depending on the scheduling algorithm or on the particular operation to be performed on the current transaction. However, this mode of operation can lead to the problem of demand overload when too many terminals request service simultaneously. In contrast, batch implies planned predictability. An operator must alert the system to begin processing a specified program and, at the same time, must make the required input and output media ready. Therefore, batch input rates are regulated and are not subject to demand overload.

It is important to remember that the work unit of real-time is an individual isolated random transaction, whereas the work unit of batch is a group of related transactions. Therefore, real-time requires a faster CPU cycle-time than batch in order to service a number of simultaneous users satisfactorily since real-time user response time is measured in seconds or minutes. Although batch response time is measured in hours or days, batch hardware efficiency exceeds real-time in that batch requires less CPU time to read a given set of input data, process it, and write the output data. Consequently, a greater rate of data throughput is possible with batch than with real-time.

Real-time requires a more powerful system interrupt mechanism than batch in order to process the more frequent and complex real-time interrupts. System interrupts are the rule rather than the exception in both real-time and today's batch. However, interrupt handling generally is more automatic and extensive in real-time than in batch in order to meet the real-time requirement of immediate system response to user demands. Both real-time and batch require priority-setting schemes for coordinating system functions, accessing transactions, and processing interrupts.

Real-time requires much less computer operator intervention than batch. However, such real-time intervention as is required must be faster and more sophisticated than for batch. Since minor errors can be more costly under real-time than batch, real-time computer-room control must be tighter and more rigid than batch and necessitates highly trained operators.

User education can be a significant real-time problem. A few computer-knowledgeable systems programmers and operators suffice for the typical batch user, relieving him of the necessity of learning how to program and operate computers. However, in a real-time environment the user himself usually must be made aware of many computer concepts in order that he may serve as his own systems analyst, programmer, and operator. His attendance is required while real-time processes his data, unlike the user-independent processing of batch. Therefore, user involvement time can be greater for real-time than for batch.

System Considerations

Unlike batch, real-time system performance may be constrained by considerations external to the system itself. For example, the nature of real-time requires large-computer centralization, whereas small-computer decentralization is possible with batch. Although the complexing of a highly general batch system may exceed that of a restricted-usage real-time system, the complexity of a real-time system will exceed that of a batch system at the same level of generality.

Real-time enhances the batch concept of data processing with the additional concept of timely control. Audit, control, inquiry, and update response capabilities for a system are faster and simpler in real-time than in batch. Real-time is actually a return to an individual transaction type of non-batch unit record processing and can eliminate the need for voluminous batched periodic reporting.

The real-time system objective of maximizing user efficiency conflicts with the batch objective of maximizing computer efficiency. The nature of the user requirements that originally necessitated a real-time system usually indicates that system failure cannot be tolerated, thus a higher degree of system reliability is required for real-time than for batch. Unlike the real-time "continuous-time" user, the batch user can "buy" more time to recover when his system fails.

The amount of necessary hardware and software system redundancy is inversely proportional to the amount of system downtime that can be tolerated. Since real-time system downtime, measured in seconds, can be significant—as in a critical chemical process—varying degrees of real-time hardware and software backup are typical. Batch system downtime, measured in hours, usually can be tolerated and therefore requires little or no backup.

Since sophisticated real-time systems may be related to profits more remotely and intangibly than batch systems, real-time user value analysis is more difficult than batch. User accounting is more difficult than batch. User accounting is more burdensome to a real-time system than a batch system because of the potentially greater number of real-time users over a given period of time. The accuracy of user accounting is proportional to the amount of system overhead that is tolerated.

Batch system modifications are much simpler to make than real-time modifications. Consequently, real-time system criteria should be frozen to a greater extent than batch when system development begins. User commitment is almost total, once real-time has been implemented. Unlike the user of a new batch system, the new real-time user may have no satisfactory way to revert back to his former batch system.

═══ 27.

REMOTE ACCESS COMPUTING: THE EXECUTIVE'S RESPONSIBILITY

By Dr. William F. Brown
and David H. Hawkins

Editor's Note: From the JOURNAL OF SYSTEMS MANAGEMENT, May 1972, pp. 12–16 and June 1972, pp. 32-35. Reprinted by permission of the publisher, the Association for Systems Management, and authors.

PART 1

Remote Access Computing can be defined as: "Making directly available, at a location remote to the computer, some or all of the functions (operations, capabilities) of the computer and software." This is not just time-sharing, but includes remote job entry from a terminal into a batch processing environment as part of the definition. Some advantages which are available to the computer executive through Remote Access Computing are:

Turnaround time is improved, in both remote job entry and time-sharing, basically because the computer job does not have to be carried to the computing center, but can be sent at telephonic speeds. The computer power is placed directly in a user's office. He does not have to wait until a report comes back to him from the data processing center. (Sending a computer output report is not really putting the power of the computer in an individual's office.)

In the time-sharing mode, programs are developed in an interactive fashion. This permits interaction between man and machine, allowing the machine to do some of the operations best suited to it and the man to do the ones best suited to him.

In time-sharing, the conversational mode can be used, which allows a non-computing specialist to address his problem to the machine, to permit editing and retrieval of information easily, and above all, allows the question-and-answer dialogue to be carried out to reduce the amount of incorrect data going into a computer.

The user has access to an ever-growing library of specialized data bases and application programs.

FUTURE POTENTIAL

The experts say that there will be an increased use of remote access computing. Currently, there are over 280,000 terminals in use. A recent report issued by Frost and Sullivan [1] states that "during the next 10 years the number of data terminals in use will increase 10 times from today's level, and that's over three times the increase in computers in use during the same period." They also project that by 1980, one-third of the dollar volume for the data terminal market will come from remote batch terminals. Others predict that by 1980 there will be a 20-fold increase in the use of data communications. Thus, in spite of the current softness in the general economy and the plight of many time-sharing and service organizations, the next decade will see many offspring from the marriage of computers and communications.

Every company will not be able to develop all of its own large applications programs, nor will they be able to afford to develop certain common data bases. Because of better data communications and improvements in hardware and software, one can anticipate a lower cost and an increased use of outside services through remote access computing. For example, the FCC has announced (May, 1971) their approval of open competition in the field of microwave and other specialized communications. Data Transmission Corp., and Microwave Communications of America, Inc., are two firms that have petitioned to offer such services and that will benefit from this decision.

Likewise, in multidivision corporations each division cannot afford to develop all its own applications. As we move into the 70's, we will also see increased use of corporate computer networks using both private leased lines and normal dial-up services. These data links

[1] "The Computer Data Terminal Market," April 1971, Frost and Sullivan, Inc., 106 Fulton Street, New York, N. Y. 10038.

are used for load leveling purposes, to balance workloads among the various divisions. They also permit divisions to specialize in certain applications, package programs, or data banks, and then provide this expertise to other divisions over the network. Both remote job entry and time-sharing are employed.

FULL POTENTIAL

In the 70's, computers must be used in solving problems with qualitative techniques rather than the quantitative techniques for which they have been used primarily in the past. In general, this requires that computing power be made directly available to the user. In this way the true power of the computer can be unleashed to meet its full potential; permitting a true intellectual partnership between man and machine, such that the special capabilities of each are best utilized.

From the foregoing it is clear that the future for Remote Access Computing is bright, but it is also clear that with all the many variations and combinations of terminals, data sets, communication lines, etc., the business of implementing Remote Access Computing is not without its technical problems. These technical considerations must be dealt with by the computer executive and those with the proper training and expertise who work for him.

There is the *data transmission problem*. Since most telephone lines are analog and not digital, they cannot provide the best possible reliability of transmission. The transmission error rates are often unacceptable for medium-speed remote job entry access over dial-up lines. Also, present telephone lines seem to be fairly well utilized. There has been a wide performance gap in transmission speeds available between medium-speed communications capability (1200 to 2400 bits-per-second) and very-high-speed communications (19,200 to 40,800 bps); a gap which is being partly closed by recent data set developments in the intervening high-speed range (3600 to 9600 bps). This gap has forced many users to pay higher rates than they should to obtain print speeds of over a few hundred lines per minute and forced many others to remain with printers whose rated speeds are far below the desired level.

There is also the line contention problem; i.e., the circuits may be busy when many users are attempting to send data. This can be due to heavy traffic on the normal switched networks (dial-up) or on the special leased or foreign exchange (FX) lines used by some service bureaus to multiplex calls between a remote city and the central computer site.

The *lack of compatibility between terminals and central computers* can also present a problem. For example, some remote (RJE) software packages are not compatible with ASCII code, only full extended EBCDIC. Software is not always available to complete the mating of terminals and central computers. It is also important to accurately estimate the "transceive time" to "compute time" ratios in remote job entry such that the proper balance of data sets and other hardware is attained, permitting reasonable turnaround times and optimizing the use of the terminals.

Also, *lack of adequate software* to permit compression of redundant data, inadequate error messages, no "request for status" capability, no local printing of output, and other undesirable shortcomings, should be avoided in the chosen systems, if possible. The coordination of multiple vendors in the event of error conditions and system downtime deserves proper pre-planning, including the setting up of definite procedures and a mutually agreed upon contingency plan.

The *availability of computer resources at the central computer* is also of major concern. There is always the question of the additional computer overhead due to remote access, although progress has been made to significantly reduce this. Also, is sufficient core storage available to the user? Are there adequate peripheral devices for data storage requirements? And perhaps most important of all, from a turnaround or response time viewpoint, is there too much contention for these resources by both batch and remote users? Is there excessive demand placed on the communications adapters and data sets, such that response to the remote user is often a "busy signal."

A further consideration involves the limitation of some of the *programming languages* made available. Is the terminal service using BASIC or COBOL, FORTRAN, APL or PL/1? Is the terminal to be used primarily by nonprogrammers or programmers? BASIC, while easy to learn, is not a powerful language and may be inappropriate. FORTRAN, while providing more flexibility and power, is more difficult to learn and may not be appropriate for the applications and persons involved.

Also, once the programs are debugged by the terminal, often they should be transferred to the batch processing mode for production. Are the languages compatible to make this conversion easy or must the job be recorded? If more than one service is used, this problem can be magnified.

OUTSIDE SOURCES

Usually, outside services are obtained because the company's computer executive cannot provide the full range of services due to a lack of power at his central computer, or the need for quick response time which he cannot meet, or requirements for special package programs or data banks. In an alarming number of cases the computer executive has not even been consulted by the user department in the selection of an outside service. In a survey conducted by Brandt Allen and reported in the Harvard Business Review [2] he states, "Of companies examined, 71% reported that time-sharing had been introduced by someone outside their own computer center. In several companies, computer center personnel actively resisted the introduction of time-sharing because they felt they would no longer retain control over company usage. In others, time-sharing terminals had been installed in management offices without the knowledge of the company's data processing center." While the percentage may be less today, the seriousness of this problem should be clearly recognized by computer executives.

Let us imagine then that a terminal has been introduced into a firm, with or without the computer executive's approval, and that the company must now deal with its control. Many of the problems are the same—whether it was introduced by the engineering department for computational work, the business management areas for access to financial or economic data banks, by parts programmers for use of APT programming services for use with numerically controlled machines, or any one of several other services. In almost all cases, a nonintelligent terminal with a typewriter will have appeared; it will usually use a dial-up line and be located external to the computer center, in the user's department.

What, then, are the true challenges which have been presented to computer management? First, they have a terminal that usually cannot be controlled by the computer department. The user may ask, "Why must it be controlled?" It will be easier for the users to misuse the service unless time limits are set at the terminal for any one user and the applications themselves are carefully and periodically reviewed to see that they are indeed worthy of a time-sharing mode. Some production applications will expand to the point where they should be transferred to the batch mode on the central system,

[2] "Time-Sharing Takes Off," *Harvard Business Review*, March-April 1969.

possibly via remote job entry. When program checkout is completed, the program can often be transferred to the in-house facility for subsequent production runs. Too often, with lack of controls, these transitions are not made and the resultant inefficiencies can soon mean that a second terminal is "required."

Many terminal users take advantage of their possession to generate applications which rightly belong on the central system, due to core and/or input-output requirements or the lack of a genuine need for the interactive or quick response mode of operation, or for that matter do not belong on a computer at all. Further, the very existence of a terminal at which the user does his own programming means that the computer executive's programming staff has been bypassed, and leads to the creation of openshop programming and systems. While this is not necessarily an inefficient practice for the scientific and engineering areas, it is generally agreed that for management information and financial systems a centralized staff is far more cost effective, preventing duplication of effort and providing the conditions for proper integration and control of the various applications.

Another important aspect of this newly arrived terminal is the security of the data which is transmitted. Some of the company's sensitive data can find its way into an external data bank which is not controlled by the computer executive or the user department, and which can be easily compromised or released unintentionally to an unauthorized person. Even with proper controls such as keywords, there are serious loopholes in the capability of the industry to provide full data security for remote access data processing. Much work lies ahead in both the physical protection and the design of hardware/software protection systems.

LEGAL ASPECTS

The computer executive should not overlook his responsibilities concerning the legal aspects of using outside services. R. Bigelow[3] has covered this subject in an article in which he distinguishes between Remote Access Service Computational (RASC) and Remote Access Service Informational (RASI). In the latter, the user cannot alter the data in file, i.e., in stock market quotation systems, real estate listing services, etc. He recommends that before entering into a contract with any remote access service, the computer executive must be sure

---

[3] "Some Legal Aspects of Commercial Remote Access Computer Services," R. P. Bigelow, *Datamation*, August 1969.

to consult with his company's legal staff to assure that he is not exposed to unknown risks. Copyright interests of data stored in computers, and the warranties of the service provided, which may or may not be implied or stated in the contract, are two important legal aspects to be aware of in procurement of outside services.

If the terminal is a more expensive one to be used for remote job entry, the opportunities for proper management involvement can be even greater. While it is less likely that this should occur, the appearance of an RJE terminal in the user department is still a real possibility. The many technical considerations mentioned on pages 14 and 15 now become even more important. For example, at the higher transmission rates the data transmission problem becomes greater; compatibility between terminals and central computers must be considered; evaluation of data sets and the various line speeds; the coordination of many vendors; these and many other factors must be considered by knowledgeable personnel—from the computer executive's department.

Finally, there are the potential limitations of the programming languages supplied by the outside vendor(s) and their possible incompatibility with in-house languages—a consideration which has more importance to both the time-sharing user and the remote job entry user, especially if conversion to the in-house machine is contemplated.

PART 2

The situation of a terminal linked with an outside service is a lead-in to the real question that should have been considered by the user's firm, and must ultimately be considered, i.e., the use of in-house facilities to satisfy the user's requirement. What challenges and responsibilities does the computer executive face in consideration of in-house sources? Many of the conditions cited for the outside sources will be the same, especially those related to control of the terminal and its use. With the central computer complex under his jurisdiction, however, the executive can incorporate better control by the use of more elaborate software techniques. Certainly the openshop programming and systems is as great a problem; also the data security problem remains, but is somewhat diminished, provided the in-house computer facility operates in a secure environment. If little attention is paid to data and file security within the in-house installation, this area may assume even greater importance. Legal aspects will change, but will not be eliminated.

Considerations of the compatibility of programming languages and their conversion to the batch mode for production will still exist, but the selection of languages may now be greatly limited depending on their availability from the vendor(s) involved at the firm's own center. What new considerations must the computer executive deal with when remote access applications are to be accommodated in-house? With reference to time-sharing, the most significant is whether the cost of additional hardware (and software, if unbundled) makes the in-house installation practical at all. If one must add costly main storage, secondary storage, communications adapters, etc., then cost justification may be difficult. If this change involves installing a completely new system, then the cost justification becomes even more stringent. Also, the thruput variance on the normal batch workload must be closely analyzed to ascertain if the regularly scheduled work can be accomplished, with a "foreground" function devoted to time-sharing.

Minicomputers are going to be considered more often in trade-off studies. The larger 16-bit word machines with floating point hardware will be offering tough competition as an alternative to the time-sharing market. Minicomputers can be used in an operations open shop mode, i.e., allowing users "console debugging" privileges and even a certain degree of man-machine interaction during production. Costly data communications, prone to error, do not have to be considered. Additionally, minicomputers serve as intelligent terminals for remote job entry purposes (and still double as an in-house computer for certain applications), communications front-ends, line concentrators, etc. The problem of control still exists but, in addition, there are the problems of maintenance and control of the software needed to run the minicomputer.

As to the general areas to which the executive must devote his attention, each executive will have to study the many considerations which pertain specifically to his particular installation. For example, the costing of the terminals and services provided to the in-house users is a major consideration which will vary in its solution from company to company. But no matter how the cost is allocated, in general, it will increase the total cost of computer services to the company.

THE EXECUTIVE'S RESPONSIBILITY

The responsibility of the computer executive is to efficiently provide all the computer services required by the organization he services. The company must recognize what the responsibilities are and then assign someone to be responsible for them. If this responsibility is not given to the computer executive, then there is a great danger to the company. For example, if left to the various user departments, the cost of purchased services can easily get out of hand and create unnecessary redundancy of computing capabilities. If left uncoordinated, these various terminal sites can each develop their own standards, making later transitions to in-house facilities a nightmare. If left uncontrolled the percentage of unjustified applications can increase. The user becomes hooked on the system and enamored with the hardware, a process which seems to be inevitable in spite of our sophistication today. This love affair is usually irreversible once started.

Thus, it is essential that there be one individual who is at all times cognizant of the overall costs of computer equipment installed, and who can eliminate the unnecessary costs of duplication or suboptimization. Effective use of this equipment requires in-depth knowledge of the EDP sciences and the proper technical leadership. One cannot expect that each functional area that uses computers through remote access will possess this expertise.

To see how the computer executive fulfills his responsibilities, assume that all requests for remote access computing are funnelled through him. If this is not the case, then this becomes the first order of business.

First, the computer executive must work with users in determining their needs. He must thoroughly and systematically evaluate the feasibility of solving their needs by using either time-sharing or remote job entry. It will not be sufficient to know what output reports the user wants—he must understand how the user's needs are to be met for carrying out special calculations, for building models, and making trade-offs. He must also know the response requirements of information for the users and how accurate they must be.

He must make the users aware of the remote access capabilities available to help them solve their problems. He must become aware of their needs, understand their problems, arrange for in-house indoctrination and vendor courses where required, and keep them abreast of technical and procedural changes. This must be accomplished in a manner which develops proper rapport and gains mutual respect for each other's contributions to the development of the total system.

A carefully conducted cost analysis should be made on the alternatives, including a comparison with the expected pay-off in dollars and convenience to the user. It will not be sufficient just to say, "The user needs good turnaround time . . . give him a terminal."

Once the feasibility of the remote access application has been worked out with the user, the computer executive must then concentrate on the "how to implement" phase. There are a number of important trade-offs to be made concerning in-house vs. purchased services. The elimination of some of the various options will depend upon the capabilities of the particular firm, such as the availability of in-house resources.

When analyzing the trade-offs between using in-house and outside remote access services, the computer executive will find several compelling reasons to at least start with the external service bureaus. The advent of time-sharing and remote job entry have removed some of the obstacles that kept many executives from utilizing outside services. The initial investment is small, and a short-term commitment can be arranged. The improvements in operating systems and transmission have opened up this service and greatly improved turnaround time; future improvements must eventually provide even better reliability and even less expensive data transmission; and computer service bureaus with dedicated and specialized service will certainly continue to offer more efficient and less expensive service.

There are, however, factors to be evaluated which are drawbacks to the use of outside services. For instance, what happens if the service firm goes out of business during your contract period? Alternative plans or contingency plans should have been developed beforehand. How much reprogramming is required to move applications? Is there adequate documentation of production systems? Also, a contract must be negotiated to protect both the executive's firm and the service bureau.

The simultaneous use of in-house facilities for the batch mode and an outside service for time-sharing is often an ideal solution. The larger computer centers can start out this way, until volume builds up to the point where internal justification can be reached; the smaller firm might never reach that point, and would continue with a combination. Even the larger centers may ultimately end up with both batch and time-sharing on their in-house equipment and use one or more outside services to access special proprietary programs and/or data banks.

In conducting these studies the computer executive must determine what software packages or special data banks are required by the user, and he must make trade-offs between in-house and purchased services for these applications, for few companies will be able to provide all the services in-house. Even with the improvement in his in-house hardware and software, there will still be cases where it will be more effective for him to purchase certain services from an outside vendor. For example, some proprietary packages and specialized data banks can only be accessed through outside services.

Finally, any trade-off study between in-house and external suppliers must consider the costs involved in the length of time required to implement the remote access service. If extensive configuration changes are involved for in-house implementation, then normally the external service can be provided in a shorter time span. For use on projects with a cut-off date, i.e., one-time applications, an outside service can also permit an earlier completion of the project.

CONTROL OF REMOTE ACCESS TERMINALS

Once the selected system is installed, the computer executive must develop a means of controlling remote access computing, particularly when the services are purchased outside. He must establish procedures and see that they are followed. Procedures should cover procurement, operation, and protection of the equipment, as well as the reviewing of the applicability of user applications and scheduling use of such terminals. This he must do in concert with the other members of management in the organization he services. He, in collaboration with the user, must determine what information shall not leave the premises of the company, and what information can.

Another of the more important responsibilities of the computer executive, which is often seriously neglected, is evaluating thoroughly and systematically, all personnel reactions. The firm should expect guidance from its computer executive, who is aware that hostilities and personal fears may develop with any change. If the executives involved are properly managing the transition, they will have considered these non-technical elements in an effort to at least reduce their adverse effects.

The computer executive must consider the many elements of programs and data security, both from the physical security point of view and the development of software utilities to protect data files from access by unauthorized persons at remote terminals.[4]

The computer executive must contact the firm's legal counsel to discuss the wording of any remote service contract before signing, and to explore problems of copyright interests, implied warranties, and proprietary data files; and if more help is needed in these areas, several law firms are now offering such services.

LONG-RANGE PLANNING

All decisions must be made in view of the needs of the business rather than merely keeping up with changes in technology for its own sake or because a competitor has made the change. Decisions should be made on economic grounds—for example, remote access to outside services involves increased communication cost and should be implemented only if analyses indicate its use is worthy of such additional expenditure. The computer executive must ultimately make use of long-range [5] and short-term planning to properly interface his firm's future requirements with the evolving rate of technological change. The industry's optimistic predictions of rapid rates of change have been wrong to a large degree. Thus, the computer executive must become sophisticated enough to place intelligent and level-headed value judgments on these predictions.

A variation of the use of remote access computing will eventually develop for the larger multidivision corporation. Each division can develop expertise in certain applications and provide this service to all other divisions over communications networks. With each division specializing in certain areas, corporate redundancy of know-how and software costs is greatly reduced. Some candidates for such a system are: APT (create tapes to guide machine tools), use of NASTRAN (structural design), GPSS, or other simulation and modeling programs.

How the computer executive goes about fulfilling this responsibility depends upon how his corporation is organized and upon its management style, but as a minimum he should keep in touch and exchange ideas with the other computer executives in his corporation.

[4] a) "Use of Software Techniques to Protect Programs and Data Files," by D. H. Hawkins, Computer Decision Magazine, October 1971.
  b) "AMR's Guide to Computer and Software Security—Protecting your Operations and Data Files," edited by William F. Brown.
[5] Also see "Long-Range Planning for the Computer Complex," by R. E. Bibaud, W. F. Brown, G. L. Hodgkins.

Finally, in order to properly carry out his responsibilities, the computer executive must remain aware of the significant developments in the remote access market. This does not mean that he has to become a specialist in it, but he must understand the general trends; what is available in services. Appropriate information must be obtained to evaluate the outside vendors and make decisions concerning their use. Since most EDP personnel do not yet have a good understanding of data communications, a specialist should be assigned as the focal point for collecting and dispersing all such knowledge.

While fulfilling his many responsibilities, the computer executive must take the leadership in approaching remote access computing and work closely with the users. He must take the initiative and not merely react to the pressures of others.

There are some pitfalls for the executive to consider about his own attitude in fulfilling the responsibilities enumerated above. There is "pride of ownership." Many executives feel that they have to own it to control it, and thus are reluctant to utilize outside services at all. Often an executive is so busy facing today's problems that no time is spent in looking to tomorrow. Unfortunately for the computer executive who does not look to tomorrow and face his responsibilities, he will find that somebody else will begin to address the problem of remote access computing, particularly when senior executives begin to ask embarrassing questions like: Why is that terminal here? What is it doing? How does it fit into the picture? Why does it cost so much? Why do I need this when I spent all of that money for my central computer center?

SUMMARY

In the 70's remote access computing will come into its own. This offers a challenge and an opportunity for the computer executive since, in all likelihood, some of his company's computing workload will be sent to outside services, and he will have to learn to control this environment. The opportunity for him is that remote access computing will permit him to truly meet the needs of the company he services in such a way that his organization will have the full authority and responsibility it needs, and its importance will be recognized throughout the company. Executives who do not seize this opportunity and challenge might become the dinosaurs of the 1970's!

The ultimate responsibility and initiative is up to him . . . to meet this new and increasingly significant challenge with the proper management involvement, control, and coordination. He must find solutions within his own company. Through awareness, further discussion, and examination, the computer executive can insure a smoother transition from the batch oriented 60's to the remote access oriented 70's, and thus protect his firm's future as well as his own.

28.

THE CASE FOR DEDICATED COMPUTERS

By Richard C. Turnblade

Editor's Note: From DATA PROCESSING MAGA-
ZINE, May 1971. Reprinted by permission of the
publisher, North American Publishing Co., and
author.

Data processing participates in business in two different ways. First,
it monitors the product of business by selecting pertinent information
from the mass of data generated (the source data base) during the
normal course of business events. From this selected data, quantitative
statements about the current status of important business parameters
are made. These lead to management status reports for reference or
management action based on approved systematic analysis. Examples
vary from cost accounting to sales analysis to inventory control. The
monitoring function increases overall visibility and management control
of the conduct and progress of business activity.

Secondly, edp supports ongoing operations, participating directly
in the line of activities of business. Examples include invoice extensions, online airline reservations, and computerized typesetting.

Under increasing loads, present central computer systems have
begun to show strain, developing several symptoms that limit their
utility and value. These limitations are self-induced, having their roots
in the intrinsic nature of the large, general-purpose, central computer
concept. The weaknesses now surfacing are more a compliment than
an indictment of central computers. These machines were designed
to be versatile, and succeed so well that people over-extend them
until inherent limits are reached.

Versatility implies compromise. A versatile tool at best only approximates the efficiency and convenience of a specialized tool. Consider, for example, the difficulties of a housewife attempting to use a single (but versatile) compressor for all the chores that the

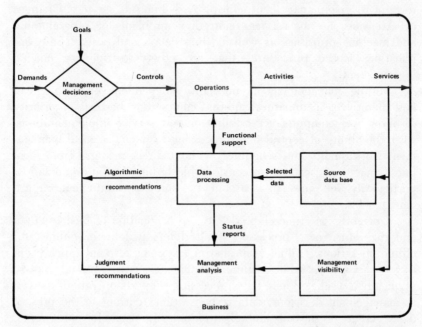

28.1 MONITORING AND PARTICIPATING. DATA PROCESSING SYSTEMS QUAN-TIFY THE CURRENT STATUS OF VITAL BUSINESS PARAMETERS, AND DIRECTLY PERFORM VARIOUS BUSINESS FUNCTIONS.

specialized refrigerator, vacuum cleaner, air conditioner, and freezer now perform. Versatile tools can be extended into applications where their reduced efficiency becomes too penalizing. They are not practical for all tasks for which they theoretically apply.

Business is characteristically a decentralized activity, segmented in several organizationally independent entities, each performing different functions—often at diverse locations. Centralizing data processing functions leads to entangling problems of:

- reduced management flexibility
- interdepartmental rivalries
- slow response times
- staffing difficulties
- vague computer costs

When line management hands over control of its data processing service needs to a centralized agency that has no competitive alternatives, it often loses control of the kinds, quality, and response time of this service. In the extreme, central data processing can impress a form of reverse management control by defining its services. Changes or extensions in this service reintroduce problems of programming and machine priorities, as well as time delays and costs. These implications freeze procedures that are otherwise ripe for needed improvement.

Middle management of normally independent operations can find themselves in unnatural internal competition because of priority disputes over computer accessibility or new service implementations. Also, the ability of central data processing to influence local management work quality and schedules, without direct recourse from local line management, can cause considerable trauma in the organization, particularly in times of seasonal pressure or equipment failure emergencies.

Currently, the time elapsed between origination of business data and the return of a processed result differs widely for online and offline operations. Online (timesharing) systems respond quickly (in a few seconds), while offline (batch) systems respond slowly (typically a week). Where data processing supports operations as well as management decisions, data response times current to the present day's activity is the substantially predominant need, for most users.

Undeniably, management decisions must be made on current information, but the degree of timeliness depends on the specific data. Some business data is no longer timely one minute later (like the volatile inventory of airline reservations), but most data is current over a daily period (like manufacturing inventory, accounting data, sales projections and goods in shipment). In fact, it is the natural pattern for business management to desire a summary update report each morning as the substantive data base for decisions throughout the remainder of the day. This need is served poorly by a batch system whose weekly reports attempt to make up for timeliness by bulk, or by an online system of much more expense whose channels are either hopelessly glutted with a morning overload or limited to supplying data piecemeal, one request at a time, without ability to display many cross-referenced implications.

Aside from the decision-making process, the data processing support of business operations is also on a day-in, day-out basis. Whether printing payroll checks or typesetting text, it's natural for people to plan work in daily cycles.

Since turnaround time is either very short or very long, suitably-handled applications are a small percentage of the total applications that computers are moving to fill. In effect, present applications skim the cream, being those most easily satisfied by currently available business computer systems. Since computers handle only a few percent of the total business data base, this situation is tolerable. But what about the future?

Achieving daily dp turnaround is not a question of business computer inadequacy; it becomes a question of applying computers to data acquisition and preparation. Today, most offline data processing methods use manual methods of data transcription—keypunch, key-to-tape, and key-to-disk equipment—to convert source data into machine-readable data. These manual methods have inherent delays which are responsible for 90% of the turnaround time. Delays could be reduced to comparative insignificance by automating data transcription with a small computer system dedicated to direct source data acquisition and preparation.

What about staffing central facilities? Today's business computer is a machine intended for operation by experts. To retain all possible flexibility for general-purpose operation, only experts can successfully guarantee machine security. Obtaining and retaining a specialized staff has often proven difficult. Personnel turnover, particularly in the middle of software developments, and confusion over the differences between computer caretakers and software developers, have contributed much to schedule losses, cost overruns, and inferior performance.

In contrast, special-purpose or dedicated computers can be operated by personnel with less training. For the dedicated application, operators need know little more than how to turn the machine on and off. Software development becomes progressively simpler because dedicated applications tend to stabilize into standard business modular functions, greatly aiding software standardization.

The training of personnel who are not oriented to computer operations has frequently proved to be expensive and inefficient. Many times a changeover to computers means substantial variations in the previous business activity pattern. Breaking up and revising already grooved and comfortable methods can create chaotic and inefficient conditions, which often endure for a long time. Dedicating computer systems to specific applications offers less compromise than a central system in adapting to the established and proven operational patterns of each application.

Another problem associated with general-purpose operations is subtle but nonetheless important. When servicing a number of different data processing needs, it's often difficult to determine the cost effectiveness of each individual application. Central system operation has served to make the computer an overhead function which buries information needed to determine whether the computer is helping or hurting. As a result, the cost effectiveness of business computers has become more a matter of faith than of fact. Clearly, dedicated computers for each major application or convenient grouping of applications would allow more straight-forward procedures of cost accounting.

Dedicated systems approach data processing applications through the use of many small computers cooperatively tied to each other

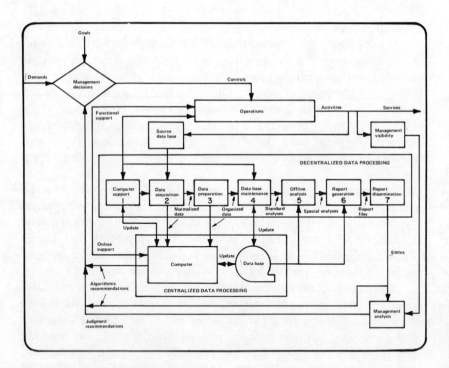

28.2 BALANCING CENTRALIZED AND DECENTRALIZED FUNCTIONS. DEDI-CATED COMPUTERS CAN HANDLE ALL OR PART OF THE SEVEN BASIC BUSINESS FUNCTIONS, DEPENDING ON NEEDS.

and to a central computer. Seven basic functions make up the bulk of data processing operations, each of which is readily handled by small, decentralized computers:

- local dedicated computer support
- data acquisition
- data preparation
- data base maintenance
- offline analysis
- report generation
- report dissemination

The Figure 28.2 shows inter-relationships among these functions, their associated business operations, and a large computer. In a balanced system each of the seven applications should be divided between centralized and decentralized processing, the choice resting upon the specific needs of each user.

1. LOCAL COMPUTER SUPPORT

Direct participation in the prime functions of a business activity is one of the fastest growing segments of computer applications. It varies from assisting point-of-sale operations to automatic process control. Some common examples are typesetting, stock transfer, and automatic letter writing.

Typesetting, including editing and composition, is a proven application for computers. Its continued expansion, however, is limited by two difficulties. First, central computers are too big for most applications; second, the general-purpose computer is foreign to type-setting people, requiring special personnel to program and operate it. A smaller, special computer system better matches the average application, making computerized typesetting available at a practical cost to the mainstream of typesetting businesses. Dedicating the computer exclusively to typeset editing and composition can simplify the operation of the machine and standardize its functions so that special personnel are not needed. So a small, dedicated computer system not only significantly satisfies a wider user segment, but also allows the computer to be absorbed directly into the business activity in a straightforward manner.

Computers could reduce the costs of stock transfer, presently a manual operation, by 30% to 60%. These costs run several hundred thousand dollars per year for the average public company. For most applications, the relatively small volume of stock transfer operations and the necessary security provisions for negotiable security handling make large computers impractical.

In automatic letter writing, a customized letter is composed from standard and special paragraphs, including personalized references unique to each addressee. Direct mail solicitation, legal documentation, proposals, and business form letters are typical. This application is always limited by output printing, making it prohibitively expensive on large computers. A small, dedicated system fits the cost scale better, yet permits a wide flexibility in letter composition.

2. DATA ACQUISITION

Currently, data is captured for computer use by manual transcription methods that represent a full 50% of the cost of data processing. Dedicating a computer to this function makes it possible to capture data at its source, directly within the normal business routine of such functions as form preparation, badge reading, and time card punching. Data costs with this method typically drop from several cents per transaction to a few tenths of a cent.

Typewritten business form data represents the single largest data base media in business operations. Forms such as purchase orders, invoices, insurance claims, financial transactions, and inventory movement are the backbone of business operations. This data base is still largely untapped even within computer sophisticated businesses. Without a significant change in data input costs, handling the full data base of business in a computer is highly impractical.

Automating data transcription requires accurate interpretation of the vagaries in the preparation of forms intended for people and not for machines. Also transactions from many different business forms must be normalized into standard output formats acceptable to downstream computer processing. These are specialized functions that, implemented separately from downstream computer analysis, can free the mainframe to serve the vastly increased data load which the reduced costs of source data acquisition will promote.

Every central computer system functions as a multi-purpose service bureau for its users. Properly implemented, source data acquisition systems must be able to reformat the data captured so that an essential flexibility can be maintained between the business source and the computer. This flexibility frees both the business and computer activities to set their formats to their personal convenience without compromise on either side. In this way business methods remain unchanged by the computer.

3. DATA PREPARATION

Continued increases in data handling, particularly encouraged by the drastically lower costs of source data acquisition, promise to saturate computers. Currently, fully 50% to 80% of all mainframe processing is devoted to the I/O limited tasks of validating, editing, and assembling, sorting, and merging.

Small computer systems can be set up with a more favorable balance between internal computing power and I/O capabilities and are generally better fitted for data pre-processing tasks. For a small investment, compared to the large computer, a small dedicated computer system can multiply overall throughput two to five times. So relieving the central computer of data preparation obligations is far more desireable than adding large machines.

Another significant benefit of specialized data preparation computers is the decreased turnaround time of invalid data entries. Coupling source data acquisition with pre-processing allows improper data to be returned to its source within a day. As an example, validating orders on a regional basis prevents attempts to consummate improper orders centrally, saving much embarrassment. Recycling the order while it is still fresh prevents serious delay in product delivery.

Corrections can be made to buffered data before it's released to final computer analysis. Once analyzed, invalid data can cause considerable trouble.

Data assembly operations, including selecting, batching and sorting, are generally economically unworthy of large central computers. These operations account for more than half the computer time. Allocating them to smaller, special-purpose machines is the least expensive method to increase computer throughput.

4. DATA BASE MAINTENANCE

Many business applications have need of an extensive addressable data base. Organized lists of mailing addresses, customers, inventories, stockholders, indices, and new accounts are major assets whose maintenance is a necessary but unchallenging computational problem. Just as in pre-processing, the use of a small computer system to perform list maintenance decreases costs significantly because a more proper balance between I/O load and central computing power results.

Updatings of master files, local decentralized data bases, and indices, along with portfolio and asset accounting, are typical applications. Each is similar to the others, with only specific recorded formats varying between applications.

5. OFFLINE ANALYSIS

Frequently a supporting small computer takes care of overload or inconvenient analysis for a large computer. Typical examples include special analysis summaries, index collations, and reorganized or cross-reference files. Also, concentration into one convenient media, such as magnetic tape from multiple diverse media (cassette, paper tape, and telecom) is more convenient and lower in cost on a small rather than a large system. Conversely, the dispersion of data from one media into several others is equally advantageous on small systems.

6. REPORT GENERATION

Reports include periodic status indications and functional business documents like invoices. Output media for reports are typically magnetic tape files and line printer printouts. Both operations are often I/O limited, and make luxurious use of central computer time. Offline service by a small computer for report generation can relieve the larger computer of a considerable nuisance load, reducing net costs and increasing throughput.

7. REPORT DISSEMINATION

The decentralized nature of business operations leads more and more into telecommunications of computer results. These communications are typically either a few large volume inter-regional transmissions, or many small volume, local terminal transmissions. The handling, addressing, error control, and routing of these telecommunications can become sophisticated and complicated. Small dedicated computer systems are beginning to take over these functions to support central computers.

Although decentralized computer systems require less capacity than the equivalent central system, individual task complexities tend to make these capacities higher than a simple division would imply. Also, successful decentralized computation rarely eliminates need for a central computer. Systems must be designed to participate cooperatively in intercomputer data communication networks.

29.

COMPUTER TIMESHARING: A PRIMER FOR THE FINANCIAL EXECUTIVE

By Timothy P. Haidinger

Editor's Note: From FINANCIAL EXECUTIVE, February 1970, pp. 26–35. Reprinted by permission of the publisher, Financial Executive Institute, and author.

The computer timesharing industry has experienced extremely rapid growth since its inception in the early 1960s. A recent report indicates that there are now over 100 timesharing firms utilizing more than 275 computer systems in their operations.[1] Services are available in 42 states and the District of Columbia, and some firms now offer nationwide hook-up to a single timeshared computer center. In less than five years, the timesharing industry has succeeded in capturing a significant share of the market for computer services, with at least six of the major hardware manufacturers selling large-scale time-sharing equipment.

Despite this rapid growth, computer timesharing has had a surprisingly limited impact on business data processing. Perhaps this can be attributed to the businessman's natural concern for reliability and continuity of service, and his consequent reluctance to adopt innovations quickly. It is clear, however, that timesharing offers a great many advantages, particularly for the smaller business, burdened

[1] Lynn Colburn and James P. Magnell, "Technology Profile: Time-Sharing Services," *Modern Data Processing* (July 1969), pp. 36–50.

with a cumbersome manual system and rising clerical costs, which cannot afford an in-house computer and is hesitant to trust its data processing to a service bureau. Often the use of timesharing services will permit such a company to automate its accounting and financial reporting systems earlier than it could if in-house or service-bureau processing were used. And automation of a company's data-processing systems may be implemented at lower cost through timesharing.

Financial executives are often required to evaluate alternative data processing methods for their companies. Timesharing is not usually a major contender in such deliberations. Few financial executives have been exposed to computer timesharing techniques, and, with few exceptions, the timesharing industry has not done a very good job of selling its wares to financial executives and accountants.

Many factors should be considered before a decision to use time-shared data processing services is made. Some of these considerations result from the unique business activities of the company; nevertheless a number of general comments can be made. The comments which follow are designed to give the reader a practical understanding of the "mechanics" of computer timesharing, guidelines for selecting a timesharing service, and system design and programming standards for business timesharing applications.

HOW TIMESHARING WORKS

The basic concept of computer timesharing is that many users, by banding together to share equipment, can have a computer capability which none of them could afford alone. Wide geographic dispersion of the users is overcome by inexpensive remote terminal devices which can serve both as input and ouput units for the central computer. Many of these terminals can be in operation at the same time, all sharing the same central processing unit. To avoid chaos, a switching and priority system in the central processing unit identifies each user and allocates a segment of processor time to him. Normally, the system responds so rapidly that the user feels he is working with "his" computer, and he need not concern himself with the fact that tens, or perhaps hundreds, of other users are connected to the same system.

Although the timesharing equipment currently available varies in many respects, there are more elements of similarity than difference.

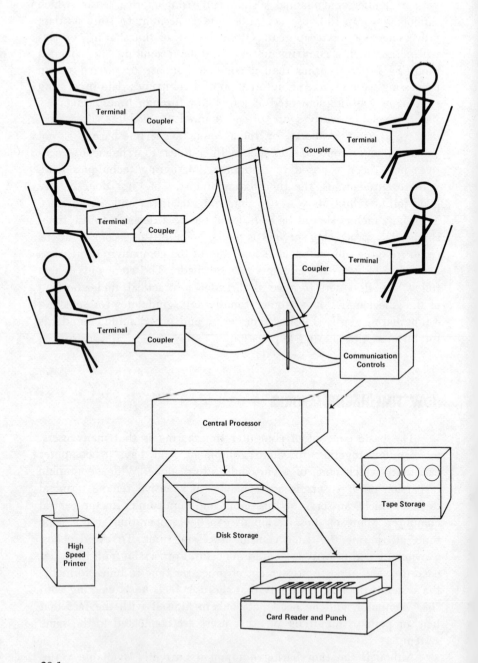

29.1   A TYPICAL TIMESHARING SYSTEM

Most timesharing systems employ the following elements:

1. A central computer, available to many users.

2. Voice-grade telephone lines for transmitting instructions and information to and from the computer.

3. Communication couplers which convert the telephone signal to terminal-compatible impulses and vice versa.

4. Remote terminals which permit the input and output of data.

CENTRAL COMPUTER

Timesharing computers are normally third-generation, and most have fairly large central processors. Large processors are necessary because a fixed number of central processing storage units (characters of memory) is normally allocated to each user when he signs onto the system; thus the number of users online at any one time is limited by the size of the central processor core storage. Also, most timesharing systems use extensive software programs, which occupy a large portion of the computer's core storage.

Peripheral devices often include all those commonly found in conventional in-house configurations, such as card readers and punches, line printers, disk and tape units, and mass storage devices using magnetic cards. Disk units are used in most timesharing systems because they make available a large amount of rapidly accessible file storage at all times to multiple users. The same is true of mass storage devices which, because of their low cost, make the processing of large business data files economically feasible. Tape units are less popular, partly because of the unavoidable delay in communicating with an operator who must mount the requested tape. To cut down on this delay, one manufacturer uses small tape reels, similar to 8-mm motion-picture film reels, which the operator mounts in response to a request from the computer terminal.

Computer timesharing equipment is produced by many manufacturers, both large and small. General Electric's 420 probably holds the greatest share of the market. Other popular systems are Scientific Data Systems' 940, IBM's 360/50 and 360/67, Digital Equipment Corporation's PDP 10, Control Data Corporation's 3300/6600, and Burroughs' B5500. Several of these manufacturers are, in effect, competing with themselves by selling timesharing hardware as well as operating their own timesharing service firms.

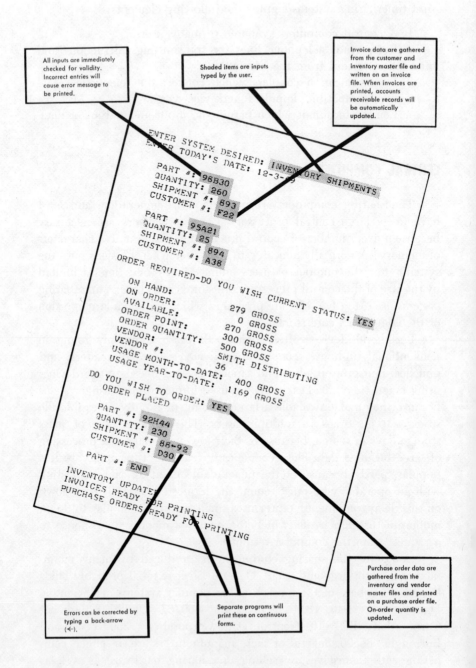

All inputs are immediately checked for validity. Incorrect entries will cause error message to be printed.

Shaded items are inputs typed by the user.

Invoice data are gathered from the customer and inventory master file and written on an invoice file. When invoices are printed, accounts receivable records will be automatically updated.

ENTER SYSTEM DESIRED: INVENTORY SHIPMENTS
ENTER TODAY'S DATE: 12-3-9
            PART #: 98B30
        QUANTITY: 260
        SHIPMENT #: 893
        CUSTOMER #: F22

            PART #: 95A21
        QUANTITY: 25
        SHIPMENT #: 894
        CUSTOMER #: A38

ORDER REQUIRED-DO YOU WISH CURRENT STATUS: YES

        ON HAND:
        ON ORDER: 279 GROSS
        AVAILABLE: 0 GROSS
        ORDER POINT: 270 GROSS
        ORDER QUANTITY: 300 GROSS
        VENDOR: 500 GROSS
        VENDOR #:   SMITH DISTRIBUTING
        USAGE MONTH-TO-DATE: 36
        USAGE YEAR-TO-DATE: 400 GROSS
                                1169 GROSS

DO YOU WISH TO ORDER: YES
    ORDER PLACED

        PART #: 92H44
    QUANTITY: 230
    SHIPMENT #: 88-92
    CUSTOMER #: D30

        PART #: END

INVENTORY UPDATED
INVOICES READY FOR PRINTING
PURCHASE ORDERS READY FOR PRINTING

Errors can be corrected by typing a back-arrow (←).

Separate programs will print these on continuous forms.

Purchase order data are gathered from the inventory and vendor master files and printed on a purchase order file. On-order quantity is updated.

29.2

VOICE-GRADE CONNECTIONS

Communication of data generally is accomplished over the common voice-grade telephone lines available in all business offices. Users near the computer center need make only a local telephone call to communicate with the computer. Many timesharing firms lease telephone lines which they make available to their users in distant markets free of cost or at a minimal charge.

Leased lines are economically practical, thanks to the technique of multiplexing. This is a method of coding telephone signals to permit the handling of many conversations (or data transmissions) over a single line. Calls from numerous users may be multiplexed at a distant location, transmitted over a single line, and reconstructed at the computer center. This procedure is generally quite effective, although in some cases the quality of data transmission appears to be better for users who are located near the computer center than for those some distance away. Operation through office switchboards also seems to cause an increased amount of transmission "noise."

Communication is conducted in either the full-duplex or half-duplex mode. In the full-duplex mode, data can be transmitted from the computer to the user at the same time that other data are being transmitted from the user to the computer. With half duplex, data can be transmitted in only one direction at a time. Full duplex results in slightly faster operation because the user can input data while the terminal is typing the response to a previous processing command. The time difference, however, is not ordinarily significant.

COMMUNICATION COUPLERS

The electronic signal carried over telephone lines consists of a "carrier" signal on which the data to be transmitted are superimposed. The data and carrier signals must be joined before transmission can take place and must be unscrambled after transmission. These tasks are performed by the communication coupler.

Couplers are of three types: acoustic, magnetic, and "hard wired." Acoustic and magnetic units make use of a telephone handset to transfer sound or magnetic impulses between the terminal and the telephone lines. The "hard wired" coupler requires an actual wire connection between the terminal and the telephone line. Such couplers are probably less subject to outside noise than are acoustic and magnetic couplers, but they may require a permanent, non-movable installation. Since all three types of couplers are permanently attached, they can usually be installed only by telephone company personnel.

REMOTE TERMINALS

A wide variety of remote terminal devices is available. Probably the most popular are the Teletype Model 33 and the IBM 2741. Cathode ray tube (CRT) terminals are not suitable for most business data processing because they do not provide output of printed copy. Even though a variety of special-purpose terminals is available, none of them has yet gained the popularity of the IBM and Teletype units. But, since terminal manufacturing companies are highly innovative, many new products will undoubtedly appear in the near future.

The Teletype Model 33 is quite similar to the equipment commonly used for sending telegrams. It prints a page 72 columns wide, in uppercase characters only, at a rate of 10 characters per second. Paper tape input and output is available on the terminal. This permits paper tape to be punched and corrected in advance, so that input to the computer can be made at maximum terminal speed. Paper tape output permits large programs or files which are used infrequently to be stored on paper tape, thereby reducing on-line file storage costs (which are often quite large). Although the unit is somewhat cumbersome, it can be moved from one location to another because it requires only a telephone line, coupler, and electric outlet for operation.

The IBM 2741 terminal is based on the Selectric typewriter. It will print 130 columns in upper- and lower-case type at the rate of 15 characters per second, and the type font can be changed easily. The unit can be used as a typewriter when not being employed as a computer terminal. The terminal can be fitted with a pin-feed sprocket which permits the proper alignment of preprinted continuous forms—a great help in preparing invoices, checks, etc. Paper tape handling equipment is not available. The installation requirements are similar to those for the Teletype 33.

SELECTING A TIMESHARING SYSTEM

Business data processing makes unique demands on a timesharing system—demands which only a limited number of systems can accommodate. A thorough evaluation of the suitability of the services provided should be made before any agreement is signed with a time-sharing firm.

The user ordinarily has the choice of proceeding with the evaluation and conversion on his own or hiring outside assistance. He will probably prefer unassisted conversion if the firm is experienced in the timesharing field, or if it wishes to develop its own expertise and is willing to pay the extra training cost which will be required. But one should keep in mind that the timesharing field is changing very rapidly. New firms are frequently being formed, and new or modified programming languages are announced daily. The computer hardware, computer terminals, and communication equipment in use are changing so rapidly that virtually a full-time effort is required to keep abreast of developments in the field. For this reason, a user may frequently be best advised to hire outside experts on a "for services rendered" basis to assist in evaluating alternative services and to prepare the computer programs.

Selection of a timesharing system should be based on a consideration of the following characteristics:

- Computer configuration
- Programming language
- Reliability
- Cost

The relative importance of these factors and the specific evaluation of them will be different for each application, but no decision should be made until all four have been considered.

COMPUTER TRANSFIGURATION

Processing characteristics of timesharing systems cover a wide range. In general, however, an extremely powerful central processor, combined with extensive peripheral devices, makes available some of the largest and fastest computer configurations now manufactured. Features of greatest interest for business applications include the numerous large on-line data files with random addressing capability, large central processor core memory, rapid computing speed, and the ability to perform "background" processing.

File Size

Most business data-processing applications require the maintenance of extensive data files. For this reason, file size and method of addressing are probably the most important characteristics of the computer configuration. The file must be large enough to handle the largest of the company's master files, with an allowance for expected

EXHIBIT 3

FILE ADDRESSING SYSTEMS EXAMPLE—PAYROLL COMPENSATION FILE

SEQUENTIAL Records not directly addressable

KEY	DATA	KEY	DATA	KEY	DATA
	Compensation record Jones		Compensation record Smith		Compensation record Brown

KEY NUMBER Records directly addressed by sequence number

KEY	DATA	KEY	DATA	KEY	DATA
	Compensation record Jones		Compensation record Smith		Compensation record Brown

KEY WORD Records directly addressed by any predetermined alphabetic or numeric key

KEY	DATA	KEY	DATA	KEY	DATA
	Compensation record Jones		Compensation record Smith		Compensation record Brown

29.3   FILE ADDRESSING SYSTEMS EXAMPLE—PAYROLL COMPENSATION FILE

growth. Also, the system should permit access to more than one file by a single program at one time. File size is normally measured in terms of the number of alphabetic or numeric characters which the file can contain, and the required size is therefore fairly easy to compute.

Random addressing

The term "addressing" refers to the method by which a computer program indicates which record of a stored file is to be read into the central processor. The most flexible system of addressing permits the programmer to use a "key word" which the system will associate with a particular record on the indicated file. This key word can be any combination of alphabetic and numeric characters. For example, a

SEQUENTIAL Records not directly addressable

KEY	DATA	KEY	DATA	KEY	DATA
	Compensation record Jones		Compensation record Smith		Compensation record Brown

KEY NUMBER Records directly addressed by sequence number

KEY	DATA	KEY	DATA	KEY	DATA
1	Compensation record Jones	2	Compensation record Smith	3	Compensation record Brown

KEY WORD Records directly addressed by any
predetermined alphabetic or numeric key

KEY	DATA	KEY	DATA	KEY	DATA
Jones	Compensation record Jones	Smith	Compensation record Smith	Brown	Compensation record Brown

part number which incorporates alphabetic and numeric characters could be used to indicate the record containing data on the price, inventory currently on hand, back order, and ordering point for the part; an employee's name or identification number could be used to indicate his compensation record.

The second common system uses a "key number" to identify each record in the master file, the key being the sequence number of the record in the file. That is, the first record has the key of one, the second record has the key of two, and so on. To recover a single record under this addressing system, the program must store a table of addresses or use some code to relate the contents of a record to its key. Although this requirement decreases operating flexibility of the system, both of these systems have the advantage of being direct-access methods in which a program needs to handle only those records for which updating is to be performed.

A third system of file addressing is "sequential addressing," in which the records of a file may be read only in strict sequence. In other words, in order to read the 30th record in the file, the preceding 29 records must first be read. Efficient processing with a sequential file addressing technique requires that the transactions used to update the file first be sorted into the same sequence in which the file is maintained. This makes it possible to update the master file in a single pass. Sorting can be a very time-consuming procedure, however, and few timesharing systems have packaged sort programs available. When transactions are prepared in the proper sequence as a matter of course, and when a large portion of the master file is to be updated, sequential addressing may not be a significant handicap. When only a small proportion of the records needs updating, the requirement that all records of the file be read may result in a considerable increase in processing time.

Processor Size

The size of the central processor available to a user is important because it determines the number of instructions which can be carried out by the computer in one operation. When a large number of steps can be performed, the need to store interim calculations can be eliminated, and the speed and ease of operation of the system are improved.

One must distinguish between the total size of the computer's central processing unit and the portion of the processing unit allocated to any single user. Many systems allocate a fixed portion of the processor to each user and this is, in effect, the size of "his" central processing unit. It is of little consequence to the user that the total processor has a capacity of several hundred thousand characters of storage if only a small part of this capacity will be allocated to him. Core storage is expensive to manufacture, and the time-sharing firm, with its high usage rate, can normally afford to purchase many more characters of storage than are economical for smaller in-house installations.

Speed

The central processors of timesharing computers are typically very large and very fast. Speed is of interest primarily when extensive computations with limited input and output are desired, or when the user is paying for central computer processor time, rather than terminal time. These conditions occur frequently enough to make speed an important consideration.

Background Processing

Some timesharing services offer what is referred to as "background batch" processing. This type of processing uses high-speed devices, such as line printers, magnetic tapes, card readers, etc., to input and output information independent of the user's terminal. Computer time is allocated to background processing only when the allocation will not interfere with on-line timesharing users. This often entails a considerable delay, but as a result of the high-speed input and output and the ability of the computer operator to make use of otherwise idle time, background processing is frequently quite inexpensive. It can best be used to process data when turnaround time is not critical and when there are large quantities of input or output.

PROGRAMMING LANGUAGE

If the user has engaged outside consultants to perform the required system design and programming, he probably will not need to concern himself with the capabilities of the programming language used by the timesharing service. Typically, the programming contract specifies that the user will own the programs once they are completed, and that the work will be performed either for a fixed price or for an agreed hourly rate, subject to some maximum. If the user plans to do his own programming, however, the characteristics of the programming language have considerable significance. It is important that the language:

1. Be easy to learn or be a language with which the company's personnel are already familiar.

2. Have instructions available which will permit terminal input and output to be formatted to the user's specifications.

3. Permit the computer program to guide its user in inputting data and interpreting output.

The last consideration is particularly important when the operator will use the program infrequently and will need coaching on the proper procedures each time it is run.

A variety of programming languages is available to the timesharing user. Many, such as Fortran II, Fortran IV, Algol, Cobol, and, more recently, PL/1, are based on languages developed in the past for stand-alone computers. Languages developed specifically for timesharing users provide extremely simple and conversational commands which can be learned rapidly. Ease of use of these languages is achieved by reducing the control the user has over the computer's operations and by employing a great deal of system software, which occupies core storage and results in higher user charges.

The most common of these conversational languages is named "Basic." This language was developed at Dartmouth University, and has since been modified into many versions, known as Extended Basic, Super Basic, etc.

A study conducted in August 1969 indicates that the vast majority of users write their programs in Fortran or Basic, with 39.6 per cent preferring Fortran and 31.0 per cent preferring Basic.[2] For business applications, Basic is probably the overwhelming choice.

RELIABILITY

Since the user does not control the operation of the computer in a timesharing system, he has little recourse in the event of unreliable service, other than transferring his allegiance to a different timesharing firm. If the programming language is unique—and nearly all programming languages are unique to some degree—the conversion may be quite costly.

The potential user can evaluate a service's reliability through inquiries to existing users and by performing "benchmark" tests of competitive systems. Timesharing firms are generally somewhat reluctant to release the names of their customers, but they will usually release the names if a sale is contingent upon satisfactory references. The program used in benchmark reliability tests should receive input data from a terminal, perform nominal processing upon the data, and return the related output to the terminal, with perhaps 50 to 100 repetitions of this cycle for each test. Testing should be conducted at the time of day when the operational programs are expected to be run, at the time when the computer center is likely to be experiencing its heaviest load, and at selected "off" times, such as the early morning or late evening hours.

When evaluating system reliability, the following factors should be considered:

Down time. The percentage of advertised operating time in which the computer is unavailable because of preventive maintenance or malfunction. This percentage may vary, depending on the time of day.

---

[2] Bolidan O. Szuprowicz, "The Time-Sharing Users: Who Are They?", *Datamation* (August 1969), pp. 55–59.

Line noise. Line noise is a communication malfunction which causes a character to be transmitted improperly to or from the computer center. This is an extremely important type of malfunction because its presence can often go undetected.

Training courses. If in-house programming is to be performed, the timesharing firm should have adequate facilities to train user personnel in the programming language to be used.

Design and programming assistance. A programmer should be on call at all times to answer miscellaneous questions on system operation and proper programming technique. A commitment to perform system design and program coding can be a very strong selling point if it is clear that qualified personnel will be made available.

Hours of operation. The number of hours per day and days per week in which the service is available may be important, particularly in applications which require a great deal of processing or where fast turnaround is needed.

Length of time in business. A timesharing firm which has maintained good relations with its customers over a period of years is usually preferable to one which has recently begun offering its services.

Financial stability. The timesharing firm should have sufficient financial strength to ensure that its operations will be carried on in a proper manner in the foreseeable future.

COST

In analyzing the economics of using a computer timesharing system, four types of cost must be considered. These are (1) conversion cost (including programming costs), (2) processing cost, (3) file storage cost, and (4) terminal rental cost.

Conversion Cost

Timesharing requires the user to pay only for the processing he accomplishes; any minimum charge is normally insignificant. This is in sharp contrast to in-house installations, which require a fairly large fixed monthly expenditure, regardless of usage. In addition, with timesharing there is no need to hire expensive and highly transient data-processing personnel or to construct the facilities in which to house a computer. At the same time, the user can retain nearly complete control over the processing of his transactions and has no outside service bureau apologizing for "unavoidable delays." A user with low transaction volume will not be forced to adapt his accounting to someone else's large-scale programming package, nor will he be a marginal client for a local service bureau.

The two primary conversion costs are for programming and input of beginning data files. Packaged internal accounting programs are beginning to appear, but none has yet gained wide acceptance. Most programs are custom-prepared, although it is often possible to adapt some program routines and input/output formats from one system to another. System programming performed by outside programmers will rarely cost less than $2,000, with $3,000 to $5,000 being an average for design and programming of a basic accounts receivable, inventory or similar system. In-house programming costs may be somewhat lower, but the difference dwindles in significance when all associated costs are considered.

Data conversion costs for specific applications can be estimated easily by computing the operator time and computer charges for inputting beginning data files. This can be done at the terminal or in punched card, magnetic tape, or other form. Ordinarily, conversion will be carried out at year-end or another time when the volume of data to be converted is low and conversion costs will not be significant.

Processing Cost

The total monthly charge a user pays for his processing is a function of two items: the cost base and the price. The cost base is normally either terminal hours used or central processor minutes used. If central processing unit minutes are the base, the rate may vary depending on the amount of core storage being used. Typical terminal rates range from $3 to $18 per terminal hour, and rates based on central processor time range from $5 to $16 per minute. A rough rule of thumb is that one CPU minute is required for each terminal hour, but the exact amount can vary greatly, depending on whether a program is oriented toward input/output or processing.

The majority of timesharing services charge on the basis of terminal hours used. Because inputting data at a terminal is a slow process, charges based on terminal input do not truly reflect utilization of the computer. This method is not, therefore, as suitable for business data processing purposes as is a charge based on central processor time. When the timesharing service charges for terminal time, the processing should be done on a batch basis, with input data prepared off-line on a paper tape which can be read by the terminal at high speed.

File Storage Cost

Most systems have a monthly charge for file storage based on the maximum number of characters stored during the month. Rates vary from several cents to as high as several dollars per thousand characters stored. The lower rates are for mass storage devices, such as the IBM data cell, and make the processing of large business data files economically feasible.

Terminal Rental

The cost of a computer terminal ranges from $100 to $120 per month. The communication coupler will add another $20 to $50, as will the cost of telephone lines, printed forms, and other miscellaneous costs. The terminal rate is for unlimited usage and includes all maintenance, which is performed by the supplier.

Cathode ray tube displays and remote plotters are available for lease at rates substantially higher than those indicated above for printed-copy terminals.

SYSTEM DESIGN AND PROGRAMMING STANDARDS

Once a timesharing system has been selected, the user must concern himself with proper system design and programming. Many of the standards used for in-house systems are applicable to timesharing systems. Since it is probable, however, that the user has had limited prior experience with computer systems, he must make a particular effort to design, program, and document his system properly.

SYSTEM DESIGN

The new system should be designed to permit easy conversion from the old system, with minimal disruption to those procedures not being changed. This will require that the analyst be thoroughly familiar with the procedures in effect, or that he work in close conjunction with financial executive. Where possible, data files should be converted at year-end or at another time when the data file is at its minimum size. As with any change in processing, the conversion to a timesharing system provides an excellent opportunity to improve existing systems. In-house or outside personnel may be effectively employed at this time to conduct an over-all system review.

Timesharing provides such extensive on-line processing capabilities that there is occasionally a tendency to neglect a proper audit trail. Both for outside auditors and for reconstruction of lost data, it is vitally important that an adequate trail be maintained. This will probably take the form of printed copy, retained on a predetermined schedule. Supplemental data files may also be maintained by the system as a part of the documentation available to permit reconstruction.

PROGRAMMING

Certain programming standards should be maintained whether the programming is done in-house, by outside programmers as a custom application, or by the adaptation of a packaged program. Some of the standards are unique to timeshared programming, and particular caution must be exercised when programming is done by those accustomed to programming for in-house operation.

Probably the most important element of a timesharing program is the set of recovery procedures to be used in case of a communication failure. Since even the most reliable communication equipment will break down occasionally, programs must be designed to permit the operator to resume processing with as little disruption as possible. Recovery procedures are also necessary to permit the reversal of transactions or data entered improperly by the operator. Such recovery techniques take many forms and are unique to each application.

There is a natural tendency to shortcut recovery in order to complete the program as quickly as possible. However, the cost of additional programming will be quickly dwarfed by the cost of reconstructing data files after the first system breakdown. Proper recovery techniques are available, but the user must insist upon them and not leave the decision to the programmer.

Programs should be properly documented and organized. The program documentation should include a program listing, flowchart (unless the program listing contains sufficient comments that it can be used as a program flowchart), sample input and output documents, layouts of all files used by the program, a directory of all variable names, and a narrative description of the processing performed by the program. If numerous programs are being developed, documentation should be maintained in a standard format and should be required before any program is considered complete. The narrative description, system flowchart, and data input and output formats should be agreed upon before any detailed program coding is begun. To facilitate future expansion or modification, the program coding should be organized in a fashion which makes it easily understood. A modular approach to program writing, in which the program is divided into subroutines, is normally the best way to assure easy expansion.

One of the great advantages of timesharing processing is that the computer program, through the terminal, can guide the user in the proper input of data. Instructions and comments printed on the terminal by the program should be comprehensive and detailed enough to keep the error rate low, but they should not be so detailed as to be cumbersome. When a particular instruction or comment will be repeated throughout the processing, it should be made brief because the operator will become familiar with its meaning. On the other hand, those comments which will be used infrequently should be made much more explicit. In some cases, it is desirable to reduce the level of instructions after an operator has become thoroughly familiar with a program. This can usually be accomplished with minor program modifications.

CONCLUSION

It seems certain that timesharing will play a larger and larger role in business data processing as financial executives become increasingly aware of its capabilities. The development of standard industry languages, improved reliability, new terminal devices, and an increased marketing effort will make timesharing a question of "when," not "if," for more and more financial executives.

At the present time the opportunities for reduced clerical costs and increased flexibility make timesharing an attractive proposition. However, the rapid growth of the industry has led to a wide variety in the type and quality of services offered by timesharing firms. The financial executive is well advised to adopt a systematic and thorough approach in both the evaluation and conversion stages to assure a system which will meet his criteria for performance and cost.

METHODS OF PROCESSING DATA: DISCUSSION QUESTIONS

1. What is the fundamental difference between batch processing and continuous or real-time processing? Is it ever desirable to perform batch processing on an on-line system capable of processing data continuously? If so, under what conditions? If not, why not?

2. Some authorities maintain that continuous, on-line processing can be less costly than batch processing with proper systems design and implementation. Explain how this could be possible.

3. Indicate whether batch processing or continuous processing is most likely to be utilized in each of the following situations. Explain fully.

   a. System operating costs are high and machine utilization is low, resulting in a need to increase capacity utilization and improve efficiency of operations.

   b. Applications processed have a high error potential.

   c. Systems storage space is limited and storage costs are high.

   d. Responses to information inquiries are needed within minutes of submission of requests. Are needed once daily.

   e. Available software and hardware resources are very limited.

   f. A large volume of transactions is to be processed but only a few records are affected (that is, activity ratio is high).

   g. A small volume of transactions occurring at irregular intervals is to be processed and the file activity ratio is high.

4. How does remote batch processing differ from standard batch processing? How are factors such as turnaround time, need for man-machine interaction, inability to collect all application data at once, existence of large volumes of data, unavailability of an in-house computer, and a shortage of qualified EDP personnel for in-house operation likely to affect the decision to utilize or not utilize remote batch processing?

5. What general characteristics do business data processing problems have that distinguish them from other types of processing prob-

lems such as scientific and engineering problems? What require-ments or restrictions do these characteristics place on the choice of data collection/transmission methods, data storage devices, or-ganization schemes, and processing methods?

6. What factors must be considered when choosing between time-sharing services of an off-premise, large-scale electronic computer and a smaller, on-site, batch-processing computer? Between an on-site continuous processing system and a time-shared system for the exclusive use of the organization operating the system?

7. Potential problem areas in the use of time-sharing systems can arise from high programming costs, time delays in program exe-cution, data security difficulties, communications problems, and data base complexities. How can these problems be overcome or at least minimized?

8. Is a time-sharing system likely to provide efficient and economical processing service for the following?
   a. Recurring, relatively standardized business data processing problems with fixed processing times.
   b. Strategic management planning problems involving the simu-lation and testing of numerous alternative courses of action.
   c. Performance reporting on the status of diverse functional activ-ities conducted by a widely geographically dispersed enter-prise.
   d. Complex scientific and engineering problems (such as, product design) requiring many calculations and large amounts of stor-age space.
   e. Industrial process-control applications in which outputs vary widely and the process itself is very unstable.
   f. Market research and stock market data supplied to a number of users at remote locations by a central data service that also col-lects some data from using organizations.
   Explain fully your answers to the above questions.

9. Which factors are likely to be most important in evaluating a time-sharing service: System availability or system reliability? Suitability of programming languages or level of user assistance and sup-port provided? Processing, storage, or data communication costs? Why?

10. What benefits can a user obtain by utilizing packaged programs in conjunction with a time-sharing service? In selecting a packaged program, which is most likely to be most important: Throughput or cost? Generality or flexibility? Accuracy or documentation? Why?

METHODS OF PROCESSING DATA: BIBLIOGRAPHY

Adams, Charles W., "Processing Business Data," *Control Engineering*, June 1956, pp. 105–112.

Adams, Jeanne, and Cohen, Leonard, "Time-Sharing vs. Instant Batch Processing: An Experiment in Programmer Training," *Computers and Automation*, March 1969, pp. 30–34.

Allen, Brandt, "Time Sharing Takes Off," *Harvard Business Review*, March–April 1969, pp. 128–136. See also "Computer Time-Sharing," *Management Accounting*, January 1969, pp. 36–38, 47.

American Data Processing, *Management of On-line Systems*, Data Processing Monograph Series, 1968, Part I, "Online Real Time Systems as a Long Range Planning Goal;" Part II, "Experimental Studies Comparing Online and Offline Programming Performance"; Part III, "Online Debugging Procedures"; Part IV, "Group Communications in Online Systems."

Amstutz, Stanford R., "Distributed Intelligence in Data Communication Networks," *Computer*, November/December 1971, pp. 27–32.

Auerbach on Time-Sharing (Phila. 1972), *Auerbach Guide to Time-Sharing Services*, 182, May 22, 1972.

Auerbach Guide to Small Business Computers, 139, May 23, 1972.

"Basic Selection of the Type of System; Off-Line, In-Line, or Un-Line?," From James D. Gallagher, *Management Information Systems and the Computer*, American Management Association, 1961, pp. 133–141.

Baker, J. B., and Nottage, K. S., "Time-Sharing: Toy or Tool for Management," *Administrative Management*, January 1973; and "Time-Sharing; Some Benchmarks," *Administrative Management*, February 1973, pp. 52–54.

Bauer, Walter F., "The Economics of On-Line Systems: Some Aspects," *Computers and Automation*, October 1965, pp. 14–16.

Bauer, Walter F., and Hill, Richard H., "The Economics of Time-Sharing," *Datamation*, Part I, November 1967, pp. 48–55; Part II, December 1967, pp. 41–49.

Blose, W. F., and Goetz, E. E., "On-Line Processing—How Will It Affect Your Organizational Structure," *Journal of Data Management,* March 1969, pp. 18–26.

Brown, Robert B., "Cost and Advantages of Online Data Processing," *Datamation,* March 1968, pp. 40–47.

Brown, W. F., and Hawkins, David H., "Remote Access Computing: The Executive's Responsibility, *Journal of Systems Management,* May 1972, pp. 12–16, and June 1972, pp. 32–35.

Canning, Richard G., "Progress in Fast Response Systems," *Systems and Procedures Journal,* July–August 1967, pp. 20–24.

Clapp, Louis C., "Time-Sharing Terminal vs. the Small Computer," *Data Systems News,* February 1970, p. 25.

Coiner, Lewis M., "Midi and Maxicomputers Expand Their Powers, Offer More Real-Time Operation and Multiprogramming," *Administrative Management,* November 1972, pp. 27–35.

Cole, Aaron W., "Coming to Terms with Data Remoting," *Administrative Management,* September 1971, pp. 63–64.

Curry, S. Y., "Strategies for Successful Computer Utilization," *Automation,* January 1963, pp. 66–71.

Daly, Diana, "How to Choose a Time-Sharing Service," *Computer Decisions,* March 1970, pp. 44–48.

Daniel, E. L., and Harris, L., "Remote Job Entry," *Datamation,* April 1969, pp. 128–131.

Datapro 70, "All About Computer Time-Sharing Services," December 1972; "All About Minicomputers," June 1972.

Dorn, Philip H., "How to Evaluate a Time-Sharing Service," *Datamation,* November 1969, pp. 220–226.

Duffy, G. F., "A Time-Sharing System for Business Operations," *Systems and Procedures Journal,* May–June 1967, pp. 20–24. See also G. W. Duffy and W. D. Timberlake, "A Business-Oriented Time-Sharing System," *AFIPS, Proceedings—Spring Joint Computer Conference,* 1966, pp. 265–275.

Emerson, Marvin, "The 'Small' Computer Versus Time-Shared Systems," *Computers and Automation,* September 1965, pp. 18–20.

Fano, Robert M., "The Place of Time Sharing," *Engineering Education,* April 1968, pp. 917–923.

Feeney, G. J., "Time Sharing, Management, and Management Science," *Management Science,* February 1967, pp. C-112 to C-116. See also Gerald H. Fine and Paul V. McIsaac, "Simulation of a Time-Sharing System," *Management Science,* February 1966, pp. B-180 to B-194.

Feeney, George, "A Three-Stage Theory of Evolution for the Sharing of Computer Power," *Computer Decisions*, pp. 42–45.

Field, John, and Stilian, G. N., "Economics of On-Line versus Offline Systems," *Data Processing*, June 1963, pp. 8–14.

Flores, Ivan, "Swapping vs. Paging," *Modern Data*, April 1970, pp. 152–157.

Forsythe, J. D., and Wilson, D. A., "Time Sharing Systems for Financial Management," *Canadian Chartered Accountant*, April 1970, pp. 239–242.

Greenless, Malcolm, "Time Sharing Computers in Business," *Cost and Management*, July–August 1969, pp. 4–16.

Grubinger, Eric W., "A Practical Look At On-Line Time Sharing," *Business Automation*, February 1967, pp. 46–54.

Greenberger, Fred, "Are Small, Free-Standing Computers Here to Stay?," *Datamation*, April 1966, pp. 67–68.

Haidinger, Timothy P., "Computer Time Sharing: A Primer for the Financial Executive," *Financial Executive*, February 1970, pp. 26–35.

Hakola, Vern E., "Computer Time-Sharing and the CPA—Opportunity or Problem?," *Journal of Accountancy*, January 1969, pp. 63–68. See also the Spring 1968 issue of *The California CAP Quarterly*.

Hammerton, James C., "Business Time-Sharing: User Economics," *Datamation*, June 1969, pp. 70–81.

Highleyman, Wilbur H., "The Economics of Business Mini's *Management Accounting*, October 1971, pp. 12–14. See also Robert L. Washburn, "Purchasing a Minicomputer," Automation, May 1972, pp. 52–56.

Howard, Phillip C., "Technology and Advantages of Time-Sharing Systems," *Data Management*, August 1969, pp. 26–29.

Huskey, Harry D., "Economics of On-Line and Batch Processing Computing in a University," *Economics of Automatic Data Processing*, A. B. Freunic, editor, North Holland Publishing Company, 1965, pp. 340–345.

Johnson, Ellsworth C., "Computer Time Sharing in Perspective," *Automation*, March 1967, pp. 92–95.

Johnson, Richard M., "Remote Computing and Its Impact on Marketing Research," *Computer Operations*, March/April 1969, pp. 10–17.

Karush, Arnold D., "Evaluating Time-Sharing Systems Using the Benchmark Method," *Data Processing*, May 1970, pp. 42–44.

Karush, Arnold D., "What Is a Minicomputer?," *The Office*, August 1972, pp. 12–14. See also Lewis M. Coiner, "Minicomputers: The Small Firm's Entree to EDP; Specialized Back-ups for Larger

Sized Businesses," *Administrative Management,* October 1972, pp. 23–29.

Katterjohn, J. M., "Batch or Real-Time Processing?," *Automation,* August 1971, pp. 61–64.

Kaufman, Felix, "Computer Time Sharing for the CPA," *Management Services,* November–December 1968, pp. 17–29.

"Here Comes Remote Batch," *EDP Analyzer,* February 1972.

Madrick, Stuart E., "Time-Sharing Systems: Virtual Machine Concept vs. Conventional Approach," *Modern Data,* March 1969, pp. 34–36.

Main, Jeremy, "Computer Time-Sharing—Every Man at the Console," *Fortune,* August 1967, pp. 88–92, 187–190.

McDaniel, Joe R., "ABC's of Time-Sharing," Automation, June 1970, p. 91–94.

Mensh, Michael, "Multiprogramming: What It Is . . . When to Use It . . . What to Look For," *Computers and Automation,* February 1968, pp. 22–25.

Miller, L., "Random Processing of Sequential Files," *Economics of Automatic Data Processing,* A. B. Freunic, editor, North Holland Publishing Company, 1965, pp. 205–209.

"Multiprogramming Does More for Less," *Computer Decisions,* June 1970, pp. 27–32.

Murphy, John A., "Minicomputers," *Modern Data,* June 1971, pp. 58–71.

Myers, Edith, "AMA Conference: Distributed Computing," *Datamation,* November 1972, pp. 133–134.

Nelson, William D., "How To Pick a Time-Sharing Service," *Computer Design,* August 1968, pp. 59–65.

Pointel, Nichole, and Cohen, Daniel, "Computer Time-Sharing—A Review," *Computers and Automation,* October 1967, pp. 38–46.

Popell, Steven D., et al., *Computer Time-Sharing: Dynamic Information Handling for Business,* Englewood Cliffs, N. J., Prentice-Hall, 1966.

Pryor, Lee, "Time-Sharing at This-Point-in-Time," *Journal of Data Management,* May 1969, pp. 30–32.

Reilly, Frank W., "Management Considerations When Evaluating Time-Shared Facilities," *Decisions from Data,* Thompson Book Co., 1967, pp. 239–246.

Rosenberg, Arthur M., "The Brave New World of Time-Sharing Operating Systems," *Datamation,* August 1969, pp. 42–47.

Rosenberg, Arthur M., "Resource Allocation and System Management in the Time-Sharing Era," *Data Processing,* May 1969, pp. 38–44.

Rullo, Thomas, "Selecting a Time-Sharing Service: The Common Sense Approach," *Data Processing*, March 1970, pp. 43–47.

Sackman, Harold, "Online vs. Offline Programming," *Data Processing Digest*, July 1968, pp. 1–14. See also H. Sackman, "Time-Sharing vs. Batch Processing: The Experimental Evidence," *Proceedings of the 1968 Spring Joint Computer Conference*, Thompson Book Company, 1968.

Samson, Thomas F., "Computer Time-Sharing: A New Tool for the Auditor," *Arthur Young Journal*, Summer 1970, pp. 41–48.

Schwab, Bernhard, "The Economics of Sharing Computers," *Harvard Business Review*, September–October 1968, pp. 61–70.

Smith, Robert M., "Two—For Less Than One," *Management Services*, July–August 1969, pp. 39–42.

Solomon, Martin B., Jr., "Are Small, Free-Standing Computers Really Here to Stay?" *Datamation*, July 1966, pp. 66, 71.

Sorensen, Jim L., "Time-Sharing or Direct Access: A Solution to the Small Company's EDP Dilemma," *Arthur Young Journal*, Autumn 1968, pp. 34–36. See also "A Solution to the Small Company's EDP Dilemma," *Journal of Data Management*, April 1969, pp. 28–31.

Spiro, Bruce E., "Processing Methods and the Systems Designer," *Journal of Data Management*, September 1968, pp. 20–27.

Statz, Robert H., "Directions In Time-Sharing Terminals," *Computer Group News*, May 1968.

Stewart, Michael, "Will Time-Sharing Help You," *Management Review*, June 1970, pp. 37–41 (condensed from *European Business*, January 1970).

Stimler, Saul, "Some Criteria for Time-Sharing Performance Measurement," *ACM Communications*, January 1969, pp. 47–53.

Sutherland, Ivan E., "The Future of On-Line Systems," *On-Line Computing Systems*, E. Burgess, editor, American Data Processing, 1965, pp. 9–13.

"The Mini's Are Moving," *Business Automation*, February 1970, pp. 46–51.

"Time-Sharing," series of articles in special issue of *Computers and Automation*, October 1968, pp. 16–39.

Turnblade, Richard C., "The Case for Dedicated Computers," *Data Processing*, May 1971, pp. 41–44.

Vance Earl E., "Multiprogramming: The New Economics," *Journal of Data Management*, May 1969, pp. 18–22.

Wald, Bruce. "Multiprocessor Operating Systems," U.S. Department of Commerce Clearinghouse, 11 April 1967, AD-651-707.

"What Every CPA Should Know about Time-Sharing," *Journal of Accountancy*, October 1972, pp. 74–76.

White, Charles H., "Time-Sharing Services," *Modern Data*, February 1970, pp. 66–74.

Wilkinson, Bryan, "Some Problems with Time-Sharing," *Business Automation*, January 1968, pp. 46–50 (condensed in *Management Review*, April 1968, pp. 52–55). See also "Some Problems with Time-Sharing: A Tale of Horror," *Datamation*, May 1968, pp. 43–45.

Wilkinson, Bryan, "Choosing a Time-Sharing Service," *Journal of Data Management*, December 1968, pp. 20–23.

Young, Neal F., "Distributed Computer Systems," *Automation*, October 1969, pp. 89–93. See also N. Nesenoff, "Design of Distributed Communications System—A Case Study," *AFIPS, Fall Joint Computer Conference*, 1969, pp. 637–653.

Yourdon, Edward, "An Approach to Measuring a Time-Sharing System," *Datamation*, April 1969, pp. 124–126.

Yourdon, Edward, "Time-Sharing for Very Small Businesses," *Computers and Automation*, October 1969, pp. 38–41.

Ziegler, James R., "What Is Time Sharing?," *Business Automation*, January 1968 (condensed in *Management Review*, April 1968, pp. 52–55).

PART VI

INFORMATION RETRIEVAL AND DISPLAY: CONCEPTS, ALTERNATIVES, AND DEVICES

The growth of specialization in subject fields and a tremendous increase in the volumes of information generated by information systems have increased the difficulties of successfully retrieving information. Problems arising in information retrieval include uncertainty as to the future use of data, very large files that are difficult and time-consuming to search, complex data structures that inhibit man-machine communication, and the marginal utility of much of the information collected. The types of systems that commonly perform information retrieval services include data base or file management systems, reference systems (which store references to materials rather than actual content), and text-processing systems (which produce reproduceable offset masters from data stored in machine-readable form).

Storage and retrieval of human knowledge is one of mankind's costliest and most time-consuming problems. Manual and automated storage and retrieval systems are now being developed to resolve this problem. Fast, direct-access computer systems now permit sequential or random searches of both structured and unstructured files on an economical and efficient basis. Currently available information services can take the form of library services (that is, in the form of documents, abstracts, or reference lists), data centers (which provide specific answers to specific questions), and analysis centers (which perform both retrieval and data analysis functions for specific data applied to a specific problem). Inquiry services, designed to minimize the effort and knowledge required for successful use of the system by the end user, can be utilized in conjunction with any of the three types of information services. Careful attention should be given to data input control, indexing schemes, methods of storing and purging data, and definition of user needs. The effectiveness of inquiry services must be judged in terms of cost per inquiry, response time to answer information requests, and the percentage of inquiries successfully answered.

Cowles emphasizes the usefulness of computer processing in storing, maintaining, and searching for documents. Major functions of information retrieval include analysis, indexing, storage, search, and selection. The computer assists in the process by working with indexes, queries, and data extraction and reporting. In creating index terms, consideration must be given to author and user viewpoints, generality or specificity of requests, semantics, and syntax. Query commands start searching operations that yield a document, its surrogate, or information that will assist the user in document location. Logical comparisons between query and stored index terms help to establish the likelihood that a "match" has been made. Once pertinent information has been selected, some manipulation of the data may be necessary prior to the output stage. Existing software packages offer a wide variety of information storage and retrieval capabilities that will satisfy the needs of many users.

A variety of output devices is available to meet user needs, as "EDP output devices: the Four Options," *Administrative Management*, points out. Impact printers are more portable, often faster, and produce more legible copies than other types of printers. The latest nonimpact printers are quieter, faster, and less expensive than ever before. Cathode-ray tubes (CRT's) are gaining favor with many users because of their fast response time, ability to scan large volumes of data rapidly, and economy and convenience of operation. For some types of quick query applications, voice-response systems have become very popular. In selecting a hard-copy printer, consideration should be given to application use, speed, cost, flexibility, reliability, and noise.

Lorber points out that in many cases, costly, high-speed printers are used to spew out large amounts of data when more selective output production would be adequate. Output printers may be characterized as serial versus parallel, full character versus dot matrix, and impact versus nonimpact. Serial printers are less costly but slower than parallel or line printers. High-speed line printers tend to be of the dot matrix variety and are therefore less suitable for multiple copy production than full copy printers. Nonimpact printers are generally faster and often more expensive than impact types. A trend toward widespread use of interactive time-sharing systems should reduce line printer batch operations and shift more of the load to real-time CRT-plus-printer terminals.

As Wolaver observes, substitution of microfilm for paper reduces filing and retrieving time, decreases storage costs and space requirements, and makes copying and distribution easier. For large-volume data retrieval and storage applications, microfilm is superior to paper printouts in terms of retrieval speeds and costs. If a microfilm system is chosen, the user must decide whether to utilize roll or unitized micro-forms, manual or automatic microfilm retrieval, or computer output to microfilm. When real-time accessing for updating or retrieval is re-quired and data volumes handled are small, an on-line system with CRT terminals will probably be preferred.

Cathode-ray tubes, computer-linked microfilm, and computer-connected graphic displays have great potential for breaking the in-formation output bottleneck but their use has been inhibited by equipment and computer programming costs, as Joplin and Pattillo note. Cathode-ray tubes permit managers to converse directly with the computer, to display alphabetic or numeric data in tabular or graphic form, and to enter new data or alter existing data in the sys-tem. CRT units are used in file-scanning systems (in which the cur-rent status of individual records is needed to make operating de-cisions) and in management reporting systems (which generate sum-maries and analyses of activities and file conditions on a periodic basis).

CRT-centered management reporting systems can display current information at a moment's notice, can update reports automatically or manually, and can produce simple graphic displays although pro-gramming requirements are very complex for graphic reporting. Effec-tive operation of such systems requires strict adherence to established rules for changing report contents or formats and controlled access to stored information. Computer-linked microfilm systems (for example, those using film rolls, microfiche, or aperture cards) use inexpensive media that can be stored easily and compactly, reproduced inexpen-sively, processed and updated or retrieved rapidly, and connected di-rectly to a graphic display device if desired. Computer graphic dis-play is particularly valuable in informing management rapidly of cur-rent developments but may require the use of digital plotters or spe-cially equipped computer printers.

Interactive visual display systems portray graphical information effectively, permit flexible interaction with the computer system in an uncomplicated manner, and allow fast and convenient access to stored data.[1] Both simple, structured problems and complex, unstructured problems can be solved faster and more effectively in many cases using interactive visual display systems. Terminal systems offer the advantages of interaction, convenience, and speed. They are most useful for applications requiring a large data base, high volumes

[1] See Michael S. S. Morton, "Interactive Visual Displays Systems and Management Problem-Solving," *Industrial Management Review*, Fall 1967, pp. 69–84 for a more complete discussion of these points.

of manipulation, analysis in stages, considerable managerial judgment, visualization of complex interrelationships, multidimensional perform- ance measurement, and group communications for effective problem solving.

The major components of a terminal system include the manager and problem area, software, the data base, visual display terminals, and a central computer. The central computer should have multiple access capabilities although time-sharing is not essential. The terminals used can be typewriters, alphanumeric cathode-ray tubes, or graphical CRTs connected to the central computer either by cables or telephone lines. In developing a satisfactory terminal system, the user must consider not only the type of input/output terminals but also the types of operating systems, programming systems, and computer processing equipment required.

Research has indicated that pictorial-verbal display makes numerical data more meaningful, that computers are better than men in aggregating probability judgments according to some formalized scale, and that display systems help to expand human problem- solving and decision-making abilities by providing memory aids and extensive data processing capabilities (see Newman). By displaying data and analyzing it at each stage in the problem-solving process, the decision-maker can guide himself to the must fruitful avenues of approach. Efficient division of processing and decision-making responsibilities between men and machines is the key to the most effective use of both sets of capabilities.

Information systems in operating environments are meaningful only to the extent they can assist humans in performing clerical, tech- nical, or managerial tasks.[2] Each individual's job position requires interaction with a limited set of variable data categories. A category domain is a category set associated with a collection of tasks per- formed by an individual or organization. This concept permits defini- tion of a practical size data base responsive to support of human tasks in an interactive manner. The size of the information system will depend largely on the size of the category domain as well as on the kinds and mixtures of tasks performed with the data base content.

An analysis of human problem-solving tasks reveals that they can be classified as simple inquiry and update, status inquiry, briefing, exception detection, diagnosis, planning/choosing, evalu- ating/optimizing, constructing (designing), and discovery. These

[2] See R. B. Miller, "Archetypes in Man-Computer Problem Solving," *IEEE Trans- actions on Man Machine Systems*, December 1969, pp. 219–241, for a fuller development of this topic.

tasks can range from simple to complex in different environments. Some common denominators in this set of tasks reveal five underlying archetypes of interaction: simple inquiry, complex inquiry and decision making, evaluating and optimizing, design or construction, and discovery (for examples, directed browsing and generalized conception). Making these archetypes explicit and consistent will permit systematic naming and ordering of data in the information system, will enable the development of manageable and meaningful parameters for data analysis, will specify ways of matching human tasks with information system capabilities, and will assist in the development of a simple, well-defined language structure for communication between the system and the human user.

═══ 30.

INFORMATION PLEASE—
STORAGE AND RETRIEVAL SYSTEMS

By C. C. Cowles

Editor's Note: From DATA PROCESSING MAGA-
ZINE, December 1970. Reprinted by permission of
the publisher, North American Publishing Co., and
author.

The originators of information cannot distribute it directly to all
users and users cannot be aware of everything in their range of
interests. Information storage and retrieval systems provide the interface between the two. It's natural to look to the computer for aid
in operating these systems. The great amounts of material that must
be stored and maintained, as well as the repetitive nature of the
searching process, lend themselves to computer control.

The objective is to simplify the retrieval of documents and text
culled from them. This procedure includes locating a document;
retrieving abstracts, extracts, and such information as bibliographic
citations that contain title, author, and publisher; and providing
complete documents.

After analysis of information to be stored, a surrogate may be
created which allows the user to survey the material quickly without
actually retrieving the document. The surrogate usually contains
document number, title, author, source, and an abstract or quotation
from the work. A set of index terms is usually assigned to the
surrogate to characterize and help locate the document. The material
is then stored, the storage location is added to the index.

When a prospective user asks for data, the computer begins by comparing the terms of the request with the index terms to locate information. In response to the search, specific information is selected by correlating it with the query and fetching it from storage. The information is integrated into reports for the user.

The major functions are analysis, indexing, storage, search, and selection. In some systems—with few documents—all data may be stored directly in the computer. Most, however, use auxiliary storage such as disks or drums; here only the index may be stored in the computer's main memory. Requests for information (queries) are processed to determine the availability and location of the data; then the specific information that satisfies the request is selected.

The central role of the computer concerns indexes, queries, data extraction, and data reporting.

An index is a table that eases information retrieval by associating sets of terms describing a document with the storage location of the document or its surrogate. In formulating a surrogate and its set of index terms, text is examined for conversion to systematic form. The basic problem of indexing is determining how to represent material to unknown users. Among the possibilities are subject, author, and numeric or alphanumeric code classifications.

To achieve the greatest degree of empathy between users and author, certain factors must be considered when creating the index term set. Viewpoints of the author and users should be studied to determine the significance of words and phrases in the document and their suitability for the index. Also, indexing methods should allow for the possibility that requests may be in terms either more general or more specific than those in the document. For example, an article indexed only by *airline, railroad* and *bus* could be sought using the query term *transportation.*

Other considerations are semantics and syntax. Semantic problems involve the association of more than one meaning to a word (homographs), association of one meaning with many words (synonyms), and various forms of a word (lexical differences). If possible, the indexing method should capture the syntactic relationship between words in a document. Otherwise, a document about fish food could be accessed by a query for fish as food.

Automatic methods can now be used to create document surrogates. These techniques can abstract, extract parts of, and index any document. They can rearrange material to ease index searches and can use statistical methods to determine word and phrase significance within the text.

One technique to control the vocabulary with which the index is formulated employs a thesaurus, which lists and defines vocabulary terms authorized for the system. The thesaurus also provides relationships between these terms, such as generic (hierarchy) and semantic (synonym) associations. The vocabulary control technique permits creation of an index that describes the information in documents more fully, at different levels of generality, and from various points of view. The thesaurus may be generated, stored, and maintained within or outside the computer system.

Having decided on the best way to represent a document, the actual structure of an index can be provided by language which contains vocabulary and syntax for writing each indexed item. The vocabulary consists of all the alphanumeric terms—natural language words and phrases that must be treated as entities—and the syntax, a set of predetermined rules for combining these terms. The most prominent indexing languages are by hierarchies, subject heading, key word, and syntax.

In a hierarchical language the index is arranged in a generic-specific array, where a class is associated with its subclasses which in turn contain subdivisions of lower-level entries. Numbers can be assigned to topical categories and to all subdivisions down to the lowest level. Here, the vocabulary consists of subjects and their associated (numeric or alphanumeric) codes. Subjects are assigned to each document to indicate its relationship to the hierarchical structure. (See Figure 30.3.) Subject heading languages offer an alternative to the hierarchical indexing methods. Here, the heading to each document is based on a list of generic terms having no relationship to each other. The index is arranged alphabetically, by subject heading, as in the example. In a third system, key-word languages, representative words are selected from the title and text of each document. Key-word indexes provide more depth than subject indexes. Also, they are more likely to consist of single natural language words than subject indexing vocabularies which use more phrases. Another advantage of key-word languages is that they require no syntax.

Still other languages use indexing methods that do involve syntax to combine terms into phrases according to a predetermined relationship. Among these methods are faceted, phrase, and permuted indexing. In faceted indexing, each position in a string of terms has a specific attribute—for example: computer, programer, FORTRAN IV or computer, operator, IBM 360. When the syntactic rules permit terms to be grouped naturally, a phrase index results. The strings can then appear—as for example, computer programers in FORTRAN IV or computer operators on the IBM 360. In other cases, each possible key-word permutation of a phrase can be represented in the index. This method allows key words to be emphasized and examined within their context.

How do you access data once the indexing method has been adopted? The query is a command that starts a computer searching its data base for information. Retrieval yields either a document, its surrogate, or information for locating the document. Like document indexes, queries are written in a specific language. When an index exists, the vocabulary and syntax of the indexing language form the basis of the query language. However, the query language is usually more complex because terms using the basic grammatical elements (vocabulary and syntax) may be combined by such connectives as logical and arithmetic operators. The result of performing logical operations on two sets, A and B, each of which satisfies part of a query, is shown in Figure 30.1.

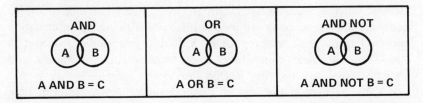

30.1   LOGICAL QUESTIONS. THE QUERY COMMAND MAY CONTAIN LOGICAL AND ARITHMETIC CONNECTIVES TO NARROW THE SEARCH FOR WANTED INFORMATION

Logical comparators involve inequalities such as equal/unequal to, greater/less than, and between. Arithmetic operators (add, subtract, multiply, divide) are well known. Other characteristics that can be included in a query language are hit (correlation) level, weighting, and relative word position. Even though it may not be necessary to satisfy all query terms, a minimum number (level) of hits may be desirable. For example, if some combination of A, B, C is sought, it can be stipulated that at least two hits occur to satisfy the query.

Each query of phrase can be assigned a numeric value (weight) that, when correlated with stored data, is added to a running sum of weights derived from all such correlations. When the entire query has been processed, this sum determines the degree to which stored data is responsive to the query. Using this technique the function

A AND (B OR C) can be processed as:

Query	A	AND	(B	OR	C)
Individual weights	2		1		1
Group weights	2		1		
Minimum sum		3			

Positions of query terms can be required to relate to one another in a particular manner within a document. Some of these relationships are word proximity (for example, the words *theory* and *number* might be required to be within two words of each other in a document or surrogate, retrieving all references to theory of numbers and number theory but not references to theory), word order (*abstract* could be required to procede *algebra* in the source material so that only references to abstract algebra would be retrieved), and words in the same sentence or paragraph.

Many systems help the user formulate queries through use of a thesaurus, intermediate output, or query enhancement. An intermediate output indicates search progress and helps the user refine his query. It allows successively more precise queries, using information obtained from prior interrogations. Valuable intermediate output is also available from computational summaries such as tallies and statistical analyses that are derived during the search.

Various methods of query enhancement involve intermediate output and successive searches, where information retrieved in any step is automatically applied to subsequent searches. Also, a query may be automatically modified before a search using a thesaurus. Guidelines for query formulation must be available to the user either by written instructions and well-defined forms or by a specialist who will write the query for insertion into the system.

Once a question has been posed to the computer it responds by searching the data base for the pertinent information and physically selecting portions of this material. The characteristics of the retrieval operation depend on whether it involves the index, source material, or both. When only the index is important, the retrieval produces a listing of document locations. When both the index and source material are involved, the index is searched to obtain document or surrogate locations. Specific source material in these locations is then selected. In systems that search such sources as documents or surrogates without use of an index, special data base construction may be needed to simplify access to the information.

After satisfying the original query, pertinent data must be extracted from the selected material and reported to the user. In some systems these functions employ user-specified report formats, requiring some manipulation of the information to group the data for output. Typically, a file could be interrogated for all documents involving space flight written prior to 1958. After selecting all documents involving space flight, their citations would be searched. Those that satisfy the query would be extracted, sorted into a list by date, and reported. The reports can contain isolated facts (primarily in data retrieval systems), textual information, bibliographic citations, or information locatives.

Applications of information storage and retrieval systems are characterized by their basic functions, techniques, and the nature

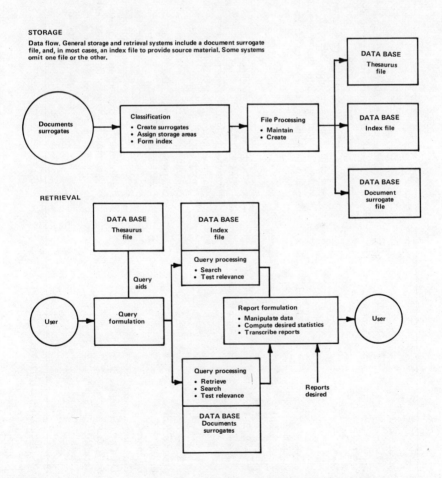

STORAGE

Data flow. General storage and retrieval systems include a document surrogate file, and, in most cases, an index file to provide source material. Some systems omit one file or the other.

30.2 DATA FLOW IN A GENERAL STORAGE AND RETRIEVAL SYSTEM

KEYWORD

A *Chicago rock-music festival* erupted into rock-throwing and gunfire, and one report said two *youths* were *shot* and *wounded*. Witnesses said the trouble began when a group of youths seized the bandshell and rampaged through *Grant Park* on the downtown lakefront last night, throwing *stones* and setting two cars afire. More than forty *arrests* were made. Police fired volleys of *tear gas* into the crowd, and a police helicopter ordered the group to disperse. The source of the gunfire

SYNTACTICAL

  FACETED:

  computer, programer, FORTRAN IV
  computer, operator, IBM 360

  PHRASE:

  computer programers in FORTRAN IV
  computer operators on the IBM 360

  PERMUTED:

computer programers in	computer operators on IBM 360
computer operators on	computer programers in FORTRAN IV
computer	FORTRAN IV
computer	IBM 360
	operators on IBM 360
	programers in FORTRAN IV

HIERARCHICAL

CODE	SUBJECT
2	Transportation
2.1	Airline
.	.
.	.
2.2	Railroad
2.2.1	Passenger
2.2.1.1	Long distance
2.2.1.2	Medium distance
2.2.1.3	Short distance
2.2.2	Freight
.	.
.	.
2.3	Bus

SUBJECT HEADING

Banks
Cashiers
Checking accounts
Data processing services
Savings accounts
Security
Tellers

30.3   INDEXING METHODS

of the data. However, to understand any system fully, you must determine the relationship between these functions. This can be done by establishing the data flow between the tasks and the general sequence of performance, as shown in Figure 30.2. Various subsets of the total set of tasks shown are used in other applications.

A survey of organizations that sell proprietary computer programs reveals relatively few packages that combine all concepts discussed here and that exclude others. Most available packages for information storage and retrieval are actually of a hybrid nature. They retrieve data from formatted files (using English-like queries that include logical operators and comparators), they sort the data, and they generate reports. Some packages perform calculations involving the contents of retrieved fields or the number of query hits. In addition to the basic functions, some offer other query capabilities and can perform document retrieval using an index.

Commercial packages do not provide the man-machine conversation normally used. These programs generally operate in a batch processing mode with no intermediate output.

Computer manufacturers and academic institutions have a larger number of suitable programs, but these are not always available to a prospective user. Despite the problems of obtaining software, available packages provide document retrieval capabilities that should satisfy many users.

31.

EDP OUTPUT DEVICES: THE FOUR OPTIONS

IMPACT PRINTERS ARE MORE PORTABLE, FASTER

Workhorse of the data processing industry is an apt nick-name for impact printers. Despite important advancements in other output technologies and glowing predictions about them from experts, impact printers will continue to dominate the field for two reasons. Most output requirements call for two to ten copies (other techniques excell only in one-time or several hundred copies and are impractical in the middle ground). And impact printers are customarily offered as part of a complete computer system by the large main-frame manufacturers.

Additionally, impact printers fit a wide range of applications, printing on virtually any paper stock. Legibility, a common criticism of other technologies (nonimpact is fuzzy; CRT isn't bright enough), is very good on most machines. Finally, some new designs and advancements have recently improved the basic impact printer technology.

Many of these advancements are represented in the following new equipment.

The Model 70-3 line printer from Data 100 Corp. has a rated speed of 300 lines per minute. Vertical format control, and a choice of one of three character sets is standard with the unit. A swing out print mechanism eases forms loading, and an 80 column print line is also standard.

From Terminal Equipment Corp., the Tycom 35/37 ASR is an

IBM Selectric typewriter configured with a Tycom keyboard, providing hard copy output or teletype reception through a desk size, compact unit. Added features encompass a 130 character line width, typewriter quality printout and low noise levels. Multiple type fonts and a special OCR font are available if needed.

A page printer from Mite Corp., the Mite 123T, is entirely portable and comes with its own carrying case. It operates in the office, at home, or nearly anywhere via an acoustic coupler that's hooked up to the telephone. In addition, Mite's Gothic type face printout speeds along at up to 110 words per minute, on ordinary 8½ × 11 paper.

Upper and lower-case printing is a new feature designed into Univac's latest impact printer, the Univac 0768. The 94 character set consists of 26 upper and lower case alphabetics each, ten numerals and 32 symbols. Printout is rated at 2,000 lines per minute with triple spacing, and the unit rents for $1,070 monthly on one-year plans.

These improvements, while only a small part of the total impact printing field, assure its bright future, and, as many industry experts agree, solidify its dominance.

NON-IMPACT PRINTERS CUT NOISE, HIGH COSTS

"Potentially the most significant imaging technology development suitable for mass printed production in the next 15 years." This is what many computer experts are saying about the latest form of nonimpact printing: ink-jet.

The reasons for such glowing reports are many. First of all, ink-jet "squirt-printing" is entirely electronic thereby eliminating the bulk, noise and down-time associated with the mechanical "hammer-striking-paper" output equipment. Ink-jet operates much the same way as a television set, with charged microparticles of ink replacing the electron beam firing at paper instead of the picture tube.

Jet printers are very fast. Typical terminals can output up to 5,000 lines per minute, 250 characters per line. Ink-jet printing also does not require any special paper, and can be used with business forms and gummed labels.

At present, two firms dominate ink-jet technology—A. B. Dick and Teletype Corp.—offering fullsized line printers.

The 9600 Videojet printer from A. B. Dick features a printout capability of about 3,000 words per minute enabling it to "eliminate most print-out bottlenecks in EDP networks," say company spokesmen. The unit sells for under $7,000.

Teletype's Inktronic will produce up to 80 characters per line and features a six-button control panel with a paper alarm lamp that signals should the paper jam or run out. In addition, an upper-lower case alphabet is available, providing full printing versatility.

The applications of ink-jet technology vary widely. According to Donald Mucha, marketing manager at A. B. Dick, "the faster printers are very well suited for use as output mechanisms for on-line computer systems in which a central EDP facility serves to process or switch information from a number of remote terminals." Ink-jet terminals are even more useful as main output printers in mini computers. "Since many of these smaller units sell for about $20,000, it makes little sense to spend $30,000 for an impact printer," adds Mucha. Two other uses for ink-jet printers include computer input when the input device includes a keyboard, and as terminal equipment for voice-grade communication systems.

But many administrative managers are still hesitant to adopt ink-jet terminals due to what they consider slightly poorer image quality. For example:

```
THE VIDEOJET 96
COMPUTER-COMMUNICATI
PER INCH IS STANDARD
CHARACTERS PER LINE
UNEQUALED OPERATING
LINE PRINTER FOR THE
COMPUTER TIME NEED N
```

Manufacturers point out, however, that the advantages of economy and increased speed far outweigh any visual imperfections. "After all," adds one, "the prime purpose of printout isn't visual perfection, but legibility."

Ink-jet printers are making the largest impact in the realm of non-impact equipment. But puns aside, they're not the only new development. There has been recent activity in electrostatic printing that's also important.

Historically, these devices "burned" images on paper electrically at high costs. Images are still "burned" onto special paper, but it's done through silicon integrated circuits. Such a circuit, made by Displaytek Corp., for OEM use, features a 5 × 7 dot printing matrix that's heated to form any of the 96 standard ASCII code characters.

The silicon chip in actual operation is claimed to achieve a print rate of up to 60 characters per second. Cost? Prices on Displaytek's chip range from $50 to $65, which means that output terminals utilizing this technology will also be less expensive.

This is true. Versatec's new 80-column non-impact printer, the Matrix 300, sells for almost half the cost of comparable impact printers: $5,500. The printer provides high contrast dot matrix characters at speeds up to 300 lines per minute, and, making use of modems operating up to 4,800 baud, is ideal for time-sharing, remote batch printing and communications output.

Little chips also enable printout terminals to shrink in size. For example, the Model 725 Portable Data Terminal from Texas Instruments. The unit is designed for time-sharing users and features a built-in acoustic coupler, printing speeds of 10, 15 or 30 cps, and is no larger than a portable typewriter. Data transmission can be accomplished over standard voice-grade telephone lines.

With so much already happening in non-impact printing, what does the future look like? A recent Arthur D. Little computer study forecasts a $125-million market for these printers in 1975, with shipments increasing over one-hundredfold by that date.

CRTs LESS COSTLY, STORE MORE DATA

One-time information represents the largest reason for the use of cathode ray tube (CRT) terminals. At the Fine Paper and Film Divisions of Olin Corp., Pisgah Forest, N.C., accessing one-time data off the CRT screen improves and speeds its manufacturing procedures.

A key step in this system is eight CC-30 Communications Stations from Computer Communications feeding two IBM System/360-30 Model F computers. When an order is received by telephone or letter in Olin's Sales Service Dept., an order clerk keys the information into one of the CRT terminals. It is processed, referenced on disk storage and displayed back on the CRT screen for verification.

Thereafter, amendments are simply coded and keyed into one of the terminals for updating. In scheduling and on the manufacturing floor, similar terminals are used to keep track of the order's status and to aid plant supervision. The process continues through production with controls for reporting quality and quantity. Upon completion of the order and its shipment, pertinent records are recalled to produce the invoice.

Says Olin: "Reports are on managers' desks when they arrive for work, giving us a growing fund of information, permitting long-range forecasting and feedback on past forecast accuracy."

Other reasons for a growing trend toward CRT terminals include:

• Speed. A good average figure for most terminals is 160 characters per second, outputting a 72 character line, about 30 lines per "page" or screen image. Many CRTS offer storage memories, however, that can remember up to 8,000 characters.

• Economy. Many of the cheaper CRT terminals available can be rented for under $100, though an average figure for many available systems that include several CRTS and a control unit is not much more than $2,000 per month.

• Peripherals. Text editing capabilities at the touch of a button, erase codes, and electronic pens for quick retrieval of reports from listings or "yes-no" communication are optional features made available by most manufacturers.

• Convenience. These terminals can be installed almost anywhere. They're no bigger than mini-televisions, and most units are just as stylish.

Reflecting these advantages are some new developments in the area of CRT: the IBM 3270 information display system, for one. Featuring buffer storage for faster response, the 3270 has a 1,920 character capacity, an electronic pen and an audible signal warning for special-attention situations.

From Video Systems Corp., a full line of new CRT units is headed by the VS-100 Inventron, a self-contained data entry and retrieval system composed of a desk top terminal screen with a standard keyboard. Also part of the Inventron: a compact data storage cabinet containing the memory.

Wyle Laboratories' Model 501 Computerminal incorporates an alphanumeric keyboard, a core memory and input/output digital computer communications capability (incidentally, more than 1,000 of these are being utilized to play the horses in New York's recently established Off-Track Betting System. A special set of keys is tagged "race/horse").

A paging feature that can store many lines of data at the display terminal with a minimum amount of refresh memory is offered in Delta Data Systems' TelTerm display. "By allowing the user to choose how much memory that he wants in the terminal, from 500 to 2,500 characters, the user can have the most economical display," company spokesmen claim. TelTerm's paging feature is complemented by a formatting and editing ability.

VOICE RESPONSE UNITS SPEAK TO MANY NEEDS

Nearly one-half billion dollars yearly is expected to be spent on voice response output terminals by 1975, according to a recent projection by the Diebold Research Program.

One reason, many administrative managers agree, is that voice response is the most convenient means of accessing data for certain businesses: airlines, financial institutions, transportation companies, to name a few. A second reason is that through use of the public telephone network, voice response units can be made amazingly portable and lightweight, a trend already reflected in new equipment of this genre.

At International Harvester's Motor Truck Div., Ft. Wayne, Ind., for example, IBM 2721 battery-powered voice terminals (built into a slim attache case for portability) are used by salesmen calling on customers to place an order or check the status of a shipment. By simply placing any phone receiver on the unit's acoustic coupler, salesmen can dial into International Harvester's central computer and obtain instant truck location or availability data.

IBM's 2721 can operate for several hours on its rechargeable batteries or plug into any 110-volt AC line; the terminal utilizes elastic diaphragm switching to eliminate mechanical keyboarding, thus removing one major cause of downtime. In addition, each 2721 can be assigned an identification code to prevent unauthorized access to stored data.

This optional security feature can be very important to firms dealing in confidential information—banks, for example. At one major New England bank such a system is used by its branches to check on the accounts or credit of customers. Again, using the telephone-acoustic-coupler hookup, bank officers enter information in alpha-numeric codes to access the computer. First they enter a special clearance sequence, and then they enter the account number in question. Instantly, a woman's voice responds with the requested data ("We use women's voices because they are very pleasurable to hear," adds a bank executive). The exact words used, though, are compiled by the central computer from a vocabulary stored in its audio response system. Storage in most voice response systems has usually been word for word on external disk or drum files, therefore somewhat limiting.

Recently Phonplex Corp. announced a solid-state voice terminal with "a virtually unlimited vocabulary due to the use of phoneme storage." These phonemes—basic voice sounds—are stored in the solid state memory and can be combined to speak words, phrases, sentences and "full dissertations!"

Voice response terminals are doing an important job, but still have many inherent problems to be solved. However, as stated in the Diebold study, "these systems can be expected to grow faster than the computer industry as a whole."

POINTERS ON PRINTERS

Searching for a hard copy printer to add to your company's data processing system? Or interested in measuring your present equipment against future needs? Here are some basic guidelines to follow before you shop.

• *Application.* How the printer will be used can narrow your choice significantly. Will the printer be used locally, on-site; or will it be used remotely with a time-sharing system? In addition, will multiple copies be needed? Most non-impact printers cannot produce more than one copy at a time. On the other hand, if multiple copies are not needed, but satellite terminals are, non-impact units provide less costly slave units since they all can work from one master unit.

• *Speed.* How fast must data be printed? Must telephone transmission speeds be matched? Two factors to consider here are speed/price rations and optimum balance.

• *Cost.* Tied in with all other guidelines, this factor is the most complex. Teletypewriter units cost up to $2,000, but print only ten characters per second. High speed line printers are much faster, and much more expensive (to $80,000). Other costs such as downtime increase with mechanical printers; but electronic printers require special paper and need added accessories. If a line printer and pen plotter system is desired, combination electrostatic printer plotters are substantially cheaper and easier to use.

• *Flexibility.* Exactly what are your formatting needs? Must your equipment have the ability of printing any line lengths up to the industry maximum of 136 characters/13.6 inch line? Many smaller impact and non-impact units are ideal for printing on an 8½ × 11 inch page; IBM Selectric typewriters are featured in some newer impact terminals. Is the communications industry standard of 80 characters per line acceptable? Again, some modern equipment can be adapted to your needs, accepting different type fonts or printing in upper-lower case.

• *Reliability.* How complex is the printing mechanism? Non-impacts are virtually downtime-free, lacking complex mechanical gear. Will required maintenance be a problem, especially regarding service contracts, location?

• *Noise.* Impact printing clatter can be a personnel problem, a distraction, a nuisance if not properly muffled. Printer noise, in fact, has reached unacceptable levels—to 94 decibels, according to National Bureau of Standards reports. Would it be a better decision to select noise-free, non-impact units?

32.

EVALUATING COMPUTER OUTPUT PRINTERS

By Matthew Lorber

Editor's Note: Reprinted from AUTOMATION, March 1972, pp. 64–67. Copyright 1972 by the Penton Publishing Company, Cleveland, Ohio.

How important are printers in the successful application of a computer system? Although printers do not get into the act insofar as system operation is concerned, they are crucial to knowing what the computer has done so as to make intelligent responses possible. True, it would be possible to see what the computer has done with such equipment as video displays and computer output microfilm. But where many departments within a company must be informed *in parallel*, for example, paper printout is about the only way to pin down all the variables. Instead of gathering management people around a CRT display to work out policy, every individual with a *need to know* would receive a printout of what might be shown on the CRT display, so that he can work on his own aspect of the problem at his own convenience.

Even when a system is based largely on time-shared computer operation—with data entered and presented via CRT terminals—it is still necessary to print out invoices, materials requirements, work-in-progress data, order acknowledgements, location-of-materials data, and information of production scheduling importance. Also, the computer might be used to generate checks for payroll and accounts payable, plus purchase orders for refilling inventory.

Though the need and operation of computer printers are straightforward, there does seem to be a gross misuse of printers in everyday systems applications. Too many firms use vast and costly high-speed printers that fill up acres of paper with printed material that nobody reads. Often, the only reason for printing-out everything is to give management the chance of spotting anomalies. For example, a printer may crank out the inventory status of all materials in stock, along with reorder comments. Materials department personnel will then scan through all the listings, noting which items need reordering. But this procedure is unnecessary because the only information required is the reordering data. The computer could have been programmed to select merely the low-on-stock items, and print-out this information only. The result would be lower cost because: 1. A small printer could be used. 2. Less paper would be consumed. 3. Management would spend less time sifting through redundant information. 4. The production of purchase orders for the selected, low-on-stock items would not be a separate operation.

An analogous misuse of computer printers occurs when a company prints out the names of *all* its customers so that someone can go over the list and cull from it the customers who have bought nothing for, say, the last six months. (Marketing people would then contact these errant customers.) A better, more direct approach would have the computer printing out only the names and addresses of the customers that had to be contacted—not the names of every customer. This concept of producing only usable information is called management by exception.

The problem of producing too much computer information can be put into perspective when one considers the actual printer capabilities possessed by some large organizations. One firm's management made a calculation of the man-hours required to read all the information that its firm's highpowered line printers could generate. It turned out that if everyone in the firm—including janitors, lawn trimmers, production people, etc.—spent their whole time reading computer printouts, they still wouldn't be able to handle all that the printers could generate. This situation is an obvious example where the concept of management by exception could trim a vast amount of printer capacity and cost, and cut down on wasted paper and manpower.

PRINTER USE IN PRODUCTION CONTROL

Order entry on a computerized basis would begin by finding parts in stock and diagnosing whether or not the order can be completed from inventory. Rarely is this mode of operation possible, however. Usually the order entry process is used to determine which items must be manufactured. A day's volume of order booking (entry) would provide a printout of the new parts to be manufactured.

A further step in the process would be to investigate the "parts explosion" for each item ordered. Usually, an assembly—say, an operational amplifier—is built up from many different parts, all of which must be available if the purchase orders are to be filled. The computer would plod through the parts explosions for each item ordered during a given day—or even on an hourly or a continuous basis—print out the "picking lists" on each customer order, and generate a list of parts that must be ordered to fill the day's bookings.

The computer might also print out copies of the parts explosions for different manufacturing and storekeeping requirements, enabling a copy of the list to accompany the parts, subassembly, and final assembly as they progress through the various production, storage, and/or shipping operations. The computer would also print out order-acknowledgements, bills-of-lading, etc.

Thus far, the computer has determined which items can be provided from stock, how many further items can be assembled from components in stock, and has printed out lists and, perhaps, purchase orders for the missing parts required to complete the orders already booked. Usually, some human intervention is required, since the purchase order should cover future parts requirements as well as those already booked. Further, the computer has printed out documentation that permits stocked components to be reserved against the booked orders, and has produced picking lists for the collection of available parts to build more inventory.

All of this computer data manipulation and the various computer printouts required are designed to keep track of parts. If the manufacturing operation is relatively simple, further processes might be manual. If, however, the manufacture of vast quantities of custom hardware is involved—such as specialized processes for the chemical industry—then further computer scheduling and an increasing number of printouts might be required to keep track of individual manufacturing operations.

You can see the enormous increase in paper-work that would result if a firm manufactures megawatt steam turbines as opposed to household door locks. In the latter case, the firm can complete manufacturing in a day or two—assuming all the parts are available—while production of custom steam turbines might take two years to fulfill each order. In the more complicated case, the computer would be required to keep a day-by-day track of manufacturing progress, predict operations during many weeks ahead, prepare materials in

PRINTER PRICE/PERFORMANCE CHARACTERISTICS

Printer Type	Price Range	Speed	Multiple Copies?	Special Paper?	Noisy?
Serial, impact full-character	$800-$4,000	10 cps to 100 cps	yes	no	yes
Serial, impact dot matrix	$2,000-$5,000	10 cps to 165 cps	yes	no	yes
Serial, nonimpact full-character	$1,000-$5,000	10 cps to 100 cps	no	usually	no
Serial, nonimpact dot matrix	$1,000-$5,000	10 cps to 100 cps	no	usually	no
Line, impact full-character	$5,000-$100,000	150 lpm to 2,000 lpm	yes	no	yes
Line, impact dot matrix	$5,000-$100,000	150 lpm to 2,000 lpm	yes	no	yes
Line, nonimpact full-character	$5,000-$100,000	150 lpm to 2,000 lpm	no	usually	less
Line, nonimpact dot matrix	$5,000-$100,000	150 lpm to 5,000 lpm	no	usually	less

advance as the turbine assembly progressed, and provide a flow of information to all working departments so that different manufacturing and purchasing procedures could be synchronized and dovetailed as required.

Owing to the complexity of this manufacturing operation, ordering of raw materials would be spread over the months of assembly time instead of having everything ordered at the time blueprints are finally approved. Further, parts and materials procurement would rest on the actual manufacturing process of each turbine, so that inventory turn-around time could be minimized.

In each production control context—whether it be complex, long-term turbine manufacture or small household locks assembly—the computer would be accompanied by an output printer or printers to provide management with key information, and to provide purchasing, invoicing, stockroom, and manufacturing personnel with daily operating instructions.

WHAT PRINTER TYPES ARE AVAILABLE?

The technology of computer output printers embraces three basic categories of choice: serial versus parallel, impact versus nonimpact, and full-character versus dot matrix.

Serial Versus Parallel

Serial machines print one character at a time, and parallel or line printers complete a whole line of output data in the same time that a serial printer produces a single character. Not surprisingly, line printers are more costly. While serial printers run from around $1,000 for a Teletype unit, line printers start at about $5,000 and go as high as $150,000. Serial printer speeds are in the 10-character-per-second to 200-character-per-second range. Line printers start around 200 lines per minute—equivalent to roughly 300-400 characters-per-second—and extend to some 5,000 lines per minute, or somewhat more than 10,000 characters-per-second.

Impact Versus Nonimpact

Not only can printers be categorized in terms of serial or parallel operation (i.e., character-at-a-time or line-at-a-time printing), but they may be classified according to whether they employ impact principles (like a typewriter) or such principles as electrostatics, ink jets, Xerography, photography, etc. The differences are more than casually important, because rarely can the nonimpact printers produce more than a single copy.

Both serial and line printers are available in impact and non-impact types. Since the impact printer implies mechanical motion —typically, impressing typewriter-like characters against the paper or paper against characters—one might expect the impact machines to be slower than their nonimpact counterparts. This is true. The fastest impacting line printers operate at speeds up to 2,000 lines/minute, whereas nonimpact versions print up to 5,000 lines/minute.

Full Character Versus Dot Matrix

A further breakdown groups printers in terms of the method used for forming the characters. Full-character machines—usually impact types—work on extensions of the typewriter principle, forming inked impressions with carefully contoured metallic characters. Dot matrix machines, by contrast, do not form smooth characters along the lines of a typewriter, but instead create the 64 different letters, numerals, and symbols by way of various combinations of dots. Dot matrix machines include both impact and nonimpact versions, although most nonimpact printers tend to rely almost exclusively on the dot matrix principle.

Many computer users prefer full character impressions, and are only deflected from this choice by an inability to obtain the desired speed/cost performance with such machines. Furthermore, because multiple copies are almost invariably required in most applications, the choice of computer output printer—especially for time-shared, multiple-terminal minicomputer-based operations—involves selecting a serial, full-character impact printer.

Two clear-cut application guidelines emerge from the above categorization. If several departments require copies of the same document, it makes sense to use an impact printer. Also, the decision to buy a line printer or serial printer depends upon the amount of material to be printed. If a timeshared system is used, then it is possible to use several remote terminals (for payroll, accounts payable, purchasing, order booking, accounts receivable, and so forth)—each with its own printer. By splitting up the printing work in this way, it is possible to dispense with a high-speed line printer, and share the printing work among the several distributed serial printers. This approach centers responsibility of EDP operations in specific departments, since there need be no central EDP room and personnel, and often no keypunch operators either. Each department assumes total responsibility for its own interaction with the computer.

This time-shared basis, for example, would center responsibility in the purchasing/inventory control department for ensuring that all parts for manufacturing were either reserved or ordered. This department would, in turn, receive its initial inputs from the order-booking department. The day's orders—culled from the centralized data base— would be displayed on the purchasing department's CRT, then purchase orders; picking lists; shipping routes; and other paperwork would be printed out on the local printer. This procedure would permit paperwork to be printed as required, instead of having to wait, in turn, to receive printouts from a single high-speed, centralized line printer operating in the conventional batch mode.

Often, it is possible to buy several serial printers for the price of one line printer, and gain the added benefits of overall operating flexibility, real-time generation and entry of data, and rapid printout of required reports and other documentation. In short, low-cost serial printers now available give a data systems designer the choice of real-time on-line data processing, instead of wait-in-turn batch operation.

SPECIAL PRINTER REQUIREMENTS

Reliability is one overwhelming printer requirement. Often, printers are expected to run with no more attention than a conventional typewriter. Modern electronically-controlled printers depend primarily on the relatively low cost of electronic logic, whereas earlier teletypewriter-like machines are primarily mechanical devices, with mind-boggling assemblies of moving linkages.

The dot matrix machine suffers from heavy wear of the delicate mechanisms used to produce character patterns. Consider the letter H, for example, as produced by a machine that simulates characters with a 9×7 pattern of dots. The horizontal bar of the letter H requires the machine to complete seven individual dots with the same hammer. Contrast this with the full-character (typewriter-like) printer, which makes the letter H with a single stroke. Thus, for a dot matrix machine to print a whole line of letter H symbols, its hammer and solenoid assembly would operate seven times faster than the comparable (same speed) full-character printer.

In print-on-the-fly machines, the print-wheel's character-set is impacted once per print-wheel revolution. This is true both for serial printers and for full-character line printers. The result is a speed limitation of one character per revolution at the maximum print-wheel speed of about 2,000 rpm.

For the serial machine with one character-set, this 2,000 rpm translates into a printing rate of one character every 0.0005 minute, or roughly 33 characters-per-second. The same limitation applies to the line printer, except that now a whole line of symbols may be printed (in the more complex machines) for every revolution of the set of print wheels (one print wheel for every column). Thus, the maximum print rate for a full-character impacting line printer is 2,000 lines per minute. Price for such a machine lies in the $60,000-$150,000 region.

Higher printing speeds can be achieved by non-impacting methods such as ink-jets, electrostatics, Xerography, photography, and so forth. Such higher speed line printers tend to be of the dot-matrix type, which almost universally confines output to single copies. Thus, further copies require duplication.

WISE PRINTER USE IS PARAMOUNT

Perhaps, if the concept of management by exception spreads, computer output printers will be used for printing out only the material that will actually be used, instead of cranking out all details for subsequent human sifting. Further, with the spread of time-shared interactive management data systems (increasingly based on minicomputers these days), several remotely located printers can be used to share the total printing job. The trend to use of time-shared systems will cut down batch operations on a line printer, and put more of the load onto real-time CRT-plus-printer terminals.

33.

INFORMATION RETRIEVAL: THREE ALTERNATIVES

By John Wolaver

Editor's Note: From HONEYWELL COMPUTER JOURNAL, Fall 1970, pp. 13–17. Reprinted courtesy of Honeywell Computer Journal, Honeywell Information Systems Inc.

A large insurance company must have all of its policies readily available for review. A multi-billion dollar corporation generates massive quantities of reports which must be indexed, filed and accessible. An airline company has 22 manuals with 12,000 pages of information from which answers to inquiries must come in minutes. For all these companies, information retrieval is a critical element of their business. In many cases a choice is available among alternate systems for information storage and retrieval. When paper becomes too cumbersome to manage, a microfilm system, or a direct access real time system may be considered. This article will compare paper and microfilm systems, discussing three different types of microfilm media. Paper print out versus computer output microfilm will also be evaluated. Finally, real time direct access will be compared to microfilm as a retrieval medium.

INTRODUCTION

One of the most urgent problems created by the information explosion is that of information storage and retrieval. For small companies or single transactions, traditional paper and manual retrieval methods may be adequate. But in a geometrically increasing number of applications, the volume of information and the need for massive amounts of computer printed documentation can no longer be handled economically with paper alone. One alternative is microfilm.

Traditionally microfilm has been used primarily for security purposes. Documents such as insurance policies are photographed and stored in vaults as archival files. Many people still view microfilm as only a medium for archival documents. Only approximately 40% of all firms using microfilm are considered to have active systems (a system in which more than 50 retrievals are made per day). Obviously even in 1970, microfilm is not generally considered to be an active retrieval medium. In actuality it can be advantageous for any organization with more paper than can be handled economically to consider microfilm as a retrieval medium. The advantages of microfilm storage over paper storage are numerous. Ease of copying and distribution, reduced filing and retrieval time are only a few.[1] With the standard 24 to 1 reduction ratio (ultrafiche with a 150 to 1 reduction ratio is also available), saving in storage costs alone can be tremendous. Because of these advantages, the use of microfilm has grown steadily over the years until it has reached at $350 million size market. Although the two largest applications areas, engineering drawing and security microfilming, which represented 80% of the 1968 market, are growing slowly, two new areas are growing very rapidly. These two new areas, computer output to microfilm and micropublishing, together will grow to 36% of the market by 1973, according to a study by Arthur D. Little.

New approaches to microfilm usage are continually being tried out. AT & T's microfilm system[2] processes over 20,000 inquiries per month from its 3,100,000 shareholders. Previously these data (stock records, dividend listings, former shareholder listings, proxy statements, etc.) were stored in 1,112 computer printout binders requiring 60 hours computer time to print and 65 square feet of storage space. Now these same data on microfilm are stored on 332 film cassettes requiring only 3.5 square feet.

At J. R. Case's component division[3] an aperture card system replaced a system of paper copying from original engineering drawings. The aperture cards are stored in a mechanized rotary tub file for quick

---

[1] One of many studies showing the greater speed of microfilm retrieval over paper systems is the Army Material Command "Report on Non-Impact Printing Project" published in January 1968.

[2] ——, "COM Helps AT & T Get Fast Answers for Millions of Shareholders," *Information and Records Management*, April/May, 1969.

[3] ——, "An Unusual Case for a Successful Microfilm System," *Modern Office Procedures*, June, 1968.

access. In addition, special self-service microfilm stations enable individual engineers to view drawings in their own department or mark
copies with the paper printing from microfilm capability which is included. With the system only 25% installed, a 20 cents per print and
2,000 man hours per year savings is estimated. The original staff of
12 is expected to shrink to 5 once the entire system is installed.

MICROFILM VERSUS PAPER

The decision to change to microfilm is nearly always based on a
volume of paperwork which is too great to handle economically. Cost
and speed of retrieval are primary considerations as are media generation and transportation costs. In general, microfilm is the preferred
medium for large volume data retrieval and storage applications. Paper is preferred for small print-out runs (invoices, for example) and
for applications where hard copy is a must. In a typical microfilm installation using motorized roll film viewers, a frame of microfilm can
be retrieved within 30 seconds. This compares with an average time
of 3 to 4 minutes to retrieve the same data when printed on paper.
Obviously when retrieval time becomes important a microfilm system is superior to a paper system.

Microfilm Media

Once the decision to use a microfilm system has been made,
further decisions remain on what type of system, manual or automatic,
and what type of microform to use.

Microforms are the various film media used to store information.
There are two basic categories: roll film and unitized records. In general the choice of microform will depend on the frequency of update
as well as on the volume and type of information to be stored. The
standard is 16mm roll film, which can store from 2,000 to 3,000 images
in a 100 foot roll. 35mm is also available, and the larger size frame
makes it attractive for engineering drawings. But both are relatively
slow on retrieval.

Unitized microforms were developed to overcome the inherent
handling and retrieval problems of roll film. In one type, aperture
cards, an image of 35 mm film is held in a cut-out portion of a tab
card. The tab card is punched to simplify retrieval. An aperture card
system is used as the medium of exchange for engineering drawings
among all Honeywell divisions. A system such as this becomes econo-

mical for larger quantities of data—a card costs only about 3.9 cents if processed in a lot of a thousand or more cards. This plus its superior retrieval speed makes it attractive for many microfilm users.

A second unitized type of microform is microfiche. Here the unit record consists of multiple pages, such as in a parts catalog or manual. The cost of a microfiche master can be as high as $15.00. However, as there are up to one hundred document pages on a microfiche, the cost per image is less than that for aperture cards. Another reason for the attractiveness of microfiche is that a microfiche viewer is less expensive than a roll film viewer, and easier to use.

Manual and Automatic Microfilm Retrieval

The choice among microfilm systems ranges from manual to fully automatic. There are some highly advanced computer-controlled systems, which combine the multiple-indexing and conversational capabilities of the computer with the advantages of microfilm, but their cost puts them out of the range of the user under consideration in this section.

Traditionally microfilm retrieval is manual, and manual readers account for the bulk of the retrieval work. In many instances manual retrieval may be very rapid. A study by a Honeywell user showed that an operator could find a frame on a roll more rapidly manually than if an automatic frame seeking technique were used, provided that the data was ordered in a reasonable manner, such as sequentially. This manual approach also saves the space on microfilm which is required by the indexing schemes of most automatic methods.

The automatic retrieval market for microfilm is extremely specialized. This results from the fact that its two advantages, relatively fast retrieval and large volume storage are not always required at the same time. Retrieval for non-automated microfilm systems usually averages about 30 seconds per line retrieved. When the faster speed of automated retrieval (generally less than 5 seconds) is required, an automatic system must be considered.

Once the question of fast retrieval becomes critical, real time computer systems also come into consideration. A more detailed analysis of automatic microfilm and direct access will be presented in a later section of the paper.

Computer Output to Microfilm

A final consideration for the prospective microfilm user is whether his microfilm capabilities should be linked to a computer system. Computer Output to Microfilm (COM) equipment is designed to read

print images stored on magnetic tape and transfer this print information to microfilm.

For the user swamped with paper printout, a COM system may
be desirable. In terms of speed, the comparison between traditional
printer output and COM is dramatic. In contrast to the maximum of
about 2,000 lines per minute for an impact printed, COM exposes
alphanumeric data on film at the rate of 20,000 to 30,000 lines per
minute. COM is also attractive when the costs of output storage are
considered. Microfilm occupies only 1/50 the space of paper or 1/5
the space of magnetic tape.[4]

When costs are compared, the COM versus printer question
changes. Figure 33.1 shows the comparison between COM and paper
printout costs as the forms volume increases. From this graph it can

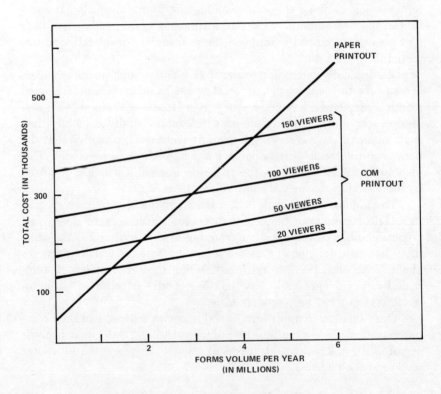

33.1   COM AND PAPER PRINTOUT COSTS VERSUS FORMS VOLUME

[4] J. E. Eichberger, "Computer Information Transformed to Microfilm," *Graphic Science*, June, 1970.

be seen that COM requires a large volume of microfilm forms to reach the cost level of paper systems. One reason for the high cost is the additional expense incurred with microfilm viewers. Although the generally purchased viewer itself costs only about $600, it requires a special work space. This floor space can usually exceed the cost of the viewer itself. The microfilm is also costly. Thus it can be seen that except for very large customers, a special application requirement in *addition* to the standard microfilm advantages is necessary to make COM a profitable alternative. In any case, COM will never replace printers. There are too many applications requiring hard copy, or low volume.

THE UPDATING PROBLEM

This comparison of microfilm and paper systems has ignored one critical factor—updating information. Updating is both slow and costly with both paper and microfilm systems, depending on how often it must be done. To ease this problem, a direct access real time retrieval system may be considered. On a casual analysis the direct access system does appear to have superior update capabilities, and greatly increased retrieval speeds. It is also more costly, and may not be reasonable at moderate levels of information volume. The analysis which follows is an attempt to replace subjective judgments with an objective, mathematical comparison of microfilm and direct access as information retrieval media.

The direct access system will be compared with an automatic retrieval microfilm system and a manual microfilm system. The three systems to be compared are:

System 1: On-line System with 2300 Honeywell Display Units

System 2: On-line System with 400 DSI Microfilm Terminals

System 3: Manual Microfilm System

In this comparison microfilm is used in its traditional character mode orientation. This analysis should not lead to the conclusion that microfilm in another mode cannot be a comparatively fast direct access medium. For example, designers can now store 1 million bits on a frame of microfilm with an access time of one microsecond per bit.

ASSUMPTIONS ON SYSTEM SPECIFICATIONS

To make a reasonable tradeoff between the three systems, a number of assumptions are made:

1. The customer size is fixed at 100,000 customers with an average of 2 documents per customer where each document requires 30 characters of storage overhead.

2. The data preparation time is not considered separately because the terminals are used to input data to the systems and the central processor time used by terminals is already considered.

3. The central processor time used for communications is independent of the number of characters stored per customer as it is assumed

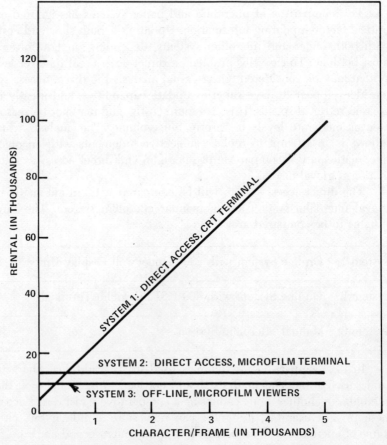

33.2 SYSTEM RENTAL PER CHARACTERS STORED (5 TERMINALS)

that of all characters stored only a few are retrieved per customer at any given time.

4. The greatest number of characters stored per document will never exceed that of one frame of microfilm or 7900 characters. This assumption means that one frame of microfilm can store all the characters of a document.

5. The initial system start-up and programming costs are not included in the model because: (a) they vary greatly from system to system, (b) the pay back period for these costs varies greatly, and (c) the percentage of costs to be apportioned to the foreground real-time as opposed to the background batch system is rarely clearly defined. In fact it can be shown that these costs have little impact on the analysis for systems with more than 20 terminals.

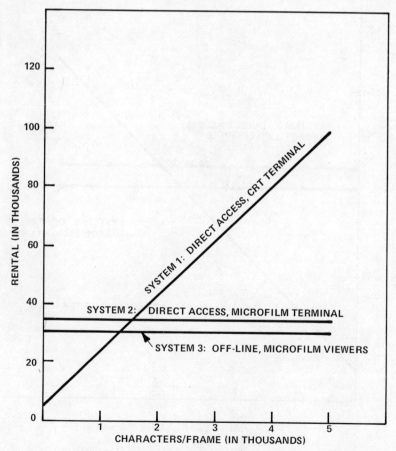

33.3   SYSTEM RENTAL PER CHARACTERS STORED (20 TERMINALS)

6. The data stored is updated only once a month. Real-time systems rapidly become more economical as the time between updates decreases.

For the manual microfilm system, besides the costs of the viewers themselves ($600), the roll film costs are $0.02 per frame on the original roll of film, and $0.006 per frame on copy rolls. It can be seen that

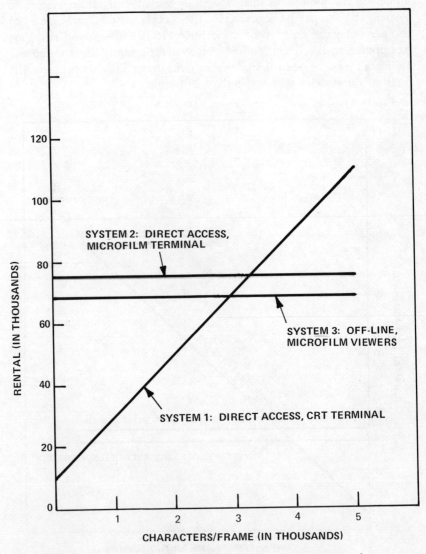

33.4 SYSTEM RENTAL PER CHARACTERS STORED (50 TERMINALS)

for the microfilm system, it is not the viewers but the microfilm itself that is the major cost. And presumably since microfilm is a relatively mature technology, these costs should not drop as rapidly as those of direct access. When this study was conducted, the direct access costs per character for the Model 258 Disk Pack Drive in System 2 were

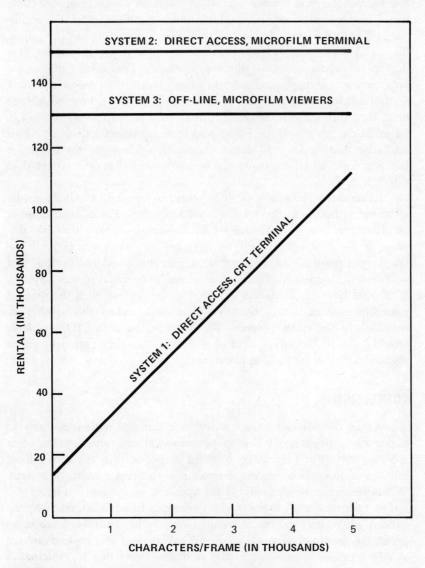

33.5 SYSTEM RENTAL PER CHARACTERS STORED (100 TERMINALS)

$0.00010 (based upon 4.6×10^6 characters) and $0.00007 for the Model 259 Drive in System 1 (based on 9.2×10^6 characters).

The graphs in Figures 33.2–33.5 describe the rental per month of the three systems for different terminal quantities. They show a very important characteristic of the trade-off analysis between direct access and microfilm. For a given number of terminals and line type, the break-even point when microfilm becomes more profitable than direct access is at a surprisingly high number of characters. For example, a 5 terminal system does not become more profitable for microfilm until a minimum of 350 characters is stored per document (i.e. one frame of microfilm per the assumptions). This means that many applications are more profitable on direct access than on microfilm. A further advantage of System 1 is that it has a retrieval time advantage of at least 5 times over System 2 and at least 30 times over System 3. In addition, only System 1 has real-time updating capability. This cost advantage in favor of direct access should increase even more in the next five years because of the technological advances expected in direct access.

In summary the following comments can be made about the trade-off decision between direct access and microfilm. For a small number of characters per customer input, an on-line system with CRT displays is the best solution. If the number of characters exceeds the break-even point for an on-line system, and the speed and flexibility of on-line indexing is a requirement, a microfilm terminal system (System 2) should be used. If on-line indexing is not critical, then the manual microfilm system should be selected. Finally, when the number of terminals in the system exceeds 50, direct access with CRT terminals would have all the advantages of real time, at lower cost than either microfilm system for most applications.

CONCLUSION

As an overall summary, microfilm is an alternative medium to paper for applications where paper retrieval or transportation costs are excessive. For very large volumes of paper printout and a fixed number of microfilm viewers, microfilm is the cost advantage system. Whenever real-time accessibility for updating or inquiry is a necessity, a direct access system is the obvious solution. In addition, many applications where only microfilm would normally be considered are more profitable on direct access than on microfilm. And this cost advantage should increase even more in the next five years due to anticipated technological advances in direct access systems.

34.

COMPUTER DISPLAYS FOR MANAGEMENT

By Bruce Joplin
and James W. Pattillo

Editor's Note: From the book EFFECTIVE AC-
COUNTING REPORTS by Bruce Joplin and James
W. Pattillo. © 1969 by Prentice-Hall, Inc. Published
by Prentice-Hall, Inc., Englewood Cliffs, New Jersey.

As more and more business data is stored in electronic computers, more efficient and economical methods of getting information out of the computer and before the manager are being sought. This article describes three computer reporting techniques that appear to have great potential for solving the information output bottleneck—cathode ray tubes (CRT), computer-linked microfilm, and computer-connected graphic display.

The cathode ray tube can display on a television screen any information stored in the computer. The information on display can be altered, added to, printed out, and returned to computer memory. Microfilm has been with us for many years as a method of storing inactive records. Now, technological advances have made microfilm a valuable reporting tool. Computer-connected graphic display can print out information on bar charts and graphs just as quickly as in tabular form. This technique enables information to be placed before the manager in a form he can quickly grasp.

These three techniques for reporting computer-stored information are being used more and more in advanced systems. The greatest inhibitors to an even greater use of CRT, microfilm, and graphics are the costs of the equipment and computer programming. Where they are currently used in management reporting systems, the initial cost of acquisition has often been borne by some other operating system; thus their use in reporting is a by-product. However, the potential of CRT, microfilm, and graphic display for reporting to management is great, and the number of such systems is constantly growing.

CATHODE RAY TUBES

The cathode ray tube has revolutionized man-computer interaction. For the first time, the manager can converse directly with the computer and thus operate in a truly dynamic environment. The instrument which has accomplished this is a small, television-like device with a keyboard attached. The keyboard has most of the characters found on a typewriter plus certain special keys through which instructions are issued to the computer. The CRT is connected directly to the computer or can be linked via communication lines. It can receive data from or transmit to the computer, and can display any data in computer memory. Alphabetic and numeric characters, punctuation marks, and specialized symbols can be displayed on some units while others are limited to numeric characters only. Usually, data is displayed in tabular form but more sophisticated units also display information in graphic form.

Up to 1,000 characters can be displayed at one time on a 9″ × 12″ or smaller screen. Each "page" may consist of as many as 30 horizontal lines depending upon the model used. Data called forth from the computer can be altered, added to, erased, and restored to its original place in memory. New data can be entered by using the typewriter to place it on the screen, sight verifying the result, and transmitting the display data to memory. Operators may be trained to use the CRT in a few hours.

Behind the extensive capabilities of the CRT is an enormous amount of systems and programming work. On-line and usually real-time computer systems are required to support CRT units. As a result, CRT installations are quite costly and are used primarily for special-purpose applications where there is a considerable payoff. However, as more CRT units are produced and experience gained in using them, the cost of such display systems will drop. Even now, most large companies are planning for CRT management reporting systems.

We will now outline the ways in which CRT units are being used and describe how such advanced reporting systems work.

FILE SCAN SYSTEMS

There are two principal ways in which CRT units can be used for reporting information: file scanning and management reporting systems. File scanning is used in those systems where the current status of individual records is required to make operating decisions. Usually, such systems are found in organizations which interact with the public —for bank customer balances and airline reservations, for example. File scanning systems are also used in production and inventory control where minute-by-minute surveillance is necessary.

Most CRT file scanning systems are designed for special purposes and are not complete information systems. They are useful in those situations where line operators or first-level supervisors need up-to-the-minute information on account balances or transactions. Higher management typically needs summaries and analyses of file conditions and activities reported on a periodic basis.

CRT MANAGEMENT REPORTS

The objective of a CRT-centered management reporting system is to make up-to-date information available at an instant's notice. Such systems are usually based on sets of reports that have been designed by the accounting department and stored in the computer. First, subreporting systems are established dealing with such categories as sales, financial, personnel, and competition. Within each subsystem the pyramid approach to reports is used. Starting from the basic file or files, successive reports summarize previous or lower level reports until the highest level is reached, as in a responsibility reporting system.

CRT reports are updated automatically by the computer, or manually. Many systems provide for the accounting department to manually control all updating of reports. Under this approach, each day the necessary data is obtained from the underlying files or other sources and, after verification, inserted via the CRT unit into the proper report stored in the computer. Usually, instead of being destroyed, the reports for at least three prior periods are retained in memory. Undoubtedly, the manual updating of reports will eventually be replaced by automatic updating by the computer. The computer will synthesize data obtained from underlying files and from figures fed into the system, and insert the resulting information in the proper report.

Each manager has access to a CRT unit either in his office or at a central "control" room. Used in this way, answers to many questions can be obtained while a meeting is still in progress. A description of how a CRT-based reporting system works is presented in the accompanying exhibit.

Despite the fact that CRT reporting systems are in their infancy, certain problems of control and operation are becoming evident. Absolute control must be maintained over changes in report content and format. Changes in the format of reports, including insertion of new reports, should be authorized by top accounting management. Changes in report content (updating) should be limited to designated accounting personnel. If these basic rules are not followed, chaos can result and the system quickly discredited. Reports on CRT should show the date to which information is current (update date) and, in many instances, the last transaction (cutoff). Any printout of information displayed must also be documented as to the effective date and last transaction covered.

Access to information via CRT must be controlled. The computer can be programmed to accept input only from CRT units in the accounting department and to permit only authorized persons access to information. For example, executive salary information can be displayed only on CRT units in the offices of top management.

GRAPHIC DISPLAY

In addition to being able to display computer-stored information in tabular form, some CRT units can project graphic information on the screen. Actually, complete pictures can be displayed but this feature has limited application for management reporting, and usually CRT graphic displays are fairly simple. A curve on a graph may be drawn, for example, and the graph can then be stored in computer memory and retrieved by management when needed.

CRT display of graphic information requires quite complex programming. Some manufacturers of CRT units have built up libraries of programs for a variety of display formats. Programs for displaying bar graphs, contour plots, and scatter diagrams are available. Most graphic displays on CRT are used for engineering or scientific purposes. While business applications have been slow in developing, the use of CRT for this purpose has obvious potential in the graphic display of relationships existing in report data.

MICROFILM REPORTING

The expanded use of microfilm for management reporting is inhibited by the fact that many people identify this process exclusively with the storage of large, inactive files. Microfilm has the image of a very slow, manually operated process that could not possibly compete with CRT display devices or even ordinary computer printing as a management reporting tool. This was true up until a few years ago. However, recent technological advances enable microfilm systems to be connected directly to the computer, thus providing speed and flexibility not possible before.

There is, in fact, a bewildering amount of new equipment and techniques being marketed by over one-hundred manufacturers. Traditionally, microfilm in reels of one-hundred feet were the standard. The filming process was slow and the retrieval process not much better. Not only have techniques for handling reels of microfilm been dramatically improved but new storage media, such as microfiche and aperture cards, have been developed.

Microfiche is a sheet of film carrying numerous micro images. There are many sizes of microfiche but $4'' \times 6''$ is considered standard. Sheets of microfiche can be coded for visual filing and retrieval. Aperture cards are tabulating cards with a frame of microfilm attached. The card is key punched for indexing. Searches for information are expedited by processing the cards through tabulating equipment. Because of the various storage media available, procedures utilizing these techniques are more properly termed "film" systems.

FILM SYSTEM

Because of the great number of film systems available, generalizations are inadequate to illustrate what can be done with this technique. We will therefore describe one typical, although advanced, system so that the potential of this new reporting medium can be appreciated. This particular system, called Micromation, was developed by Stromberg-Carlson, but any organization interested in using film should thoroughly review all applicable systems and decide which one best meets its needs.

Normally, in order to be used in a microfilm system, computer-generated data must be produced first in paper form and then photographed by various cameras. While fairly well automated, these cameras nevertheless cannot keep pace with the ever-increasing speed of data processing machines. Micromation eliminates the need for first producing paper records. To accomplish this, the system depends upon one of several electronic printers which accept computer codes, either on-line or from magnetic tapes. The codes are fed into the electronic printers which automatically translate the codes into ordinary language. The data is then displayed briefly on a special cathode ray tube. The tube is built into the printer and in its operation is not visible to the user except for monitoring purposes. Instead, a microfilm camera is focused automatically on the tube face. As each page of data appears on the tube, the camera snaps a picture and automatically advances the film to the next frame. Then another page of data is presented on the tube and the picturetaking process is repeated.

Currently, three types of film can be produced with this system. The most popular form is 16mm microfilm which is stored in plastic cartridges or magazines after processing. Then there is 35mm film which, normally, can be cut into individual frames and attached to aperture cards. The third form and one which is growing in application is microfiche. Instead of one frame or page of data being reproduced on each card, many pages can be recorded. For example, 72 pages could be recorded on the microfiche sheet by using 6 rows of 12 pages each. These microfiche sheets are sufficiently rigid to be filed just as aperture cards are now handled, except that less space is required and more pages of data can be extracted from the files with a single card.

In most business applications today, only letters, numerals and some special symbols are required, but the user normally wants this data recorded on some special business form. For example, a firm might want its computer-generated data printed over a report form bearing various headings, lines, boxes, and perhaps its company logotype. In the past, vast inventories of many different variations of such forms had to be preprinted and stored. The system here described eliminates this expense. Instead of preprinting the forms, a photographic slide is made of each desired form, and this is then inserted into a special holder inside the printer. Simultaneously with the microfilming of the data on the tube face, light is passed through the slide containing the business form. In this way the camera records the lines and other static data on the form at the same time it records the computer-produced data.

The following are some additional important features associated with film systems:

- *Graphics on film.* More sophisticated printers are capable of turning computer-generated data directly into graphic forms. In this case, management may desire charts showing sales or inventory curves, for example. The computer can be programmed to extract this information from its memory, and then the cathode ray tube can draw the chart on the face of its tube where it can be recorded by camera. The speed possible with the cathode ray tube surpasses that of any other method. A complex chart, for example, can be drawn in a fraction of a second, making it feasible to put many composite reports in graph form which would have been impractical before.

• *Processing speeds.* One way of describing the speed of microfilm systems is in terms of $8\frac{1}{2}'' \times 11''$ pages of information translated from computer codes and recorded in a work day. The lower cost machines can record 20,000 pages or frames of data in one eight-hour shift while other equipment can increase this speed to 70,000 pages per shift. With these speeds, even the most comprehensive system of management reports can be reproduced frequently. Because film is relatively inexpensive, reports which were formerly updated monthly can be reproduced weekly or even on a daily basis. Thus, management and clerical help can have up-to-the-minute reports that were not available previously.

• *Duplicate and "hard" copies.* Once the film is exposed, it must be processed. This is done automatically by special processors. If duplicate copies are needed they can be produced rapidly on automatic film copiers. Because of the low cost of film, an organization can afford to send duplicate reports to many different executives or offices, often to locations in other cities. Even the cost of postage involved in mailing film to locations in other cities is cheaper than sending paper records or using communications lines. Even with filmed data, some organizations may require or desire paper copies of all data. Where a paper copy is required, the film may be run through another machine. This machine will handle microfilm at a rate of 60 feet per minute, producing report-quality paper records in page form of all the filmed data, whether it is in alphanumeric or graphic form.

• *Paper reports.* Most firms, however, will eventually dispense with bulky paper records entirely. Instead, they will equip all possible users with inexpensive film-viewing consoles. Each manager may have a viewing device in his office or located nearby. At these stations the user has all the up-to-date records in film form, either in 16 mm cartridges, 35 mm aperture cards, or on microfiche. When he wishes to refer to a given record, the manager merely selects the cartridge or card containing that particular page and inserts it into the desk-top viewer. The record is displayed on the screen and the data noted by the user. Should the user have need for a paper copy of that particular record, viewers can be installed which have a paper-producing capability. By pushing a special control, a paper copy of the record is displayed on the screen. In this way, paper copies are made only when needed, rather than producing hard copy records of all data. The storage savings alone can be sizeable.

• *Updating and retrieval.* In one company, information for management reports is maintained on magnetic tape files. Each week, the computer-stored reports are updated and the changed records are microfilmed. Inquiries can be processed by first locating the report number on an index which is also on microfilm. The index shows both the number of the film magazine and the location of the frame that contains the microfilmed report. Retrieval is made on high-speed reader/printer systems that make paper copies for return to the requester. If required, a report can be retrieved in less than one minute. A compute system without on-line retrieval capabilities can, in most instances, only provide overnight services.

While not applicable to organizations producing only a few reports daily, microfilm systems are rapidly becoming accepted by firms inundated with voluminous reports. In many cases, the users can obtain more up-to-date reports faster and at lower costs by using microfilm than by relying on paper printers. Cost savings come in the form of reduced paper inventories, storage costs and labor involved in handling records. In the near future most managers and supervisors, even factory foremen, may have viewers at their desks for reading reports. Business use of CRT units is inevitable where instant access to a computer memory is required. However, in many organizations CRT costs are prohibitive in the foreseeable future for business applications. Film generally provides a cheaper storage medium than computer memory, and film viewers are far less expensive than providing a CRT display for every user.

COMPUTER GRAPHIC DISPLAY

Most methods of retrieving computer-stored business information provide for numerical tabulations in one form or another. This is not always the most useful format. Graphic display of information is often easier to understand, and hence of more use to busy managers. In the past it was necessary to have a clerk transfer information from lengthy computer runs on to hand-prepared charts and graphs. This process took considerable time, was subject to inaccuracies, and was not always attractively done.

A number of devices are available that will allow computer-synthesized data to be printed out in graphic form. These devices can produce bar charts or graphs on stock paper, graph paper, or custom forms in the time it would take to print the same information in tabular form. Displays range in size from 5" × 5" to 20" × 100" and can be printed in a number of colors and different line types. Some graphic display devices can "draw" curves as well as straight, point-to-point lines. If desired, graphic display can be connected directly to a computer-microfilm system of the type previously described.

The most advantageous use of computer-connected graphic displays is to quickly inform management of current developments. By a glance, the manager can identify trends and potential trouble spots. Usually, actual data is plotted against planned or budgeted figures, and any significant deviations spotlighted on the graph. A frequent use of graphic display is for projecting operations into the future. Variables can be introduced, and the computer quickly and accurately plots the effect of assumed changes in values. Graphic displays are often used to plot breakeven points and other widely used business measurements.

Basically, two types of devices are available for graphic display of computer-stored data. The digital plotter is the most widely used instrument for this purpose. Digital plotters can be operated on-line or off-line and can be used in a card-only system. The capabilities of plotters vary widely, as do the prices. Most plotters are used primarily for engineering and scientific purposes, and few are installed for purely business information display. However, definite thought should be given in appropriate circumstances to utilizing their capabilities for management reporting. A graphic report, for example, might be prepared by a digital plotter to evaluate the progress of branch offices, the status of each branch being plotted for many different categories.

Charts and graphs can also be prepared by specially equipped computer printers. These are not as widely used as digital plotters for graphic display although the use of both is increasing. One factor inhibiting the use of computer-connected graphic display is the cost of programming such a system, which may exceed the cost of the additional equipment needed for graphic display. Manufacturers of digital plotters are developing packaged programs for certain types of graphs and charts. If these "canned" display formats can be utilized for management reporting, substantial costs can be avoided.

CONCLUSION

The computer is almost synonymous with innovation. The foregoing discussing has presented simply a few illustrations of current trends in computer reporting. The field continues to grow. One recent development, for example, is the emergence of time-shared computer graphic displays. A computer manufacturer and a maker of digital plotters have joined forces to set up a network of computer-connected digital plotters throughout the nation. Organizations may purchase only the time they need for graphic display work, thus avoiding the purchase price and upkeep expense on equipment. As the use of time-sharing increases, more companies may avail themselves of this means of producing graphic information for management decisions.

HOW A CRT-BASED REPORTING SYSTEM WORKS

First, an executive activates the CRT unit by inserting an instruction code through the keyboard. An index of subreporting systems which are available to him is flashed on the screen as in Frame I.

Frame I

	Code
Sales	100
Production	200
Personnel	400
Financial	600
Equipment	800
Profit Control and Analysis	900

Each subreporting system has numerous computer-stored reports that provide information in increasing detail about the general topic. Assume that the executive wants to review financial reports. He inserts Code 600 into the CRT and Frame II appears. The data at the bottom of the frame indicates that the report is updated every seven days and that the last update was on August 21. Also, note that *Sales* is cross-indexed to Frame I.

Frame II

		(*thousands*)
610	Cash	4,820
620	Receivables	16,830
630	Inventories	20,100

640	Fixed Assets	40,082
645	Other Assets	8,921
650	Current Liabilities	20,921
655	Long-Term Liabilities	30,112
660	Equity	39,720
100	Sales (Net of C.G.S.)	90,821
680	Budget Controlled Expenses	71,020
690	Fixed Expenses	10,200

U.D. 8-21-70 (7)

The executive is interested in the company's cash position. He inserts Code 610 into the CRT and Frame III appears showing a breakdown of *Cash* in Frame II. The total of *Cash* in Frame III does not equal *Cash* in Frame II because the former is updated daily and $400,000 has been added since August 21.

Frame III

		(*thousands*)
611	Cash Budget 6-Month Projection	
612	Demand Deposits	3,320
613	U. S. Securities	1,400
614	Time Deposits	500
615	Source and Application STMT	

U.D. 8-24-70 (1)

The executive can review the projection of cash needs by inserting Code 611 or review the prior twelve months' source and application of funds statement by inserting Code 615. If he wants a breakdown of maturities of U. S. Securities he inserts Code 613 and Frame IV appears. By inserting 613.2, a detail listing of securities maturing within 15 days would appear on the screen.

Frame IV

	Maturities	(*thousands*)
613.1	7 Days	—
613.2	15 Days	100
613.3	30 Days	300
613.4	60 Days	400
613.5	90 Days	200
613.6	120 Days	400

U.D. 8-24-70 (1)

The CRT reporting system allows the manager to browse through each subsystem picking and choosing the information he needs for decision-making. The information is always up-to-date and can be displayed as fast as the keyboard can be activated. If desired, a hard copy can be printed of any report appearing on the screen.

35.

EXTENSION OF HUMAN CAPABILITY THROUGH INFORMATION PROCESSING AND DISPLAY SYSTEMS

By J. Robert Newman

Editor's Note: From SYSTEM DEVELOPMENT CORPORATION REPORTS, September 1966. Reprinted by permission of the publisher and author.

INTRODUCTION

The number of basic facts we have about how human beings interact with that fascinating piece of equipment—the digital computer—is rapidly growing, as is the whole area of man-computer technology, i.e., the scientific development of ways for men and computers to work together to solve problems and make decisions. I will concentrate at this time on one aspect of this technology—that of extending an *individual's problem-solving capability*—and will refer primarily to the man who is in a fairly high-level work position, such as the scientist, corporate executive, or military commander.

Man-computer technology has grown so rapidly that very few of its accomplishments have been described in the general literature. They can be found for the most part in reports from university, government, and industrial laboratories, and are too numerous to review here. Rather, I will concentrate on a few representative examples, which illustrate some important concepts and principles, and, whenever possible, will discuss the implications of these principles for the industrial and business community.

BASIC TECHNIQUES AND CONCEPTS

Since this discussion concerns a special type of man-machine inter-action, it is important to list the three major concepts underlying such an interaction.

1. On-line Computer Usage

The first concept is that of the *on-line* use of computers. This means that a user is able to sit down at a console and communicate directly with it. No intermediate programming or coding is needed (although a great deal of sophisticated programming *is* necessary to make this possible). The physical means of communication between man and machine is the computer interrogation and display console, which at the least consists of a teletypewriter and a matrix of push buttons. There are some far more sophisticated display consoles available, however, which have been programmed to allow a person to ask questions, perform various functions, and have the results displayed almost immediately. The important idea is that one can sit at this console, just as at a desk, and use the computer as an obedient and willing servant. Information that used to be in filing cabinets and libraries is now stored in the computer, where its retrieval is easy and almost instantaneous. Complicated data manipulations, which heretofore were drudgery, are now quite easy and much more flexible.

2. Time-Sharing

The second concept arose from the sheer economics of using a computer on-line. These machines are expensive to purchase, maintain, and program. That a single person should tie one up for several hours at a time was just not economical. The practical answer was the development of *computer time-sharing*, which enables many people to utilize the computer simultaneously, although independently. Computer time-sharing, which was just a dream about six years ago, is now an operational reality, in existence in several centers across the country.

3. Step-Display-Look Cycle

The first two concepts, of *time-sharing* and *on-line* computer usage, are essentially concerned with organization of computer hardware, with its programming, and with how it will be used. The third concept is more psychological in nature. It is called the *step-display-*

look cycle and, as far as I know, was first stated by Douwe Yntema of Lincoln Laboratories (Yntema, 1964).

The word *step* is used in a very special sense. It means the unit action that the user wants taken by the computer, whether it be performing some calculation, rearranging data, or merely inserting or deleting data. When a person has taken a *step* he usually wants to see the results of what he has done, so he *displays* the results and *looks* at them. After he has looked at them, he may want to do something else, or perhaps to look at them in a different way, in which case he will take more steps, display their results, and thus repeat the cycle. The *look* phase is by far the most important of the three. During this interval, the user is not only staring at the display and absorbing what he sees; he is also considering his next step. It is during this phase that creative thinking is going on and the man is utilizing his best talents. This aspect of the cycle is the key to extending man's capability via computer and display systems. At the present there is often a great disparity in time between *step* and *display*. It takes much longer to tell the machine what you want done than it does to get the results back. What we aim for—and are, I believe, achieving—is a rapid reduction in the time between *looks,* i.e., a reduction in the time it takes to make steps and have the results displayed. This may sound straightforward and simple. Its implementation is far from simple, but space prohibits discussion of that here. I do want to emphasize the importance of reducing the time between looks, for by such reduction, it seems to me, we accomplish at least two things that are important for problem solving and decision making.

First, we reduce the amount of *preplanning* or *foresight* a person must engage in or have. Foresight, and therefore preplanning, are often difficult for human beings. Most of us are really not sure what we would like to have—what kinds of data and what organization we need—until we start working on a problem. By taking a few steps and seeing the results almost immediately we reduce the number of possibilities that might otherwise be anticipated. It is much more efficient to proceed sequentially, a few steps at a time, in the fashion indicated by the *step-display-look cycle.*

Second, we reduce the problems connected with the phenomenon of *psychological set,* the tendency to guide one's thinking along the lines of what one expects or is *set for.* It is well known that one of the worst things that can happen to a problem solver is to get into the *wrong set,* i.e., to persist in activities that are not fruitful and do not lead anywhere. In our SDC laboratory we have gathered evidence that this tendency is reduced via the *step-display-look cycle.* If the steps are not appropriate, looking at the resulting display often reveals this very quickly. Furthermore, if it is easy to take a few more steps, one is more apt to do so and to get a new display—a new way of looking at the data—that might be more revealing. Perhaps a simple example will illustrate this. Consider an economist trying to analyze a complex economic time series. In such work the choice of scale in which the data is plotted is critical. Certain patterns or trends that are not revealed on, say, a linear scale may become apparent on a logarithmic scale. The ability to switch from one scale to another, *to take that step, display the results,* and *take another look* enables the analyst to get off one track quickly and onto another, perhaps more fruitful, one.

REPRESENTATIVE EXAMPLES

Three specific examples come to mind in which human capability has been enhanced by computer and display systems. These three have been purposely chosen from widely different areas in order to emphasize the extraordinary range of application that lies open to man-computer interaction. The examples also illustrate some additional basic concepts about man-machine problem solving that may have important implications for industrial psychologists.

The first example is taken from the area of logistical planning and maintenance schedules, an area of vital importance to military and industrial organizations. Sweetland, of the Rand Corporation (Sweetland, 1964), has described a computer and display system designed to improve the quality of Air Force maintenance engineering, i.e., the determination of failure rates, types of failure, recurring failure, and in general identification of "sick" aircraft. The interesting aspect of Sweetland's approach is its psychological nature. Maintenance analysis was viewed as a problem-solving process, and he started from the hypothesis that computer-retrieved displays of appropriate data would significantly raise human problem-solving capacities. He and his colleagues reasoned, on the basis of psychological theory, that the display should emphasize spatial and verbal rather than numerical elements. This approach was highly successful and also produced an unanticipated effect: *The pictorial-verbal display apparently made numerical data more tolerable.* Given the general picture, the maintenance personnel persistently requested, and were able to use, more detail. Apparently the pictorial-verbal elements allowed observers to comprehend a larger number of numerical elements and to assimilate considerably more detailed information. This is an important point, which I will return to shortly.

The second example is taken from a relatively new and rapidly developing area of research and application growing out of Bayesian statistics (Edwards, 1962). It is important to note that the basic ideas involved were developed for, and have had their greatest impact in, the area of business and economic decision making. These ideas are easy to state:

(1) Human beings have a high tolerance for ambiguity, vagueness, and uncertainty, and they can effectively translate uncertainty into probability.

(2) Probabilities are best considered as "orderly opinions" about the likelihood of the occurrence of certain events important to the decision maker. Another way of stating this is to say that human judgment or expert opinion can and should be expressed in probabilistic terms.

(3) Statistical information processing is or should be a tool for revising opinions of probabilities in the light of new information.

(4) There are or should be normative rules (of which Bayes's theorem is one) that guide the process of such revisions.

What this theory and body of research has emphasized, from a practical standpoint, is that while men are excellent at handling uncertainty and can effectively translate uncertainty into probability, they are not very good at combining or aggregating probabilities in subjective decision problems. Computers, on the other hand, cannot deal very well with uncertainty, but are far superior to men in taking probability judgments in some suitable numerical form, and aggregating them according to some formal rule. My own research, as well as that of Edwards at the University of Michigan and of Shum and his colleagues at Ohio State University, has utilized the formal rule of Bayes's theorem as the means of aggregating human judgment (see Edwards, 1966, for a review of this research). This is not, however, the only rule that can be used. Roger Shepard, now at Harvard University, has described a system for combining human judgments with the aid of a computer (Shepard, 1964), and his system is based on nonmetric scaling theory. Ward and Davis (1963) have demonstrated that human judgments involved in the employment problem (that is, the problem of finding an optimum assignment of N candidates to K vacant positions) can be effectively combined in a digital computer by a fairly straightforward multiple regression approach. The technique advocated by Ward and Davis does not replace human judgment but rather captures or reproduces the human's implicit strategy within the computer.

Whatever the procedure, the significant aspect of these investigations is the following: Human judgment can be translated into probability or into some comparable weighting index. These indices can then be inserted into a computer, which aggregates them according to some formal rule and displays the result to the decision maker. The result can be a powerful decision-making system.

The third example is taken from some work Miles Rogers and I [1] have been doing recently at SDC. We have been investigating computer and display aids for humans who are trying to solve extremely complex problems that require the subject to make an inference or discover a rule using a relatively small amount of data. Our approach was as follows: We presented subjects with a series of problems varying widely in difficulty. Each problem consisted of a set of displayed symbols that were multidimensionally defined. Each symbol could be uniquely defined by a value on each of four different attributes or dimensions. The displayed symbols were organized according to a definite rule or pattern. The subject's task was to discover what that rule or pattern was.

Each subject was allowed to manipulate the set of symbols via a number of computer and display aids. These aids were designed to reflect or represent a set of processes known or thought to be useful for human problem solving, and were suggested by theoretical and empirical research. For example, we know that people do not have very good short-term memories, so we provided a memory aid. It has been stated that the presence of too much detail or irrelevant information usually slows down performance, so we provided a capability for getting rid of information that was thought unimportant. We know that humans are capable of reducing the complexity of their environments by recoding raw data into other units, so we provided a capability for recoding the symbols. Other aids were available but these examples illustrate the flavor of our approach.

We called these aids *symbol manipulation functions*. Perhaps their utility can best be summarized by saying that our subjects were provided with computer representations of at least some of the things they would normally have available to them when solving difficult problems.

Essentially, the display and computer provides a type of electronic

[1] Newman, J. R., and Rogers, M. S. Experiments in computer aided inductive reasoning. SDC document TM-3227 (in publication).

chalkboard for the subject as he tries to solve the problems presented to him. The initial problem sequence represents the raw information, and the symbol manipulation functions can be considered as a series of transformations on that raw information. These transformations include selection, deletion, counting, adding, and combinations of these. Also, just as a person working at a chalkboard or with paper and pencil can erase or throw away and start again with a modified attack on the problem, so could our subjects erase or clear their displays and start again.

We are still analyzing the results of the last series of experiments but the main trends can be summarized:

(1) Subjects using the computer and display aids solved more problems, solved them faster, and made fewer errors than did subjects in a control group that did not have the aids available. This, of course, is not too surprising. A man with a pick and shovel is not as good at digging ditches as is one with a power shovel.

(2) There was tremendous transfer of problem-solving ability both within and between levels of problem difficulty. There was a definite learning-how-to-learn or "learning set" phenomenon operating. This was evidenced in both groups, but the effect was *much stronger in the aided group.* In this group, there is some evidence that skills developed while interacting with the computer will carry over even when the subjects do not use the aids; i.e., that whatever skills they developed while interacting with the computer will carry over to situations in which they solve similar problems without computer aids.

(3) The computer and display aids that allowed the subjects to transform and recode the basic data were used more frequently, and apparently more effectively, than other aids. This way of reducing complexity seems to be preferred to that in which information is gotten rid of, for example. Incidentally, reducing complexity in this fashion does not mean that there are fewer elements in the display. On the contrary, the displays often got completely filled with data as a result of the subject's manipulation of the basic symbol set. This may have been an artifact of our experimental situation, but that is doubtful. In the logistics study referred to earlier, Sweetland found that properly formatted displays allowed people to tolerate and absorb much more information than would normally be expected.

There seems to be an important principle operating here, one of considerable generality: People don't mind dealing with complexity if they have some way of controlling or handling it. I agree with Bill Howell,[2] who has discussed some of these factors, when he says that if a person is allowed to structure a complex situation according to his perceptual and conceptual needs, sheer complexity is no bar to effective performance.

CONCLUSION

Finally, there are three main points to bring out concerning some implications these topics have for industrial psychologists.

(1) More emphasis will be placed on improving high-level human performance, i.e., improving the effectiveness of people engaged in planning and executive decision making. On-line computer systems will play an important role in this emphasis. In this context, human factors engineering and system analysis procedures will probably be used more commonly. Most of the work in on-line computer usage was done to improve the efficiency and operation of high-level military command centers. Systems analysis and human factors engineering played an important role in the development of those systems. A great deal of this work has a straightforward application to industry.

(2) There are now, or soon will be, models and techniques that handle decision problems once presumed to be incurably subjective. These are the kinds of decision problems that, it was thought, could be handled only by human beings. In certain areas this will still be true for some time to come, but the human beings will be directly aided and assisted by computer and display systems. The distinction between objective and subjective decision making is disappearing—in all probability largely because of the kinds of man-computer systems that have been briefly discussed here.

(3) We are going to have to revise our thinking about the limitations of human performance. A great deal of recent research has yielded data suggesting that humans are very limited in their capacity to absorb and use information. This viewpoint is probably correct for tasks in which speed of performance is critical. However, for higher problem-solving tasks, in which time and resources are

[2] W. Howell, *Perceptual Factors in Personnel-Equipment Interaction*, Paper prepared for Division 14 Symposium: Constructs Concerning Human Performance in the World of Work II: Personnel-Work Equipment Interactions, American Psychological Association Convention, New York City, September 1966.

available for the manipulation of data, I am not convinced it is true. To state the point differently: If we concentrate on providing people with computer and display aids that overcome their limitations—for example, by providing memory aids, and extending the ability to manipulate, recode, and transform data—then problem-solving and decision-making abilities can be expanded tremendously. In the work we have been doing at System Development Corporation, we presented our subjects with problems considerably more difficult than those normally used in psychological experiments. Even so, we found that these problems could be readily solved, using the computer and display aids, and we had to increase the level of problem difficulty far beyond what we had at first anticipated in order to keep the subjects challenged. There are undoubtedly upper limits to man's intellectual ability, but we are a long way from determining just where those limits are.

INFORMATION RETRIEVAL AND DISPLAY: DISCUSSION QUESTIONS

1. How can the major problems of uncertain information requirements, excessive volumes of stored data, the difficulties of properly
   classifying data, and slow or inconvenient access to data by the
   user be resolved by designers of information retrieval systems?
   What hardware, software, and data organization techniques are
   available to assist in this endeavor?

2. What benefits can the systems designer and/or the user attain
   by storing and retrieving documents and processed data within
   the same system? What problems must be overcome in order to
   implement such a combined system satisfactorily.

3. What criteria are most appropriate for judging the effectiveness
   of inquiry services from the standpoint of the user? From the viewpoint of the centers providing such services? Are there any
   conflicts? Explain.

4. What are the major benefits and limitations of using computer
   output to microfilm in conjunction with graphic display devices
   such as cathode-ray tubes and digital plotters? For what kinds
   of applications is the microfilm medium likely to replace hard-
   copy output? Why?

5. What factors should be considered in selecting the most suitable
   type of display device for an information system? To what extent
   must some factors be sacrificed (for example, cost and complexity)
   in order to achieve a higher degree of performance from others
   (for example, fast response times and flexibility)? How important
   is the volume of data to be processed? The use to be made of the
   retrieved information? System reliability?

6. To what extent can automated information display systems be
   used to solve simple, structured problems? Complex and structured
   problems? Complex and unstructured problems? Explain fully.

7. On what basis can the cost and complexity involved in developing
   a computer graphics system for business decision making be

justified? For what types of decisions or problems is a computer graphics system best suited (for example, terminal costing, economic forecasting and analysis, product scheduling, capital investment planning)? Why? Explain fully.

8. How does a personalized data system differ from more generalized information systems? What benefits should the user expect to attain from such a system in order to justify the time, money, and effort required for successful system development?

9. How can an on-line information display system help the manager to utilize more fully and to expand his decision-making capabilities? What are the practical limits of such extensions?

10. What types of problem-solving tasks can be handled satisfactorily by machines? What kinds of tasks are better left to man? What factors should be considered and how should they be balanced in achieving the optimal combination of man and machine efforts in problem solving?

INFORMATION RETRIEVAL AND DISPLAY: BIBLIOGRAPHY

Albert, David, "New, Low-Cost Interactive Graphics," *Machine Design,* January 25, 1973, pp. 97–101.

Aronson, R. L., "Applying CRT's to Control," *Control Engineering,* 1972.

Auerbach on Computer Output to Microfilm, June 1972; *on Alphanumeric Displays; on Microfilm Readers/Printers.*

Avedon, Don M., "An Overview of the Computer Output Microfilm Field," AFIPS, *Fall Joint Computer Conference Proceedings,* 1969, pp. 613–623. See also, J. K. Koeneman and J. R. Schwanbeck, "Computer Microfilm—A Cost Cutting Solution to the EDP Output Bottleneck," pp. 629–635, and S. A. Brown, "The Microfilm Page Printer—Software Considerations," pp. 625–627.

Bird, Michael G., "Indexing Is the Key to Retrieving COM-stored Data," *Computer Decisions,* May 1971, pp. 30–33. See also J. Burt Totaro, "Microfilming Cuts Computer Data Down to Size," *Computer Decisions,* March 1971, pp. 22–27.

Brooks, Stanley A., "A Microfilm Primer," *Journal of Systems Management,* February 1970, pp. 28–31. See also December 1969 issue of *Datamation* devoted primarily to computer microfilm units.

Chu, Albert L. C., "COM Takes on an Active Image," *Business Automation,* April 1972, pp. 30–38.

"Computer Gets Faster Running Mate," *Business Week,* June 8, 1968, pp. 84–85.

"COM: The Prospects Take Another Look" (Tom McCuster), *Datamation,* November 1972, pp. 166–169.

"Computer Output Microfilm Systems," *Data Processing Digest,* February 1971, pp. 1–4 (condensed from *Modern Data,* November 1970, pp. 78–90).

Cowles, C. C., "Information Please—Storage and Retrieval Systems," *Data Processing,* December 1970, pp. 29–32.

Curry, W. C., "CRT Displays," a three-part report appearing in the

July, August, and September, 1968 issues of *Modern Data Systems.*

"Data Display with CRT's," *Control Engineering,* June 1968, pp. 108–110.

Datapro 70, "How to Select and Apply CRT Terminals," January 1972; "All About Computer Output to Microfilm," November 1971; "All About Voice Response," March 1972.

Davis, Ruth M., "Man-Machine Communication," *Annual Review of Information Science and Technology,* John Wiley & Sons, 1966, pp. 221–254.

Davis, Sidney, "Printer Selection Factors," *Computer Design,* December 1972, pp. 45–54.

"Design and Applications of Automated Display Systems," and "High Speed Printers: A State of the Art Report," *Auerbach Standard EDP Reports,* 1968.

Deahl, Thomas F., and Rauzine, Vincent, "Computer Output Microfilmers." *Data Processing,* Part I, August 1969, pp. 34–39; Part II, September 1969, pp. 60–64.

"EDP Output Devices: The Four Options," *Administrative Management,* June 1971, pp. 76–81. See also Sam Bellotto, "EDP Output Devices Go Portable, Get Smaller as Computer Users Seek Decentralization," *Administrative Management,* May 1972, pp. 33–42.

"Evaluating COM Costs," *Data Systems News,* December 1970, p. 24 (condensed in *Data Processing Digest,* March 1971, pp. 13–15).

Furth, S. E., "Information Retrieval and the Computer," *Data Processing Yearbook,* American Data Processing, 1966, pp. 189–194.

"Graphic Data Processing," special collection of articles in *Computers and Automation,* November 1967, pp. 16–36. See also the November 1968 issue, especially "Interactive Computer Graphics," by J. J. Guenther, pp. 14–17.

"Graphic Terminals: Man's Window to Interactive Computing," *Computer Decisions,* November 1971, pp. 10–15.

Harmon, George H., "Microfilm Update," *Data Processing Magazine,* May 1971, pp. 36–38.

Hayes, Robert M., "Information Retrieval: An Introduction," *Datamation,* March 1968, pp. 22–26.

Hobbs, L. C., "Interactive Man-Machine Systems," *Ideas for Management,* Systems & Procedures Association, 1967, pp. 168–173.

"Interactive CRT Terminals," *Modern Data,* Part I, June 1971, pp. 44–55; Part II, July 1971, pp. 62–76.

Johnson, C. I., "Interactive Graphics in Data Processing: Principles of Interactive Systems," *IBM Systems Journal,* Nos. 3 and 4 (combined issue), 1968, pp. 147–173.

Joplin, Bruce, and Pattillo, James W., "Computer Displays for Management," *Management Controls,* July 1970, pp. 142–147.

Lachter, Lewis E., "Four New Forms of EDP Output," *Administrative Management,* July 1969, pp. 36–40.

"Large Data Base Tapped Interactively by Storage Terminals," *Computer Decisions,* June 1970, pp. 21–26.

Lehman, David A., "Tomorrow's Manager and Displays," *Data Processing,* Vol. XI, 1967 DPMA Conference Proceedings, pp. 524–537.

Levine, Joel H., "High-Speed Line Printers," *Modern Data Systems,* May 1968, pp. 36–43.

Loewe, R. T., and Horrowitz, P., "Display System Design Considerations," *Computers: Key to Total Systems Control,* Joint Eastern Data Processing Conference Proceedings, 1961, pp. 323–331. See also pp. 15–37 of *Electronic Information Display Systems,* James H. Howard, Editor, Spartan Books, 1963, by same authors.

Lorber, Matthew, "Evaluating Computer Output Printers," *Automation,* March 1972, pp. 64–67.

Martin, J. Sperling, "How Document Retrieval Systems Work," *Computer Operations Journal,* August 1969, pp. 58–65.

McGrath, James D., "Does COM Eliminate the Output Bottleneck," *Data Management,* May 1971, pp. 14–20. See also, "Will COM Remain a Marketable Product?," *Data Management,* June 1971, pp. 28–33.

Mezei, Leslie, "Computer Graphics for Society," *Computers and Automation,* Part I, October 1970, pp. 28–30, and Part II, November 1970, pp. 30–35.

Miller, Irvin M., "Computer Graphics for Decision Making," *Harvard Business Review,* November–December 1969, pp. 121–132. See also "Economic Art Speeds Business Decision-Making," *Computer Decisions,* July 1972, pp. 18–21.

Miller, Lee D., "Information Displays," *Automation,* June 1968, pp. 72–80.

Miller, R. B., "Archetypes in Man-Computer Problem Solving," *IEEE Transactions on Man-Machine Systems,* December 1969, pp. 219–241. See also L. P. Schrenk, "Aiding the Decision-Maker—A Decision Process Model," pp. 204–218. Reprinted from *Ergonomics,* July 1969.

Mills, R. G., "Man-Machine Communication and Problem Solving," *Annual Review of Information Science and Technology,* John Wiley & Sons, 1967, pp. 223–254.

Minor, William H., "A Practical Approach to Information Retrieval," *Datamation*, September 1969, pp. 109–124.

Morton, Michael S. S., "Interactive Visual Display Systems and Management Problem Solving," *Industrial Management Review*, Fall 1967, pp. 69–84.

Morton, Michael S., and McCosh, Andrew M., "Terminal Costing for Better Decisions," *Harvard Business Review*, May–June 1968, pp. 724–737.

Mumma, Fred W., "Progress with Displays," *Data Processing*, October 1969, pp. 34–42, 68.

Murphy, John A., "Computer Output Microfilm," *Modern Data*, November 1971, pp. 48–52.

Nauer, Richard S., "Reference It; Retrieve It; Reproduce It," *Systems & Procedures Journal*, March–April 1968, pp. 32–36.

Newman, J. Robert, "Extension of Human Capability through Information Processing and Display Systems," Systems Development Corporation Reports, December 1966 (SP-2560/000/00).

O'Brien, B. V., "Why Data Terminals?," *Automation*, May 1972, pp. 46–51.

"Plotting for Business," *Journal of Data Management*, August 1970, pp. 18–20.

Pratt, Alan D., "Computers and Information Retrieval," *Ideas for Management*, Systems & Procedures Association, 1965, pp. 52–61.

"Progress in Information Retrieval," *EDP Analyzer*, January 1970, and "Computer Output Microfilm," *EDP Analyzer*, June 1970.

Rinder, Robert, "Hard Copies from CRT Terminals," *Datamation*, April 1969, pp. 64–66.

"Scanning the CRT Picture," *Journal of Data Management*, June 1970, pp. 33–35.

Schroer, B. S., "Interactive Computer Graphics," *Journal of Systems Management*, May 1972, pp. 17–21.

Schussel, George, "Advent of Information and Inquiry Services," *Journal of Data Management*, September 1969, pp. 24–32.

Showalter, A. Kenneth, "Display Systems," *Datamation*, November 15, 1971, pp. 28–32.

Sprague, Richard E., "Personalized Data Systems," *Business Automation*, October 1969, pp. 42–51.

Stephenson, Andrew, "Planning Interactive Communication Systems," *Modern Data Systems*, November 1968.

Stieffel, Malcolm L., "Digital Plotter Terminals and Systems," *Modern Data*, September 1971, pp. 48–57.

Stotz, Robert H., "Directions in Time-Sharing Terminals," *Computer Group News*, May 1968, pp. 12–18.

Summit, Roger K., "Dialog: An Operational On-Line Reference Retrieval System," *Proceedings—ACM National Meeting*, 1967, pp. 51–55.

Swets, John A., "Information-Retrieval Systems," *Science*, July 19, 1963, pp. 245–250.

Technology Profile: Interactive CRT Display Terminals, *Modern Data;* "Part 1—The Technology and the Market," May 1970, pp. 62–69; Part 2, "Alphanumeric CRT Terminals," June 1970, pp. 70–84; Part 3, "Graphic CRT Terminals," July 1970, pp. 60–68.

Technology Profile: "Digital Plotters," *Modern Data*, July 1970, pp. 72–83.

Theis, D. J., and Hobbs, L. C., "Low-Cost Remote CRT Terminals," *Datamation*, June 1968, pp. 22–29.

Weisberg, David E., "Graphic Displays: Matching Man to Machine for On-Line Control," *Control Engineering*, November 1968, pp. 79–82. See also "Man-Machine Communication and Process Control," *Data Processing*, September 1967, pp. 18–24.

"What's the Status of MIS?," EDP Analyzer, October 1969, and "Technical Support for an MIS," *EDP Analyzer,* November 1969.

"With COM, More Than Meets the Eye," *Administrative Management*, January 1973, pp. 38–39.

Wolaver, John, "Information Retrieval: Three Alternatives," *Honeywell Computer Journal*, Fall 1970, pp. 13–17.

Workman, William E., "The Picturephone Puts Data at Management's Fingertips," *Computer Decisions*, October 1970, pp. 35–39.

INDEX